4 00

The Agitator

A Collection
of
Diverse Opinions
from America's
Not-so-Popular
Press

Edited by
Donald L. Rice   comp.

A Schism Anthology

American
Library
Association
Chicago 1972

Library of Congress Cataloging in Publication Data

Rice, Donald L   comp.
    The agitator.

    (A Schism anthology)
    Articles compiled from Schism, v. 1-2, 1970-71.
    1. U. S, Social conditions—1960–   —Addresses, essays,
lectures. 2. U. S.—Economic conditions—1961–   —Addresses, essays, lectures. 3. U. S.—Race question—Addresses,
essays, lectures. I. Schism. II. Title. III. Series.
HN65.R52   309.1'73'092   74-178271
    ISBN 0-8389-0114-X

International Standard Book Number 0-8389-0114-X (1972)
Library of Congress Catalog Card Number 74-178271
Copyright © 1972 by the American Library Association

                    Printed in the United States of America

Contents

Race Relations

Women's Liberation

Foreword

In 1948, on the recommendation of the Intellectual Freedom Committee, the Council of the American Library Association adopted the Library Bill of Rights as the Association's basic policy on intellectual freedom. Included in the document was Article II: "There should be the fullest practicable provision of material presenting all points of view concerning the problems and issues of our times. . . ."

Recognizing that every question and issue has many sides, the committee chose the phrase, "all points of view," rather than *both* points of view. Between the absolute right and the absolute left lie many shades of opinion, and writers sometimes move across the median line in erratic patterns.

Presenting all points of view, however, often is a physical and practical impossibility, and most libraries have tended to settle for the relatively middle of the road or "popular" opinions. The extreme right and the extreme left and opinions close to these polar opposites have generally been underrepresented in library collections. THE AGITATOR offers all libraries an opportunity to provide a variety of viewpoints concerning contemporary issues.

While some of the views expressed in the anthology will undoubtedly be repugnant to many Americans, the strength of our form of government rests on the belief that if all sides of issues are presented, the best will eventually be chosen. This belief is conditioned on the existence of the ability to utilize choice effectively. Should this ability be allowed to atrophy because of limited availability of varying points of view, our system of government will inevitably suffer. THE AGITATOR, by offering opinions not only from the "right" or "left" of questions, but from many intermediate positions provides an occasion for libraries to give support to the Library Bill of Rights.

JUDITH F. KRUG, Director
ALA Office for Intellectual Freedom

Preface

The articles collected in this anthology were taken from volumes 1 and 2 of *Schism: A Journal of Divergent American Opinion,* published by the Schism Publishing Co., 1109 West Vine Street, Mount Vernon, Ohio. *Schism* reprints without condensation or editorial comment articles appearing in a wide spectrum of important but ephemeral journals, all of which in some significant respect diverge sharply from the standards and values of what may be designated, for want of a better phrase, the American establishment consensus. *Schism,* the quarterly journal, fulfills the preserving function of gathering together in one vehicle articles which might otherwise vanish without leaving a bibliographic trace. THE AGITATOR, on the other hand, makes possible a still more permanent record of dissident voices from America's not-so-popular press. Furthermore, THE AGITATOR presents this material in a systematic arrangement whose categories reflect broad topics or areas of social concern but *not* ideology or doctrinal commitment. The substantial Introduction, written for this anthology, seeks to provide the reader with a theoretical overview of the interplay of consensus and dissent in American society today.

Acknowledgments

Acknowledgments are hereby made to the following authors and periodicals:

Anderson, Tom, "Straight Talk," *The Kentucky Farmer* v.106, no.5 (May 1970).

Bayes, William W., "What Is Property?" *The Freeman* v.20, no.7 (July 1970).

Bell, Daniel, "Social Trends of the 70s," *The Conference Board Record* v.7, no.6 (June 1970).

Black Politics, "On Police Murder," v.2, nos.13–14 (Mar.–Apr. 1969).

Bodian, Stephan, "Eldridge Cleaver: A Man to Believe," *Lancaster Independent Press* v.1, no.25 (Jan. 31, 1970).

The Brian Bex Report, "Marihuana," v.5, no.24 (Oct. 15, 1970).

Chamberlain, Park, " 'Justice'—A Tragedy in One Act," *Human Events* v.30, no.6 (Feb. 7, 1970).

Christenson, Malcolm, "Government by Science . . . or Chaos," *The Technocrat* no.236, v.36 (June 1969).

Christian Anti-Communism Crusade, "Are the Black Panthers Being Persecuted?" (Jan. 1, 1970).

Christian Crusade Weekly, "The Tragedy of Misguided Idealists," v.10, no.49 (Oct. 18, 1970).

Clamage, Dena, and Murray Bookchin, "The Anarchist Revolution," *The Fifth Estate* v.4, no.6 (July 24–Aug. 6, 1969).

Cleveland, Ray L., "The Fallacy of Race and the Arab-Israeli Conflict," *Issues* (Winter 1969).

Counterattack, "Quality Education or Craven Accommodation," v.24, p.13 (Feb. 23, 1970).

The Dan Smoot Report, "Our Tax Money Breeds Misery," v.16, no.46 (Nov. 16, 1970).

Danby, Charles, "The Face of Fascism in the U.S.," *News and Letters* v.15, no.6 (June–July 1970).

Davis, Angela, "A Growing Awareness among the People," *People's World* v.33, no.46 (Nov. 14, 1970).

Dellinger, Dave, "Memoir of Czechago," *Liberation* v.15, no.2 (Apr. 1970).

Dohrn, Bernardine, Jeff Jones, and Bill Ayers, "Weatherman," *Spokane Natural* v.4, no.22 (Oct. 30, 1970).

Duke, David Ernest, "The White Power Program," *Racialist* special ed., 1970.

Eddy, T. R., "Resignation from the John Birch Society," *National Chronicle* 1969.

Ginsberg, Allen, "Ginsberg Talks about Speed," *Door to Liberation* v.2, issue 8 (Sept. 10, 1970).

Hall, Gus, "Marxism-Leninism: The Star of Revolutionary Transition," *New World Review* v.38, no.1 (Winter 1970).

Harrigan, Anthony, "A Profile of Defeatism: Dismantling the Nation's Defenses," *Life Lines* v.12, no.68 (June 1970).

Hazlitt, Henry, "In Defense of Conformity," *The Intercollegiate Review* v.7, no.1–2 (Fall 1970).

The Herald of Freedom, "All Shades of Revolutionaries," v.18, no.5 (Oct. 2, 1970); and "The Battle of the Sexes," v.18, no.2 (Aug. 21, 1970).

Hillegas, Jan, "Mendenhall: Old-Time Violence," *The Southern Patriot* v.28, no.3 (Mar. 1970).

Hoffer, William, and Sen. Sam J. Ervin, Jr., "The Good Lord and the Government," *Liberty* v.65, no.6 (Nov.–Dec. 1970).

Hoops, Walter, "Religion and American Foreign Policy," *The American Rationalist* v.14, no.2 (July–Aug. 1969).

Hoppe, Arthur, "The 'Latest' Book in Sex Education," *Liberal* v.24, no.3 (Mar. 1970).

Hummel, Jeffrey Rogers, "Legalization of Heroin," *The Torch* v.3, no.1 (Oct. 12, 1970).

Ivie, Wilton, "Revulsion against Social Change," *The Technocrat* v.37, no.234 (June 1970).

Johnson, Dr. Thomas L., "Welfare and the Constitution," *Freedom Magazine* v.15, no.3 (Autumn 1970).

Leviathan, "Thy Brothers' Keeper," v.1, no.8 (Feb. 1970).

Lightfoot, Claude, "Black Liberation Impossible without Communists," *Political Affairs* v.48, no.9–10 (Sept.–Oct. 1969).

Madole, James H., "America at the Crossroads: Authoritarianism or Chaos?" *National Renaissance Bulletin* v.20, nos.1–3 (Jan.–Mar. 1969); and "Is the Concept of Race Evil?" *National Renaissance Bulletin* v.20, nos.10–12 (Oct.–Dec. 1969).

El Malcriado, "The Army Buys Up Grapes . . . to Defend the American Way of Life?" v.3, no.7 (July 1–15, 1969).

Manas, "The Decline of the 'Official,' " v.23, no.38 (Sept. 23, 1970).

Manion, Dean Clarence E., "Will the Workers Revolt?" *Manion Forum Newsletter* v.9, no.13 (July 1969).

Manis, Rod, "Poverty: A Libertarian View," *The Davis Arena* v.2, no.2 (Feb. 2, 1970).

Marra, William A., "The Case against Sex Education in the Schools," *Christian Economics* v.22, no.13 Oct. 1970).

McGee, The Rev. J. Lester, "Have Churches Carried Social Action Too Far? Some Have!" *Life Lines* v.2, no.83 (July 14, 1969).

Munn, Melvin, "Compare the Results," *Freedom Talk* no.86 (Mar. 27, 1970); "The Grape Boycott Farce," *Freedom Talk* no.92 (July 11, 1969); and "What Being an American Should Mean," *Freedom Talk* no.15 (Nov. 11, 1970).

National Chronicle, "J. Edgar Hoover and the Jews," v.19, no.3 (Jan. 29, 1970).

The New Right, "White Reply to the Black Manifesto," v.1, no.8 (Sept. 1969).

Opitz, Edmund A., "The Quiet Revolution," *The Freeman* v.19, no.10 (Oct. 1969).

Peter the Hermit, "State vs. Racial Nationalism," *Trud!* (1969).

Rat, "We Took What We Needed . . . ," issue no.16 (Nov. 17–Dec. 6, 1970).

Russell, Randee, Jerry Salak, and Kathy Rakochy, "Resolution on Women's Liberation," *New Left Notes* v.5, no.8 (Dec. 22, 1969).

Scahill, Mike, "Up from Nonviolence," *Catholic Worker* v.36, no.5 (June 1970).

Sexton, Brendan, " 'Middle Class' Workers and the New Politics," *Dissent* v.16, no.3 (May–June 1969).

Sharp, Gene, "National Defense without Armaments," *War/Peace Report* v.10, no.4 (Apr. 1970).

Sibley, Mulford Q., "Violence and Democracy," *New America* v.9, no.7–8 (May 15, 1970).

Siegal, Bob, Fred Kushner, and Carol Schik, "Lessons from the Summer Work-In, *SDS New Left Notes* v.5, no.4 (Sept. 20, 1969).

Social Questions, "Hysteria," v.60, no.6 (Summer 1970).

Sons of Liberty, "Proposed Constitutional Change on Voting," (Aug. 1970).

Stevenson, Ronald, "No Justice for Black People," *People's World* v.32, no.31 (Aug. 2, 1969).

Sweezy, Paul M., "Toward a Critique of Economics," *Monthly Review* v.21, no.8 (Jan. 1970).

Tornquist, Elizabeth, "Police Crush Freedom House," *The North Carolina Anvil* v.4, no.158 (June 6, 1970).

Veracruz, Phillip, "Racism in Agriculture," *El Malcriado* v.3, no.25 (May 15, 1970).

von Epp, "New Right Report," *Trud!* no.38 (1970).

Weisskopf, Walter A., "Science, Technology, and Rebellion," *Manas* v.22, no.30 (July 23, 1969).

The Western Socialist, "Nationalism," v.37, no.277 (no.5, 1970).

White Power, "Lessons from *Mein Kampf*: White Racial Solidarity," no.12 (Mar.–Apr. 1970).

The White Sentinel, "Why Some Whites Are Arming," v.19, nos.9–10 (Sept.–Oct. 1969).

Woodworth, Fred, "The Case for Anarchism," *The Match!* v.2, no.1 (Mar. 18, 1970).

Young, Patricia, "Hoax of Marxist Economics," *Christian Economics* v.22, no.4 (Mar. 3, 1970).

Introduction

Agitation for social change has become the preoccupation of our age: participating in it, writing and talking about it, or merely observing it. A disproportionate amount of mass media reporting is devoted to this phenomenon—disproportionate to the actual number of active participants, though the more popular the pastime becomes, the greater the percentage of activists becomes. It can hardly be refuted that the number of people signing petitions, sending letters, marching, demonstrating, engaging in court battles, making speeches, and pamphleteering is greater all over the world than ever before in history.

What is happening? The clichés about mass communication and transportation making the world smaller are probably true, and they in turn are compounding aggravations. What is often overlooked is that the same mass communication and transportation that cause unrest and mobility are also acting as catalysts among far-flung interest groups and individuals who are now realizing for the first time just how greatly their tribes have increased. The "Woodstock Nation" was discovered in this way.

Also probably true is the commonplace about the acceleration of the rate of change. There was a time when what we call an "age" lasted a long while: the Ice Age lasted 500,000 years; and the Iron Age, 1,100 years. Even the Industrial Revolution was evolution, an explosion in slow motion, by today's reckoning. Ages, of course, are not absolute divisions of time, but rather periods of culture, overlapping by centuries from one portion of the world to another. They are becoming universal in the twentieth century, more frequent, more concentrated, and even more overlapping. We seem to be living, concurrently, in the Atomic Age, the Jet Age, the Space Age, and the Age of Aquarius, among others. The Atomic Age began officially on August 6, 1945; within days almost everyone in the world knew about it. How many people living in 500 B.C., say, were aware that they were living in the Iron Age?

The Time for Change

Every generation thinks that it is facing unique problems. The problems are not new; they are unique because they have not existed before under precisely the same conditions. When have there not been war, poverty, crime, corruption in government, social injustice, a decline in morals, the enemy within, tigers at the gates, and the end of civilization as we know it? Somehow things manage to work out, though often at great cost in human lives and suffering.

We may take the social evolutionist's view that events occur when they do because it is their time and place to do so. This belief should not be fatalistic license, though, to sit back and let history take its course; things might happen when they shouldn't.

Every idea must have fierce proponents and still fiercer opponents to assure that its time has, in fact, come. In 1970 abortion was made a legitimate exercise of individual right in New York State. For this law to have been enacted, very powerful forces had to confront and to overcome moral, ethical, and expeditious arguments that such a law should not be. The notion of legalizing abortion is certainly not new; for it finally to prevail over powerful, dedicated, and determined opponents is a sure indication that this generation was prepared to legitimize an act contrary to seemingly well-established mores. This is not to say that the legislation is good—or that it is bad—but only that it is a fact. All one can do now is to acknowledge that fact and, depending upon one's feelings, fight to maintain it, merely accept it, or fight for its repeal. The number of legal abortions performed within months after passage of the New York law, indicated that such a law was long past due. Yet other laws have come and gone, and it is a simple mental exercise to imagine a time when abortions will again be illegal.

National prohibition required superhuman effort to become a law, but it wasn't a fact. Passage of the Eighteenth Amendment not only did not prohibit "the manufacture, sale, or transportation of intoxicating liquors" in the United States, it seems to have encouraged these acts. Almost fifteen years of further superhuman effort were required to repeal the amendment. But the repeal came, as it had to. Clearly, it was not the time for Prohibition.

The so-called no-knock law, passed by Congress in 1970, applies only to Washington, D.C. It gives police with a search warrant the right to enter a house without announcing themselves. This is an idea that has long been repugnant to Americans and they have resisted it vigorously. So distasteful was the idea, that it was rarely suggested. But its time has come— or so it seems—and it too is a fact.

How one chooses to dress and to groom one's self is a perennial subject for debate. Right now, some females are discarding their bras, and some males are letting their hair grow long. Almost everyone has read newspaper accounts or knows through personal experience of actual court cases involving the length of a boy's hair. A heavyweight boxer in Argentina was suspended from the ring in that country because his hair was longer than the boxing commission thought reasonable. No doubt twenty-five years from now people will read such things and laugh at the stupidity of our times because we wasted so much energy on so trivial a matter. Consider this: In 1956, George Gallup conducted a poll to inquire into the attitudes of Americans. One of the questions asked was, "Do you approve or disapprove of men wearing [Bermuda shorts] to their place of work?" Who would bother to take the time to ask such a question today?

There is nothing new under the sun we hear. Well, yes and no. Whether an old idea can be considered new depends, as army privates like to put it, on the situation and the terrain. Prostitution may very well be the world's oldest profession, but there were some strains of gonococci in 1970 that did not respond to antibiotics as one would have wished them to. Venereal disease in 1970 was not what it was just ten years before. (And, of course, before Dr. Fleming presented us with penicillin, one had to take one's chances anyway.)

Critics of American society are fond of comparing it with ancient Rome: bread and circuses, welfare, taxes, war, a strong central government, etc. "History repeats itself," they say.

Such a view of history makes life seem so futile. What is the point in one generation's sweeping out the stables if they have never been kept clean before and never will be? What we must hope is this: that while the work seems repetitive, the nature of what must be swept out is improving and the quantity decreasing. And, too, that what is malodorous to one generation is inoffensive to another.

When William Jennings Bryan was campaigning for the presidency in 1896, he attempted to make a speech in New Haven. Yale University students in attendance were solidly behind McKinley and had little use for Bryan's populism. They gaily hooted and hissed while he spoke—an especially effective technique back when a politician had to depend upon the volume of sound that came out of his mouth, rather than out of loudspeakers. A marching band was practicing at some distance. Possibly by accident, probably by design, the band marched up to the edge of the crowd to continue its practice, drowning out Bryan's speech altogether so that he was forced to stop. The New York *Sun* commented on the students' rudeness:

What did these students really do? On the day that Yale University opened its new college year, Bryan came to New Haven and prepared to address a great crowd at the green adjacent to which are the college buildings of the center of university life, in a town of which the university is the great and distinguishing feature. The students gathered in strong force, as was natural. Practically, they were on their own ground. They expressed their feelings with the vigor and vociferousness of youth; and they had a right to do it.

They ought to have done it; and the sentiment to which they gave utterance was honorable to them. The boys made a great noise, cheering for McKinley and yelling and jeering at repudiation, so that Mr. Bryan could not be heard for several minutes. If they had applauded him incessantly for even a full half hour, would there have been any complaints of their preventing him from starting out in his speech? Has not a crowd in the open air as much right to hiss as to cheer? At what period in our history was that privilege taken from Americans?

Professor Henry P. Wright, acting as president of the university, in a statement the following day said:

Boys will be boys, you know, and it was really nothing more than a boyish outbreak. Students are forever doing such things, thoughtless enough I am sure. I am very sorry indeed that it should have happened, for it places the university in a false light, where the antics of college boys are not understood.

Bryan himself said this:

Do not criticise the boys too harshly. I am not inclined to criticise them as severely as some others have. Having been a college boy myself, I attribute their interruption more to youthful exuberance then to any intention to interfere with free speech.

It is difficult to imagine a politician today displaying such tolerance. Since the temper of our times does not encourage it, there is no reason he should.

One more reaction provides an interesting sidelight to the students' behavior. At a mass meeting of the Cherokees, Creeks, Choctaws, and Seminoles that was being held about that time in Muskogee, Oklahoma (then Indian Territory), the following resolution was unanimously adopted:

Resolved, that we contemplate with deep regret the recent insulting treatment of William J. Bryan by students of a college in the land of the boasted white man's civilization, and we admonish all Indians who think of sending their sons to Yale that association with such students could but prove hurtful alike to their morals and their progress toward the higher standards of civilization.*

The whole incident can hardly qualify as even a spot on the stable floor, but it does demonstrate how prevailing attitudes determine what should and what should not be swept out. That students shouted down politicians in 1896 and shout them down today is no more a repetition of history than the Second Coming will be a repeat of the first.

Forces for Change

Things change quickly these days. Attitudes can't really be counted on from one year to the next. As president, Richard Nixon would like the government to guarantee a minimum wage for all Americans. Had you suggested this notion to him twenty

---

*All references here to this incident are from *The First Battle* by William Jennings Bryan (Chicago: W. B. Conkey Co., 1896), pages 484–88.

years ago, he would have laughed. Yesterday's "crackpot" ideas are today's political realities.

What is it that changes people's attitudes? What command is it that can order a cultural about-face? Sometimes it is simply a matter of being physically able to do something that couldn't be done before. But something had to make that change possible. Perhaps we can credit—or blame—the beginnings of any social change to unreasonable people. At least to their contemporaries they appear to be unreasonable: unwilling to listen to reason, irrational, and impractical. They want to fly heavier-than-air machines, they want to desegregate public schools, they want to conquer other nations, they want to go to the moon. They are extremists. In an attempt to achieve their goals, they argue, cajole, agitate, and propagandize to try to increase their influence over other men's minds. At first they are disregarded and then dismissed as cranks, but as their influence grows, so too does the strength of their opposition. Every new idea must pass many tests; it must prove itself. This isn't to say that acceptability proves the worth of an idea any more than rejection proves its worthlessness, but that at that moment in history it either can or cannot find favor.

Every person in every society affects, to some degree, the rate and direction of social change. In a relatively stable society—and this does not necessarily exclude one with an accelerated rate of social change—each individual has an important function. The tory is just as necessary as the revolutionary. The extremists are important because of their polarizing effect; the sympathizers lend their strength; and the apathetic offer no resistance. Whichever camp gains the most strength is the one that ultimately wins.

That there are not more revolutions in the world can be credited to the genius of national leaders; maintaining a stable government in a country in which there are violently opposed forces is no task for a minor-league politician. The administrative duties of a president are important, but they are still incidental to his main function: the prevention of a revolution. A president, after all, is created in the image of his electors; otherwise he wouldn't be there. Once elected, he must sense any changes in this image and adjust his own countenance accordingly. This is not entirely a one-way street. A president, if he is clever enough, can shift the majority a few degrees in any direction to suit his purpose. The easiest course is to follow rather than to lead one's constituency. President Nixon is a master at this. The majority of Americans can hold him up and ask, "Mirror, mirror, on the wall, who's the fairest of us all?" Lyndon Johnson wasn't as willing to be a mere reflection, and he wasn't clever enough to remake America in his image.

There is always the danger that the leader may do too good a job. Hitler did this in Germany. He rightly sensed the then current disposition of the majority of the German people. Rather than contenting himself with being just their reflection, however, he chose also to lead, to exaggerate that reflection. Emotions are not subject to the law of the conservation of matter; through the interaction of the parts, the whole can be increased. Just as lovers in the heat of passion disregard all practical considerations and consequences of their relationship, so can a nation and a leader.

The same is true for any politician who would be successful. Although, individually, each isn't as important as the national leader, the proper men filling the lesser ranks will shore up a society, stabilizing it even if they oppose the national government. In fact, the "loyal opposition" is a vital part of the governmental structure, often preventing its collapse. The opposition gives a voice to otherwise frustrated and potentially dangerous minorities. Bureaucrats and civil servants manipulating the red tape of government tie everything together, preventing any drastic moves in one direction or another; though the strictures of a bureaucracy can also be too confining, not allowing for the necessary shift of the central government. Generally, however, the unwieldiness of government helps maintain stability since only slow, orderly changes can take apart and reassemble its interdependent network.

This aversion to social change that characterizes bureaucracies is precisely why they have survived as an institution in governments. And it is why those who desire rapid social change instinctively damn bureaucrats. Any would-be revolutionary (violent or otherwise) can further his cause early by destroying the bureaucracies—except that this is nearly impossible. It would be better to encourage a bureaucracy to follow its natural bent to overwhelm and strangle the rest of the government.

The motto of a revolutionist must be, "The worse things are, the better they are." It is impossible to create a revolutionary climate among fat and happy citizens. It is the government's job, then, to avoid the blunders in judging the tactics of a sophisticated revolutionary force. Tactics that invite indiscriminate repression are calculated to make things worse for everybody but the revolutionists. For them, the climate for revolution has improved, and their chances for success have increased.

If there were only one faction pressuring for drastic social change and if it were far outside the mainstream of the majority opinion, the government's solution would be simple: ruthless extermination. But this is rarely the case. There are always many divergent factions, some of them diametrically opposed, with the government in the middle. They all have sympathizers of varying degrees, not only among the general population, but also within the government itself. While all this tends to make the elimination of the factions nearly impossible, it does not necessarily indicate an unstable society. If the sympathizers within the government have strength and numbers fairly representative of the various factions, they cause the government to be always moving toward the center of gravity, maintaining a balance that would otherwise be difficult to achieve.

This can be demonstrated schematically: Imagine that society is a disc resting upon a pillar of government (fig.1). If the pillar is in the center, all is well.

Fig. 1

But suppose that the disc is not uniform—that certain areas have more weight than others. Then the pillar must shift to the new center of gravity if all is not to topple (fig.2).

In a society such as ours where special interest groups sprout like mushrooms after a spring rain, the president has to be something of a social acrobat to be able to maintain his administration at the center of gravity. He has to lie, change his

Fig. 2

mind, occasionally tell the truth, contradict himself, and use every other device necessary to accomplish his balancing act.

Now suppose that the president disregards the weight of the majority and supports only one small pressure group. With the help of the "loyal opposition," the society may keep an uneasy balance (fig.3). But eventually, what happens is revo-

Fig. 3

lution. Collapse of the government and perhaps the whole structure of society as well (fig.4).

Fig. 4

A government must react positively to important shifts in the thinking of the governed or it will not be tolerated. Just as important, it must be able to distinguish between fundamental changes in thinking and mere fads. To have passed laws in 1956 regarding the wearing of Bermuda shorts in places of business would have been frivolous. Worse than that, it could have been dangerous. Frivolity and caprice on the part of the state can give to those who oppose it a rallying point otherwise unavailable to them. Jimmy Durante put this succinctly when he said, "Don't put no constrictions on da people. Leave 'em ta hell alone."

A few years ago, Alan Abel formed a national organization to put clothes on animals. It started as a practical joke but soon grew into a full-blown hoax. He was interviewed on television shows and written about in newspapers and magazines. The whole thing was totally foolish (offering free patterns for dog pants and picketing the White House demanding that Caroline Kennedy's horse be clothed), but many people were taken in. Suppose that a high government official had been among them; suppose other government officials had believed Abel when he claimed that the Society for Indecency to Naked Animals (SINA) had 58,000 supporters and $500,000 in financing? Too farfetched, you say? Crazy laws have been passed in this country before and will continue to be. (It was once illegal in Providence, R.I., to wear nylon stockings.)

Such laws didn't just spring forth out of the febrile brains of crackpot legislators. At the time of their enactment, there was a rationale behind them which made them seem perfectly reasonable. There had to be forces at work agitating for such legislation, much as Abel rallied SINA to pressure the government into clothing animals. Before a legislative body takes the drastic step of prohibiting or requiring any human activity, it must first be convinced that such a need exists. An elected official who depends upon the vagaries of his constituency to keep his job must be persuaded that his livelihood depends upon his support of this or that measure. One thing that he must do is to divine the political direction in which those who elected him are heading. This isn't always easy.

Political Classifications

For nearly two centuries people have been relying upon the left-right scale to measure politcal proclivities. This scale was first used to designate liberal and conservative members of European parliaments (principally, England and France) in the late 1700s. The more liberal members sat to the left of the presiding officer and the conservatives sat to the right. In high school Problems of American Democracy classes, most of us were given a demonstration of this scale on the blackboard. On the far right, we were told, is the reactionary; next comes the conservative; next, the liberal; and last, the radical. Most of us, we were assured by our teachers, were comfortably settled somewhere in the middle of this scale. The definitions of these four classifications were usually quite glib: Reactionaries yearn for the good old days. (It was never explained just what "good old days." Those of King Arthur? Cro-Magnon man? Harry Truman?) The conservatives do not want to change anything. (Traffic deaths? Heroin addiction?) The liberals want to change things, and the radicals want to change everything now.

In spite of these definitions, Stalin ended up on the far left, and Hitler ended up on the far right. Some people felt that there wasn't enough difference between the two men to warrant their being at extreme ends of a scale, and the "great circle" theory was proposed. According to this theory, the continuum isn't a straight line at all, but a circle (fig.5). As

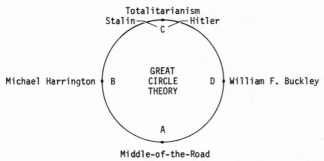

Fig. 5. Diagram of the "great circle" theory

one leaves point A in either direction toward point C, one approaches totalitarianism. Now since opposite poles on a circle ought to be just that—opposite—we find that totalitarianism is opposite middle-of-the-road. There is no room on this scale for anyone who wants fewer restrictions than are wanted, at any given time, by those in the middle-of-the-road. When we divide the circle through the north-south axis, we find that Michael Harrington is on the same side as Stalin, and that

William F. Buckley, Jr., is on the side of Hitler. None of the four would appreciate the comparison.

Right and *left* are convenient terms, but they don't really work. There isn't just one scale on which to measure political philosophies, but many. I am going to suggest four: the Right of Access, the Individual versus the State, Racial Equality, and a Supreme Being.

The Right of Access. To what extent should all human beings, regardless of station in life, talents, age, political loyalties, race, etc., be allowed free access to the earth's wealth? Examples of free access are public libraries, public parks, and homestead lands. How far should it be extended? To include hospitals, universities, mass transportation, grocery stores—everything? Or should it be severely restricted?

The Individual versus the State. To what extent should the right of the individual take precedence over the will of the state? Should it extend to occupational qualifications? style of dress (or undress)? attendance in grade school? political activity? participation in war? everything? Or have we already gone too far?

Racial Equality. Are such qualities as intelligence, physical abilities, adult possibilities, etc., equal at birth? Do they vary only by individuals or are they determined by race? Are certain races inherently superior?

Supreme Being. To what extent is man's conduct subject to the approval of a higher intelligence? Assuming that a Higher Power cares little about which shoe a man puts on first, how far should a "captain of my fate, master of my soul" philosophy be extended? To include all personal conduct? Or is that too far?

Attitudes toward these four subjects, and certainly some others that could be suggested, combine to form most political philosophies and personal stances. There are thousands of possibilities if we combine various ups and downs of the four scales; many of them are represented by formally organized groups in the United States. People who are used to classifying in traditional left-right terms will often be surprised to see how their own philosophies compare with those of others whom they now automatically call friends or enemies.

How can one find just where a group falls on any of these

scales? First, by reading their literature. Second, by trying to find unbiased reports of what they actually do. The second is almost impossible. A friend of mine claims that, with the exception of the *Statistical Abstract of the United States,* everything that is written is biased—and he has grave suspicions about the *Statistical Abstract.* A start toward an understanding is to read what these people are writing. That is what this collection is all about.

The Pamphleteer

The one word that characterizes most, though certainly not all, of the contributors to this collection is *pamphleteer.* I am not using this word in any contemptuous sense; it is, I think an accurate description of a certain type of political activist that has had a long and distinguished tradition. A pamphleteer is a person who, with little or no thought of immediate personal profit, writes or disseminates printed matter that is intended to effect particular social changes. Occasionally the pamphleteer may profit financially from his activity, but this is incidental. Usually any such profit is not retained for personal gain; rather it becomes a means for further circulation and improvement of the pamphlets. No longer is the pamphleteer limited to printed matter; other media such as radio and television are now in common use. In fact, in many cities one can even dial a telephone number to hear a recorded political or religious message. Using these media is a modern and logical extension of the earlier methods of pamphleteering; the motivations are the same.

The word *pamphlet* has its roots in the title of a twelfth century Latin amatory poem (*Pamphilus seu de Amore*) and has little to do with what we consider a pamphlet today. Its earliest recorded use to describe printed, bound literature was in Richard de Bury's *Philobiblon,* a treatise published in 1344 on the care and study of books. In the fifteenth and sixteenth centuries pamphlets were concerned generally with religious controversy, although at that time religion and politics were often part of the same struggle. During the next two hundred years, however, pamphlets became a means of disseminating the persuasive political and social opinions of such men as Addison, Burke, and Rousseau.

Many pamphlets published before the twentieth century are of great historical significance. Thomas Paine's *Common Sense* published in 1776 has been credited with being the most important single morale factor in the winning of the American Revolution. (More than 100,000 copies were printed.) Proudhon's anarchist pamphlet *Que'est-ce que la Propriété?* ("What Is Property?"), published in 1840, established in print the philosophical basis for the activities of many of today's young anarchists, whether they know it or not. Émile Zola intended to publish his famous open letter to President Faure, *J'Accuse*, as a pamphlet. Before doing so, he showed it to George Clemenceau who gave it its title and published it in his newspaper. Even so, it remained pamphleteering in spirit and electrifying in effect. Perhaps the one pamphlet whose influence has been felt, for better or for worse, more than any other has been *The Communist Manifesto* by Karl Marx and Friedrich Engels.

It is difficult to name any pamphlets of modern times that have had such influence. Many of today's pamphlets are published as books: Edmund Wilson's *Cold War and the Income Tax* and Phyllis Schafly's *A Choice, Not an Echo,* for example. But the influence of any single pamphlet today is nothing compared to those of the past. What has happened in the last century? Have the writers changed? Or the readers? Years ago, people were not bombarded as we are today with printed matter, and any literate person was probably anxious to exercise his reading skills if a pamphlet appeared. In the eighteenth and nineteenth centuries the random distribution of printed political opinions received a higher percentage of readership than do their twentieth-century counterparts.

Even though the current flood of printed literature has apparently lessened the effectiveness of each individual piece, it has not discouraged an increase in volume. Pamphlets have increased not only in the total number printed per capita, but also in variety. Books, broadsides, and periodicals may now also be included in the definition given for *pamphlet*: printed matter intended to effect certain social changes without also bringing immediate financial profit to authors and distributors. To account for this flood of paper, we need look no farther than the convenience of modern printing, manufacturing, and distribution. It was no coincidence that in the past many revolutionaries and popularizers of novel social ideas were printers by trade or else were rich; few ordinary citizens had access to printshops or could afford to have printing done otherwise. But today, the situation is different. Anyone with a typewriter, scissors, and cellophane tape can publish a pamphlet. It is very unlikely that any printer is crying for paper and ink today, as was Bobby Bell, publisher of *Common Sense*; we have solved the problem of production. Mailing lists are readily available, and second and third-class mailing permits greatly reduce the cost of distribution. (Holders of third-class "junk mail" permits show a profit to the Post Office, according to the *Wall Street Journal*.)

True, it still takes money, but anyone with a steady job can easily afford to buy printing. With the advent of the offset press, publishing one's opinions became available to anyone who wished to do so. A Multilith 1250 has become standard equipment in the headquarters of hundreds of social-action groups. The greatest advantage of offset printing over letterpress was the lowering, if not the elimination, of typesetting and engraving costs. Letterpress printing requires an expensive Linotype machine and an operator. To reproduce artwork, an expensive zinc or copper engraving is necessary. Offset printing requires only that the material to be reproduced be capable of being photographed. Text can be typed directly on certain of the offset printing plates.

Years ago, one man would write and distribute a pamphlet. This is still being done today, but organizations have usually taken on the obligation of publishing writings by their members and supporters. Many political-action groups offer, at a nominal price, whole libraries of pamphlets. More often than not, these organizations also issue a periodical, that is, a regularly published collection of articles by many authors.

The subscribers to these periodicals, with the exception of libraries and collectors, invariably agree with the general editorial slant presented. The relationship between subscribers and publishers of these periodicals is quite different than that between the subscribers and publishers of, say, *Time*. There are many loyal *Time* readers, but how would they respond to a request for donations to keep the magazine alive? Would *Colliers* or *Look* magazine still be published today if their subscribers were asked to give money for that purpose? It is unlikely. But many of the small journals of opinion survive almost solely on donations—donations of time, talents, and money. In many cases, writers are not paid for their articles and the actual business of publishing and mailing the periodicals is carried out by volunteers. This haphazard financing is what accounts for the constant founding and failure of political journals. Some of the long-lived journals survive only because they are subsidized by a few individuals. Usually the better periodicals will survive and the cruder will fade away, though there are surprising exceptions to both these rules.

The physical qualities of the journals range from badly mimeographed to slick four-color printing. The writing within them ranges from inane, hysterical ramblings to thoughtful, imaginative expositions. The influence of the journals is as varied as their contents. Some have only tiny circulations; others circulate in the thousands. Since most go only to those who are already sympathetic to a particular political philosophy, the journals act as sounding boards for new ideas, testing them to see if they are compatible with that philosophy's current thinking. While the periodicals themselves make few new converts, they do provide ammunition for their readers to use in the ideological battle for political power.

Harry Zitzler, a *Manas* correspondent, once suggested the formation of a mind-to-mind community based on letter writing, a suggestion patterned after one made by Sherwood Anderson to Theodore Drieser. Although Zitzler was discussing letter writing, he incidentally was describing another function of political journals:

We, who are interested in these problems and searching for a better life, are separated from one another, and do not know others like ourselves. We plod our individual paths in silence. For while the world is big, the world to which *we* belong is microscopic, and we hardly ever encounter other members of that world, in our daily lives. Indeed, it sometimes seems that the world to which we belong is only populated by one, with, as it were, vague voices from afar breaking in, on occasion, to let us know we are not alone.*

*"A Mind-to-Mind Community," *Manas*, v.14, no.40 (Oct. 4, 1961).

The main value of the journals, however, is to put new ideas into currency and to provide a means to sustain old ideas that might otherwise be lost.

This selection of articles doesn't pretend to give a complete overview of all the many social problems facing America or of the myriad solutions offered for them. Although some of the writers selected may seem to be offering simplistic answers, it is because they are represented by only one short article. Most of them realize that their battles must be fought on many fronts. Some subjects are overemphasized, others neglected. Indeed, a Martian reading these articles would barely be aware that the Vietnam war is in progress.

A social problem doesn't exist in a vacuum. None of society's ills can be cured by surgery. Racial tensions, campus unrest, unemployment, and drug abuse are not benign cancers needing only to be cut out of an otherwise healthy organism. So inextricably combined are most social issues that it is hard even to distinguish among causes, symptoms, and cures. Etiology is difficult to apply to the ills of society. Is the Vietnam war a cause of campus unrest? Or are both war and unrest merely symptoms of yet another sickness?

There are many ideas and attitudes presented in the following pages. Not all of them will come to pass; they conflict too greatly for that. But some of them will be adopted, and they need to be studied and considered now—in some cases so that they can be combated. Virtually all the organizations and individuals represented here won't like at least half the company they are keeping. Collectively, however, they act as foils, offering alternatives in the competition for power as we approach the last quarter of the twentieth century. Some of the ideas are startingly new, and some comfortingly old. There are a few surprisingly good, and a few appallingly bad. All need to be read and considered.

Social Change

WE DEMAND:

1 That the United States government end its systematic oppression of political dissidents and release all political prisoners such as Bobby Seale and other members of the Black Panther Party.

2 That the United States government cease its escalation of the Vietnam War into Cambodia and Laos; that it unilaterally and immediately withdraw all forces from Southeast Asia.

3 That the universities end their complicity with the United States war machine by the immediate end to defense research, ROTC, counterinsurgency research, and all other such programs.

STRIKE!

Reprinted in *Schism* v.1, no.3 (Summer 1970) from *Spokane Natural* v.4, no.10 (May 15—28, 1970).

Social Trends of the 70s

Daniel Bell

This society, within the last two decades, has become a *national* society for the first time; that is the fundamental context of change framing the way we perceive our problems. It was always a nation with an identity as a nation, but not a national society in the sense that a high degree of interdependence is achieved.

By the magic of jet transportation, by the modes of communication (particularly television), coast-to-coast dialing, and the simultaneous publication dates of news magazines, we have become truly a national society.

That means there is a sense of instant awareness of change from one part of the society to the others. It means a pressure to equalize standards in different parts of the society. It means, to some extent, a reduction of regionalism, and many of the problems that we have arise from the fact that we don't have a set of institutions for dealing with national problems in a national way.

The second context of change is in the rise of non-market public decision-making—the fact that more and more of the problems confronting us cannot be settled by the market, cannot be settled by the private sector, but involve community decisions. The problem of clear air, for example, cannot be solved by each individual buying his share of clean air at the marketplace, but involves the introduction of communal decision mechanisms.

The virtue of the market is that it disperses responsibility. But with public decision-making—where to locate a jet port, which part of town a road should go through—the decision-

Schism v.1, no.4 (Fall 1970)

makers are visible. The consequences are clear; one knows whose ox is going to be gored. For this reason, we must expect more and more community conflict arising as a result of non-market public decision-making.

The third dimension is the fact that, increasingly, we must face the claim of group rights rather than individual rights. Blacks, for instance, who on the basis of culture disadvantage make a claim for compensation, preference, quotas, etc., do so on the basis of membership in a group rather than as individuals, and this creates, equally, conflicts with others.

So the prognosis for the future is a difficult one. It is a prognosis of more and more community conflict, more and more group conflict—unless there are some mechanisms for bargaining, which is the only way to settle these things.

One of the ways of seeing where we stand now is to make a very simple comparison with the New Deal of the 1930's. The New Deal arose in response to the need for some management of the economy on a national scale. The states could not handle the kinds of economic problems generated in the 1920's and 1930's. The rise of such mechanisms as SEC and NLRB was, in effect, an effort to manage a national economy.

In the 1960's we began to confront the fact that we had to manage not just a national economy, but a national society. Poverty, the situation of the blacks, the role of the city, the problems of education—these could no longer be handled by the states, any more than the states had been able to handle the economy in the earlier period. To that extent, we now begin to have various programs for the management of the society as we then had programs for the management of the economy.

Predicting Future Social Problems

Looking ahead at the 1970's, it is relatively easy to predict social problems. But one doesn't know, in a sense, how the problems may be solved and where they will go, and one can't, therefore, predict politics. But one can predict the kinds of social problems we will face. What one cannot predict within social problems is the degree of attention one or the other issue might get.

themselves upon the public consciousness can be listed in four areas.

The first of these issues is what may be called social costs. It is realized more and more that private parties in their own transaction can generate costs which are borne, in a sense, by the rest of society. Pollution, of course, has been the chief example of such a social cost, but it is not the only one. The cost of noise created by jet planes is also a social cost that has to be borne or mitigated by various individuals who live near the new jet airports. And, by and large, the question of who will pay for these external costs generated by private companies will be, its seems to be, one of the major problems of the 1970's.

One of the difficulties is, of course, that these external costs differ from company to company, and it is very difficult for single companies to try to undertake the task of internalizing these external costs. They live in competitive situations, and this simply means adding to their own costs while their competitors may not have to take on these kinds of burdens.

More and more in these areas, there will be a push for Federal standards in an effort to create industrywide conditions for external costs. And it seems that any industry would be unwise to try to resist that kind of effort.

A second issue, and I suspect perhaps the next one which is going to receive large-scale public attention, is housing. Housing in many respects is the great pinch confronting this society. In the next decade there will be about 30 million more persons added to the society, and that 30 million is a net increase. Actually, in terms of births, there will be many more. There will probably be 47 million births in the next decade, but about 21 million deaths, and about 4 million immigrants, leaving a net increase of 30 million. Over the next 30 years there will probably be 140 million births in this society.

So in the next decade the major problem that we will confront is essentially the fact that we have been lagging in housing, and this will be multiplied by the fact that there will be an increase in household formation.

While one cannot be sure which issues will be the most salient in 1970, I think the kinds of problems that will force

There are already 20 million persons who occupy shelter

that falls below standards of decency in our society. Some live in places without toilets, or share them with other families. Some have no running water; some live in buildings or shacks that are beyond repair.

Second, there are perhaps 60 million persons who live in obsolescent houses in aging city neighborhoods and towns. The dwellings may have plumbing, the roofs may not leak, but they constitute neighborhoods far below the image of the American way of life. Schools are old-fashioned, play space is scarce, streets are cluttered with traffic and parked cars. European visitors express surprise that the United States has such extensive areas like this in its cities and towns.

Tomorrow's Children

Third, there are tomorrow's children. Within a decade, 47 million children will be born. Over the rest of the century about 35 million households will be added to our present population. These future families will be insistent claimants for housing and all that goes with it—water, waste disposal facilities, roads, schools and recreation areas.

In 1968 the Congress set a ten-year production target of 26 million homes, with 6 million earmarked for poor and moderate-income families. To achieve this and related goals, the Department of Housing and Urban Development has more than 70 programs—but in 1969, in the first year of the ten-year target period, housing starts were a half million below the 2 million mark that had been hoped for by the target centers. Given the problems of increasing costs, the problems of selling sites, etc., this deficit will continue over the decade.

Not only do we fail in building houses, we also fail in handling the social costs which are involved—cost of about $4 to 6 thousand per dwelling unit which, in a sense, are operating expenses paid for by the locality. The present method of meeting these local costs (about two-thirds from local property taxes and the rest from a patchwork of Federal and state aids) is neither sufficiently responsive to the needs nor effective in tapping the income stream. On set of social statistics will illustrate the point.

Perhaps 20 to 25% of post-war housing developments were initially built without community sewer systems. Even in 1962, 37% of the residences in America were still not connected to municipal sewers. Of the 63% with connections, almost one-fifth discharged untreated sewerage into the area, and a large art of the treatment (about 40%) was simply primary treatment—that is, the trapping of sewerage in catchments and exposure to open air.

Just taking care of this auxiliary amount of sewerage alone would mean spending about $2-3 billion a year for the next 15 to 20 years rather than the current billion which we now spend.

A second problem which is crying for attention is health. In 1950 the U.S. ranked fifth in infant mortality; in 1969 we had fallen to 18th place, behind expectancy; in 1965 we were 22nd. The number of doctors caring for private patients declined 10% relative to the population between 1960 and 1965 —to 92 per 100,000 Americans.

A third area, small in detail and yet symbolic in our sense of the nation is something that very few people think about— the performing arts; live theatre, opera, music, symphony orchestras, dance. The simple problem is the nature of technology. For the economy as a whole, productivity has risen at an average rate of between 2 and 2½% a year. In the technology of live performance, there is little room for labor-saving innovation; one can't speed up a 49-minute Beethoven symphony. Large-scale industry costs can be met through labor-saving innovations. One can't do this in the performing arts.

In the next decade there will be large deficits, and a question arises: Will there be sufficient attention to a viable culture and a willingness in this society to support, in effect, live theatre, music, dance, and, of course, museums?

A fourth area is the increasing schism in black life. In many respects, there has been remarkable progress in the advance of the black community, but only in one sector; among those who have been able to go to college, and those entering professional and technical employment.

Between 1960 and 1969 the number of blacks in these areas increased 109%—to 692,000. Blacks today constitute 6½% of the total in this category as against 4½% in 1960. So, in the middle-class sector of society, there has been a sizable increase in the number of blacks.

But against this is a deepening schism, for there are large numbers of the black community, particularly among those headed by females, for whom things have been getting worse, not better. Where there has been a persistence of long-term unemployment, it has been greatest among the blacks. Among the black unemployed, 20% are without jobs 15 weeks or more, against 12% of the whites.

The real problem is deterioration in the situation of Negro families headed by females. Through 1959 and 1968 the number of blacks in poor, female-headed families increased by 24% and, if you take a look in absolute numbers, the increase amounted to almost 600,000. Even though the blacks today constitute 11% of the population, more than 2.3 million poor children are in female-headed families, and 52% of all such children are in black, female-headed families. This is fundamentally the welfare problem that confronts the Nixon administration, and this is the problem which to some extent the Nixon administration's new proposals are designed to try to meet.

The major problem that we have is a multiplication of social problems for the one simple reason that the growth of the society has been primarily in the private sector and in private consumption at the expense of public services. To some extent this is due to an attitude toward taxes which is very strange in any rational society, for we tend to think of taxes as money taken from us by "them," rather than as taxes for the necessary purchase of public services which people can't pay for by themselves.

The Political Overload

The major problem facing the United States in 1970, therefore, is an overload on the political system as a result of the multiplicity of social problems that can't be managed. So far, the political system has not been effective in dealing with these issues for several reasons. First, the shortage of money as a result of the Vietnam War. Second, the administrative failures in carrying out programs, particularly in housing and health.

And thirdly, the lack of social science knowledge adequate to the task.

To date, we lack any comprehensive social accounting scheme which assembles all of our needs in one social budget, seeks to establish priorities, monitors performance, and evaluates the consequences. To that extent, we may need a council of social advisers similar to the Council of Economic Advisers, or at least an expanded council of economic and social advisers to deal with these problems.

Revulsion against Social Change

Wilton Ivie

It is obvious that people do not welcome social change. A few resist it vigorously; some oppose it with a cold resentment; most go along with it, regretfully; and a few help to facilitate it. People are not against 'progress,' of course; but what they regard as an interest in progress has scant relationship to any active support for fundamental social change. What they tend to support are those things that will enhance their own positions in the status quo; that is, they want to climb economically and socially in the system, but they want the system to remain much as it is. When they become 'socially minded,' it is usually through the technique of identifying their personal frustrations with the 'unjust' suppression or persecution of some minority group and through developing a crusading zeal for elevating the status of that minority group as a whole, but themselves in particular. The crusader wants his group to rise higher in the system than it is, but he wants his own position to rise higher than the general rise of his group.

Militant crusades for social reform do result in changes of a sort, but usually in terms of philosophical concepts rather than in the structure of the social foundations. Women have been accorded the right to own property, to participate in business enterprise, to engage in a wide variety of remunerative employments, and to vote in political elections. Labor has won the right to work fewer hours, to receive higher pay, to live in better houses, and to own more gadgets. Farmers have been socially and economically advanced by gaining more government paternalism, granted in exchange for votes and a quiescent attitude regarding the status quo. Little businesses have been granted considerable protection from competition. The claims of religious and racial minorities for more tolerant recognition have gained much support. Crusades for these and many other causes have been productive of some results; although in most cases the alleged 'results have been nothing more than the *effects* of a more fundamental change introduced by the application of science to the problems of man and society. Without a concurrent advance in the use of technology, it is doubtful that any of the 'results' mentioned here would have been achieved by crusading alone.

In fact, it is very doubtful whether the social gains from all of the crusades for piecemeal social reform that have been waged were worth the effort expended on them. At best, the direct results have been merely ripples on the surface, and these are capable of receding even faster than they arose, as illustrated by the barbaric social degradation that accompanied the upsurge of fascism in Europe just before and during World War II. *Any social reform* which depends upon human consent and continued vigilance is, indeed, fragile. *To be effective and permanent, the change must occur as a fundamental alteration of the structure and function of the social mechanism.* Such changes are dreaded by the people (before they happen) and are almost always introduced without popular consent. But, once they have happened, they are proudly lauded and tenaciously defended by the same people.

Conservatism is strongly imbedded in the chromosomes of the human race; hence, social change is not inherit in human nature. Through the hundreds of centuries that the human race was struggling *not* to rise about its existing social level, the social rewards went to the conservative, conventional imitator of the existing social patterns. The innovator was the dread heretic. If his innovations did not eliminate him, the chances are his fellow men did. The slowness of the rise of man was not due to the lack of ingenuity or inventiveness, but rather to the conservative traditions of the prevailing social orders. The introduction of change came through accident; not so much the accident of innovations as the accident of their survival and acceptance. The great responsibility of the presiding guardians of the social groups was not that their social entities should progress, but rather that they should avoid progression, and that would-be progressives should receive the proper 'treatment.'

Future Frightens Intellectuals

Thus, through the process of natural selection, the human tendencies to remain the same have been preserved in the chromosomes, and the tendencies to seek something different have been culled out. A general revulsion against social change and a nostalgia for the ways of the recent past are deeply ingrained aspects of human nature. This phenomenon, along with the fact that we are now experiencing the most rapid change in man's social history, accounts for the epidemic of intellectual vomiting that is going on among the would-be protectors of man's social destiny and human values. Thus, such writers as Francois Mauriac, George Orwell, Kurt Vonnegut, Aldous Huxley, and many others view the future of 'materialistic progress' with a dim eye and seek retreat into the haven of the social mores, customs, and values of their own youths.

It is amazing, yet understandable when one knows the biological basis for it, that these people who most fear future social change are just as reluctant to abrogate post social change as they are to accept the new. They never advocate a return to the life of the cave man, for example, or even to the customs and values of a few centuries ago. Their nostalgia hovers about the customs, ideals, and values which prevailed in the locality and days of their own childhoods. Those are the things they grew up with and which they understand. When they review the present or look into the future, the customs and values look different from those they have known and they become frightened, or at least apprehensive, about their effects on the 'spiritual side' of man. Rather than seek a new understanding, they, in their conservatism, retreat subjectively to the more pleasant memories of their childhood and feel that 'too much' mechanical progress is somehow 'not good' for man. *They feel that we should declare a moratorium on all progress and repudiate some of that which has already occurred.*

These intellectual conservatives usually have a root in some ecclesiastical creed, which, by virtue of its 'infallibility,' cannot adapt to changes of a degree that is obvious to the individual during his lifetime; and, therefore, it follows that the change and not the creed must be rejected. Even so, many changes in beliefs (such as beliefs regarding the shape of the earth and the nature of the sun have been quietly instituted after the defensive battles have turned from them to some more recent controversy and the leading protagonists of the old beliefs have died off.

What are some of the things about the future that frighten the professional intellectual conservatives and turn them into reactionaries? What is it they yearn for in place of what they fear will come? The field of their revulsion is wide, so we shall take only a few representative examples.

One of the things that frightens them most of all is *the idea of freedom from toil for the human being.* They argue that the normal human likes to work; that, if you take him away from his work, he will become bored with his freedom, will sicken with ennui, and will become a ripe dupe for anyone who comes along and advocates the destruction of the machines that have deprived him of his cherished drudgery. Destroying some of the machines would be all right in their estimation, but they are afraid that the momentum of the mob reaction may go 'too far.'

For some reason hat would seem strange to the logician, but not to the biologist, their yearning for the past does not go back so far as the days of universal slavery, nor even to the 84-hour work-week; rather, it goes back only to the 40- or 44-hour week (plus some overtime, maybe). In the same way, we can anticipate that similar writers of the future will become nostalgic about the 24- or 28-hour week (with no overtime). The writers of today have graduated from the revulsion over workers being demoralized by the 8-hour day, which was the pet peeve of their predecessors on this same theme. It is not the 8-hour day, *but the 4-hour or 2-hour workday that bothers them now.*

Factories Without Men 'Evil'

The intellectual reactionaries of a few decades ago deplored the passing of the small home workshop with its handicraft industries, and they resented the creeping 'evil' of the factory assembly line, lamenting that it was turning human beings into mere cogs in the machine. It was reasoned that the human being, doing only one small detail in the production of something, could not have a constructive pride in his work or feel that he was really making something that reflected his personality, like in the handicraft days when the same individual made all parts of the item he produced. That phase of nostalgia has now nearly passed. The present crop of writers tends to feel a pride in the assembly line that employed thousands of happy workers, who left that they were, personally and with their own hands and skill, contributing to the manufacture of automobiles, radios, washing machines, and other gadgets—who felt that they were needed and that their work was useful to mankind. What this crop of writers wails about is *the automatic factory—the factory that turns out an abundance of complex things—without any men at all!* You can hear them crying out their souls: How can people feel pride in things that are not made by human hands? Automatic factories will soon deprive people of the privilege of using their muscles and skills in production. And the automatic factories will de-humanize the home. The joys Mom has in washing the clothes and hanging them out on the line, of cooking meals on the semi-automatic electric range, of sweeping the floors with a vacuum cleaner will become only memories; after a while, then, people won't remember those things at all.

A generation ago, their predecessors wailed because the delightful home, wherein Mom churned butter, baked bread, knitted stockings, and made clothes for the family (without benefit of Soap Operas on the radio to relieve the monotony), was fading memory, and they were shedding tears over that. In the near future, Mom will have no work to do and few decisions to make around the home. Home won't be like home anymore, will it? Poor Mom! How can life possibly be worth living for her? Wouldn't it be grand if she could go back to doing something about the house so that she could feel that she was needed there and belonged there? No, not back to scrubbing floors on her knees, or rubbing clothes clean on a washboard, or firing a woodburning cookstove with pieces of wood carried in from the pile out near the backhouse—we don't have to go back that far; after all, we've made some progress since then. But it would be nice, wouldn't it, if she could go back to the kitchen stove with controls that are set by hand, and the floor-waxing machine which she can guide across the floor while an electric motor does the work, and the washing machine that will let her do *something* (so she could take a break from watching television during the Soap Opera commercials). Ah, those were the good old days, we'll proclaim. That was when Mom felt that she was somebody; that she was needed; and that her work was appreciated because she had given of herself to it. Now, what is there in life for Mom? No work. A house that takes care of itself. Appliances that do their own thinking and turn themselves on and off. No maids to instruct, or worry about, or scold for incompetence.

Fear Life-Long Security

Well, so much for Mom. Suppose you are a man who is living a half century from now. What will you be doing? There will be no work in the factories for you. Nor in the offices; in fact, very few offices will be needed. All that paper work that required the employment of millions will be unnecessary, or it will be done by machines that don't make mistakes. You won't be wondering if the time is opportune for you to sneak out for a smoke or a cup of coffee on the boss's time, or if it is near enough quitting time for you to leave without being conspicuous. It is true for a period during the prime of your life you will have a functional designation and will give a few hours of attention per week to some operation of the functional mechanism that provides for the requirements of the population, but you could hardly call *that* a job. What are you going to do with the rest of your time? Wouldn't it be nice if you could go back a few decades, to working those four six-hour shifts per week, with a pay envelope every Thursday afternoon; and the long evening at the bar celebrating the end of the four-day work-week; and the long week-end, puttering around the house, doing chores for the 'missus,' and taking that annoying drive through the countryside in congested traffic on Sunday afternoon? And that happy feeling of going back to work Monday morning?

The intellectual reactionaries have a fear of what abundance will do to the character of future man. What incentive will a person have, if he receives a folder of Certificates every month, winter and summer, so long as he lives, and no questions asked? With them he can purchase anything he can use, and all he can use; and everyone else can do the same. You would feel like a parasite (or a politician), wouldn't you, taking income that you have not earned? You will miss the joys of counting your dollars and dimes (after tax deductions) to determine what bills you can pay now and what things you can make down payments on, and which ones you will have to postpone until another month or another year. Think of the great ecstacy that used to come with the realization that you had saved up enough for a down-payment on a new car. That won't happen anymore; for, you can have a really functional car anytime you want one, merely by presenting your driver's license. Further, you will always have a dwelling to live in, with no rent and no dickering with landlords; and you won't even have the privilege of ordering and paying for fuel oil, like in the good old days. Ah, that was the time, when a man had a few things to keep his mind occupied, like, for example, how long would he and his family be able to stay in the place where they then lived, or would he be able to keep his job until the worst of the bills were paid?

The one haunting thing that always lurks in the background of the specious arguments against social change is the fear that, if human beings have abundance, life-long security, and freedom from toil, they will cease to pay enough homage to the gods who preside over scarcity, poverty, property values, and untimely death. They fear that it will not be so easy to sell people promises of a favored position in a Free Enterprise Price System hereafter. If the underprivileged 'masses' do not have a duty and obligation to earn their sustenance with sweat and blood and tears, they might develop the concept that they have a Divine Right to life, liberty, and the pursuit of happiness. Imagine the problem of trying to tell such 'misguided' people that members of 'their class' are not entitled to the finer things in life unless they can establish title to them through inheritance, successful predation, ingenious chicanery, or singular luck. Such an effort, we suspect, would be about as fruitful as attempting to explain to the postwar debutante that a modern home, a new car, a fur coat, and a diamond ring should not be hers by right of marriage, but only right of long-term toil and sacrifice.

It is so easy for people to lose sight of the 'true values' and 'immutable verities.' People find it very easy to forego their poverty, their toil, their insecurity, and their yearning for a decent status in the hereafter, if the alternative is abundance of the material things of life, plenty of leisure, and security for the rest of their lives. *The moralists are not in favor of improving the general human welfare, but only in persuading people that they should be more content with their hardships and misfortunes;* and, if necessary (as it seems always to be), that they should share their scarcity a little more equitably with those who are still worse off—through organized charity institutions, of course.

Yes, it is verifiable that people do not welcome social change; but the change that they welcome least of all is a change from a higher to a lower socio-economic status, and doubly so if this change is accompanied by increasing toil and insecurity. How many wealthy people have you known who burned down or abandoned their swank houses, gave away their money, and dismissed their servants, so that they could return to the joys of living in a small, unpretentious house, working long hours for a low wage, and doing their own chores, in order to escape the ennui of being rich and idle and to recapture the simple values of the common man? Maybe it happens in fiction books (written by moral philosophers), but, if it happens in real life, we have yet to see an example.

The present generation of Americans has experienced the most profound and the most rapid social change of any generation since the beginning of man. This generation has had to witness the disappearance of more old things and the introduction of more new things and methods than any other generation to date. Hence, it is only natural that the people now living lack a feeling of social stability. The past has gone out from under them, never to return; the present is in a state of flux, with the reference points changing constantly; and the future is cloudy and full of questions. It's enough to make one's chromosomes turn over in their cells.

'Good Old Days' Gone

The capacity of the human being to tolerate change, however, is great, as has been demonstrated on many occasions. Man's ability to adjust to change when it comes is not the problem that concerns us. We know that he can meet almost any probable change and make a good 'go' of it. What we are discussing here is his psychological attitude toward change before it happens, particularly fundamental changes in the function and structure of the social order.

While there is a general resistance to change, which may on occasion develop into overt antagonism, this resistance has no definable course, it is not against any particular type of social structure nor in favor of any particular type of status quo, Man's inertia favors that which he has gotten used to and opposes anything that is appreciably different from that. For example, living in a large city apartment would be just as repugnant to a Navajo Indian as living in a desert hogan would be to a socialite born and raised in a large city. Farmers and city dwellers do not readily adapt to each other's pattern of life. In other words, the individual tends to prefer the pattern to which he has become familiar, although he does have a urge to rise at least one step above where he is within that pattern. Thus, adult immigrants to America from Europe never fully abandon their European culture, psychologically, even though their conditions here are immeasurably more comfortable than they were in place of origin as 'Home,' and to retain a nostalgic longing to revisit the land of their youth. Their descendants, having had no contact with the early 'alien' environment of their parents and grandparents, prefer to stay where they are, in the culture and surroundings with which they themselves have become familiar. In a similar manner, the older people who have grown up in America speak authoritatively and appreciatively of the 'good old days' before all these dubious 'new-fangled' changes came about; *but their children and grandchildren have little appreciation for the way of life about which they are talking.*

Rapid social change, we can be sure, will continue for another generation or more on the North American Continent. From then on, the rate of change probably will level off to a low incline. The Americans who are now growing up will not live out their lives in any pattern much resembling that of their youth. Theirs will be the burden of carrying the greatest degree of social change of any generation, past or future. But the generations following the next one or two will find conditions much more stable and, hence, more psychologically satisfying. They will accept and approve of their circumstances and wonder about the sanity of their ancestors who would endure the 'primitive' and 'barbaric' culture of the mid-Twentieth Century, with its wars, its Free Enterprise, and its political party conventions.

The culture of the New America must contain a number of fundamental changes from that of the old America and of the present transitional America. Among other things, there will be an abundance of goods and services available to everyone, without price. There will be ample free time at the disposal of the individual to do things of his own choosing. There will be much greater security from economic, criminal, 'psycho,' and legal hazards, and from external wars. *But we can be sure that the people of that day will not sit around feeling that their lives are empty, longing for the return of crime, predatory enterprise, political elections, human toil, and scarcity.* The people of that time will have vital interests, enjoyable pursuits, and individual probems. There will be more for them to gain in the way of 'human values' than they will lose. The people will be very similar to the people of today, biologically and psychologically, but they will approach the problems of life with different concepts and different backgrounds of experience. Our descendants also will not have the same values and imponderables that we have today.

In America, today, there are many who resent the social changes that are coming. They want to feel that what they cherish will be the same things that their children and grandchildren will cherish. They do not want to feel that the ideals and traditions that they worship will become rubbish tomorrow. Although present day Americans do not live up to the ideals of thrift, hard work, and piety that their grandparents had hoped they would perpetuate, still, they do not want their descendants to cast away the 'true values' which they, themselves, have happened to acquire by circumstances. Many of them would die in battle (or at least sacrifice their sons in battle) to uphold the virtues of debt, corporate enterprise, a republican form of government, and the right to buy real estate in the hereafter. But this generation, with its values and concepts, is a unique generation. There was never one like it before and there will never be one like it again. But the individual homo sapiens, instead of feeling honored by such a unique position in history, prefers to feel that he is the embodiment of the past, present, and future, all molded into one eternal verity.

Change from Pressure of Events

Any person in tolerable circumstances tends to be egotistical about his own way of life and to delude himself into the belief that other people, living in quite different circumstances, would readily and of their own free will change from their 'unfortunate' way of life to that of his own, given an opportunity to do so. *This is one of the greatest fallacies that at present plagues the American departments of psychological warfare.* If only the people behind the Iron Curtain could be informed of The Truth about our way of life, they believe, the poor souls would enthusiastically overthrow their leaders and rush with open arms to embrace a way of life that is strange to them— the way of Western Freedom. It is incomprehensible to many of us that people 'suffering' under conditions prevailing in Poland and Hungary, for example, should not welcome the 'blessings' of Freedom enjoyed by, say, the Italians and Britons.

It is inevitable that some of the older residents of Eastern Europe, who have had a new pattern of life suddenly imposed upon them, should yearn for the type of business enterprise, political regimentation, and church worship that prevailed in their youths, and that they should be susceptible to being lured with lush promises into fleeing across the border and into the hands of a new tyranny, which they are led to believe more closely resembles that of their youth. But we doubt that any worthwhile proportion of the younger people, conditioned to the 'other' way of life, can be seduced by promises of Western Freedom to come over to our side. We say this, not from the standpoint of appraisal of the relative merits of the two ways of life, *but from an understanding of the way human beings behave.*

When amateur 'authorities' on human nature dogmatically assert that we can't have social change because 'you can't change human nature,' you can be sure that they are expressing merely their subjective desires and not a resume of scientific knowledge about human behavior. *You can be sure they have a stake of some kind in the status quo,* if nothing more than a psychological addiction to its professed values and traditions. *But it so happens that social change is not dependent upon a change in human nature.* Sure, human nature resists social change; but, once the change is made, the same kind of human nature will hold onto the new milieu and in turn resist further changes from that.

Even though the human being has an internal inertia against change, he is on the whole more apathetic than stubborn. He will go along with change if he is pushed into it, and once this has happened his inertia will prevent his readily going back to the original circumstances. *The great majority will not fight against social change actively.* There will be demagogues who will put up a show of fighting change, in order to protect some 'investment' in the status quo; and there will be those who will fight for a 'return' to some particular pattern, such as laissez faire Free Enterprise, or States Rights. But the advocators of change, whether it is progressive or retrogressive, will find little popular support—that is, active support—unless the immediate conditions are intolerable and the people *have to* move somewhere. When that time comes, the people can just as easily be incited to take destructive action as to move to an improved position. The intellectual reactionaries take the view that destructive action would be for the better—providing it doesn't go too far. They would welcome a restrained destruction of the automatic factories, huge public works, and any strong centralized social control (except the spiritual). Then the world could be 'given back to the people' and all could work long hours producing the requirements of life by hand tool techniques. Their characters would develop, their souls would be saved, and they wouldn't have time to be bored with living.

Technocracy knows the psychological and biological factors which affect human beings who are faced with social change. We know *that people can and will change,* not readily and spontaneously, of course, nor as a result of ordinary means of intellectual persuasion, *but under the pressure of events.* Even under stable conditions, they will gradually accept that which appears to enhance their lot, such as the automobile, the telephone, the radio, and the bathtub. They will tolerate almost anything and eventually accept it as a matter of fact, if it is introduced quietly and gradually enough; for example, smoking of cigarettes by women, or income taxes. Although people do not purposely seek social change if what they have is not too burdensome, still, they will demand a change in the face of a major failure of the existing system. *Once the social emergency becomes acute, the demand for change will become epidemic by contagion.* Then, you better stay out of the road, Bud, or you'll get trampled under.

Technocracy is aware that the contradictions within the Price System are such that it has become self-destructive. Like the lemmings going down to the sea, the Price System cannot stop or turn back; it can only hurtle forward to total destruction. Its demise is merely a matter of time, and not very much time at that. As its malfunctioning accumulates, an increasing number of people will find their hopes and their planned patterns of life disrupted and their circumstances rendered intolerable. Then they will demand change, not from a desire for change, but from compulsion. And, since they have to change, and as the demand intensifies into a mass emotion, they will want a big change while they're at it. They might as well take the best that is 'on the market.'

Technocracy Offers More

Technocracy offers the people of North America far more than any other organization. In the field of social change, nothing can compete with Technocracy. It offers the people more in the way of material abundance, comfortable living, and long-range security than anything else yet proposed; and it has a sound technological basis, which none of the other movements have. It is 100 percent North American and is tailor-made for this Continent.

Technocrats have a big job ahead of them—the job of giving direction to the greatest mass-movement in history. They are tightening their ranks and getting prepared for the time when a common inquiry on the street will be: *'Listen, Mack, I want to join Technocracy; where do I go to sign up?'*

The Quiet Revolution

Edmund A. Opitz

The great naturalist, John Burroughs, wrote that "in the ordinary course of nature, the great beneficent changes come slowly and silently. The noisy changes, for the most part, mean violence and disruption. . . . The still small voice is the voice of life and growth. . . . In the history of a nation it is the same."

This is a time of noisy change, a time of violence and disruption, a time of perpetual crisis. There is, we are told, a crisis in family life, a crisis in the cities, a crisis in race relations, a crisis in religion. Doubt has been cast on all the old certainties; nothing appears fixed except change—and the inmates are trying to run the asylum. The present mood has been captured in the familiar lines by William Butler Yeats:

Things fall apart; the centre cannot hold;
Mere anarchy is loosed upon the world. . . .
The best lack all conviction, while the worst
Are full of passionate intensity.

A bill of particulars is not needed; any man can supply his own, from any newspaper, any day of the week. And the feeling grows among us that the whirlwind of change which has scrambled our value system has erased all guidelines, all benchmarks, all standards.

The 1960's have not dealt kindly with Americans, and our magnificent accomplishments in outer space serve but to highlight the tragic ruptures which mar our social life. We are bogged down in a land war in Asia, as a phase of the cycle of wars into which we have been locked since 1914. Whereas America was once regarded by the world's peoples as "the last, best hope of earth," it is now reviled in many quarters. Latin American countries ask a Presidential emissary to call off his tour because they cannot guarantee his safety. The nineteenth century trend in the direction of constitutionally guaranteed liberties of the citizen in his personal, his social, anl his economic affairs slowed to a halt in the twentieth. The tide of totalitarianism began to rise, and communism in Russia has recently celebrated its fiftieth anniversary, confident of its strength, sure of the future, able to count on the disaffected of all countries—including our own—as allies.

We are uncertain about the philosophical basis of our own form of society; Adam Smith seems almost as remote as the original Adam, and who reads *The Federalist Papers* nowadays? The Executive branch has become semi-autonomous, and the Supreme Court usurps a legislative function. At the level where most of us live there is mounting concern over increased crime and the open incitements to violence—to which certain sectors of our society respond by displaying a paranoid sense of collective guilt. And then there are the demonstrations, the riots, and that crushing blow to our spirit—three tragic assassinations.

What has happened to people? What will become of America? What of the church in all this?

Outward Signs of Inner Turmoil

I take it as axiomatic that external disorder and social strife is a reflection of disorder in the mind and soul. For it is in the nature of the human condition that man forever seeks a harmony within himself, that is, an ordered soul; and secondly, he works for an outer order of society. Thomas Aquinas put it this way: "Man has a natural inclination toward knowing the truth about God, and toward living in society." This is to restate the Great Commandment given to us by the Master when he said: "Thou shalt love the Lord thy God with all thy heart, and with all thy soul, and with all thy mind, and with all thy strength. . . . And thy neighbor as thyself." (Mark 12:30-31) The inner and spiritual liberty proclaimed in the Gospels must seek to realize itself and find proper expression in outer and social freedom. Christianity penetrates society and creates the appropriate political and economic structures by means of Christian persons who are citizens or magistrates. The earth will never witness a fully realized Christian society, for this would mean the Kingdom of God, and God's Kingdom is beyond history. But what we can hope for is a society Christian in its norms, Christian in its understanding that man is formed to serve a transcendent end, to fulfill a purpose beyond society.

Biblical religion understands the world as the creation of God who looked out upon his work and called it good. It regards man as a creature who bears a unique relation to this God, being formed in his image—meaning that man possesses free will and the ability to command his own actions. This free being is given dominion over the earth with the admonition to be fruitful and multiply. He is commanded to work in order that he might eat; he is made steward of the earth's resources and held accountable for their economic use. He is to respect the life of his neighbor and not covet his goods; theft is wrong because property is right. When this outlook comes to prevail, the groundwork is laid for a free and prosperous commonwealth; the City of Man is not an end in itself, it is the proving ground for the City of God.

"Secular Christianity"

The comtemporary outlook is quite different. It excludes God from its reckoning, and in a sector of the church we witness the paradox of a school of thought proclaiming "secular Christianity." The present outlook views the world as self-existent and man is reduced to a mere natural product of natural forces—autonomous man, stripped of all attachments which were thought to bind him to a transcedent realm of being. Shorn of his cosmic dimension, man is depersonalized; no longer the creature of God, he is reduced to a mere unit of mass society struggling to retain vestiges of his humanity as his world goes through a time of troubles.

Secular trends have acquired such a momentum that religious movements tumble along in their wake. Theologians talk about the death of God and the new morality. The New Clergy tell us that *the church must go,* as they rush out to man the barricades; they preach violence and the overthrow of society. "The New Clergy intersects with the New Left," declares a writer in a recent *Harpers.* "These men are out to remake the world," some wit remarked, "as God would have made it in the first place—except he lacked the funds!"

Politically-minded churchmen seek to shape the churches into an ecclesiastical power bloc which would reduce religion to a mere instrument of revolutionary social change. We witness the growth of organizations, agencies, and councils designed to bring ecclesiastical leverage to bear on society, in a manner indistinguishable from the efforts of secular collectivists. Chief among these is the National Council of Churches and the World Council. If social salvation were to be had from large, powerful, and prestigious ecclesiastical organizations, then we should have been saved already. But provide a religious organization with wealth and power and it begins to change into a secular agency. The church in every age has come under the spell of secular movements and enthusiasms, to the detriment of spiritual religion. Churchmen dream of a large and powerful organization, both for the sake of the church itself—as they think —and for the sake of what that church might accomplish by its influence on government. In former days, churchmen invoked government to guarantee purity of doctrine by punishing those who deviated into some heresy. The aim was to get more souls into heaven. Today, churchmen seek to strengthen the hand of government and give it the power to manage the economy and control, where needed, the lives of the citizenry. The aim is to guarantee economic security from cradle to grave.

Mistaken Methods

It is easy for us now to see that medieval churchmen were mistaken in thinking that souls could be shoveled into heaven by the forced repetition of some incantation. Someday it will be just as evident that present-day churchmen are sadly misguided in their preoccupation with the reshuffling of the existing stock of economic goods. Like the secular liberals and collectivists, these churchmen expect to overcome economic disabilities by political interventions. They'll never achieve prosperity by taking this tack. Poverty can be overcome by increased productivity, and in no other; and a society of free men is more productive than any other. It follows that we maximize production and minimize poverty only as men are increasingly free to pursue their personal aims—including their economic goals—within the framework of law. Prosperity, in fact, is a by-product of liberty. Limit the government to its proper competence, so that men are uncoerced in their interpersonal relations—including their economic arrangements—and the general level of well-being rises.

A generation ago, Dean Inge of St. Pauls foresaw a "reversion to political and external religion, the very thing against which the Gospel declared relentless war." It is not that Christianity regards social progress as unimportant, the Dean goes on to say; it is a question of how genuine improvement may best be promoted; "the true answer . . . is that the advance of civilization is a sort of by-product of Christianity, not its chief aim; but we can appeal to history to support us that this progress is most stable and genuine when it is a by-product of a lofty and unworldly idealism."

The church is *in* the world, but it is not wholly *of* the world. Whenever it seeks to further social progress by embracing the currently fashionable political nostrum, it not only fails to achieve its social ends by politicalizing its gospel, but it betrays its own nature as well. The church's job is to remind man, in season and out, who he really is and what he may become; and this task, in every age, means some resistance to "the world." The church must never marry the spirit of the age, Dean Inge used to say, for if she does she'll be a widow in the next.

The Saving Remnant

Sometimes we despair of the church, but we must not forget that in every age there has been a creative and self-renewing activity at work within it; and it's at work there today. This is the saving Remnant. The seventeenth century Church of England Bishop, Richard Warburton, pondered these matters. Is the church worth saving, he wondered? Whimsically, he compared the church to Noah's ark, and concluded that the church, like the ark of Noah, "*is* worth saving, not for the sake of the unclean beasts that almost filled it and probably made much noise and clamor in it, but for the little corner of rationality [Noah and family] that was as much distressed by the stink within as by the tempest without."

The French have a saying: "The situation is desperate; but it's not serious." The human venture has always been an up-hill fight. The biological odds were against the emergence of man, and the scales have always been weighted against man's survival. But these facts, in themselves, have never been grounds for widespread or long-continued despair; certainly not wherever the Christian faith has taken hold.

A certain seventeenth century New England Puritan left a journal, in which was found this entry: "My heart leaps for joy, every time I hear the good news of damnation." Now the Puritans were a peculiar people, and this one had an odd way of putting things. But perhaps he is telling us something, in his oblique way. It *is* good news that man possesses the gift of freedom so far-reaching that he is personally responsible for the ultimate fate of his soul. This is not to say that man saves himself; it is to say that the individual may choose to accept or reject the means of grace made available to him, and that his act of choosing is determinative.

Responsibility Implies Freedom

This old doctrine says, first of all, that Somebody in the universe cares for us individually, one by one. Such is the basic implication of any system of rewards and punishments based on merit or demerit. The conviction that this is a universe where, in the long run, we *do* get our just deserts implies that we have a responsibility for our lives; that nobody really gets away with anything.

No man is held accountable for an outcome which his actions did not affect one way or the other. Responsibility implies freedom. To say that man is a responsible being is to say that his freely made choices do cause things to happen this way rather than that. Life's alternate possibilities of reward and punishment imply that men *must* choose. And because the universe does not jest, it has not given man the freedom to make a choice as to how he will commit his life without at the same time equipping that choice with power to affect the ultimate outcome. This is the core of the Doctrine of Election which a hillbilly preacher explained to his flock in this fashion: "The Lord votes for you; the Devil votes against you. It's the way *you* vote that decides the election." Even if you do nothing, your very inaction becomes a form of action, affecting the outcome one way or the other.

The Power behind the universe has so much confidence in man that it has made him a free and responsible being. This is a basic premise of our religious heritage, but our generation, like each before it, must earn its heritage anew before we can make it our own.

The rest of creation is complete; we alone are unfinished. The Creator has given the animal world all the answers it needs; answers locked up in instinctual responses as old as time. But man has *not* been given the answers; before *our* eyes the Creator has posed a gigantic question mark. We are handed a question, and the answer is ours to give. We have the responsibility, the freedom and the power to respond.

If these things are true at all, they are true for everyone, but not everyone is equally able to grasp them as truths. Organizations that are equipped with the blinders fastened on them by wealth, power, and success are handicapped; they come to care more for their image than for the truth. It is sad to observe that nothing fails like success. But organizations and individuals who are *not* drawn into the power-and-success game may advance the truth without encumbering it with themselves. They may become part of the saving Remnant.

"Be still, and know that I am God," sang the Psalmist (Ps. 46:10). "In quietness . . . shall be your strength," said Isaiah. (Isaiah 30:15) Victory for the things we want victorious comes not with noisy demonstrations, clamorous agitation, bustling campaigns, shouted slogans, heated discussions, passionate arguments, emotional debates, demagogic harangues;

neither will it come by a display of power or a show of strength. The only victories worth winning arrive quietly, by the slow progress of thought, by the refinement of moral values. "Nothing is so powerful as an idea whose time has come," and the ripening of ideas in the corridors of men's minds and the translation of these into appropriate action when ready is the only way man may advance. It is in the intellect and in the moral imagination—that is, in the human spirit—that men may "wait upon the Lord and renew their strength."

The great Swiss economist, Wilhelm Roepke, was also a deeply religious man. He fought in World War I and was the first intellectual exiled by Hitler. "For more than a century," he writes, "we have made the hopeless effort more and more baldly proclaimed, to get along without God. It is as though we wanted to add to the already existing proofs of God's existence, a new and finally convincing one; the universal destruction that follows on assuming God's nonexistence. The genesis of the malady from which our civilization suffers lies in the individual soul and is only to be overcome within the individual soul." And if the care of souls is not, first and foremost, the province of the church, what—in God's name—is the church's main business?

Disorder in society reflects a disorientation in man's inner life. If there is confusion as to the proper end, aim, and goal of personal life, then bizarre social ideologists will prove irresistibly attractive and a sickness spreads in society. A healthy society, on the other hand, is the natural consequence of sound thinking and right action among men and women who are pursuing the life-goals proper to human beings.

The church is a means for ends beyond itself; and our lives contain potentialities which can never be fully realized on the biological and social planes alone. We are involved in lost causes; but take heart from St. Paul, where he speaks of foolish things confounding the wise and weak things confounding the mighty. Paradoxically, there *is* a kind of wisdom in foolishness. And there are victories in lost causes, because God may choose them to work out his purposes.

Science, Technology, and Rebellion

Walter A. Weisskopf

Science and technology are supposed to increase man's power to understand, to predict and, thereby, to control nature. But science has shown us a universe so vast and complex that it defies comprehension. It has demoted man from what was previously conceived as a central position to a haphazard, accidental freak of creation whose role in the universe seems without any meaning. Everything that was supposed to give meaning and purpose to his life such as religious and philosophical ideas and ideals has been debunked by science. It cannot be denied that we know much more than our ancestors about the universe; but this kind of knowledge has not increased control of our destiny; on the contrary it has only uncovered our exposure to unknowable and uncontrollable forces. Real self-determination would require the discovery of meaning in the universe and in history; science has made both more meaningless and incomprehensible.

This conclusion is not contradicted by our enormous scientific and technological "accomplishments." Every step towards more control through science and technology has implicit destructive results; every step forward is accompanied by negative effects. Improvement in health and longevity brought about the population explosion; economic growth is tied in with urbanization and its over-crowding, ghettos, traffic jams, ugliness and discomforts. Some of the greatest advances in technology have been connected with wars and the making of destructive weapons. Every new factory not only produces more goods but pollutes air and water and destroys the landscape. Pesticides remove harmful insects but poison nutritious plants. Cars transport us faster to points which become more and more undesirable to reach because the countryside is covered with cement and habitats have become unlivable.

Bureaucratization is not in conflict with science, technology and their industrial application, but is their necessary consequence. The enormous literature on mass organizations, including Galbraith's *The New Industrial State,* has made it quite clear that the requirements of modern technology for large capital investments and technological and managerial expertise push inevitably in the direction of more bureaucratization, and the domination of mass-organization in industry and government.

All this works against self-determination and individual autonomy. It is obvious that individual autonomy is best served in small communities with *direct* democracy. Even direct democracy reduces autonomy if it applies majority rule. *Representative* democracy weakens individual autonomy further; and in a mass society where the individual can participate only by going to the polls once in two or four years, and is subject to the rule of agencies over which he has little control, there is preciously little autonomy. To be optimistic about individual self-determination in a time when the secret decisions and mistakes of a few presidents and their advisers got us into the most insane war of our history seems almost ludicrous.

What the economy of mass consumption does to our standards of living has been pointed out by Galbraith. It has subjected us to the imperative of producing and consuming more and more goods regardless of the importance for our individual and national goals. As he says:

> More die in the United States of too much food than of too little. Where the population was once thought to press on the food supply, now the food supply presses relentlessly on the population. No one can seriously suggest that the steel which comprises the extra four or five feet of purely decorative distance on our automobiles is of prime urgency. For many women and some men clothing has ceased to be related to protection from exposure and has become, like plumage, almost exclusively erotic. Yet production remains central to our thoughts.

And more and more weapons and missiles bring us closer to the possibility of final destruction. We are getting accustomed to a way of life which seeks its ultimate meaning in the pursuit of elusive possessions and comforts. Under the impact of these material standards—from which some claim we gain more autonomy—the consumer has been subjected increasingly to the domination and seduction of advertising and salesmanship and has become unabel to develop and apply any individual standards for what is good and what is bad in consumption. Under the impact of an economistic, materialistic, life-style which meets the alleged needs of corporate and aggregate economic growth, we have accepted the insane idea that having and consuming more and more is a good thing.

The psychological wisdom of all ages shows that the contrary is true and that moderation and balance in consumption and possession is the road to mental health and well-being. How one can maintain that our so-called high standards of living are mentally and physically healthy in view of the facts shown to every psychiatrist by the occupiers of their therapeutic couches: the boredom, the alienation, the meaninglessness, the self-accusations and complexes of the rich, the powerful and the upper classes can only be explained as conscious or unconscious subservience to the industrial establishment. That does not mean that the fight for greater equality of income distribution is meaningless; under the given conditions the glaring differences between standards and styles of life are a deep source of alienation and unrest; but without moderating the drive of the affluent majority for more and more income, such equalization is condemned to failure.

It is sometimes argued that the present-day rebellions are a continuation of the development towards modernization. There is, however, a deep conflict between the attitudes of the new rebels and all the technological and economic values of modern society. One of the most penetrating studies of the new rebels (Kenneth Keniston, *The Young Radicals*) talks about the ambivalence of post-modern youth towards technology. The young rebels reject "Bureaucratization, impersonality, regimentation . . . conformity, its bigness, stratification, fixed roles, . . . efficiency, quantification, and measurement of human beings"—all unavoidable traits of technological society. But the rebels have to use technology, especially its mass media, and their rebellion is partly made possible by the affluent economy. There can be no doubt, however, that, in spite of this ambivalence, the rebels feel little or no optimism concerning the existing society, and that they do not see a direct line of progress from technology, science and affluence to self-determination and autonomy. Their very rebellion is directed against the lack of participation which technological society has brought about. What the young ones rebel against is science, technology, and economic growth as ends in themselves, as ideologies.

This is the end-result of a long dialectical process in the West in which the very instruments of progress have brought about an alienation from meaning, goals, purpose, and values. The process started with the secularization of religious beliefs; Western ideals such as dignity of the individual, autonomy, freedom, self-determination, were derived from religious beliefs. But during the eighteenth and nineteenth centuries these ideals were translated into secular thought, and based on the idea of natural law and inalienable rights.

This basis was destroyed by the very factor now held to be conducive to the actualization. Technology fostered a pragmatic attitude towards ideas and values; in technology, the ends are not questioned, they are given by technical requirements, and only the appropriate means are considered. Science destroyed the realm of ideals because the normative seems to have no place in the world of scientific facts. Science and technology implicitly led to a disintegration not only of ideals and values but removed them from their universe of discourse and activity altogether. In science, technology, and business, ideals and moral principles have no place or are subordinated to production, consumption and the profit motive. Thus, in the fields which predominate in modern society, ideals are homeless; and all other dimensions of life in which ideals may have been formed—such as religion, ethics, moral thought, art, became of secondary important and were neglected and emptied of values. What originally were means—science, technology, and economic activity—became, in the absence of any belief system about ultimate values, ends in themselves. The realm of means was elevated into the realm of ends. Science, technology, and economic action became ideologies. Thus we arrive at a situation in which economic growth and technical change are the ultimate goals of business *and* of society.

This is the main cause for the anomie, apathy, meaninglessness, and lack of purpose in Western life which is so widely discussed today as alienation. It is against this alienation that the radical rebellion of the young is directed. Therefore, this rebellion is also directed against the values which stem from technology, business, and a science empty of values. This science, together with mass society and the conformity of organization men in science, industry, government and in the universities, is the butt of the attack. That the rebels are ambivalent about the robots does not contradict this fact. What matters is that the rebels aim at the humanization of the robots: they want them to be means to ends which are not dictated by them and by the technocracy which serves them. Whether this is possible is the great question of post-industrial society. The solution to this problem, however, will not be promoted by closing our eyes to the detrimental effects of science, industry, and technology on the human condition and their dialectical conflict with freedom, self-determination, and autonomy.

America at the Crossroads: Authoritarianism or Chaos?

James H. Madole

A glimmer of light has finally appeared in American scientific circles which previously have always elected to sacrifice the pure truth of scientific fact on the altar of political expediency. At this point three recognized scientific and educational authorities have actually dared to question the sacred Liberal domga that all racial groups are inherently equal. Dr. William Shockley, a Nobel Prize winning American physicist at Stanford University, has stated that our nation is undergoing serious "down-breeding" of its racial stock by the huge illegitimate birth rate among Negroes of low inborn intelligence. Shockley also pointed out a somewhat lower increase among illegitimate children born to Whites of low intellect. Secondly, Shockley stressed that Blacks are, as a rule, born mentally inferior to Whites and that our educational system should reflect this simple genetic fact rather than lowering America's standards of intelligence to meet the needs of aborigines. As an immediate example of this practice, a passing grade in High School geometry was 75% in 1945; it became 65% after the 1954 Supreme Court decision on school integration; and in June 1969 it was lowered to 55% so that 14,000 black geniuses could be released into the American intellectual community!

Meanwhile the Russian and Chinese educational standards are both state-subsidized and require ever-greater degrees of scholastic achievement on the part of their students prior to the granting of any degree. Ultimately this idiocy of accommodating the American educational system to the mental needs of hopelessly primitive racial groups will spell disaster to America's ability to compete with Soviet Russia and Red China both in nuclear research and in the exploration of Outer Space. There is no room for misguided sentiment on the part of Christian zealots when their pious whimperings about "human equality" endanger the welfare of Aryan Man's destiny in the SPACE AGE. When Dr. Shockley presented his views to The National Academy of Sciences, the leading scientific body in the United States, and requested that a study of heredity and its effect on the Race Question be undertaken by that eminent body, he was refused by a vote of 200 to 10! In a similar vein Dr. Herbert E. Warfel was forced to resign his position as superintendent of Caribbean Consolidated Schools in San Juan, Puerto Rico because of a speech delivered to the Rotary Club in which he blamed the violence on American university campuses to the hereditary inferiority of Negro students. Dr. Warfel attributed his information to an article in the "Harvard Educational Review" by Dr. Arthur Jensen, a professor of educational psychology at the University of California, which stressed that Negroes are genetically, and therefore mentally, inferior to White. Tremendous pressure is being exerted by the tax-exempt Ford and Rockefeller Foundations as well as Jewish millionaires who subsidize American educational institutions and scientific research projects to stifle these voices of rebellion in academic circles. Only by understanding the Messianic religion of World Jewry based upon ancient Talmudic doctrine can we gain an insight into the maniacal will of "God's chosen people" to break down all racial and class barriers in the Gentile World. It was best expressed in a letter from Baruch Levy to Karl Marx as follows:

"The Jewish People, taken collectively, will be its own Messiah. It will attain to mastery of the world through the union of all other human races, through abolition of boundaries and monarchies, which are the bulwarks of particularism, and through the erection of a universal Republic, in which the Jews will everywhere enjoy universal rights. In this new organization of mankind the sons of Israel will spread themselves over the whole inhabited world, and they, since they belong all to the same race and culture-tradition, without at the same time having a definite nationality, form the leading elements without finding opposition. The government of the nations, which will make up this universal Republic, will pass without effort into the hands of the Israelites, by the very fact of the victory of the proletariat. The Jewish race can then do away with private property, and after that everywhere administer the public funds. Then shall the promises of the Talmud be fulfilled. When the time of the Messiah has come, the Jews will hold in their hands the key to the wealth of the world."

The Jew, because of his messianic Talmudic beliefs, will always be the spiritual enemy of Aryan Man. By his very nature the Jew must work for the ethical, cultural, and racial destruction of Aryan society. Democracy, or rule by the politically unsophisticated mob, is the tool used by the Hebraic leadership to fuse the hordes of primitive, illiterate Negroes and half-castes, the social outcasts and economic failures in the lower echelons of the White Race, and the starry-eyed religious zealots and budding social reformers among the upper class of White society into the massive base needed to uphold the pyramid of Jewish political and economic power in the Western World. Read again the text of Baruch Levy's letter to Karl Marx and you will grasp the basic psychology of the Jewish mind which makes him forever the mortal antagonist of Aryan Man.

If Aryan Man is to survive and multiply he must learn to see the universe in the light of Cosmic Law rather than devising ridiculous anthropomorphic Gods, shaped from the Hebrew fantasies of the Old Testament, which in turn were plagiarized from still more ancient Babylonian, Assyrian, and Akkadian myths of the Great Flood, Adam and Eve, etc. Under the poisonous opiate of Judeo-Christian mythology our Aryan manhood has been corroded into accepting as virtues such despicable, effiminate characteristcs as humility, meekness, glorification of cowardice and weakness on the part of the individual, and love for those who have sworn to destroy us! We forget that 500 million years of organic evolution on this planet demonstrates the inflexible Cosmic Law of necessary struggle between different species of plants and animals coupled with a process of Natural Selection to weed out the unfit and thus assure the *survival of the fittest!*

Aryan Man, under Hebrew guidance, has chosen to accept an Old Testament anthropomorphic God, shaped in his own image, and then given further affrontery to Cosmic Reality by placing words in the mouth of their man-made "God" which directly contravene the Laws of Nature, which we assume must be the Laws of the true Cosmic Divinity else they could not exist! Because Racial Nationalists must learn to combat with logic the delusions of well-meaning Christians who have been ruthlessly deluded into fighting against their own racial interests by a profit-minded Church Hierarchy, I strongly suggest that our readers purchase copies of "The Great Secret" by M. Maeterlinck, a Belgian Nobel prize winner, who traces the history of religion and the true nature of that Cosmic Force we call "God." I might also suggest "The Twilight of the Idols" and "The Anti-Christ" by Friedrich Nietzsche and "Imperium" by Francis P. Yockey as the foundation stones of a needed philosophy for Aryan Man. All can be found on our book list this month.

The myth of racial equality promoted by fuzzy-minded clergymen on soul-saving missions to Africa, by reactionary business entrepreneurs seeking new consumer markets without regard to the racial welfare of America, and by Jewish pseudo-scientists like Ashley Montagu (Ehrenberg), Sir Basil Davidson of "The Lost Cities Of Africa" fame, Ruth Benedict and Gene Weltfish (whose works are usually sponsored by the Anti-Defamation League of B'nai B'rith) has brought Aryan Society to the brink of doom on the North American Continent. Honest scientists like Dr. William Shockley, Dr. Herbert Warfel, and Dr. Arthur Jensen are fired from their eminent positions or ridiculed into silence by the kept media of communication with the American public. The results of downgrading the racial stock in our nation may be seen by the astronomical rise in the crime rate, particularly in major urban centers where Blacks are fast becoming the chief inhabitants, and in figures put out by the U. S. Census Bureau which point out that approximately 141,000 White Americans were fleeing our cities yearly in the period 1960-1966 but in the period 1968-1969 they are leaving at a rate of 500,000 per annum. With the productive racial elements fleeing to Suburbia our cities can no longer meet their financial needs since the colored population are totally unskilled and a burden on the few remaining taxpayers. Hence Aryan civilization is dying a slow death in the United States as the colored birth-rate soars and the White birth-rate steadily diminishes!

Those who oppose the NRP because of its authoritarian nature must eventually come to grips with the fact that Conservative leadership comprised of men like George Wallace, William Buckley, Jr., and Strom Thurmond is ideologically enslaved to the principles of 19th Century Constitutional government and the Judeo-Christian ethic. If one of these products of a bygone age were placed at the helm of our Ship of State, what steps could he take, under the provisions of Constitutional Law, to halt the Black birth-rate and remove 25 million racial inferiors from our American shores? What remedial action could be taken, under the aegis of that Constitution which our immature Conservatives idolize as a semi-Divine document, to smash the political and economic influence of American Jewry which has proven so detrimental to Aryan interests? Only a dictatorship has the unlimited power to act against those racial elements whose very existence within our nation endangers the future survival of Aryan Man? If they continue to breed like rabbits we shall find that under the democratic principle of "One Man, One Vote," with the Constitution still intact, our racial inferiors will vote Aryan Man out of existence or into slavery to primitive savages! Mssrs. Thurmond, Wallace, or Buckley would simply be voted out of political office by the future Black majority.

Because I do not subscribe to the ridiculous Judeo-Christian concepts of love, compassion, and mercy toward my enemies and the sworn foes of Aryan Man, I feel uniquely qualified to build this movement. I want the young men in the National Renaissance Party to have the unbridled pride of Lucifer who, upon his defeat by the hosts of Heaven, hurled his defiance in the phrase "Better to reign in Hell than serve in Heaven," I want them to have the physical stamina and relentless perseverance of a pack of timber wolves, I want them to cultivate wisdom and desire for knowledge which can raise their minds to a God-like level and, above all, I want them to hate with a passion to match the fiery pits of hell; for only those who can hate their enemies with a vengeance can know true love for their own Race and Nation! From these young Americans who join us now we shall create a superior race of human beings hampered by the false virtues of humility, love for enemies, meekness, compassion toward inferiors who menace the future of Aryan Man in the Space Age, and charity towards failures. Instead Aryan Man will have the true virtues of courage, devotion toward duty, a mind which seeks out the hidden facets of Nature and uses them to enrich the Racial Community, and pride in his personal and collective achievements. Thus the NRP sends out its challenge to the people of America: *authoritarianism or chaos!*

Proposed Constitutional Change on Voting

Sons of Liberty

Regardless of your political affiliation or preference, I am sure that you are as concerned as I am over the political stagnation in the United States of America.

The Establishment in Washington has done all in its power to make sure that all political dissent at the polls is stifled.

Every two years Americans are urged to vote for tweedle dee and tweedle dum.

The same group of dullards from the Republican and Democratic parties run for office. If the trend seems to be going to the left, they come out leftist; if the trend seems to be going to the right, they come out rightist. Our Congressmen (and Senators) are mere political prostitutes without an ounce of courage, philosophy, or idealism.

Any idealist who tries to run for Congress or the Senate is quickly smashed by the Establishment.

The present electoral laws make it almost impossible for any new party to get on the ballot and make it almost impossible for new candidates to win.

While members of many political groups live *across the U. S.* not enough people of many minor party live in *one concentrated area* to elect even *one Congressman.*

The views of at least 40% of all Americans are not being heard. People, both left and right, are continuously being forced to vote for the "lesser of two evils" instead of for candidates that represent their viewpoints.

All Congressmen in Washington are compromisers. They all vote for each other's bills and make behind the scenes deals. They all believe in live and let live. Their motto is don't do anything to upset the boat. Their master program is to do just enough to fool the people back home and get elected each time. Their key issues are health, wealth, and social welfare bills. They go to great pains to avoid taking a stand on controversial issues. None of them seem to have *true* principles or political philosophies.

We believe that all *political viewpoints should be heard.* No matter how radical or how different from our own. We believe that the people have a right to vote for the candidate or party of their choice.

As a start in modernizing our outdated Congressional election system we advocate the following:

1. A law should be passed or the people should get a Constitutional Amendment to add 100 Congressmen to our present Congress.
2. These Congressmen would be elected *at large* nation wide.
3. This would be done in the following way:

The names of regular candidates of the major parties would appear on the ballots in each state as usual. This would mean the normal 538 Congressional candidates now elected from the Republican and Democratic parties would still run from their respective districts against candidate nominated in the normal procedure.

Any minor party wishing to run Congressional candidates *at large* would have to get a minimum of 1,000 certified signatures in each state.

Any minor party qualifying with the 1,000 names would have their *party name and emblem* prominently displayed on the ballot on a *special* line with other minor parties. People voting for any of these parties would be doing so *nation wide at large*.

Voters would be voting for *parties* instead of individual candidates from designated areas. The total vote of each party from all 50 states would be added together and the parties would get their Congressmen according to the total national vote they received. Using the 1968 voting pattern it would run something like this: 25 Democrats, 20 Republicans, 13 American Independents, 6 Peace and Freedom, 2 Communists, 3 States Righters, 10 Black Militants, 2 Socialists, 10 Independents, 1 Prohibition Party, 2 Anarchists, 3 Conservative Party, 3 Liberals.

What would happen, in effect, is that people would be allowed to vote for their philosophy, ideals and true convictions. Candidates from any minority radical party could more or less depend on 80% of their hard core vote staying with them permanently. Therefore, once elected to the Congress they could speak without fear of reprisal and intimidation. They would *not* have to back the establishment or compromise.

Along with this, any minor political party polling 5% of the vote nation wide would (if the party requested it) have its candidates for the regular Congress, Senate, State offices and local offices placed on the ballot in individual states without further red tape.

Once a minor party reached the 5% it could then contest Congressional seats in selected areas against named candidates of other parties which qualify. Therefore, if any party should have a program which would merit the support of more than the normal hard core of voters it would eventually grow into a major party.

In the *at large* Congressional elections candidates would be elected on the party *label* and not as individual candidates. Therefore, the *parties* would *appoint* their nominees to sit in the Congress under their party name.

The minor parties would also have the right to withdraw the name of the nominee after his two year term and name another to take his place.

Petitions that the minor parties would use to run their candidates at large would be provided by the Secretary of State in the several states.

The wording on the petitions would be simple and to the point. Petitions could also be typed or mimeographed or printed by offset or letterpress as long as the correct wording was used. One original petition from any state could serve as an example.

Petitions could have the name and address of the party distributing them on them so they could be returned to the proper people distributing them. The information pertaining to when the petitions should be turned in could also be included on the bottom of the petitions. Each petition should be printed or drawn up using one side only with space for at least fifty signatures. Petitions do not have to be completely filled out with the maximum number of names to be turned in.

Any citizen of the United States would be eligible to circulate and turn in the petitions.

Qualified voters would be eligible to sign the petitions. Each qualified voter would be eligible to only sign a petition for *one* political party in each pre-election petition drive.

Petitions would not have to be notarized but the several states would be obligated to check on the validity of the signatures obtained.

Petitions would be made available to the respective parties within ninety days after the passage of the voting bill.

Petitions could be completed and turned in anytime up till ninety days before the next Congressional election.

Party names would only be included on the ballot in states where the petitions with the proper number of signatures have been turned in and validated by the state.

The Federal government will make available funds to the

respective states to cover cost of validating signatures and setting up the proper levers on voting machines. No charges whatsoever will be made to the new parties.

If the bill is passed within six months after the swearing in of a new congress, Congress will call a special election six months from the date of the passage of the bill.

The next election of at large congressmen will take place at the regularly scheduled Congressional elections.

The parties will be required to hold a national convention of the national central committee at a designated place and time within twenty days after the federal count of percentage votes and nominate their number of congressmen.

The names of the nominated congressmen will then be turned over to the Clerk of Congress and preparations will be made to swear them in to take their seats.

After the first election when at large candidates run at the same time as regular Congressmen, the minor parties will be required to submit their at large congressmen's names to the Clerk of Congress twenty days before the official swearing in of the new members of Congress.

In the event of two or more minor parties not receiving 1% of the vote, they may call and hold a joint convention and merge into a single party under one party name with new officers elected and combine their total popular vote to qualify for one congressman or more. This is to insure that no voter will lose his vote in the election.

Any minor party upon receiving 5% or more of the popular vote will qualify to receive the same equal time through radio, T.V. and newspaper coverage as any other party that has been established.

Candidates nominated for Congress by the parties must meet all the standard voting qualifications and be citizens of the United States.

This letter outlines the basic proposals for an *at large* addition to Congress to represent the views of all the people.

We urge all those organizations receiving this letter to do what they can to improve the content and to give it maximum publicity and editorial support. Only by combined action of concerned Americans of Left, Right and Center can we hope to get these proposals acted upon.

If Congress will not promptly act on these proposals then we urge that an Amendment to the Constitution be used to make these proposals law.

The Case for Anarchism

Fred Woodworth

Why should you work for anarchism? What's in it for you? Hasn't "Democracy" worked well enough?

The proof of the exact nature of the democratic system as practiced in the United States is all about us—we have only to consider it. Consider Chicago. Watch Julius Hoffman sentence seven men and their lawyers to long prison terms on charges of contempt of court (who can fail to have contempt for it?) and charges of crossing state lines with intent to incite a riot. Why state lines? Why not county lines or municipalities? Isn't it possible that tomorrow you might be confined to your own block or face charges of carrying a subversive idea across the street? And who knows what intent lurks in the mind of a man? Well, the government does now, and if it doesn't, it *invents* an intent. This is *thoughtcrime,* (1894). Orwell ought to have entitled his book, America, 1970.

Then we have people all over the world in military bases never getting to enjoy the "freedom" they supposedly have under this system, they are so busy spending their lives fighting for the *freedom* of all other peoples everywhere, so that (presumably) they, too, will be able to spend their lives in involuntary servitude for grinning military task-masters who delight in keeping wars going on all over the Earth. Meanwhile, back in the States, the people at home, (whom the government lulls with bread and circuses and welfare and television) are having the life taxed right out of them to pay for this kind of lovely "freedom."

At the same time we find the Congress on one hand hypocritically reassuring us that we have the right to privacy which is protected by the Constitution, yet on the other hand considering measures to legalize hithertofore unconstitutiònal unwarranted knockless nighttime entry into private homes. (What if you're *not* smoking, or tripping, or dropping, or injecting when they come crashing in? What if you're taking a bath? Or clipping your toenails?) And even if you *were* tripping out—it *is* your body, is it not? No, come to think of it, it isn't. The government regulates what substances you may place within your private body, tells you where you may travel to, and in what ways you may enjoy that aging mass of nerve fiber you call your own, so perhaps you don't really own it after all. At least not under the present system.

Government *leaders* (who would be called "followers" if Democracy were *really* rule by the people) arroganty force upon you a census designed to "find out how many people there are," yet which asks you from forty to sixty personal questions. (Yes Ma'am, only sixty of 'em this time. Oh, you're too busy with your own private affairs to answer them? Hmmm. What are your private affairs, anyway? But don't worry, Ma'am. Nobody will know your answers to these *personal* questions—nobody but, giggle, you and me and the *census bureau*.

And why shouldn't you answer? What have you to hide? Are you a Communist sympathizer or what? Why should you be embarrassed or reluctant to tell the census people how many times a week you do it with your wife? (She *is* your wife, isn't she? The Census will want to know.)

And we have increasing pollution, but let's be thankful to the government which is cracking down on people doing naughty things like burning garbage in their back yards. They leave the big smelters alone, though . . .

Don't forget about the Panthers, either. (Oh, sure, they were fighting back when the police raided their place at three o'clock in the morning. Resisting arrest. Yes. Funny about all those bullet holes in the beds . . . but who cares about those unpatriotic Niggers, anyway?)

America has Nixon, now, too. But what can you say about him? He will issue a proclamation about every conceivable subject from the beneficial aspect of Coca-Cola to the importance of the peanut crop in Tanganyika, but will never say anything at all. He just smiles and shakes hands and goes to church and still sends thousands to their deaths uselessly every month.

Agnew? He'll call you a gibbering little snotty loon, but you must respect him. After all, he's your *leader*.

Why should you work for anarchism? What more do you need? Do you really think this is a great system we now have? Perhaps others are worse, but is that any reason to regard the corruption here as less reprehensible?

Don't fall for the Statist line that it is immoral to work to bring about Anarchy. There is nothing in the soil or trees of this country—no intrinsic thing which orders "Democracy" to persevere throughout the ages, oppressing people . . . clenching minds through unspeakably dark centuries. Anarchy must prevail—without casting away the hulk of the outmoded established system, liberty will remain an ever-elusive phantasm.

In Defense of Conformity

Henry Hazlitt

I cannot remember ever having read any essay, article, or book in defense of conformity. From my earliest days, I have found it disparaged or derided. Two of my favorite writers, in my teens and early twenties, were John Stuart Mill and Herbert Spencer. Spencer was the son of a Nonconformist (in the religous sense); Spencer's first article was even written for a magazine called the 'Nonconformist'; and Spencer constantly lauded nonconformity in thought and action. Nonconformity was also one of the key virtues in John Stuart Mill's code of ethics. His essay, "On Liberty" (which appeared in 1859), is

Schism v.2, no.1 (Winter 1970)

Reprinted with permission from *The Intercollegiate Review*, v.7, no.1–2. ©1970, by the Intercollegiate Studies Institute, Inc., 14 S. Bryn Mawr Ave., Bryn Mawr, Pa. 19010.

a paean in praise of variety, diversity, even eccentricity, in both behavior and thought. "In this age, the mere example of non-conformity, the mere refusal to bend the knee to custom, is itself a service. . . . It is desirable . . . that people should be eccentric."

Mill and Spencer, in their time, were really expressing a minority view, even among intellectuals. But their disparagement of conformity has become a deeply embedded part of our literary and philosophical tradition. It is now, ironically, the fashion; and it has been the fashion for at least the last quarter century. It would be hard to recall a college commencement address in all that time which has not deplored and warned against conformity. The only judicial opinions which we ever hear praised are the dissents. The highest honor which his admirers could think of bestowing upon the late Justice Holmes was to dub him The Great Dissenter.

What we find extolled and rewarded today seems to me to be more and more dissent for its own sake. The college president or the commencement orator assures himself a reputation for liberality and sagacity by suggesting that the students who riot, seize administration buildings, smash windows, burn files, and kick deans down stairs are more to be praised than those who are trying seriously to pursue their studies, because the rioters are Dissenters, alive to the new revolutionary tides in the world, resentful of the injustices going on everywhere, and determined to bring about—ah! magic word—Change. So the youngsters who get adult attention and newspaper headlines are not the quiet students who do well, even extraordinarily well, in their studies, but those who dress filthily, refuse to get haircuts or shaves, and make nonnegotiable demands.

I should like to put forward what may today seem the perverse suggestion that there is a case for Conformity—conformity in dress, speech, manners, morals, action and thought. I would go even further, and suggest that without this basic conformity civilized society could hardly survive.

The essence of society is cooperation among individuals for the achievement of their common purposes. And conformity to accepted rules is an indispensable element of all cooperation.

I do not here attach to the word conformity any unusual or strained definition. The first definition of "conform" in the

Random House Dictionary is: "to act in accord or harmony; comply."

If we want concrete illustrations we could hardly do better than begin with traffic rules. The purpose of traffic rules is to maximize the flow of traffic and to minimize snarls and accidents. All such rules demand conformity: conformity to accepted and specified speed limits, to the rule of driving on the right side of the road (or the left in Britain), to the rules on right, left, and U-turns and one-way streets, to all legal signals and signs. When any driver insists on deciding for himself just which rules to conform to, he increases the probability of an accident. If every driver insisted on deciding for himself which rules, if any, to conform to, there would be traffic chaos.

But the traffic rules, in addition to their own inherent importance, symbolize all the rules by which society works and lives. As Henry Sidgwick remarked a century ago: "The life of man in society involves daily a mass of minute forecasts of the actions of other men." These forecasts are necessary to human cooperation. We can make them correctly in so far as others conform to generally accepted rules. Every automobile driver depends on his ability to forecast accurately what the other fellow is going to do. This forecast is most often based on the assumption that the other fellow is going to conform to the established practice or rule applying to that situation.

Such conformity is indispensable for most of our daily actions. It makes life smoother and pleasanter even in trivial matters. The actions of men in modern society are synchronized by clocks and watches and set schedules. We depend on each other's punctuality. A worker gets to the factory at 8:00 and stays till 4:00 on the understanding that his co-workers and foreman will be there from 8:00 to 4:00.

The enormously increased efficiency and productivity brought about by the synchronization and division of labor are made possible only by this conformity to set time schedules. When a man takes the 8:17 to the office and the 5:26 home he depends on the railroad's conformity to this pre-advertised schedule; the railroad depends in turn on a sufficient number of commuters' adhering to it. If a dinner invitation is for 7:00, you get there at 7:00. If the symphony concert begins at 8:15 everybody is supposed to be in his seat by then.

In short, a great society can function, in its diversions and pleasures no less than its work, only by the daily, hour-by-hour, and often minute-by-minute cooperation of its constituent members, their willing subordination to a common time-schedule that will enable them to synchronize their individual contributions. A business firm—a large newspaper, for example—can function and succeed only if each employee, reporter, re-write man, photographer, editor, printer, columnist, copy-boy, proof-reader, advertising solicitor, artist, layout man, delivery truck driver, newsstand operator, carries out his special function on schedule.

This is what it means to be that now much derided creature, an Organization Man. The performance of any great constructive work whatever, the very survival of society, depends on the organization men and women. Modern society functions by the division of labor. The division of labor is only possible through cooperative organization. Cooperative organization is only possible through the mutual voluntary meshing and conformity of one man's contribution with that of others.

This must occur on both the largest and smallest scale, in university life, scientific research, business, sports, amusements. If a symphony concert is to give pleasure to anyone, then every player of every instrument in the orchestra must conform with the utmost precision of tempo and note to both the score before him and to the conductor's baton. Every performer, in addition to having the skill and training to do so, must willingly subordinate his individual contribution to the collective result that all the performers are trying to achieve. Each instrumentalist must be, not least of all, a superb Organization Man.

Conformity in manners, through the tendency of so many of the young today is to deride it as adherence to a needless and silly ritual, also makes daily life enormously smoother and pleasanter than it would otherwise be. Take the understood rules for precedence through a doorway: the guest before the host, the lady before the man, the older before the younger, and so on. Or take even the rules of dress: Most of us dress not merely to please ourselves, but to please others; so that if we accept an invitation to a formal dinner we put on the conventional formal wear. General recognition of these and similar rules obviously makes for more harmonious human relations.

Many readers will readily grant that such conformity to established rules, written or unwritten is necessary or at least generally desirable in matters of behavior; but surely, they will protest, not in matters of thought and opinion. Yet here it is necessary to make some very important distinctions.

Progress in any of the sciences is only possible, of course, if at least some individuals make discoveries that change a hitherto accepted view. But these discoveries are not made by those who dissent simply for dissent's sake. They are made, in the overwhelming majority of cases, by men who have arduously studied what has already been learned or discovered by their predecessors. It is only then that a thinker, however original, is in a position to understand the problems and difficulties and to propose or achieve a new solution. When he does this, he may be said to be "dissenting" from the previously accepted view, though "disagreeing" would be a more appropriate word. His disagreement, moreover, is merely incidental to his discovery. (Perhaps from here on out we should adhere strictly to the vital distinction recently made by Daniel J. Boorstin: "People who disagree have an argument, but people who dissent have a quarrel. . . . A liberal society thrives on disagreement but is killed by dissension.")

What has been said about the conditions for true progress in the sciences applies also in the arts. The architects of the ancient Greek temples, and of the cathedrals of the Middle Ages, had none of the uneasy struggle for "originality" that marks the architects of our own age. They were not determined that this year's temple or cathedral should be strikingly different from last years. Architectural styles did change; but by centuries rather than by years, and one style almost imperceptibly evolved out of its predecessor. El Greco, the archetype of the great original painter, began as a student of Titian, and mastered the style of Titian before he developed his own daring innovations. The earlier compositions of another great innovator, Beethoven, were in the style of Haydn, one of his teachers. True originality usually grows out of the mastery of a tradition.

The modern penchant for innovation for its own sake, in art, science, and philosophy, is mainly a symptom of restlessness. As Morris R. Cohen pointed out in 1931: "The notion that we can dismiss the views of all previous thinkers surely leaves no basis for the hope that our own work will prove of any value to others."

Even the most independent and original thinker in his own field is compelled to assume provisionally the truth of the prevailing opinion in areas in which he is not an expert. It is absurd, even impossible, to challenge every accepted belief at once.

One fundamental reason why we follow custom is that we cannot make a fresh, original, and unique decision for every situation or contingency. We must economize our time and thought to meet situations for which no tests and customary response has been established. This applies to our conclusions as well as our behavior. As Bertrand Russell once remarked: "The average man's opinions are much less foolish than they would be if he thought for himself." And there is a limit to the number of subjects on which even the most brilliant man has time and knowledge to bestow independent thought, or challenge the accepted opinion.

I hope that at this point I may be allowed a personal note. I have thought of myself in the past as primarily a libertarian, but not as a conservative. And if the conservative position is interpreted as saying: Whatever is, is right; let us keep the old ways, the old institutions, the old beliefs, whatever they are; let us not change—then I am certainly not a conservative. But this picture is a caricature. The conservatism I have come to accept says, rather: Let us change our moral codes, our laws, our political institutions, when we find this to be necessary, but let us do so cautiously, gradually, piecemeal, making sure at each step that the change we are making is carefully considered and really represents a progress, not a retrogression. Let us beware always of sudden and sweeping change, of "wiping the slate clean," of "making a completely fresh start," of root and branch upheaval. That way lies chaos.

I will offer only a single illustration, from the field of law. There prevailed for generations, in the courts not only of this country but in responsible courts everywhere, the doctrine of stare decisis: "Stand by what has been settled": Let the principles of law established by previous judicial decisions be accepted as authoritative in cases similar to those from which such principles were derived. When the Warren Supreme Court contemptuously disregarded stare decisis it was at sea; and the Court is still at sea. Without this doctrine no one knows what the courts will decide or what the law is.

It is the increasing disregard of stare decisis, or its equivalent, in nearly all social areas today—in morals, manners, dress, in the legal, political, and economic field—that is now leading to such a chaotic result, to the disappearance of standards, to immorality, confrontations, riots, and crime. The glorification of "dissent" has turned into glorification of "protest," and finally into a glorification of lawlessness and nihilism.

Nothing is easier than to destroy. The tree that has taken half a century to grow can be sawed down in less than an hour. The cathedral that took generations to build can be demolished by a bomb in a minute. And without having a single building demolished, a great university can lose within a few months, by capitulating to some senseless student demand, everything that made it worth respecting. But when the problem comes of supplanting what has ben destroyed, the rebels have only a hollow rhetoric for answer.

Ironically, what emerges is a new conformity, less tolerant than the old, and without redeeming social utility. As the sociologist Charles Horton Cooley was pointing out more than forty years ago, there is "nothing more sheep-like than a flock of young rebels." This is glaringly evident in the hippies of today: the prescribed dress—uncut hair, untrimmed beards, boots, tight jeans with paint splotches, dirty over-sized sweaters, bodily filthiness, pot, guitars, rock, free sex, mutual imitation in everything; and ridicule and intolerance of good manners, neatness, cleanliness, patriotism, work, saving, self-discipline, responsibility, and everybody over thirty.

And in the realm of ideas (as Cooley was also pointing out forty years ago) young radicals, trying mainly to be unlike others, fall into a "subservience of contradiction." They take their cue from their "orthodox" opponents, and grab the other end of the same rope, so that in every age the conspicuous radicals are likely to be contradictors and hence subserivent, while real changes gestate in obscurity.

Let me not be misunderstood. This essay is in defense of conformity because, to repeat, a prevailing conformity is essential to mutual cooperation, and cooperation is essential to the achievement of our common ends. But in pointing to the indispensableness of conformity, or diversity, or independence, and certainly not individuality or originality. It is mainly a question of emphasis. What I am suggesting is that, in a turbulent and revolutionary year like the present, it is not especially helpful to keep praising nonconformity, dissent, and protest as if they were absolute virtues in themselves, regardless of what belief or practice is being protested or dissented from. We must always try to judge each belief or practice (if it lies within our own individual sphere of competence) on its own merits, rather than in conformity or nonconformity with what other people think or do. It may possibly have been true, when Mill wrote it more than a century ago: "That so few now dare to be eccentric, marks one of the chief dangers of our time." But that so many now try to be eccentric, marks one of the chief dangers of our time. Nonconformity, dissent, and protest are in themselves disintegrative. True individualism and originality can flourish only within a basically cooperative system.

In sum, in the interests of social harmony and genuine progress, conformity must be the rule, and nonconformity the exception.

The Decline of the "Official"

Manas

This may be the first time in history when large numbers of people are turning away from the "official" ways of doing things, and in noticeable contrast to similar mass rejections in the past propose no new "official" program to replace the one now in force. "Official" is a word usually taken to mean having the backing of established political authority, but here we use it as including the restrictive and coercive aspects of social

habit or custom—what Ortega termed "binding observance."
As he explains:

> Now, the greater part of the ideas by which and from
> which we live, we have never thought for ourselves, on
> our own responsibility, nor even rethought. We use them
> mechanically, on the authority of the collectivity in which
> we live and from which they waylaid us, penetrated us
> under pressure like oil in the automobile. . . . No one
> thinks of uttering them (these ideas) as a discovery of
> his own or as something needing our support. Instead of
> saying them forcefully and persuasively, it is enough for us
> to appeal to them, perhaps as a mere allusion, and instead
> of assuming the attitude of maintaining them, we rather
> do the opposite—we mention them to find support in
> them, as a resort to higher authority, as if they were an
> ordinance, a rule, or a law. And this is because these opin-
> ions are in fact established usages, and "established" means
> that they do not need support and backing from particular
> individuals and groups, but that, on the contrary, they im-
> pose themselves on everyone, exert their constraint on
> everyone. It is this that leads me to call them "binding
> observances." The binding force exercised by these ob-
> servances is clearly and often unpleasantly perceived by
> anyone who tries to oppose it. At every normal moment
> of collective existence an immense repertory of these es-
> tablished opinions is in obligatory observance; they are
> what we call "commonplaces." Society, the collectivity,
> does not contain any ideas that are properly such—that
> is, ideas clearly thought out on sound evidence. It con-
> tains only commonplaces and exists on the basis of these
> commonplaces. By this I do not mean to say that they
> are untrue ideas—they may be magnificent ideas; what I
> do say is inasmuch as they are observances or established
> opinions or commonplaces, their possible excellent qual-
> ties remain inactive. What acts is simply their mechanical
> pressures on all individuals, their soulless coercion.

In this passage—from *Man and People*—Ortega goes on to
distinguish between general "public opinion," which has the

force of binding observance, and the "energetic, aggressive, and proselytizing" opinion of a rebellious group. The generally prevailing opinion, he says, needs no special defense: "so long as it is in observance, it predominates and rules, whereas private opinion has no existence except strictly in the measure to which one person or several or many people take it upon themselves to maintain it."

The all-pervasive schemes of binding observance are of course subject to change, but their alteration is almost imperceptible except in the climactic time of revolution, when the sudden collapse of many familiar structures of habit makes deep anxiety, if not actual terror, an obsessive factor in the lives of many men. The more theoretical and unpracticed the revolutionary ideas, the fewer the people who will have the inner resources and stabilities to sustain them during the period of rapid change.

Studies of past revolutionary epochs show that the victorious leaders find it immediately necessary to fill the vacuum left by these lost stabilities with new binding observances. So it is that the ecstasy of "revolutionary love" cannot last, since it is released in crisis, and when the crisis is over the love has no form. Then the Napoleons and Stalins add compulsion to the definitions of the new order, and the people are obliged to adapt and conform as well as they can to its ideologically binding observances. Yet often there are gains. There are gains to the extent that areas are widened where self-reliance can be exercised and private thought pursued without official prescription. There are gains to the extent that areas are widened where self-reliance can be exercised and private thought pursued without official prescription. There are gains if there is a growth in individuals which is recognized as a deepening sense of the meaning of life—a development which cannot be mechanistically caused by turbulent historical events, although it is associated with them.

We started out by saying that the present may be the first time in history when large numbers of people are withdrawing from the patterns of established observance yet plot no campaigns for a new or better "officialdom." This is a movement of the human spirit, a "tropism" which has had illustrious forerunners, Thoreau being a notable example. Gandhi, who recognized in Thoreau a spiritual kinsman, is another. The "official," as Gandhi saw it, becomes the inhibitor of authentic human growth by replacing its initiative and absorbing the field of its exercise. And Vinoba, in some respects Gandhi's successor, said recently that it is no part of the government's duty to spread revolutionary ideas, and that, in fact, when it attempts to do this, or pretends to, it emasculates both the theory and the practice of revolution. Revolution, in short, in the eyes of such men, must be unofficial. Could we say, then, that some of the confusing and increasingly "unorganized" aspects of the changes now going on are due to the fact that they mark the beginning of the age of "unofficial" revolution? That the cadres of this revolutionary society-to-be remain authentic only so long as they continue to be unofficial, self-defined, and in some sense "unique."

But what about the apparent inevitability of the rule of "binding observance?" In Ortega's definition, they seem mainly oppressive, yet they must also be a device of Nature, since no society is without them. One thing seems clear: we seldom even notice the binding observances which operate in our own lives until the loss of their meaning begins to be manifest, or until they have self-evidently destructive effects. Pursuing "progress," for example, has long been a binding observance in America, but when it brings universal pollution in its train questions begin to be asked. Another means of making binding observance "objective" is the sudden impact of another culture—the result of war, conquest, or colonization. In 'Man in a Mirror,' Richard Llewellyn dramatized the intrusion of white civilization on African tribal culture by comparing their binding observances. An educated Masai leader, a man who had the role of intermediary between his people and the white administrators, broods on the differences:

> Nterenke began to realize with increasing dismay which he found almost comical that the Masai intellect held not the least notion of physical science, no philosophy, or sense of ideas in the abstract, or any mathematical processes higher than the use of the hands and fingers. He amused himself in trying to imagine how he might teach

Olle Tselence the theory of the spectrum. Yet every tracker knew the value of sunlight in a dewdrop because the prism told where the track led and when it had been made. How the eye saw the colors or why the colors were supposed to exist was never a mystery or problem. They had no place anywhere in thought. But all male Masai, from the time they were Al Ayoni, had a sharp sense of color from living in the forest and choosing plumage for the cap. Color became a chief need in the weeks of shooting, and comparing, and taking out a smaller for a larger bird, or throwing away a larger for a smaller, more colorful. He wondered where the idea of color began, or why a scholar should interest himself. Mr. James had taught that sound politics led to a rich economy where people earned more money for less hours of work, and so created a condition of leisure needed by inventors, whether mental or physical. The Masai had always enjoyed an ample economy, if it meant a complete filling of needs, and after the animals were tended, there was plenty of leisure. Yet there were no inventors of any sort. There was a father-to-son and mouth-to-mouth passing of small items that pretended to be history, and a large fund of forest lore that might pass as learning, but there were no scholars, no artists, no craftsmen in the European sense.

The effect was to lock a growing mind in a wide prison of physical action and disciplined restriction that by habit became accepted as absolute liberty.

Today, as we read this perceptive description, we may experience a wave of nostalgia for a simple life like that of the Masai. It seems so natural, so good, while our own civilization, as we have recently discovered, has been in the charge of sorcerer's apprentices and scientific boy Fausts. Already the longing for an eternal Peter-Pan career is strong in the young, and while their vitamin-nourished glands make this unlikely they can at least dress up like Indians, romance about the "tribes," and do what else they are able to screen out the ugliness they see and feel.

It may be natural enough for the young to react by feeling

to the present scheme of binding observances according to a good/bad scale of judgment; in this they are only repeating history, and they are after all young; yet there is another way of looking at these things. We learn from medicine and the new psychology, for example, that the symptoms of illness may be best understood as the body's or the mind's strenuous if failing effort to get well. A neurosis is a distorted healing process, a defense against what seem dangerous enemies, a struggle of the psyche for survival. If we look at "binding observance" with this in mind, we may be able to find a better solution for its evils.

Binding observances are unquestioned social habits. What do we know about habits? Well, we know that we can't get along without them. So far as the life of the physical body is concerned, we certainly couldn't do without its physiological habits, which we call instincts. Suppose we had to make our hearts beat with a continuous act of the will? Or give precise instructions to the cells along the margins of a gash on how they must heal the wound? The "binding observances" of the body come very close to being perfect as well as indispensable. This reliance on the services of habit applies in all directions. We don't feel that we really possess a skill—like driving a car—until we can use it without thinking about how it works. An artist can't really profit by his "technique" until he is able to forget it—forget, that is, that it's in his fingers and at his service. A good habit is an extension of human function which has become second nature. Once the function took concentrated attention, but not after it has been made into a habit.

Actually, there may be a vast natural ground for this idea. In his remarkable book, 'Instinct and Intelligence' (Macmillan, 1929), Major R. W. G. Hinston expresses the view, based on a great deal of personal observation, that "instinct began in a reasoned act which gradually became unconscious." While there may be little room for this opinion in modern evolutionary theory, it certainly fits with what we know about the formation of our useful habits, and the entire subject of how evolution takes place is still mysterious enough to allow consideration to the idea. Further, it has the advantage of supporting the conception of human life as a self-determined expression of nature; as A. H. Maslow has put it, we are "self-evolvers."

If one looks closely at this question of habit and freedom, or habit versus freedom, it gets very metaphysical indeed. A habit is a way of acting, a form of behavior, an instrument of the will. Nobody acts without instruments. By confining (conserving) and directing the energy of action, an instrument makes the action possible. A habit, you could say, is the endowment given an instrument for relatively independent behavior, freeing the individual for other, more demanding activity. A bad habit is an endowment which makes you do a thing you no longer want to do, or which prevents you from doing something else which is more important. Obviously, then, a good habit is a habit which will not get in the way of a man's capacity to innovate, yet will efficiently take over on functions which are his habits by this criterion.

A great many of the social habits which men acquire—and which become binding observances, or are incorporated in constitutions—are prescriptions for the not yet wise. The wiser a man is, the less his need for or dependence upon such habits. But if he is really wise, he seldom insists that other people change their binding observances. Instead, he writes a 'Bhagavad-Gita' or conducts a Socratic Dialogue. He knows that people whose habits are suddenly taken away from them by fiat will either become enraged, succumb to fright, or lapse into apathy, because their familiar modes of action have been destroyed.

If the prevailing set of binding observances in his society add up to intolerable evil, he may contest them non-violently. The most deep-seated observances are below the threshold of rational inquiry. They are taken for granted; as Ortega says, they make the ground of assumption with which you demonstrate arguable matters; you don't have to prove them. The need of the Spanish conquistadores to convert the heathen Indians to the one true religion was not open to debate for these invaders. They were Christian and right. The need of the South Africans to discriminate against Indians and blacks involved the very identity of the ruling race. They might be obliged to talk about the question, but they couldn't really reason about it. Their racism was a binding observance impenetrable to rational communication. Gandhi saw this. Explaining why he believed that non-violent action was needed, he said:

Because human beings are not always ready for persuasion. Their preconceptions may be so deeply rooted that arguments do not touch them at all. Then, you must touch their feelings. Nothing else will change their minds.

One might say that non-violence was for Gandhi an appeal from a stance above the threshold of reason to those whose behavior, in a given situation, was below it. He met one extreme with another.

But this is the requirement of a crisis situation, when men are ruled by passion and fear, as is usually the case when their deepest binding observances are challenged, and it probably takes a Gandhi to turn such confrontations into mutually educational experiences. Without Gandhis to lead, there may be a tendency to think of "action" as taking place only in crisis situations, making this idea into a "radical" binding observance, while neglecting multitudinous other processes of natural human awakening and growth. These processes thrive in the interstices of society, and on the fringes. There are those who, today, instead of migrating to "new lands," are finding ways to live without official guidance. They have performed a kind of inner emigration, but you couldn't say they have "opted out." A happy instance of this new social tendency was reported in the Los Angeles Times for Aug. 15, by John C. Waugh. The story tells of twenty-two men and women who have joined to create New Mexico's Theater of All Possibilities on 160 acres of flat and open land near Cerillos. The players live in the stalls of an abandoned stable and the yard makes an outdoor theatre. Benches for the audience seat two hundred. Mr. Waugh relates:

> In the festival season in the late summer, the troupe sets up tents for playgoers who wish to camp overnight or take in the group's repertoire of seven plays.
>
> The commune dwellers are all artisans practicing a dozen theatre-related crafts—among them a leathersmith, a wood carver, printers, a blacksmith, table-makers, potters and photographers.
>
> One of the four co-directors—they also double as actors—is the commune butcher. Another is an adobe build-

er. Maria Allen, the commune leader's wife, is also a potter and the overseer of the group's livestock—hogs, chickens, guinea hens, horses and one mule.

One way or another, each member of the commune must earn $75 a month. The $900 a year they must each contribute to the commune treasury is enough to feed and board the members, run the theatre, build new buildings, plant and maintain orchards and gardens, husband livestock, hold a theatre festival, take three plays on tour once a year and pay off the mortgage.

John Allen, a former engineer now in his thirties, is apparently the moving spirit in the group. The Times writer says he "looks and talks like a stern pilgrim just landed on a rockbound coast."

Having rejected the Establishment, he is convinced that communal living is the only social form left that makes sense. A family of four, he points out, spend $10,000 to $20,000 a year living a non-commune life. On his commune, the same family can live for $2,000.

The members, who in age range from eighteen to forty-three, have no use for drugs, which are banned, and outlaw drunkenness. The plays in the repertoire include Shakespeare, Sophocles, Moliere and Brecht, and some dramas by members of the group may be added. The actor-craftsmen prefer not to be called a "commune," because of the term's associations, but a reporter has to use a generalizing noun now and then.

Well, artists, as we have before suggested, are naturally stalwarts in the rejection of the "official." They develop their conventions, too, of course, since they are human, yet the weaknesses of unthinking conformity show more quickly in the arts than in other areas of enterprise and can be guarded against. This example may not be world-shaking in implication, but it illustrates a great many basic changes in attitude and objective among a disciplined group of people. There are other such groups, and many such individuals. The energy which is turned toward the future is not going into "official" alternatives, but into extraordinarily diverse individual transformations and dramatically original enterprises, none of which looks forward to power, status, or acquisition as the climax of their achievement. It might be said that even if we could collect many such accounts, our samples would remain statistically insignificant, compared to the population of the world. That would be true enough, but we are sampling germ cells, not somatic cells. This objection reminds one of what Faraday said to Gladstone when the latter commented on the scientist's first model of a dynamo: "Very interesting, sir, but what good is it?" The inventor replied: "What good is a newborn baby?"

What Being an American Should Mean

Melvin Munn

We hear orators speak and we read dissertations upon what it means to be an American. Let's think for a few minutes on what it should mean to every man, woman, and child in the United States to be an American.

Being an American should mean many wonderful things to you. Does it?

At the risk of being accused of preaching a bit, we would like to think with you for the next few minutes about what it ought to mean to be an American. Unfortunately there are those in our land today who place very little value on being an American—so little, in fact, that they would betray their country and destroy its government and its way of life.

Being an American ought to mean that we are proud of our history and of the heroes whose deeds of valor and service to their fellow-man are the high points in that history.

No other nation on earth has a history which will compare with ours. There are nations much older. They may have longer histories, but not nearly so filled with illustrious deeds and with the ideals of freedom which have been the foundation of our nation since colonial days.

No other nation has ever been able to afford its people either so great a measure of individual freedom and dignity or such a luxurious standard of living. We have a right to look back and to be proud of the past which has given us the blessings of today and, if preserved, the promise of a wonderful future.

We should, first of all, be grateful for the hardy breed of pioneers who braved the dangers of the New World and an uncharted wilderness to settle this great land. They were a courageous, dedicated, and religious people seeking something they were unable to find in their native lands.

Then we remember that when the English king sought to lay taxes upon the American colonists without due representation the Americans dared to stand up for principles they believed to be right. Such men as John Hancock, Benjamin Franklin, Patrick Henry, George Washington, John Adams, Thomas Jefferson, and Alexander Hamilton were men of courage and conviction. They declared independence, fought for independence, and set up our government after independence had been won.

It was a great gamble these men took. England was a strong nation at that time, and if England had won the war instead of losing to the colonists and their French helpers, they would have lost everything, including their lives and families. But to them the principle of freedom was worth risking their lives, their fortunes, and their sacred honor, as they stated when they signed the Declaration of Independence.

Being an American means we should be proud of this bit of our history and those men who played the leading roles in it, but this is only one part of our history. Down through the years the nation has grown and prospered, and in every time of crisis there has been a leader who helped to bring our nation through successfully.

The United States of America has not only met crises in her own development, but has fought to perpetuate freedom for others and to defeat aggressors seeking to enslave the world. The world looks to America as the principal bastion of freedom today because of what we have done in the past and what we have been in the past.

In the past, certainly until relatively recent years, we have known just where our leaders stood and what our policy was with regard to the rest of the world. Our nation stood four-square and commanded respect. That, too, is part of the greatness of our history.

Being an American ought to mean many more things. It ought to mean that each of us thrills at the sight of Old Glory, that seeing the red, white, and blue rippling on the breeze has real meaning for us.

For Americans who have followed this great flag in time of national emergency—World War I, World War II, in Korea, or in Viet Nam—one need not urge reverence for the flag. They know what the flag means, and any attempt by anybody to dishonor Old Glory will bring a quick protest from a veteran. But far too many of the rest of us take Old Glory for granted. It has flown over us ever since we can remember, and we never really took the trouble to think about what it means. It is time we did consider what this symbol of our land means and just what a terrible thing it is when the flag is dishonored.

Being an American ought to mean that we love our country and that the United States means a great deal to us as individuals, along with our families and our church. Physically and geographically, this is a great land, a country blessed with wonderful natural resources, pleasant climate, and a variety of nature's greatest beauties.

What is this land we call America? It is a broad land, stretching from the stormy Atlantic to the blue Pacific and from the Great Lakes to the Gulf of Mexico and Mexico itself. It has vast green plains and valleys, blue and purple mountains rising into the sky, and mighty rivers flowing endlessly to the sea, and crystal lakes filled with shiny fish. It is towering green forests and lush fields of corn. It is seaports haunted by the blast of the freighter's horn and it is industrial cities teeming with hurry and bustle.

It is ribbons of superhighways and hundreds of airports where the giant planes thunder and roar as they land and take off. It has a great throbbing heart and great capacity for work and production. It is huge fleets of trucks and thundering trains on silver rails.

Most of all it is people—a people with a great heritage—

a people born to a greatness because of what their forefathers were. It is people who love to live, who spend more time in recreation and luxury than any people before them, but a people who can rise to meet any emergency and go forth into any battle ready to make whatever sacrifice is necessary to vanquish the enemy and win the victory. We are a people accustomed to winning and not ready to settle for anything less. Being an American ought to mean loving the nation and its people—for what they are.

America has been known for a century as the land of opportunity. Millions of people in other lands, given the opportunity to come to America to live, would fling off all connections with their native lands and rejoice in the chance to become American citizens.

Being an American, then, ought to mean taking advantage of our opportunities. Our free enterprise economic system gives to each person the right to choose his vocation and his job. He may seek any job he chooses, and in that job he can rise to whatever level he deserves, based upon his ability and his willingness to work. Success may be harder to achieve today than it was a half-century ago when competition was maybe less keen, but it is still possible.

Those with ability and willingness to work are still finding opportunities that open the doors to success—and some of them to fame and fortune. There is still a demand for a top-flight with ideas who can lead.

Being an American ought to mean being a self-reliant individual, and it does for most Americans today, just as it always has. But a growing number of people have gotten the erroneous idea that the world owes them a living—a good living—regardless of whether they work and produce or not. They have surrendered their self-respect and sold their self-reliance for a mess of security pottage, just as Esau sold his birthright to Jacob.

Until very recent years, willingness to accept charity, except in times of real need, was frowned upon. It was considered disgraceful. A family prided itself upon being self-reliant and self-supporting. To infer that it was otherwise was an insult of the gravest kind.

Unfortunately, some of that idea has been lost, and the nation is the worse for its passing. We would hope, moreover, that being an American will long continue to mean being self-reliant for most American citizens.

Being an American ought to mean that we participate in our government. The founding fathers wisely established a constitutional republic, in which citizens elect their representatives to make laws and to administer the affairs of state. Only when the people in general participate in their government, as intended when the Constitution was written, will the government function properly. This means we have not only a privilege but a duty and a responsibility to vote and to vote intelligently.

We should take part in party affairs and exercise a voice in formulating the party platforms. We should communicate as much as possible with our elected officials and let them know our opinions on issues which arise. Only if this is done can they represent us as they should.

We have the constitutional right to criticize acts by our government with which we do not agree, but our right to criticize skates on very thin ice if we do not participate in choosing and helping to direct government.

Americans ought to love the freedom they have as citizens of this great land. Nowhere else does the individual have so much freedom as is guaranteed under our Constitution. The objective of the Constitution, in addition to providing a framework for our government, is to protect the freedom of the individual against encroachments from the government. No other constitution is based upon such an objective.

Somehow, never having know what it was to live without these freedoms, we tend to take them for granted, and we don't realize that people in other lands do not have them.

If we, then, are proud of our heritage, our history, and the heroes that helped make this nation great, if we get a real thrill at the sight of Old Glory, if we truly love our great land, and if we participate in our government and practice self-reliance, seeking to take advantage of the opportunities it affords, it follows that we should know who our enemies are.

We do have enemies. The followers of Marxism cannot stand idly by and see our great nation at work. They detest it as a bastion of freedom—opposed to the system for which they stand. Being an American means we should inform ourselves about our enemies and how they operate.

Being an American should also mean that we are willing to make whatever sacrifices may be necessary to preserve our heritage of freedom for our children. We today hold in our hands the keys to the future of this great nation. It has been well said that freedom must be rewon with every new generation, and our time of testing is now.

Pressure is growing within from those who profess to follow communism. The hordes of communists in other lands are watching with anticipation for the moment when they think our nation is ready to fall or can be overcome by military or other means.

Americans have in past risked boldly for freedom, both for themselves and for others. Today, being an American should mean we are still willing to stand foursquare for freedom of the individual and the dignity of man.

The call today is for patriotism to be revived and love of freedom to be reviewed, for in America lies the hope of man for a bright future.

Nationalism

The Western Socialist

Flag Day 1970 is now water under the bridge. As usual on this day (or at least since 1916), communities throughout the land paid tribute to the American Flag.

In Chicago this past Flag Day, June 14, Mayor "Club 'em" Daley issued a proclamation wherein he is quoted as having said: "It is well for us all to proudly rally behind our flag, the emblem of justice, freedom and democracy." That very same day one of Daley's finest, a Chicago police officer, arrested a 17-year-old lad for desecrating the flag by appearing at a North Side beach with the flag draped around his shoulders. The naivete of this young lad is indicated by the remark he made on being arrested: "In America, you can do what ever you want. It's a free country." In the hands of one group of protectors of surplus value, the police, this young lad undoubtedly learned that the freedom he spoke of is more substantial in theory than in practice.

In Rome, N.Y., where Francis Bellamy, the author of the "Pledge of Allegiance," lies buried, and where this writer happened to be on Flag Day, Col. Robert C. Mathis, commander of Rome Air Development Center, using a flag kit offering of a local newspaper as a basis for his address to a modest gathering, had in part this to say: "The American flag is a simple symbol, complete with aluminum pole, for three dollars and fifty cents. But it represents the soul of America." Socialists wouldn't know about the flag representing the "soul of America," but they do know that the three dollars and fifty cents" represent the exploitation of labor.

Paying tribute to the American Flag is all part and parcel of nationalism—a yearly ritual encouraged and supported by the ruling class—the capitalist—for psychophysiologically reinforcing in the ruled, the workers a fight-and-die, my country, right-or-wrong orientation.

Historically, the growth of nationalism goes back to the seventeenth and eighteenth centuries when feudal states were united to form nations. Nationalism may be defined simply as an acquired strong feeling of devotion of people toward their "own country"—its language, culture, customs and traditions, and the unification under a single government of the geographic area occupied by a people. Or it can be defined in these words which tend to bring its essentially dangerous character to the fore:

> Members of the national unit recognize their likeness and emphasize their difference from other men . . . The fact of nationality is urgently separatist in character . . . It is exclusive and it promotes a loyalty which may often, like family affection, live its life independent of right and truth. (H. J. Laski, *A Grammar of Politics*, p. 221.)

International Capital

In this contemporary world of interdependence, feelings of nationalism are decidedly immature, infantile and archaic. But since it is recognized by our rulers that nationalism remains a great political force and a powerful political reality, they unceasingly encourage their political factotums to promote and make shrewd use of it. Though our rulers, for ulterior motives, would have their wage slaves subservient to nationalism, they themselves do not personally subscribe to such idiocy as evidenced by their ramified international financial involvements. When it comes down to the nitty-gritty, they recognize but one flag—the $ flag. We refer here, of course, to the rulers—the 1.6 percent who own 80 percent of all stock—and not to the petty business man whose products cannot be exported abroad and who therefore may be a rabid nationalist, and who may actually credit his devout patriotism to ideological reasons and not to the material fact that his patriotism pays handsome dividends for him. Nationalism today, in some respects, is a hindrance to our rulers, for it serves in some measure to limit their freedom of action. They seek to by-pass their creation—nationalism—without, however, seriously weakening its emotional status in the minds of workers nor arousing their antipathy by actions which might be constructed by the latter as being unpatriotic.

Former U.S. Undersecretary of State, George W. Ball, highlighted this hindrance in these words as quoted in *Business Week,* February 17, 1968:

> There is an inherent conflict of interest between corporate managements that operate in the world economy, and governments whose points of view are confined to the narrow national scene.

What our rulers now seek is a global corporate law. Writes *Business Week*:

> Their companies operate in a world economy and mobilize and deploy capital, labor, raw materials, plant facilities, and distribution according to the most efficient (profitable) pattern. They plan globally, sometimes manufacturing in one country products to be marketed only in others. . . . For such a company, the prospect of an international corporations act offers one extraordinary ad-

vantage: "a chance to leapfrog serious obstacles"—(taxes, impediments to mergers, employment regulations, the manner in which capital is employed, etc.)—occasionally thrown in its path by single nations motivated by narrower, national considerations.

According to McKinsey & Co.'s Managing Director Gilbert H. Clee, these multinational corporations, as they are called, want room "to move around the world with some degree of assurance—(government support and protection)."

As quoted in *Business Week,* Ball issues this warning:

> Conflict will increase between the world corporation, which is a modern concept evolved to meet the requirements of the modern age, and the nation-state, which is still rooted in archaic concepts unsympathetic to the needs of our complex world.

Since our rulers indirectly but none the less decisively rule the government—the state—it is a foregone conclusion that the latter will accelerate its present support of these multinational corporations in their global economic ventures. By so doing, politically, economically, and militarily, the impediments to foreign governments can be frequently overcome.

But this by no means indicates that there will be a lessening of nationalistic fostering by our rulers. Actually, nationalism will be intensified. It will take on an added hue, as it has commenced to do of late, to accommodate the ambitions of the multinational corporations.

"Our" Foreign Investments

The gearing of national policies and opinion in the West in support of multinational corporations has for some time been apparent in official pronouncements no less than in economic writings such as was quoted above. For instance, Eisenhower, in his State of the Union Message in 1953, defined the aims of American foreign policy as

> doing whatever our Government can properly do to en-

courage the flow of private investment abroad. This involves, as a serious and explicit purpose of our foreign policy, the encouragement of a hospitable climate for such investment in foreign countries.

The added nationalistic hue of which we spoke consists of a total and sustained effort by the government of the U.S. to assist in achieving, by snarl or smile, a suitable foreign climate for multinational corporations.

The primary media for fostering nationalism are the school, the press, and the parson or priest. As for the latter, we can make short shift of him by pointing out that as a servant or as a commission agent of God, he ought to be anti-nationalist by profession. But this is not the case. Using the opportunities he has for expressing his opinions, taking full advantage of his ready made audience, and making clever use of the prestige of his Church, he is invariably found peddling nationalism like a Madison Avenue huckster peddling an antiperspirant. There are those, of course, a mere handful or more, who reject outlandish displays of nationalism, and who preach to their flock in terms of curbing pollution and inflation, of fighting for social and economic justice, of exposing corruption in public office, and in general pointing out other areas for improving the quality of life in the U.S. But as every socialist knows, such actions are historically endless and the sought goals impossible of reasonable achievement under capitalism.

Headfixing (the Big Lie)

The school is an ideal setting for fostering nationalism. As an agent of nationalist propaganda, it is most effective because it is general; because school attendance up to a certain age is compulsory, and because it catches the individual at an impressionable age. Its curriculum permits easy injection of nationalism. History and geography, for example, are taught from a strict national point of view, directly and indirectly: directly through emphasis on the national interest, the result of which is that the U.S.A. emerges as the finest country in the world, and indirectly by teaching history and geography at the expense of world history and world geography. Literature is another subject through which the doctrine of nationalism is inculcated.

Occasionally one is pleasantly surprised to run across a teacher who has had it up to his eyebrows with the propagation of nationalism and other falsehoods which pass under the guise of education. He knows nationalism to be, like religion, a disease for his students and for the working class in general. He rebels and pays the price. And the price of his nonconformism and noncompliance with capitalist-dictated mores is loss of professional employment; social ostracism, and endless harassment from the minions of class society. But compensatory, he has shed his anxiety and fear of what other people think of him and enjoys basking in the refreshing atmosphere of following the dictates of his own conscience and complying in thought and action with the factual socio-economic structure of the world.

The Press

Coming now to the press, it can unquestionably be stated that it is a most important and effective fosterer of nationalist propaganda. The press carries out this propaganda in the service of powerful private interests—our rulers—under the cloak of national interest. And since the press is first and foremost a profit-making industry, with the reporting of news being of secondary or minor importance, the propagation of nationalism is also self-serving. Like politicians, the press realizes the potentialities of the already existing nationalism and is quick to cash in on it.

In *The Rich and the Super-Rich,* Ferdinand Lundberg, scholarly forthright but somewhat conservative, speaking of the mass media—newspapers, magazines, radio and television—had this to say:

> The dependence upon corporate advertising of the . . . newspapers . . . make them editorially subservient (and even to the point of slanting their news columns), without in any way being prompted, to points of view known or thought to be favored by the big property owners. Sometimes, of course, as the record abundantly shows,

they have been prompted and even coerced to alter attitudes. But the willing subservience shows itself most generally, apart from specific acts of omission or commission, in an easy blandness on the part of the (newspaper) toward serious social problems. These are all treated, when treated at all, as part of a diverting kaleidoscopic spectacle, the modern Roman circus of telecommunication.

Being enterprises of Big Business, newspapers are indeed powerful purveyors of nationalism. They control the exchange of news throughout the world; they command the resources of space and time; and they affect in a thousand subtle ways the thought of the working class who, for the most part, rely on this medium to keep them informed. Not consciously knowing that what is presented as news is so limited, colored and distorted by capitalist interests as to be falsehood in the guise of truth, the workers are deceived as to the true state of socio-economic affairs.

Nationalism will slowly but surely follow the demise of the socio-economic order—capitalism—to which it owes its genesis and crystallization. Having in its rise developed nationalism, capitalism has also produced the conditions for its ultimate disintegration and disappearance. Capitalism

has through its exploitation of the world market given a cosmopolitan character to production and consumption in every country. To the great chagrin of reactionists, it has drawn from under the feet of industry the national ground on which it stood. All old-established national industries have been destroyed or are daily being destroyed. They are dislodged by new industries, whose introduction becomes a life and death question for all civilized nations, by industries that no longer work up indigenous raw material, but raw material drawn from the remotest zones; industries whose products are consumed not only at home, but in every quarter of the globe. In place of the old wants, satisfied by the productions of the country, we find new wants, requiring for their satisfaction the products of distant lands and climes. In place of the old local and national seclusion and self-sufficiency we have intercourse in every direction, universal interdependence of nations. And as in material, so also in intellectual production. The intellectual creations of individual nations become common property. National one-sidedness and narrow-mindedness become more and more impossible, and from the numerous national and local literatures there arises a world literature. (*Communist Manifesto.*)

With the end of capitalism and the exploitation of one class by another, "the exploitation of one nation by another will also be put to an end." With the coming of socialism and our entrance into a world without mental or physical frontiers, the capitalist created concept of nationalism with its barbaric features will be but a historic legacy found only in the dusty pages of history books.

Confrontation

Reprinted in *Schism* from *The Bond* v.4, no.2 (Feb. 18, 1970).

Violence and Democracy

Mulford Q. Sibley

This is an era in which many—and not only the younger generation—seem to have developed an extraordinary confidence in violence as a method of fundamental social change and of defending whatever may be good in the existing social order. Thus Mao Tse-tung tells us that "Political power grows out of the barrel of a gun." And elsewhere he writes: "The seizure of power by armed force, the settlement of the issue by war, is the central task and the highest form of revolution." Thousands of youth have come to idolize Che Guevara, whose notion of social change gave a central role to violence. Among the so-called black "militants" in the United States, mass violence is sometimes seen as both a way of defense and a method for achieving equality.

Nor is the so-called "liberal" attitude to matters of this kind radically different. To be sure, professions of faith in non-violent change are abundant and those among the radicals who appeal to violence are often severely criticized by the liberals. Yet liberals themselves, when the chips are down, are generally committed to the notion that "Democracy" can be defended by violence against the attacks of "totalitarians."

It was a liberal administration which carried out the "Bay of Pigs" expedition—whose ostensible objective was to weaken or overthrow an alleged tyranny—utilizing methods very similar to those which are advocated by professed revolutionaries. It was the liberals who initiated or—for the most part—at least condoned the invasion of the Dominican Republic under Lyndon Johnson. It was under professed liberal leadership, too, that the United States utilized violence in World War I, World War II, the Korean War, and, most recently, the Vietnamese war.

Schism v.1, no.4 (Fall 1970)

To be sure, it can be argued that the liberals in actuality often employ violence for other than their professed goals, which constitute a kind of cover-up for actual ends which are less than noble. Nevertheless, it remains true that both contemporary revolutionaries and self-professed liberals state their aims in much the same way and appeal to very much the same means. Thus, if one compares the words used by Lyndon Johnson when he formulated his aims for the Vietnamese war with the words employed by the Democratic Republic of Vietnam and the National Liberation Front, they are amazingly alike: self-government, national self-determination, basic economic change, an agrarian revolution, and so on. And the means both sides use rely heavily on violence: napalming and fragmentation bombing by the Americans and what the newspapers call "terrorism" by the forces of Ho Chi Minh and the National Liberation Front.

In general, it is usually taken for granted by both Western "democrats" and Western and Eastern "communists" that violence has liberated man in the past. Our histories are written as if this were true and our children—whether in China, or the United States, or the Soviet Union—grow up believing that certain wars were "liberating" and others were "enslaving." American children are taught that the Civil War "freed" the slaves; but the monumental costs of that frightful bloodletting in treasure, human lives, and long-term bitterness are usually not emphasized. And the kind of "freedom" supposedly gained by blacks in the Civil War has, at least until recently, been hardly ever analyzed.

This paper questions the appeal to violence, whether uttered in the name of some proposed egalitarian revolution or on behalf of the defense of democracy. Although we may well understand why men may, in desperation, turn to violence, that has nothing to do with a possible justification of violence. And it is very far removed from the fairly common contemporary tendency—reflected, for example, in the followers of Franz Fanon—to make a mystique of violent action.

Here we ground our argument against violence not on some ultimate religious commitment (although that can certainly be done) but rather upon the practical imperatives which utilization of violence sets up for those who employ it. Those imperatives, we contend, demand a structure of action and a set of immediate objectives which tend to undermine ultimate revolutionary or truly democratic goals—of those goals embrace such ends as social equality, radical redistribution of power, and genuine fraternity. The utilization of violence is stupid, in other words; and while it may at points be called heroic, the heroism is blind and pointless. Che Guevara, whatever his personal courage, was amazingly naive about the means of fundamental social change.

The utilization of violence tends to set up a kind of social logic that emphasizes class differences, promotes inequality, destroys the possibility of reconciliation, and, in general, undercuts the goals of revolution. The greater the violence, other things being equal, the less the revolution; the less the violence, the greater the possibilities of revolution.

Violence, once employed by the revolutionist, has a tendency to so enamor him of its use that he becomes unaware of other possibilities. It is so dramatic and seemingly so effective in the short run, that if it becomes a mainstay of action, the revolutionist tends to become uncritically attached to it. Other means seem tame, slow, and ineffective by comparison. A ready gun attenuates the use of intelligence. The tumult, conspiratorial atmosphere, and shouting so often associated with the employment of violent means delude the user into believing that "something is being done" and that the opponent can, in fact, be overcome by these means.

The initial excuse for the use of violence, of course, is that the opponent is employing it (and he usually is) and that one has to "fight fire with fire." This was true in the French Revolution after 1789; in the Russian Revolution after November, 1917; and in the Spanish Revolution of the thirties. And one could cite many other examples.

What was the effect of revolutionary violence on its users? Any assessment will, of course, require the weighing of many factors and the evaluation of evidence that is by no means conclusive. The tangled skein of human affairs, particularly in crises, is never easy to unravel. In revolutionary situations, incidence of violence is only one of many factors which are responsible for particular results. Nevertheless, it would seem that when French revolutionists turned to violence, it became much easier for them to compromise their original ideals, especially after they turned to that master of violence, Napoleon, to "save" the revolution. In Russia, Bolshevik reliance on violence sharply checked egalitarian tendencies, as the hierarchy and secret police necessary to wield violence gained in power. The psychology of violence in the defense against Franco made it less difficult for the Spanish anarchists to surrender certain of their revolutionary principles. The violence of the two sides became indistinguishable; and it is a fair guess to say that had the Loyalists triumphed, their regime might have been virtually as repressive as that of Franco: similar means tend to lead to similar ends, however, much the professed goals might have differed from each other.

This is not to deny that revolutions in which violence is employed may accomplish useful objectives, as was true, in some measure, of the French Revolution. What we question is whether the social and other costs of violent revolution (the mountain of corpses produced by the French Revolution, for example, and the enormous social dislocations) do not always far outweigh any gains. We also ask whether the use of violence in itself does not set up and necessitate goals (bitterness, hierarchical structures, authoritarian patterns of conduct, and so on) which tend to persist and which become far more significant than the social gains.

The critic may, of course, claim that it is conflict itself which tends to destroy community. The answer is that while certain varieties of conflict may indeed have this effect, not all types do. It is conflict carried on without any sense of limits, conflict which has as its objective the destruction of human lives, violent conflict, which is mainly responsible.

If the logic of violence is physical destruction of the opponent, what becomes of such demands as equality, respect for personality and other revolutionary claims? Dead men cannot be equal—for they are now mere things and not men at all. The use of violence, in the context which usually accompanies it, tends to make both its wielders and its recipient unjust. The former discovers that his devotion to reason is eclipsed and that he becomes a slave to the violence which he thinks will emancipate him, while he who suffers from the violence finds his qualities as a human being disregarded, and he is tempted to retaliate in kind, thus perpetuating the cycle.

Search for Non-Violent Power

How do we break through the never-ending cycle of violence which appears to have held captive so much of human history? How are we to make the means of revolution accord with the spirit of its ends?

It is questions of this kind which egalitarian revolutionists —whether white or black—must increasingly ask themselves. They must search for forms of non-violent power and conflict and reject the violence which will inevitably defeat their ends. Such experiments as those of Martin Luther King in the United States and, earlier, of Gandhi in India, point the way, although we are only just beginning to study seriously the potentialities for non-violent revolution. Unless we find methods of non-violent power we are doomed to be disillusioned endlessly: wars of liberation will turn out in the end to have created new tyrannies; wars for the defense of democracy will be shown to have weakened democracy; and violent revolts in South America, in the ghettos of the United States, and in Asia, will contribute to new racism, new exploitation, new authoritarianism, and new social inequalities.

Up from Nonviolence

Mike Scahill

> Behold, he is coming with the clouds, and every eye will see him, every one who pierced him; and all tribes of the earth will wail on account of him. Even so. Amen.
> > Book of Revelation.

This essay is to be a chronicle of impressions I have from a two-month visit to Cuba as a member of the Venceremos Brigade. I will caution you at the beginning of the particular biases I bring to the subject by first informing you of my credentials. They are, to be honest, quite modest. The preceding months before I journeyed to Cuba I worked with The Catholic Worker in New York City. My concerns there were of an eminently practical nature, as they must be if one is to daily practice the works of mercy: peeling potatoes, making soup, putting out a monthly newspaper, and providing hospitality. It was the days spent at the Catholic Worker which formed the convictions I brought to Cuba; it was time spent in the Bowery—which the Catholic Worker serves—that gave me a contempt for the theoretical and the abstract. I took offense at men of thought who dared to enter and explain that mysterious realm of individual human destiny, as if sociologists and theologians could rationally explain away how men and women born with obvious gifts and talents can suddenly abandon themselves and give way to waste and indulgence. In grasping this I began to grasp the meaning of revolution. One does not necessarily enter into revolution by reading Marx or Lenin; men will know and fight their oppression whether or not they have read the fathers of revolution. One enters into revolution only by first entering into that strangest of all riddles which is the common, ordinary, transient life of the world and entering into the souls of the people who such such a world its life. Not only to enter into it, but once there to put to a full and creative use the faculties given a man by God so that it is obvious both to himself and others that he has eyes and ears and a heart. These are the only credentials any man brings anywhere; these are the credentials I brought to Cuba. That being said, let me tell you how I used them.

The Venceremos Brigade consisted of about nine hundred American citizens (and also a group from the U.S. colony of Puerto Rico) representing every age group, every racial and ethnic group, and every political passion. The purpose of the trip was to participate in the historic harvest of the ten million tons of sugar which would hopefully be a big step in pulling Cuba out of underdevelopment. There were two trips to Cuba by the brigade. One took place in November of last year; the other, which I attended, went in February of this year. Each group stayed in Cuba for two months; cutting sugar cane for six weeks and touring the island for two.

The origin of the Venceremos Brigade is rooted in two ideas. The first is the economic blockade which the government of the United States has imposed on the people of Cuba. Given the nature of the Cuban economy, given the underdevelopment and the medical, educational, and technological needs, such a blockade is a crime. This name is economic aggression. Thus, for me to go to Cuba was to merely be consistent with the protest I voice against the crimes the United States daily commits against the underdeveloped world. Secondly, the Venceremos Brigade is rooted in solidarity with the Cuban Revolution. In 1970 work is the meaning of the revolution in Cuba. To be a revolutionary in that land today means to be a worker with a machette in your hand. We actively participated in the work of the revolution, and by so doing said it was right and good for the people, that such a revolution should even happen elsewhere. Since most of my time in Cuba was spent in the canefields, and since most of my impressions were formed simply by working by working in them, it might be of benefit to record a "typical day" in the camp of the Venceremos Brigade.

Our day began at five a.m. with a bugle reveille "De Pie" (meaning "on your feet" in Spanish), breakfast, consisting of coffee and a roll, then off to your machete rack where along with the other thirty members of your work brigade you sharpened your machete. There were twenty-five work brigades, each consisting of about twenty-five Americans and five Cubans. At six o'clock we were off to the canefields and cut until nine, at which time we had a "merienda" for fifteen minutes (equivalent to the American coffee break at which a pastry and cool drink were served). Back to work until eleven then to the camp for lunch and a break until two-thirty. During the break you either slept, read, wrote in your journal, chatted, or listened to the news which was daily broadcast over the loudspeaker in the camp. I particularly enjoyed the news every afternoon because it was so informative about events receiving little or no publicity in the States, especially accounts of guerrilla struggles in Latin America. At two-thirty we again made the long walk to the canefields (sometimes as far as two miles). It was in the course of these long walks that I came to know and become good friends with the Cuban students in my brigade. Wilfredo, Rafael, Cristobal, Maria, and the rest of us would pass the time away singing or discussing numerous political questions. At six-thirty we came back to the camp, washed up, and had dinner. Three evenings a week we have films in the camp. A number of them were documentaries by the Cuban director Santiago Alvarez. Most of the films were on various aspects of the revolution ranging from the early days in the mountains to agricultural experiments and to the history of Cuban ballet. After the film it was usually right to bed. (We lived in tents with bunk beds to house twenty-five).

We worked five and a half days a week and on Saturday afternoons we had a "production meeting" with the entire camp in attendance. This was to discuss the work of the week, whether or not each work-brigade met the quota they set, and also to set work goals for the following week. It was meetings such as these that made me more enthusiastic about the work and more conscious of its importance. I have worked at many jobs in the States, ranging from office work to construction, and I can recall that every time I reflected on the meaning and value of my work and who it benefited, I became terribly depressed and even felt like quitting. Not so when I worked in Cuba. The more I learned of the purpose of the sugar harvest, of its importance for the economy, of what it would do for the people—the more my sweat and fatigue took on meaning. For the first time in my life I was employed to labor for people.

Without a doubt I can say I experienced the very essence of the Cuban Revolution in the canefields. In fact as we rode into camp that very first day I was to learn the basic lesson upon which that revolution and all others like it are founded. It was a lesson which the United States would learn by its embarrassing defeat at Playa Giron in 1961; a lesson which Fidel would stress with all the clarity and passion that is his; a lesson which the mother of Camilo Torres would explain in a manner so convincing and gentle that she could have been your mother or mine; a lesson, finally, which the Vietnamese testify to simply by their history and their lives. Let me go through with you, step by step, how this lesson was taught to me; for whenever it is asked of me, "What did you learn in Cuba?" my reply is "I have learned the meaning of la lucha armada—the armed struggle."

Riding into the camp on that hot February day, the first person I spotted was the armed guard at the entrance. There were two others elsewhere. During my stay in Cuba I was to see innumerable arms: guns, machine guns, and pistols worn by young men and women as well as old men and women. I would swiftly learn the meaning of all this artillery. Not only would I learn its purpose but I would come to appreciate and condone its use. I think the meaning of all this military preparedness was best put at Playa Giron, the first step of our tour. Playa Giron is now a school and a museum displaying tanks, jeeps, army fatigues, machine guns—all made in the U.S.—captured in the U.S.-financed and supported mercenary invasion of Cuba in 1961. A major who commanded a battalion in one of the battles spoke to us. "A people who have built up a happiness have a right to defend that happiness," he told us. On our two-week tour of Cuba we had an opportunity to see the happiness which the revolution is building up. We spent three days on the Isle of Youth (formerly the Isle of Pines where Fidel Castro was once imprisoned) where agricultural experiments are being tried by groups of students in the hope that a more original form of socialism or communism can be achieved. The experiment on the Isle of Youth reminds me, oddly enough, of one of the basic ideas of Peter Maurin—founder of the Catholic Worker—who wrote that "workers should become students and students should become workers."

From the Isle of Youth we went on to many schools and universities. As we traveled through the five provinces of Cuba I began to feel a strange sensation, as if for the first time in my life, I was discovering the meaning of patriotism. People exhibited a certain pride, a sense of purpose and vision in their lives. All this came out when they spoke of the need to defend the happiness they were building because all I spoke with—from fifth graders in Havana to simple farmers in the mountains of Oriente—had a vivid recollection of the past and never, never again, they vowed, would that return.

It was to this very point Fidel addressed himself upon his visit to the camp.

Keep in mind as I offer a description of Fidel that it is a very superficial one since I only had contact with him on the one day he was cutting cane with us and conducted a lengthy question and answer period. On the one hand he is a very shrewd Marxist theoretician, a near genius; on the other hand he is like a fiery baptist preacher, possessing that rare brand of charisma which excites men to follow him.

He has that coveted gift of being able to speak to people of their problems in their language. Keeping in line with the point I am pursuing, he said that if one wished to find out why Cuba is striving to arm itself so heavily one should not ask the Cuban government but should instead ask the government of the United States. While Fidel spoke, my own thoughts drifted back to the Mexico City Airport a few weeks previous.

As we waited the Cuban plane to take us to Havana, numerous government agents scrupulously observed us and took our pictures, agents of a frightened and desperate government. I began to wonder how anyone could be so angry and disturbed with me for going to Cuba because my motives were of the most innocent nature. It seemed to me that any person who has even minimally witnessed the events of the past few years in America should eagerly want to see Cuba, to see a society which has resolved many of the basic ills currently rending this nation asunder. But as Fidel spoke I began to understand why he is a threat to the United States. Not military or economically—that is certain. Fidel is a threat because of his example. Here is a man who can not be bought off, who has no price, who, as the saying goes, does not live on bread alone. If the rest of Latin America and the rest of the world were to take up this example—as they are now doing—then the American way of life, a way of life based on cash registers, stocks, and multi-million-dollar businesses—in short, a way of life based on greed—if the rest of the world were to follow his example then that way of life would quickly perish from the earth.

The mother of Camilo Torres also picked up on the idea of example in the life of a revolutionary as she spoke of why her son, a priest, took a gun and went off to fight in the mountains. He really had no hope of winning but only sought to show others the way.

If Fidel and Cuba now set the example for the rest of Latin America, the Vietnamese certainly set the example for Cuba. Everywhere we went in Cuba billboards and posters could be seen with the saying, *Como en Vietnam*. It means to imitate the Vietnamese in all that you do; in your life, your work, your study. A poster in our camp went like this:

Como en Vietnam
tenacidad, orgonozacion,
disciplina
heroismo diario, en el trabajo
diez anos de lucha antiyanqui
del pueblo vietnamita diez
millones de toneladas de
azucar

I had the occasion to experience the content of such a statement in a unique and moving way. On one of the visits of the
Vietnamese to our camp my work brigade was one of the ones
they worked with. Each of us had one of the Vietnamese for
a cutting partner. There were five worker-students from Hanoi
and five fighters from the National Liberation Front of South
Vietnam. My cutting partner for a good part of the morning
was one of the fighters from the NLF. A Vietnamese girl named
Susan, who is studying at the University of Havana, translated
for us. Carlos is his name in Spanish (I can't recall his name
in Vietnamese). He is twenty-two years old and has been
fighting with the Front since he was fifteen. Both of his parents
were killed in the course of the war. He holds the rank of
captain in the NLF and has won seven out of thirty-two battles. We spoke a little of one of the battles he was in where
he led an attack on an air base, was wounded, but still managed to capture the base. Much of our conversation was on
the politics of the war—common knowledge to most of us by
now—but a more horrible tale when it is spun from the lips
of a man who has lived his life in the midst of it. Needless to
say, the morning spent with Carlos brought the war to a new
point of unbearableness in my life. Think of the finest person
you know being executed for a crime he did not commit. Think
of the Vietnamese.

More than anything else it was the conversation with Carlos
that inspired the title of this piece. I did not intend the title
to be witty or clever. It would, I hope, connote a new understanding of certain issues on my part; as if for the first time
I was seeing and feeling within my own guts what was taking
place in the world. I mentioned earlier how prior to going to
Cuba I worked with the Catholic Worker. I mentioned how
my main concern was with the tradition and life of the Cath-

olic Worker, that is, with nonviolence. Yet in Cuba I found some of my basic premises for nonviolence to be shaken. A violent revolution seemed to produce a decent society. Guns and coercion were not necessary to preserve the revolution. Workers preserved it. Still, even questions as these approach the issue vaguely and theoretically. There was something which pushed me beyond all theory in speaking with this little man with the almond-shaped eyes, the high cheekbones, and the speech that was more like song than speech. Something about the compassion expressed in being overly apologetic for having killed American soldiers; a compassion so vast a number of Americans fail to show. Finally, in his constant distinction between the American government and the American people there was a great similarity to that command given in one of the Testaments about separating the sin from the sinner. In learning this I was to learn to see the issue of Vietnam and even Latin America in a more profound way. What exists in these lands is not so much a revolution in the sense of a planned and calculated overthrow of a tyranny, as it is a classical case of self-defense against an oppression so sophisticated that its means range from corporations to napalm. So, to support the Vietnamese and the National Liberation Front is not so much to support a people striving to bring on a new society; no, it is a far deeper issue, of saying they have a right to be men, a right to the most venerable and ancient of all aspirations—the right of a man to live as he wants. In such a context not only do the Vietnamese have a right to shoot down B-52's; they have a moral obligation—out of demands of justice and charity—to do so.

I suppose in light of the foregoing and my obvious affirmation of Carlos and the cause he represents that it means I support him and the NLF. If that be an abandonment of nonviolence, so be it. I only intended to state in this essay all I saw and felt and learned while in Cuba.

The final word I have to offer is taken from a meditation I recorded in my journal upon the first visit of the Vietnamese to our camp. Speaking of the Venceremos Brigade they referred to it as "an act of militant friendship." Somehow that is the only way to describe the bonds and ties which were formed between myself and Cubans and Vietnamese, bonds and ties which neither time nor distance can separate. The significance of the Venceremos Brigade, at least to me, is that a friendship has happened between citizens of America and victims of America. No longer is it a case of the United States government committing aggressions against faraway lands which many of us could barely write in single page essay on at one time. It is now a case of aggressions against our friends.

My thoughts this moment are of the Cuban students I worked with. Suppose Rafael, Wilfredo, Cristobal, or Maria are killed the next time the U.S. finances an assault on Cuba? And Carlos. What awaits him on his return to Vietnam? I call these questions to mind with you because the degree of intensity and spirit, the degree of courage and hope with which a man struggles is incredibly heightened when a man struggles on behalf of his friends. Since the struggle of today is no different from any other struggle, in any other place, in any other time, it means that at some point the ultimate act of friendship will be demanded—the laying down of one's own life for one's friends.

And so, in the year nineteen hundred and seventy, Richard Nixon being president, the whole world at war, we pray for the strength to accept that demand.

Weatherman

Bernardine Dohrn,
Jeff Jones and Bill Ayers

(LNS) Chicago, 1886. Union organizers and revolutionaries were building towards a May 1st strike which would win workers an 8-hour day. But the McCormick Reaper Works began a lock-out in February, shutting down the plant, with 58,000 workers out. On May first, the day of the planned strike, the city was tense. On

May 3, locked-out workers from the McCormick plant held a mass rally, which ended in a fight with scabs. Police arrived on the scene and fired into the crowd, killing six workers and wounding many more.

To protest these killings and to support the 8-hour movement, a rally was called the next day at the Haymarket Square. It was raining, and the crowd was small and peaceful. As the last speaker was concluding a speech an army of police descended on the square and ordered people to disperse. There was a moment of confused silence. Suddenly a bomb was thrown close to the speakers stand not far from the police, who responded by firing indiscriminately, even at each other. When workers returned shots, the police charged, emptying their guns on the people.

Seven policemen were killed and 60 officers wounded; the toll of murdered workers, estimated at three times that number is still unknown.

Without delay, police rounded up labor organizers all around the city. With the help of the daily papers, eight revolutionaries were then tried and condemned to death. (Three were finally pardoned.) The bomb thrower, whether a radical or a police provocateur, was never identified.

Shortly after, a memorial statue was erected in Haymarket Square. It is a uniformed policeman with his arm raised, commanding "Peace."

Chicago, October, 1969. Just prior to the SDS Weatherman "Days of Rage" demonstration, a dynamite blast demolished the police statue. After some time, a new statue was erected on the same site.

On Oct. 5, 1970, exactly one year later, dynamite again toppled the policeman in Haymarket Square. A few minutes after the explosion, the Chicago Tribune, whose columns in 1886 supported the police attack on the workers, received a phone call:

"We just blew up the Haymarket Square statue for the second time in a row to show our allegiance to our brothers in the New York prison (the Tombs, in revolt for the second time this year) and our black sisters and brothers everywhere.

This is another phase of our revolution to overthrow this fascist society."

Chicago Mayor Richard Daley hurriedly reassured the world that the downtown statue would again be replaced: "We admire the statue for what it depicts and represents—men who gave their lives for the people of Chicago."

Sgt. Richard Barrett of the Chicago Sergeants Association warned that the "blowing up of the only police monument in the USA is a declaration of war by radicals."

The following statement about the bombing—the "fifth communication from the Weatherman underground"—was signed by Bernardine Dohrn, Jeff Jones, and Bill Ayers. A tape of the same message, recorded by Bernardine, was released to the straight media.

Sisters and Brothers

A year ago we blew away the Haymarket pig statue at the start of a youth riot in Chicago. The head of the Police Sergeant's Association called emotionally for all-out war between the pigs and us. We accepted. Last night we destroyed the pig again. This time it begins a fall offensive of youth resistance that will spread from Santa Barbara to Boston, back to Kent and Kansas, for we are everywhere and next week families and tribes will attack the enemy around the country. It is our job to blast away the myths of the total superiority of the man.

We did not choose to live in a time of war. We choose only to become guerillas and to urge our people to prepare for war rather than become accomplices in the genocide of our sisters and brothers.

We learned from American history about policies of exterminating an entire people and their magnificent cultures—the Indians, the blacks, the Vietnamese. We are making plans to resist with all of our creativity.

Students and hippies who now hear peace talk from the white man must remember how talk of peace was used against the Indians and preached to the blacks.

Today many students leaders have cut their hair and called for peace. They say young people shouldn't provoke the government. And they receive in return promises of peaceful change. Promises of peace from a government that bombs Cambodia while talking about an end to war, that killed students at Jackson and Kent while calling for responsibility on campus, that murdered Fred Hampton and hundreds of blacks while calling for racial harmony. Remember that American pigs have already dropped more bombs on a piece of land about the size of Florida than the entire tonnage dropped during World War II.

Don't be tricked by talk. Arm yourselves and shoot to live!

We are building a culture and a society that can resist genocide. It is a culture of total resistance to mind-controlling maniacs, a culture of high-energy sisters getting it on, of hippie acid-smiles and communes and freedom to be the farthest-out people we can be. It's culture that can take care of its people; Rosemary and Tim are free and high.

J. Edgar himself admitted that "Under-ground radicals" were the hardest group to infiltrate. That's because the culture and ideals we want to live by can only be lived in total resistance to Imperialism.

If Nixon invades Cuba, bombs North Vietnam, intervenes in the Middle East, we must all move fast. Figure out strategic weak points of the enemy. Look at the Arabs. With the underground and mass movement responding together, we could shut down every international airport in Amerika within 24 hours. Every long-hair is a YIPPIE! every militant woman a Leila Khaled.

Surround every armed attack with rallies, phone calls, posters and celebrations. We are not just "attacking targets"—we are bringing a pitiful helpless giant to its knees.

We invite Ky and Nixon and Agnew to travel in this country. Come to the high schools and campuses. But guard your planes, guard your colleges, guard your banks, guard your children, *GUARD YOUR DOORS*.

> (signed)
> Bernardine Dohrn
> Jeff Jones
> Bill Ayers

This is the fifth communication from the Weatherman underground.

The Tragedy
of Misguided Idealists

Christian Crusade Weekly

A major cause of the guerrilla warfare plaguing our nation today is misguided idealism. Communists and Communist sympathizers have long been quite effective at taking advantage of youthful idealists and misguiding them into supporting Red objectives. The key to this Communist success is the fact the 'uniformed' people, especially youth, are easily 'misinformed.' Most Americans go through high school and college with little or no understanding of our Communist enemies and little appreciation of our nation's heritage.

Youth, with little or no faith in God combined with lack of appreciation for our nation, are plagued with a spiritual vacuum. They know something is missing—they want to do something for the good of mankind but are in utter confusion which way to turn. Into the lives of these young idealists Communists and pro-Communists move with their evil propaganda and fill the vacuum. We are now reaping the fruits of many years of such efforts. Young do-gooders are misled into paths which lead to evil, not good. More background in relation to this process is contained in our booklet, "Campus Radicalism —Prelude to Disaster?" (Copies may be ordered at 50 cents each from Christian Crusade, P.O. Box 977, Tulsa, Oklahoma 74102.)

The Remaking of Diana Oughton

It seems that a significant proportion of America's young radicals come from well-to-do families. The story of the molding of one of these tragic youths was presented in a series of five articles by Lucinda Franks and Thomas Powers of United Press International, which was carried in many newspapers across the nation during September.

The authors pointed out that when this young lady, Diana

Oughton, enrolled at Bryn Mawr in the fall of 1959, she was a midwestern Republican who was against anything "which smacked of 'liberalism' or 'big government.'" In 1961, when she was 19, Diana went to Germany to spend her junior year at the University of Munich. According to the authors, she "made close friendships with German students and would sometimes remain late into the night at student cafes, discussing over cigarettes and coffee the social problems in the United States which she later was to feel could be solved only by violence." While in Germany she was quoted as saying, "Hurrah for socialism!"

She came back to Bryn Mawr for her senior year during 1962-63. The UPI writers explained "Diana's senior year at Bryn Mawr . . . was a year of change for young people throughout the country. John F. Kennedy's promise in 1960 to 'get the country moving again' had set young people to thinking about America. They found it fell short of what they had always been taught to believe it was. So they went on freedom rides in the South, joined voter-registration projects and picketed stores which discriminated against Negroes.

"Students of fashionable schools like Bryn Mawr talked about social justice and racial prejudice, and turned away from deb parties and champagne in the back of a fast car. During the same period, a kind of genteel Bohemianism was becoming fashionable in the colleges. Diana was among the first students, inspired by the beatniks of the 1950's who grew their hair long and traded their shirtwaists and circle pins for sandals and suede jackets.

"A book which made a deep impression on thousands of white students was John Howard Griffin's "Black Like Me," an account of a trip the author made through the Deep South disguised as a Negro. Diana was strongly affected by it and joined a project in Philadelphia to tutor black ghetto children. . . . Like thousands of other students touched by the new mood in the country, Diana often spent long evenings discussing what was wrong and how to make it right. . . . She shunned college mixers and proms, and listened to Joan Baez albums by the hour . . ."

After her graduation from Bryn Mawr in June, 1963, Diana went to Guatemala for the Quaker-run Voluntary International

Service (VISA) program. Her thinking was seriously affected by the poverty in Guatemala and her time there was apparently an important turning point in her conversion to a revolutionary.

In the third of this series of articles, the authors stated: "The Diana Oughton who returned from the poverty of Guatemala in the fall of 1965 was not the same young woman who had graduated from Bryn Mawr two years earlier. . . . Friends said she had become disillusioned with her country's role in Guatemala and increasingly critical of its policies elsewhere, particularly in Vietnam."

In the spring of 1966 she left Philadelphia for Ann Arbor to enroll in the University of Michigan graduate school of education to get her master's degree in teaching. At this time, according to the authors, a "darker vision of America was emerging in the minds of many young people . . ."

As time went on, Diana became more and more deeply involved in the Students for a Democratic Society (SDS) and eventually went with the Weathermen faction which turned to terrorism. The "Weatherman manifesto" was partly written by her boyfriend, Bill Ayers.

A Father Balks at Financing His Own Destruction

According to the UPI writers, eventually "Diana's father canceled a gas company credit card she had been using on behalf of SDS." They then quoted from a letter written to her by her father in which he declared:

"You speak of a revolution against capitalism. This can only mean that you are developing forces against me and the rest of your family. The oldest and most reasonable form of capitalism is the ownership of agricultural land, and this is what your family has been involved with for a hundred years.

"I will resist any effort to change the basic ideology governing my own life, and it should be obvious I do not want to support any movement that would develop into violence against me and my family." The article continued:

"The passionate intensity with which the Weathermen took their political ideas created a state of mind in Diana which her father later called 'a kind of intellectual hysteria.' He found her less and less willing to really talk about politics, increasingly heated when she did. She finally refused to discuss the subject altogether. 'I've made by decision, Daddy,' she said. 'There's no sense talking about it.' . . ." Here is a typical example of a closed mind, totally brainwashed by the enemies of our nation and mankind.

Tragic End to a Misguided Life

The tragic end came to this one thoroughly misguided idealist on March 6, 1970, when a bomb exploded, killing Diana and two other Weathermen in New York City. In short, she was killed while manufacturing a deadly weapon to use in war against her own country and, as her father stated in the above mentioned letter, against the interests of her family.

Bill Ayers—a Major Influence

According to the UPI writers, a major influence on Diana was Bill Ayers: "After she arrived at the University of Michigan in 1966, Diana joined the Children's Community School, founded by a group of students the year before. There she met Bill Ayers, son of the chairman of Commonwealth Edison Co. of Chicago and one of the Weathermen later indicted on bomb conspiracy charges. Ayers probably exercised the single most powerful influence over Diana until her death. . . ."

As a Weatherman Bill Ayers was totally dedicated to destruction of the United States government. For example, in a speech at the Midwest National Action conference of SDS held in Cleveland August 20-September 1, 1969, he proclaimed: ". . . We have won, we won in Vietnam . . . and we shall continue to win, continue to defeat U.S. imperialism. . . . We're not just saying bring the troops home . . . we're saying bring the war home . . . increasingly this country is going to be torn down . . . we're going to create class war in the streets and institutions of this country, and we're going to make them pay a price, and the price ultimately is going to be total defeat for them . . ."

There Are Many Others

Diana Oughton and her boyfriend, Bill Ayers, are merely two examples of many well-to-do young Americans who have gradually had their minds poisoned to a vicious hatred of their own nation. This mind conditioning which is so detrimental to our country is not limited merely to those who have gone far enough to engage in violent warfare to achieve this "change" but include many more who ideologically support the militant revolutionaries and also those who support their goals of "change" in a Communist-Socialist direction but do not approve of the violent warfare.

The great tragedy of these misguided idealists is that if they are successful, they will create a situation in our nation far worse than that which they seek to cure. Far-left Liberals only see America's faults, real and imagined ones. They do not see its positive points which put it far ahead of nations toward which these leftists look as examples we should follow.

Guatemala—What Diana Did Not Know

The personal tragedy of Diana Oughton is compounded by the fact that the nation where conditions influenced her thinking so strongly towards a militant Communist viewpoint has actually suffered under communism. Under the great delusion that it would bring some kind of utopia to that nation and others, young leftist radicals such as the late Diana Oughton would put all nations under Communist rule. Guatemala was under an all-out pro-Communist government during the years 1950-54. A sample of this supposed utopia under which Guatemalans lived during those years was described in an Associated Press article datelined Guatemala in the Washington *Evening Star* of July 2, 1954:

> Handkerchiefs to their noses, a long line of men, women and teen-agers filed past a row of mutilated bodies in tropical Guatemala's capital today. The smell of death was overpowering as the curious populace lifted the lids of the crude wooden coffins to peer at some of those the

new military government says were tortured to death by deposed President Jacobo Arbenz Guzman's secret police. Some of those who looked fainted. Others vomited at the stench. Most fled . . .

The gruesome display was part of the drive by Guatemala's new government against Arbenz' Communist backers, who sparked the terror wave which preceded his downfall and who now are reported stirring up peasant opposition to his conquerors. In the weeks just before and after Col. Carlos Castillo Armas' 'liberation' army of exiles invaded from neighboring Honduras, the police rounded up hundreds of anti-Communists and opponents of Arbenz' Red-backed regime.

Of those picked up, the bodies of some 60 so far have been brought to the capital—torn, battered and broken by police torture. Six of these, brought in yesterday from the little village of Villa Lobos, were typical. After several days of working over by the police, they were machine-gunned on June 24 and left in a shallow grave.

All were men. Their bodies were purple from beating, slashed and cut by floggings. Eyes were gouged out and teeth were kicked in. The groins had been a favorite target. Each man's hands were tied behind him . . .

This article went on to report that many of the bodies were "tossed in front of their homes or left in the streets," and that "More are being discovered daily."

Nationally syndicated columnist Jim Bishop wrote of some of the atrocities of the Guatemalan Communists in the February, 1955, issue of *The Catholic Digest*:

. . . On June 9 (1954), they took an old man named Filemon Meza to the ornate police headquarters and, after darkness, they stretched him on his side and took turns kicking him in the face and stomach. Some of the police turned away . . . Senor Meza's offense seemed to be that he was on the side of God, and opposed to communism . . . Pedro Arriaga . . . used to be head of the city slaughterhouse. He was a little younger, a little stronger. During the torture, he screamed. When he stopped screaming, they filled a *pila* with water. A *pila* is a huge stone tub where clothes are washed. They tied Arriaga's hands and feet and threw him into it. The trick was to watch him struggle for air, and then to get him out just before he drowned. This man was strong. He kept on living. He lost his mind, and when he began grinning foolishly they finished him by having the young cops form a circle and kick him to death . . .

Mr. Bishop described several other cases, including that of Col. Chua. The Communists attempted to get him to reveal the location and number of units of the anti-Communist army of liberation. When the colonel refused to cooperate, he was given the following treatment:

They dropped him to the floor, and they kicked him until it began to look as though they might lose him. The colonel was bound hand and foot, and dropped into the *pila*. When he recovered, he was carried into the cell, and leather thongs were tied to his thumbs and run through steel rings in the ceiling. As he was lifted off the floor, he began to scream and beg for mercy. They left him there . . .

Of course, eventually the colonel, along with two members of his staff, was killed, but not before much additional cruel, inhuman torture was inflicted.

Surely few college students would turn to any form of communism if they were taught the cold, hard facts of Communist terrorism and inhumanity such as that detailed above.

Vietnam

Vietnam has for some years been a major cause of misguided idealists. Undoubtedly, there is a far larger minority in our country supporting Communist victory in Vietnam than has ever been the case with an enemy of our nation. Once again they ignore the facts of life regarding Communists atrocities at Hue and throughout South Vietnam. They ignore the fact that when Vietnam was divided into two countries, masses of people in North Vietnam attempted to flee south but there was very little traffic in the other direction. Among voluminous printed material relating to Communist atrocities in Vietnam was an article by John G. Hubbell in the November, 1968, issue of *Reader's Digest*. Lt. Gen. Lewis W. Walt, U.S. Marine Corps (Commander, I Corps Area, South Vietnam, 1966-1967), made the following remarks regarding the authenticity of this article:

> This article accurately depicts the true nature of the enemy in South Vietnam. I saw the little boy with his hands cut off. I have seen heads impaled on stakes, and disembowled bodies. I learned early in my two years of duty in South Vietnam, fighting and working alongside the South Vietnamese forces, that the Communist terrorism described in this article is no mere accident of war but a program of systematic butchery. This deliberate and brutal assault against the grassroots citizenry is one reason why we who have responded to South Vietnam's call for assistance believe devoutly that our efforts to save this nation are worthwhile, necessary and important.

The article described the case of the little boy mentioned by General Walt as follows:

> The village chief and his wife were distraught. One of their children, a seven-year-old boy, had been missing for four days. They were terrified, they explained to Marine Lt. Gen. Lewis W. Walt, because they believed he had been captured by the Vietcong.
> Suddenly, the boy came out of the jungle and ran across the rice paddies toward the village. He was crying. His mother ran to him and swept him up in her arms. Both of his hands had been cut off, and there was a sign around his neck, a message to his father: if he or anyone else in the village dared to go to the polls during the upcoming elections, something worse would happen to the rest of his children.

The article continued discussing communism's total inhumanity: "The VC delivered a similar warning to the residents of a hamlet not far from Da Nang. All were herded before the home of their chief. While they and the chief's pregnant wife and four children were forced to look on, the chief's tongue was cut out. . . ." Then the article described an unspeakable atrocity too horrible for us to print and continued: "As he died, the VC went to work on his wife. . . . Then, the nine-year-old son; a bamboo lance was rammed through one ear and out the other. Two more of the chief's children were murdered the same way. The VC did not harm the five-year-old daughter—not physically: they simply left her crying, holding her dead mother's hand.

General Walt tells of his arrival at a district headquarters the day after it had been overrun by VC and North Vietnamese army troops. Those South Vietnam soldiers not killed in the battle had been tied up and shot through the mouths or the backs of their heads. Then their wives and children, including a number of two- and three-year-olds, had been brought into the street, disrobed, tortured and finally executed: their throats were cut; they were shot, beheaded, disemboweled. The mutilated bodies were draped on fences and hung with signs telling the rest of the community that if they continued to support the Saigon government and allied forces, they could look forward to the same fate.

These atrocities are not isolated cases; they are typical. For this is the enemy's way of warfare, clearly expressed in his combat policy in Vietnam. While the naive and anti-American throughout the world, cued by Communist propaganda, have trumpeted against American immorality in the Vietnam War . . . the Communists have systematically authored history's grisliest catalogue of barbarism. By the end of 1967, they had committed at least 100,000 acts of terror against the South Vietnamese people. The record is an endless litany of tortures, mutilations and murders that would have been instructive even to such as Adolf Hitler. . . . It is long past time for

Americans . . . to take a hard look at the nature of this enemy. . . .

To this last sentence, informed Americans can only say Amen!

Other atrocities were detailed in this article and the author stated: "The full record of Communist barbarism in Vietnam would fill volumes. If South Vietnam falls to the Communists, millions more are certain to die, large numbers of them at the hands of Ho's imaginative torturers. That is a primary reason why, at election times, more than 80 per cent of eligible South Vietnamese defy every Communist threat and go to the polls, and why, after mortar attacks, voting lines always form anew. . . . It is why those who prance about—even in our own country—waving Vietcong flags and decrying our 'unjust' and 'immoral' war should be paid the contempt they deserve. . . ." We might add that they should also be treated as allies of the worst enemy our nation has ever faced and prosecuted for giving aid and comfort to that enemy.

Other Atrocities

These atrocities and acts of terror in Guatemala and Vietnam are merely a tiny sample of what goes on all over the Communist empire, including the Soviet Union itself. A recent report on atrocities there appeared in an Associated Press news item in the Tulsa *Daily World* of July 28, 1970:

> In a taped message Monday, smuggled from the concentration camp where he is held by the Soviet government, writer Alexander Ginzburg charged that "16 political prisoners have perished recently" for lack of medical care.
>
> In another message, Vladimir Bukovsky described tortures inflicted on dissident Russian intellectuals held by Soviet authorities in insane asylums. . . . Bukovsky . . . said that prisons and concentration camps were not the worst punishments possible. Insane asylums, he said, were worse. The 27-year-old Russian had spent a total of six years in all three.

He described one torture. "It involved the use of wet canvas, in which the patient is rolled up from head to foot," he said. "As the canvas began to dry out, it would get tighter and tighter and make the patient feel even worse. There were medical men present while it was taking place who made sure that the patient did not lose consciousness." . . .

They Will Suffer Too

Most of the misguided idealists who are deceived into working with Communist groups for the destruction of America would suffer under communism the same as other citizens. There have been a number of such incidents in countries which have fallen to communism. One of these was discussed in a book published during 1956 entitled *The White Nights—Pages from a Russian Doctor's Notebook*. The author, Dr. Boris Sokoloff, was acquainted with a number of "Liberals" who helped the Communists take over and knew some in prison camps. In regard to the original Communist takeover in Russia, he wrote:

> . . . The role of the left-wing Socialists had been pathetic enough—and their fate was tragic. Although admitted to the Soviet of People's Commissars, in which they received a few seats, they were mercilessly liquidated as soon as their usefulness as appeasers had ended. Boris Kamkoff and many of their leaders, who had given so much help to the Communists during the October 'coup d'etat' and the days preceding the Constituent convention, were among the first victims of the Red terror . . .

Later Dr. Sokoloff related his experience in prison with left-wingers:

> Paradoxically, I was in the midst of left-wingers. Out of twenty men in Cell 17, fourteen were men who only two years before had ardently promoted and defended communism. Two were maximalist Socialists, two Social-

Democrats, six Left Socialists, two followers of Tchernoff, and two fellow-traveling Liberals. All were filled with hatred for the Soviet government. They claimed they had been betrayed, in the most outrageous manner, by Lenin and his comrades. "Without us," they reiterated, over and over, "the Communists would never have been able to overthrow Kerensky's government or disperse the Constituent Assembly. We believed them. We trusted their honesty, their integrity, their promises to adhere to democratic principles and respect freedom. We realize now that it was all a fraud. We realize now that they wanted power and nothing but power." Again and again, they discussed among themselves the ignominy of their own conduct, which had helped to bring disaster to their country.

The first to die were the two Liberals. Called by the warden soon after I arrived at Boutyrki, they walked out of the cell crying, "— the Communists." Next, one after another, the Left Socialists were taken. They went forth with murder on their lips, cursing their former comrades and associates, the Communists.

Dr. Sokoloff himself was spared because Nicholas Morosoff, president of the University of Lesgaft, had personally intervened in his case and begged Lenin to "save the life of a promising young scientist." Later he managed to escape from Russia along with Alexander Kerensky's wife and two sons, all traveling under the guise of Estonians.

It Always Has Been Evil

Communism has always been an inhumanely evil force. The late Allen Pinkerton, founder of the famous Pinkerton Detective Agency, warned of this evil many years ago in his 1878 book entitled *Strikers, Communists, Tramps and Detectives.* In regard to the Paris Commune he wrote:

> With a grim sort of humor, the Commune abolished public executions, while foully murdering scores of victims in prison. . . . It destroyed public buildings, and de-

molished monuments. It levied upon the rich, and encouraged rapine upon both rich and poor. Incendiarism, robbery and murder were its constant practices. It brushed out of existence nearly a hundred great newspapers, and brought into existence nearly a hundred sheets which for vileness were never equalled. Unbridled license was the crowning feature. All that is held by mankind as execrable and infamous was enacted by it. . . . Its lesson is not one for Paris . . . (but) for the entire civilized world. . . . Give it time and let it alone, and it will lift its red hand with all the savage ferocity with which it struck Paris . . . (Communists) are a class of human hyenas worthy of all notice and attention. . . ." Later in the book he rightly contended that communism "calls for as prompt an extermination as we would give a deadly reptile. . . .

Mr. Pinkerton's warnings were absolutely correct some 92 years ago and they are still correct today. Truth, instead of misinformation about communism, can lead more of our nation's idealistic young activists to work "against" this evil instead of helping to bring its terror upon an unsuspecting American populace.

A Growing Awareness among the People

Angela Davis

The bourgeois press seized upon my recent capture by the Federal pigs as an occasion to inject more confusion into the minds of the American public.

Focusing the bulk of its articles on my personality and background, the press has clearly attempted to camouflage the political issues involved in my case.

Regardless of what degrees I may have, regardless of my external appearance and psychological make-up, the reality of my present situation is this:

The reactionary pig forces of this country have chosen to persecute me because I am a Communist revolutionary, participating together with millions of oppressed peoples throughout the world, designed to overthrow all of the conditions that stand in the way of our freedom.

While newspapers and magazines wasted pages upon pages, attempting to resurrect my past, they should have instead been cognizant of hundreds upon hundreds of American revolutionaries who have been confronted with a fate no different than mine.

Government agents incessantly employ the most devious and barbarous means to rid the country of all those who are challenging racism, exposing capitalist exploitation, and working, organizing and fighting for freedom.

Scores of members of the Black Panther party have been mutilated and murdered, hundreds from among their ranks have been shoved into the nation's prisons; and still others have been forced into exile.

And the Soledad Brothers continue to battle with the representatives of the repressive prison apparatus, programmed to offer death by gas to anyone who dares to speak out against racism and propagates the idea of freedom among captives.

Ronald Reagan and the State of California, having first demanded my job because I am a member of the Communist party, are now demanding my life. Why?

Not because I am the dangerous criminal they portray; not because I am guilty of their framed-up charge for which there is no evidence whatsoever, but because, in their warped vision, a revolutionary is, a priori, a criminal.

Turning myself in to Ronald Reagan and his accomplices would have been equivalent to placing my head voluntarily on the executioner's block.

The death of Jonathan Jackson at San Rafael was not only a deep and crushing blow to me, his family and friends, but a profound loss to the world revolutionary movement.

No black man or woman can fail to understand the unbearable pressure which led Jonathan to his death, struck down in the midst of battle.

His courage and self-sacrifice leave us with a legacy which no force can eradicate.

My flight was unsuccessful. I have been captured. To me, this means I must strengthen my will to fight this monstrous system.

One more is being held captive, but more importantly, the revolution continues to grow in vigor and verve.

Our enemies find themselves confronted with a growing awareness among the people that the concentrated effort to maim and murder revolutionaries is just another form of the daily genocide of police brutality, and impoverished living conditions of ghettos and barrios.

If masses of people will fulfill their obligation to protect the men and women who have devoted their lives to the struggle for equality and freedom, let there be no doubt about it—victory will soon be ours.

Long live the memory of Jonathan Jackson.

Free Erica, Bobby, the New York Panthers, the Soledad Brothers and all political prisoners.

Power to the people.

Angela Yvonne Davis
Women's House of Detention
New York, N.Y.
Nov. 10, 1970

All Shades of Revolutionaries

The Herald of Freedom

The Black Panthers have it made from a revolutionary point of view, with the Communist Party and the obedient knee-jerk "liberals" rushing to their support whenever problems arise with the law. Coming on strong are two other organizations to take care of other segments of the population in respect to organizing them for revolutionary activity. The Young Lords are to the Puerto Ricans what the Black Panthers are to the Blacks, while there are now White Panthers working on white youth who have dropped out of normal society to form the "Woodstock Nation." An official report of the California Senate (15th report of the un-American Activities Sub-committee) was recently released and made the accusation, based on its investigations, that the Communist Party had taken over the Black Panthers and was using them as "shock troops on the front line of the revolution." This is, of course, what we have been saying right along while the Panthers were pretending to be an independent organization. A report from an undercover agent in the militant radical movement fingers Angela Davis as the "personality" around whom the Communists built their control of the Panthers. She has now gone into that vast and well organized underground to which so many radicals wanted by the FBI have fled. This is as a result of the kidnapping and murder of a California judge with weapons which she purchased and owned. The Black Panthers have been involved in many other recent "shoot-outs" which have been well publicized.

The White Panthers are not so well known on the East Coast but they are working on it. Their program closely resembles in language and purpose those of the Young Lords and the Black Panthers. They are working to politicize the alienated youth who presumably have nothing but drugs and rock music on their minds. They are armed, as are their Black and Puerto Rican counterparts. Their national headquarters is in Ann Arbor, Michigan, but they have branches in other cities. Their Portland, Ore., headquarters was recently raided and police uncovered an arsenal which included rifles, shotguns (one sawed-off), a telescopic sight, a bayonet and ammunition.

The White Panther Party was founded in 1968 by Chairman John Sinclair and Minister of Defense Pun Plamondon; they are both now in jail. Magdalene Sinclair is Minister of Propaganda. She was born in Communist East Germany and "escaped" in 1958 at the age of 18. The remainder of her family still lives in the Communist country. She has a younger sister, Uta, and a brother Erhard, now 19 and a private in the East German Army. In writing about her return to her homeland for her mother's funeral, she makes it quite clear that she did not leave the Communist country because she was anti-Communist. She writes concerning the funeral. (*Sun/Dance,* Vol. 1, No. 1, July 4, 1970):

"The funeral was a drag. An insult to human dignity, to say the least. My mother . . . worked for the collective ever since it was formed back in 1951. . . . Always, the collective came first, then her family and last herself . . .

"And here . . . this preacher starts talking about how her illness was God's punishment, how she always let her work be more important than the worship of God . . . the whole Christian-guilt trip.

"I looked around and studied the faces of the people. Did they feel as insulted as I did by the theologian up there, spouting counter-revolutionary bulls—t? No reaction. I felt like getting the record straight—'She was no "sinner," she was a revolutionary, we should give honor where honor is due . . .'"

Mrs. Sinclair writes about the young people in East Germany who "are watching us." She states: "They know all about the Black Panther Party, they know all about the Conspiracy trial, they know about Timothy Leary. And they know that Rock 'n' Roll is not a decadent western art form, as their government tries to tell them. . . . Just as they are for us, rock 'n' roll and long hair are symbols for them. In fact, just like here, they ARE freedom. What is needed then is a truly international youth party, or Youth International Party, in East and West Germany, Czechoslovakia, Amerika, Canada, Japan, or any other western, highly industrialized mother countries. My brother wants to start a chapter in East Germany and call it the Red Panthers."

The "Rock Festival" which occurred at Woodstock has evolved into what is known as the "Woodstock Nation," which denotes solidarity among the hippie-type youth of the country. The White Panther Information Service (*Sun/Dance*) carries "Woodstock Nation Notes," in which we read: "Brother Jerry Rubin, is right now in the hands of the pig in Cook County Jail, Chicago, serving charges stemming from the Pentagon (remember that?) and from Chicago. He'll be there about two months, and brothers and sisters should write him and let him know we love him. Write: Jerry Rubin, c/o Frank Oliver, 30 LaSalle St., Chicago, Ill."

A musical (?) group known as the Up has been associated with the White Panther Party since it was founded. This "Up" is described by them as "the guerilla arm of the White Panther Party Ministry of Culture, and as such its function is aggressively to seek out Amerika's children in the death culture's own territory and to move them to come over to the side of the revolution." The WPP publication states:

"The White Panther Party believes that the cultural revolution and the social political revolution are inseparable. . . . The four men in the Up live communally with about 25 other White Panthers at National Headquarters, taking part in the collective life of the Party and in the process of criticism and self-criticism that is the Party's fundamental method of development."

The "lead singer" of Up is Frank Bach who was made Minister of Culture and Up manager David Sinclair is Chief of Staff of the WPP *Sun/Dance* states:

> As Minister of Culture, Frank reports on developments in the youth culture and in the music industry for various revolutionary publications . . . and he takes an active part in the organization of community cultural events. As Ministry of Culture cadre, Bob Rasmussen, Gary Rasmussen, and Scott Bailey work on the production and promotion of these events. . . .
>
> Through the White Panther Party Ministry of Culture and in alliance with other revolutionary organizations and people's bands, the Up aim at building up a people's recording company, a people's booking agency, people's printing presses, etc., so that the people's music can always be presented in a revolutionary manner and so that the music can give economic support to Woodstock Nation, instead of that other one . . . On their own Sundance label, they recently released the first pressing of their single (record). . . . More information on the Up, including booking and the purchasing of the record, may

be obtained by writing Rejuvenation Society, Up, 1520 Hill St., Ann Arbor, Mich. 48104. . . . All Power to the People! Long Live Rock and Roll!

The program of the White Panther Party (July 4, 1970) is as follows:

We have seen the future—we ARE the future—and we know that it is not only ours, but that it likewise belongs to all the people on the planet. We know that the age of capitalism, competition, consumerism, and the class society is finished, and we demand total entrance for all people into the New Age of common wealth, cooperation, communalism, and the classless society which is now possible . . . Everything belongs to everybody, and we all share a common interest, a common wealth and a common fate. We demand the end of the present control system with its consumerism and war and its death-culture, and the beginning of a continuous human revolution based on the free exchange of energy and materials, the free passage of people and goods from place to place as demanded by the absolute needs of the people, the free use of the energies and resources of the planet and its people within the context of a free social order based wholly on the needs of all the people all the time, and free development of a new Life-Culture which will give voice to the highest spirit of mankind. These are our most basic demands.

What We Want/What We Believe

1. We want freedom. We want the power for all people to determine their own destinies.

We believe that we will not be free until all people are free, and that there will not be world peace until all the people of the world have their freedom. . . .

We believe further that all oppressed peoples have the absolute right to national self-determination, and that they are not bound to recognize or respect the so-called laws of the oppressor. In this connection, we support the national liberation struggles of the black, brown, yellow, red and youth colonies on the North American continent, of the Provisional Revolutionary Government of Vietnam, the Pathet Lao in Laos, the Khmer Rouge in Cambodia, the revolutionary peoples of Thailand, Malaysia, Japan, and the Philippines, the Palestinian Liberation Front, all African, Asian and Latin American national liberation movements, and the struggles of all other peoples throughout the world who are fighting for their liberation from the forces of modern imperialism. We unite particularly with the revolutionary youth of the western world who are struggling with us to bring the New Age into being on this planet.

2. We want justice. We want an immediate and total end to all political, cultural, and sexist repression of all oppressed peoples all over the world, particularly the repression of women, of black people, young people, and all national minorities within the confines of the United States of America. We want the complete transformation of the so-called legal system in the United States so that the laws and courts and police and military will function only in the best interests of ALL the people. We want the end of all police and military violence directed against the people of the earth right now!

3. We want a free world economy based on the free exchange of energy and materials and the end of money. . . .

4. We want a clean planet and a healthy people. We want to eliminate all industrial and military pollution of the land, the water, the air, and the universe itself, and of the people of the earth whose minds and bodies are now polluted by the products and the propaganda of the consumer/war society. . . . We believe that the present state of disaster on planet earth is a direct and inescapable result of the irresponsible capitalist system and the greedy conduct of the "ownership" class . . . We believe that control of the planet's resources must be placed entirely in the hands of the people. . . .

5. We want a free educational system that will teach each man, woman, and child on earth exactly what each needs to know to survive and grow into his or her full human potential . . . A free revolutionary educational

system is central to the development of a free revolutionary society, since the people have to be fully informed and made fully aware of the possibilities open to them. . . .

6. We want to free all structures from corporate rule and turn all the buildings and land over to the people at once . . . We believe that deeds, mortgages, leases, rents, liens, all of those things are simple phony means of control through which the "ownership" class exploits the rest of the people.

7. We want free access to all information media and to all technology for all the people. . . .

8. We want the freedom of all people who are being held against their will in the conscripted armies of the oppressor throughout the world. We believe that the only legitimate armed forces are those which can only be defined as people's armies. . . .

9. We want freedom of all political prisoners of war held in federal, state, county, and city jails and prisons. We want them returned to their communities a once! We believe that the government of the United States and its various agencies and subsidiaries is presently carrying out an organized, calculated, wide-ranging program of political and cultural repression and terrorism against the revolutionary peoples throughout the world . . . We believe particularly that John Sinclair, Huey P. Newton, Bobby Seale, Erika Huggins, the Panther 21, Timothy Leary, Ahmed Evans, Mortin Sostre, Lee Otis Johnson, all marijuana prisoners, all draft resisters, all deserters and resisters of illegitimate authority within the mother country armed forces must be released from all jails at once. . . . We believe that prisons and jails have nothing to do with the "crimes" committed by their inhabitants, and that all prisoners should be released and given a chance to prove themselves as free citizens of the New Age. If there are "criminals" who cannot restrain themselves from harming other people, they must then be brought before juries of their *peers* and, if convicted, sent to real rehabilitation centers which will teach them how to live in the New Age.

10. We want a free planet. We want free land, free

food, free shelter, free clothing, free music, and culture, free media, free technology, free education, free health care, free bodies, free people, free time and space, everything free for everybody!

Those running the WPP (Central Committee) are as follows: Chairman, John Sinclair; Minister of Defense, Pun Plamondon; Minister of the International Affairs, Gene Plamondon; Minister of the Interior, Skip Kelley; Minister of Education, Magdalene Sinclair; Minister of Art, Gary Grimshaw; Minister of Culture, Frank Bach; Minister of Communications, Lynn Schneider; Chief of Staff, David Sinclair. The Editorial Staff of *Sun/Dance* (Jointly edited by the Central Committee, White Panther Party) consists of Ken Kelley as Editor and Gary Grimshaw as "Revolutionary Artist and Layout"; while the Production Coordinators are Marsha Rabideau, Al Shamie, Terry Taube, and Peggy Taube. Distribution Manager is Judy Janis and Hiawatha Bailey is in charge of Circulation. Headquarters is at 1520 Hill St., Ann Arbor, Michigan.

The females of the White Panther Party call themselves the Red Star sisters because "the Red Star is a universal symbol of *commune*ism, of living and working together, coming together, a symbol of righteous revolution and love for *all of humanity*." They state: "We, the sister of the White Panther Party, take the Red Star as the symbol of our own liberation and align ourselves with all oppressed people on the planet. . . . We, the Red Star sisters of the White Panther Party, are a cadre of sisters united and dedicated to serving the needs of the people, with a specific purpose of educating and organizing more revolutionary sisters into the White Panther Party. . . . We call on all revolutionary sisters to unite with us to make the White Panther Party a truly revolutionary Party . . . *power to the Red Star sisters. Revolution is the way of life.*"

The Young Lords Party was established July 22, 1969 with the merger of two groups of Puerto Rican youths in New York City. One was composed of college students and called itself Sociedad de Albizu Campos (SAC) and the other was a street gang called the Young Lords which name it took from the Chicago gang of the same name. The new unified group made its first appearance as the New York State Chapter of the Young Lords Organization at a solidarity rally for Cuba on July 26th. The first issue around which they began to organize and draw attention to themselves was garbage with which they barricaded the streets. They continued to organize and set up Free Breakfast (and Indoctrination) Programs. They received much publicity when they occupied the First Spanish Methodist Church on Dec. 28, 1969, remaining until Jan. 7th. The church had been a Young Lords target since October when they asked the church board for space for their breakfast program, a medical clinic and a "liberation school." The board, not being sympathetic to the left-wing orientation of the Young Lords, had refused them permission to use the premises which were new and on which the congregation of 123 members gladly paid $642 per month on the mortgage in addition to the other financial demands made upon them. After disrupting church services a number of times, the Young Lords moved in and took over, renamed the church the "People's Church" and put their "community" programs into action. They were finally evicted when police came with a court order; they left peacefully and were arrested. No punishment was meted out to them for their action by the courts, however.

The hierarchy of the Methodist Church was quite conciliatory and sympathetic to the Young Lords, with Bishop Lloyd C. Wicke writing in a letter to his clergy in the N.Y. Conference on Jan. 12th:

"December 11 Dr. Osborne and I met with the minister of defense of the Young Lords and discussed various program possibilities . . . We assured the Young Lords we would meet with the congregation and employ every persuasive power toward involving the church more widely in the life of the immediate community. We agreed to strive to establish a dialogue between the Board of the church and the Young Lords . . . And we promised to meet with the members of their group any time, anywhere. . . ."

The bishop pointed out that the First Spanish UMC was not the only church that was irrelevant to its community and that there was an imperative lesson in this "unfortunate situation" for all churches to begin to find ways to deal with the (physical) needs of their communities. In this letter the bishop stated:

"The church membership agrees that it has not been as faithful in serving the community as the occasion and opportunity demanded. It has set in motion processes to inaugurate more adequate social services. . . .

"The church acknowledges its flaw in the past. It pledges itself to consult with and involve community leaders as it seeks to serve its immediate neighborhood."

The Young Lords, however, are a revolutionary socialist group. They do not aim to make their people "happy," but wish to keep them unhappy in order to organize them for use as a revolutionary "people's army." A member of the Young Lords, Rafael Viera, was arrested for the murder of a Detroit policeman during a National conference of the Republic of New Africa which he attended. The results were reported in the Young Lords "Latin Revolutionary News Service," *Palante*:

> Rafael Viera, revolutionary member of the Young Lords Party, arrested last year, March, 1969, for allegedly offing a pig in Detroit during a national meeting of the Republic of New Africa, was set free June 16. Rafael and two other brothers were found innocent of those ridiculous charges after the pigs realized they couldn't make the charges stick even in Detroit. . . . Rafael Viera, a solid and strong member of the Young Lords Party, was singled out as a target because he was the only Puerto Rican at the . . . convention. After months in jail, awaiting trial, Rafael Viera, the Young Lords Party's first political prisoner of war, is free and on the streets continuing his work as a freedom fighter for his nation. . . .

The National Headquarters of the YLP is at 1678 Madison Avenue, New York. The Central Committee is made up of Felipe Luciano, Chairman (recently ousted); Juan Gonzalez, Minister of Education; David Perez, Field Marshal; Pablo "Yoruba" Guzman, Minister of Information; Juan Fi Ortiz, Chief of Staff; and Denise Oliver, Minister of Finance. Announcement was made on Sept. 4, 1970 that Luciano had been ousted as National chairman by the central committee for "male chauvinism, unclear politics, political individualism and lack of development." In a statement or news release concerning the ouster it was stated that "the ouster was seen by informants as moving the Young Lords party into an open 'nationalist position in relation to the struggle for the independence of Puerto Rico.'" The release also stated that the Lords had recently opened branches in Hoboken, N.J., and in Philadelphia and that it "expects to receive the original Chicago-based group (from which it had separated—Ed.) back into the fold as a chapter."

The Young Lords Party has a 13 Point Program and Platform which closely resembles that of the Black and the White Panthers and which states specifically (Point No. 11):

> 11. We fight anti-Communism with international unity. Anyone who resists injustice is called a communist by "the man" and condemned. . . . No longer will our people believe attacks.

The Young Lords also have rules of Discipline which require "criticism and self-criticism," political education classes, learning to operate and service weapons. The rules state: "All Traitors, Provocateurs, and Agents will be subject to Revolutionary Justice."

These Black, Brown and White organizations are actually Red and should be recognized as such and not as heroes trying to help the "oppressed" (although in a "misguided" way) as the news media would have us believe. Their organization around a "Central Committee" is patterned after the Communists and they consider themselves international also in their "solidarity" with the exploited peoples of the world. The Black Panther Party has recently opened up an "international section" in Algiers and the BPP has been accorded the status of a "liberation movement" officially by the Algerian Government. The new section was formally opened by Eldridge Cleaver, just returned from his tour of Asian Communist capitals as a member of the "United States Peoples' Anti-Imperialist Delegation."

Those people who are waiting for a revolution to happen some time in the future should look a bit more closely at what is happening. The revolution is here now. The revolutionary Blacks, Browns, Whites and Reds are not playing games . . . they are deadly and serious.

Hysteria

Social Questions

The Rev. William M. Holman, MFSA friend, pastor of the Tarrytown (NY) UMC, was involved in a disruptive situation in the Tarrytowns: The village was planning to celebrate its Centennial this summer, and the Centennial committee asked the Clergy Association, of which Holman is president, to prepare an opening open air service Sunday evening, June 7. The clergy decided upon a musical program. Camilla Williams, black soprano from the Metropolitan Opera, would sing. The local cantor would bring a 78-voice choir. Pete Seeger consented to come and do his Hudson River Ballad. Each of these artists offered to donate his services. With the word that Pete Seeger would be on the program, the VFW said that if he were, they would pull their bands and floats out of the parade, would counteract with blaring sirens and would destroy the Centennial. The Centennial committee weakly gave in to the VFW, and told the clergy they would have to drop Seeger from the program, for Seeger is a "Communist."

Some years ago Seeger was summoned before a subcommittee of HUAC. He did not take the Fifth Amendment—on his Constitutional rights. He was cited in contempt of Congress on ten counts. He spent a period in jail. Later a federal Circuit Court of Appeals dismissed all charges against Seeger, and said the HUAC subcommittee did not even have a legal right to sit on the Seeger case. The National Laymen's Council of Edgar C. Bundy's (Rightist) Church League of America, Wheaton, Ill., did a smear job on Seeger because of his experience at the hands of HUAC. The Tarrytown VFW based their case on Seeger's "Communism" on this material from Wheaton.

Holman did some research on Seeger's "communism." He asked his Congressman Richard L. Ottinger to check it. Ottinger checked with the Department of Justice—Seeger was given a clean bill of ideological health. (Seeger should be allowed to sing even if he were a communist.—LHB).

Schism v.2, no.1 (Winter 1971)

Interestingly, while the Tarrytown VFW was raising such strenuous objection to Seeger, he was singing at Marymount College (RC) in Tarrytown. He sings for the National Park Service. He sang recently in the House of Representatives. Seeger's campaign to clean up the Hudson River is helped by the Rockefeller, Ottinger and DeWitt Wallace (Reader's Digest) foundations. The Tarrytown Daily News gave fair coverage to Seeger's exoneration from the charge of communism in a 7-column front page article. The VFW still said No!

In consideration of the research which revealed Seeger's "clearance," the Tarrytown clergy voted 10-1 to keep him on their part of the Centennial program. To accede to the demand to bar him from the program would, they held, violate both the First Amendment, and the Ninth Commandment against bearing "false witness." A "Citizens Against Censorship in the Tarrytowns" was formed. Petitions were circulated; 600 signatures were affixed in the schools, 1600 families signed. Still the VFW was adamant, refusing even to meet with the clergy to talk about the issue, and the Centennial committee still tamely submitted to the intimidation of the VFW. The village was divided, families were divided, the churches were divided. The clergy were put under heavy pressure from their congregations to compromise their stand. A church woman was heard to exclaim, "We should do away with the First Amendment!"

Tarrytowners for Peace were preparing a float on which they proposed putting Mark Twain's prayer against war, as Mark Twain had lived briefly in Tarrytown. The Centennial committee said Mark Twain's prayer would be subversive and unacceptable. Then the Ten Commandments were proposed, with the words, "Thou shalt not kill," underscored. The Centennial committee held that this also would be controversial. A third proposal was put forth, that simply the name, "Tarrytowners for Peace," be put on the float. This also was denied—"no messages or slogans of a controversial nature" would be permitted. So "peace" is controversial, in the view of the Centennial Committee. At length CBS aired this controversy. Under threat of a lawsuit the Centennial Committee did permit a peace contingent in the parade. 'Elaine Urbain' reported that 100 men and women, wearing white and carrying white balloons, started in the parade, behind a banner, "People for Peace." They marched to the accompaniment of applause, and a hundred bystanders came off the sidewalks to join them!

This Tarrytown incident deserves attention because it is a symbol of what will happen increasingly across this country under the aegis of Nixon-Agnew-Mitchell. The American Middle is disappearing. The country is being tragically polarized into Right or Left.

New Right Report

von Epp

At a time when the youth of the West seems irreversibly sunk in the pit of democracy, degeneracy and drugs, a flash of lightning has illuminated the bleak horizon, giving hope for the survival of our race.

The emergence of the Skinheads in England should indicate that all is not lost, and should serve as fresh inspiration for those of us who have long struggled in Racial Nationalist ranks.

England, as the home of money politics and economic thought (democracy), has long been in the vanguard of Culture-distortion. The debauchery of hippidom, rock music, idiotic gurus and the other assorted fads and freaks, all originated in the sewers of Soho, and subsequently spread throughout the rest of the White World.

The rush toward race-suicide in England has somewhat abated. It has been replaced by a new awareness, a new spirit. It has not come from the "respectable" bourgeoise, nor from the "responsible" conservatives who are still mesmerized by such things as "money" and "votes," but from the one source of health left in the White Race: the Productive Classes.

The skinheads know that life is a struggle, that the strong survive and the weak go under, that courage and strength are

worth more than intellect and reason, that beauty is not gro-
tesqueness nor degeneracy health. They have looked on the
hairy, dissipated, tacky-skinned lizards in power and have been
rightfully repulsed. The sons of the White Productive Class
have not replied with silly arguments, but with fists and clubs.
Dialogue has given way to the sounds of Jew and negroid
cranial cavities progressively collapsing under the rythmic impact of deftly placed boots. Smashed bottles dragged across
pale, fungi-infested faces have convinced more than one of the
"flower children" that the future does not belong to them,
but to the strong—the truly "beautiful people," the White Race.

The Skinheads are drawn from the age group of 15 to 25
years. They all work for a living. The spirits, to quote Spengler,
"Have not lost the old triumph-feeling of the beast of prey
as it holds the quivering victim in its claws." Bricks, rocks,
bottles, meathooks, chisels and pipes have all been talentedly
utilized on scum, Jews and other assorted Culture-distorters
who currently infest their homeland. Skinhead minds have not
been infected by "progressive education." No brotherhood garbage or guilt feelings have warped their psyches. Their disdain
for the social parasites who run the edjewcation system is
truly profound. Like Nietzsche's Zarathustra, they have indeed
"broke the tyranny of reason." This contempt was expressed
by one such street fighter who stated, "All I did in school is
kick the teacher." The do-gooder and the bleeding heart do
not have a healthy existence in skinhead environments!

Like all associations of young warriors, the Skinheads have
their own uniform. They wear blue denim shirts and work
pants with red suspenders. Steel-toed boots are de rigeur for
stomping on flabby physiognomies. These young men respect
their women, who they call "birds," and treat them with a
civility and kindness unknown in England since the gentility
of the Cavaliers. Woe be to any sub-human sophisticate who
approaches a "bird"—multiple contusion, skull fractures and
snapped spines are the least they can expect!

Despite the good and wholesome traits displayed by these
young beasts of prey, they lack the organizational structure
and ideological underpinnings for their actions. Outside of an
instinctive disgust against those races "unloved by the gods,"
there is nothing. The absence of unity and direction means

that much effort will be wasted in non-essential squabbling and dead-end projects which will cause the downfall of that which has appeared. Our forces must not let this happen. Here is a heaven-sent opportunity to build a fighting cadre from the most idealistic elements of the White Race. If not, another opportunity for Race-Victory will be squandered. Creative violence, if channeled into correct, consistent programs of activity could produce effective results. Perhaps the vision of united White fighters demolishing the shaggy outpourings of democracy will inspire our own Authoritarian Racial Nationalists to set to work organizing American Productive Class youth to do likewise.

The Face of Fascism in the U.S.

Charles Danby

Nothing in the history of this country has divided the minds and thinking of the American people as much as the Vietnam war. And nothing has pushed their thinking and action further apart than Nixon-Agnew's remarks about people who have opposed the war.

Never before have so many innocent young people been murdered on the streets and on school campuses. The Birchites and the KKK who have infiltrated all the law agencies in this country have been more than willing to carry out the hints that Agnew and Nixon have thrown out in their speeches about student dissent. What else did Nixon mean when he called them "those bums in the colleges," and said that the only good young people are the boys in Vietnam, that they are the only ones "standing tall."

Schism v.1, no.4 (Fall 1970)

Wasted for Nothing

There are about 20 workers in one group in our shop, who work the same job. The majority are black, but there are several young whites, and most of the black workers felt they were racist and supported Nixon's policies—until a week ago. Then one of these young white workers came in and told us that one of his younger brothers had been killed in Cambodia. One of the black workers said sadly, "Will Nixon say his death was because he was standing tall?"

This young worker said that his mother received the news while she was in a hospital. He said, "She used to oppose those who demonstrated against the war. She resented hippies. She always talked of how proud she was of her son in the service. But now she said that if my two younger brothers are called she may take them to Canada, or let them take their chances in prison, instead of wasting their lives for nothing."

All the workers in the department pitched in and collected money for flowers for the family, and when this worker returned after the funeral he shook every worker's hand and thanked us all warmly.

Words with No Meaning

When Nixon was campaigning for the presidency, he kept yelling that what this country needed most was a leader who could pull the people of the country together. What he did not say was that he wanted to pull them together in line with a fascist philosophy. He said he had a plan to end the war in Vietnam. One of the workers in our shop said he read an article that words will not have any meaning by 1978, and another worker said Nixon has beat the gun because his words have no meaning now. Workers call Nixon the greatest liar who has ever held office.

When the news broke about the murder of the students at Kent State, and we discovered that they were white students, black workers were predicting that the next demonstration black students held would be mowed down. When the news broke about Jackson State, we knew that the blood-thirsty cops in Mississippi had got the Nixon-Agnew message. So had the

KKK cops in Georgia, who killed six blacks and wounded 25 more, shooting them all in the back to show the fascists in this country how brave they are.

One worker said, "When I hear Nixon claim that violence invites tragedy I want to know what violence were the four young black children causing in the First Baptist Church in Birmingham, Alabama, when they were bombed while they were sitting in Sunday School? What violence were the Kennedy brothers causing? What violence was being committed by all the blacks who have been lynched throughout the South because they were black? Nixon has caused more violence than any other president in the history of this nation."

Nixon's Violence

Several weeks before the invasion of Cambodia, Nixon was saying that he was not going to send troops there, nor even supply that country with ammunition. After the American people revolted so strongly against his decision he said the Army was there to protect Cambodian neutrality. How can a country be neutral when it is being torn to pieces, when thousands and thousands of innocent women and children are being killed— and most of them by an armed force that has been sent from ten thousand miles away? The worker was right—Nixon's words have no meaning.

Nothing would please the Nixon Administration more at home than to be able to drive a wedge between white students and black students and start a war of racist whites against those he calls radicals. The Administration must have found joy and happiness from the Mafia-controlled, racist white construction workers in New York. This is the same union that has barred black workers for years. When black workers demonstrated, they were treated to the same violence as the young peace marchers just received.

I can never believe that all white workers feel the same as the construction workers in New York. What Nixon is afraid of is that the student movement will find allies among the working people. This is a much needed alliance for the anti-war movement, and all efforts should be made to unite these two forces and the Women's Liberation movement. Unless that happens the fascism that is on the forward move in this country will strangle us before we strangle it.

Revolution and Legality

National Socialist World

Two classes of concepts which are fundamentally different in nature, yet often confused, are those having to do with *doctrine* and those concerned with *tactics*. The former are independent of changing circumstances and conditions, the latter are strongly dependent on these things. We make an extremely grave error when we treat a doctrinal point as if it were a tactical matter, but we also make a serious error when we assign to some tactical consideration the attributes of a point of doctrine.

The National Socialist movement has generally been considered to be an element of "the right wing," albeit an extreme element. Indeed, we apparently share a number of things with the other right-wing elements, such as anti-Marxism, a respect for tradition, and support for the forces of law and order. This last has meant, among other things, that we have constrained ourselves to the use of "legal" methods only in our struggle.

Now, whereas our anti-Marxism is implicit in our National Socialist doctrine, our self-restriction to legal methods is tactical in nature.[1] Because the Movement has, however, since 1923, insisted upon "legality" in its relationship with constituted authority, some may have fallen into the error of thinking that this insistence stems from doctrinal considerations about the sanctity of "law and order." Under certain conditions this error can lead to disastrous consequences. Since the occurrence of these "certain conditions" in the foreseeable future is by no

Schism v.1, no.2 (Winter 1970)

[1]And our respect for tradition is often tactical rather than doctrinal; it makes a great deal of difference about *which* traditions we are talking.

means a merely academic possibility, it may be worthwhile to examine this problem in detail.

In terms of the most fundamental National Socialist criterion, the question is: Is the support of the constituted authority and the maintenance of law and order in the best long-term interest of the race? And the self-evident answer is, that this depends upon the nature and the aims of the particular constituted authority in question. For while it is true that when a State is fulfilling its proper function as defender and champion of the racial interests of its people the aims of race and of law and order become identical, those aims no longer coincide when the State strays from its proper role. In this respect the teachings of the Leader are quite clear:

> The State is a means to an end. This end is the preservation and advancement of a community of physically and spiritually homogeneous living creatures. This preservation itself includes, firstly, subsistence as a race and thus permits the free development of all powers slumbering within that race.
>
> . . . States that do not serve this purpose are mistakes, nay, monstrosities. The fact of their existence does not alter this any more than the success of a crew of buccaneers can justify piracy.
>
> . . . We must make a sharp distinction between the State as a vessel and the race as its content. This vessel has a purpose only so long as it can preserve and protect the content; otherwise it is worthless.[2]

Strictly speaking, *only* a National Socialist State can fully satisfy our criterion; any other State formation can only approximate the ideal role of the State as the defender and champion of the racial interests of its people; and in this light the present-day Western democracies can only be described as monstrosities.

If a State can be carried through a peaceful evolution toward its proper role, then this course should be followed, for we certainly do not seek a state of anarchy and chaos as an

[2]Adolf Hitler, *Mein Kampf,* II, chap. 2.

end in itself. There are always dangers inherent in such a situation: more than one revolution has gone astray during its violent phase, emerging from the conflict with an altogether different character than upon entering.

On the other hand, neither must peaceful evolution be sought as an end in itself. Where it does not provide a realistic and practical course of action, it must be abandoned without hesitation for other means.

Considering the present array of State formations with which we are faced, the question which naturally arises is this: Is it conceivable that any of these criminally degenerate and racially destructive entities can be smoothly transformed into a National Socialist State? Or must we think in terms of a total leveling of the present structures before we can hope to begin building a new structure on sound foundations? *Whatever our answer, it must be based only upon an evaluation of the possibilities inherent in the various paths leading to our ultimate racial goals, and not upon any false conception of our obligations toward any presently existing State authority.*

Again, the Leader has spelled this out for us:

> State authority cannot exist as an end in itself, or every tyranny in this world would be sacred and untouchable.
>
> If, by the instrument of governmental authority, a people is being driven to its destruction, then rebellion is not only the right but the duty of every member of that people. . . .
>
> In general, it must never be forgotten that the highest purpose of man's existence is not the maintenance of a State, let alone of a government, but the preservation of his own kind.
>
> Let that be in danger of suppression or destruction, and the question of legality is but subordinate. Then, though the methods of the ruling power be a thousand times 'legal,' the self-preservation of the oppressed is always the noblest justification for a struggle using any and every weapon.[3]

---

[3]Adolf Hitler, *Mein Kampf*, I, chap. 3.

Why, then, the insistence up till now on "legality" in our struggle? The answer is that we are faced with the same difficulty today that confronted the Movement forty-five years ago in Germany: the enemy, with all the repressive powers of the State at his disposal, is far stronger physically than we. In any shooting match with the State authority, we are bound to lose decisively, just as we lost on November 9, 1923.

The fact that the anarchist elements among the Jews are able to use illegal means with relative impunity in their assault upon "the Establishment" should not mislead us into thinking that the same tactics will work for us. In the first place, we do not have the allies in the Establishment that they have. We cannot provoke large-scale violence and disorder and receive only a gentle slap on the wrist in reprisal, as they can. In the second place, we and they have entirely different aims. Since their purpose is, above all, to destroy the existing order of things, they have a much greater freedom of action than we have; they can carry out their purpose with a much looser organizational structure than we can ours, and thus they are relatively less susceptible to counterattack.

We are "legal" now because we dare not be otherwise; we are yet too weak to defy the State authority successfully. At the same time, as long as we are weak and ineffective the State feels no real threat from us and, therefore, no pressing need to destroy us. But our relationship with the State is changing, and we are entering a new and critical phase of our development—one in which we are becoming too strong for the State to ignore, yet not strong enough to defend ourselves from its attacks. These attacks will progress from quasi-legal harassment, intimidation of our members and supporters, and interference with our mail to illegal arrests and criminal charges based on falsified evidence, the withdrawal of police protection, and—eventually—outlawry through special legislation. Whenever in the course of these developments we allow ourselves to be provoked into illegal counteraction, we provide the State with the powerful weapon of self-justification.

Yet, the conflict seems inevitable, for before our struggle is over each and every criminal comprising the present System will have a pretty good idea just what fate awaits him at our hands. Very few are likely to deceive themselves into believing that we are "just another Party," with which they can reach an "understanding" which will leave the System largely intact. They will almost certainly realize that a triumphant National Socialism will mean not only a permanent end to their whole way of life, but an end to life itself for many of them. This knowedge will not incline them to yield gracefully to us.

Despite what lies ahead, however, we must strenuously avoid yielding to the temptation to retaliate prematurely to the provocations which daily beset us. When we do take the very grave step of illegal action, it must only be because the further progress of the Movement demands it—not because we can no longer repress the urge to gratify ourt thirst for vengeance or because irresponsible elements in the Movement have not been kept under close enough rein.

Thus, the key to success in the struggle ahead is *self-discipline*. While it is the time to be "legal" we must stolidly endure whatever the State sees fit to inflict upon us. And when it is time to revolt, we must be prepared to unleash all the furies of hell on the State until it yields.

Memoir of Czechago

Dave Dellinger

The Chicago Conspiracy trial was lengthy and complex— 5 months, 190 witnesses, more than 22,000 pages of transcript. In varying degrees, the future careers of the prosecutors, the political viability of the Daley machine, the success of certain Nixon-Agnew-Thurmond-Mitchell initiatives for getting rid of the last troublesome vestiges of democracy in the country, the integrity of the defendants (not to mention 10 years of our lives) and the future directions of some sections of the antiwar movement and other rising insurgencies all hung in the balance. Not on the verdict alone but on the cumulative impact of everything that happened.

Schism v.1, no.4 (Fall 1970)

Rubin

Bobby Seale as witness

Dellinger

In my own mind, the case should not have assumed such importance. Not a country where prosecutions and guilty verdicts are routine for draft resisters; anti-war G.I.'s; black, Mexican-American and Puerto Rican liberation fighters; rank-and-file violators of the property fetish; token individuals apprehended for possession of marijuana. Now while a hundred G.I.'s and a thousand Vietnamese are being killed every week (and approximately 5½ times that many wounded) and most people are too bored by now with war and anti-war to pay attention.

Every day during the trial, I received a dozen or more letters, most of them from strangers. About 80 to 90 percent of them were favorable, 10 to 20 percent hostile. After my bail was revoked and I was imprisoned in Cook County Jail, the number of letters doubled but the proportion of favorable to unfavorable stayed about the same. Both times that I was sentenced, first for the contempt of court, then for the guilty verdict on the riot charge, the number of letters increased, the proportions held steady. A surprisingly large percentage of the friendly letters were from writers who identified themselves as members of the "silent majority" who vowed to remain silent no longer, in face of the government's repressiveness and our "courageous" response. Practically all the hostile letters bore no return address and promised that if I got out of jail I would be assissinated. I should mention that two or three letters a day invited me to seek salvation in Jesus Christ, while two or three others offered the opinion that whatever Judge Hoffman did to me was too good for a Jew like myself. It didn't seem to matter that Judge Hoffman is Jewish (along with Assistant Prosecutor Schultz, who handled most of the government's case) and I am not. My prison mail was censored, but no government agency offered to trace the threatening letters or provide protection. Nor did I ask any such "assistance."

Not surprisingly I find myself emerging from the over-all experience with a wide range of reactions—conclusions, if you will though some are tentative and others require refining. The lessons I draw concern national politics, the courts, bail, prison,

John Froines

Davis

Tom Hayden

**All Conspiracy
Trial Sketches by
Elizabeth Langer**

Lee Weiner

the press, the movement and the nature of the economy and culture in which these institutions operate and from which they take on their character. Let me in the present article write mostly about the courts and the inevitability of the clashes that occurred.

The court system in this country is, on the whole, a faithful example of the anti-democratic institutions of the society, both in its internal procedures and in its broader, social function. Of necessity, it was only a matter of time until the movement that is challenging a series of other authoritarian institutions—including the country's military imperialism, its domestic racism, its bureaucratic and inegalitarian corporation economy (here the challenge has barely begun), its hypocritical electoral processes, its anti-educational school system—should come into open conflict with the judiciary. At the first glance it would seem that if the government were wise it would not have staged a show trial of movement leaders in its highly vulnerable courts, which simply cannot stand the light of public scrutiny.

Could the government have been counting on the traditional subservience of the intended victims? Their willingness to acquiesce in the rules of the game, as laid down by the executioners. In support of this hypothesis, the power of the courts to consign its opponents to hell is awesome, being both more immediate and more certain than that of the Pope. And it has been a well-known watchword in the movement that the duty of a revolutionist is to stay out of jail.

More likely, the Nixon strategy calls for a series of assaults on traditional liberal values and is prepared for whatever dramatic showdowns this entails. There are many signs, from the Supreme Court appointments to the speeches of Agnew, that the Administration welcomes an intensification of the conflict, polarization, and the introduction of as much Law-and-Order-Minus-the-Bill-of-Rights as may prove necessary to smash the democratic rebellions that have been spreading under partial adherence to constitutional guarantees. In a way I hesitate to call this policy by its proper political name, fascism, because the word conjures up visions of the secondary German or Italian characteristics of the period before World War II. Obviously, like everything else in the United States, from Hamberg(ers) and Bologna to religion and militarism, American fascism will reflect (already reflects) peculiarly American charasteristics.

Weinglass   Kunstler

Whatever it is called, the new policy represents little more than a firming up and extension into new areas of the Johnson-Humphrey-Daley policy at the Convention itself. The Walker Commission described the Convention disturbances as a "police riot." In doing so, it accomplished a remarkable triple play, whose brilliance was largely wasted because, politically, the Report straddled the polarization that was taking place. In the first place, it described the immediate events accurately; secondly, it conveniently drew attention away from the top-level decision-makers who set the stage for the riots; and finally, by putting the blame on the police, who carried out the new policy, rather than on the demonstrators, who were its victims, it indicated its own implicit disapproval of this top-level excursion into new forms of repressiveness. But the Walker Report may well have been one of the last gasps of the sophisticated liberals before the coming power of the police state. In any event, we were not allowed to introduce into evidence at the trial—not the report itself, not a single sentence or phrase from it, not even the name or the fact that such an elaborate study and analysis had been made. There is a great gulf between the politics of the Walker Report and the politics of defendants, but it was a relatively honest, liberal effort to describe and explain what happened. As such it was considered too dangerous to be laid before the jury. As is normal procedure in such instances, the jury was dismissed from the room before the arguments on its admissibility took place. The American court system used the Memory Hole long before George Orwell invented the term.

Similarly, Ramsey Clark, the head of the Justice Department that tapped most of the defendant's phones and kept us under electronic surveillance, the government official in charge of prosecuting Dr. Spock, William Coffin and the other members of the Boston Five, was considered too dangerous to be allowed to appear on the witness stand. Although he was the top law enforcement officer of the country at the time of the Convention; although, prior to the Convention, he carried out elaborate investigations of the plans of the Mobe and the Yippies; although he held conferences with President Johnson and other government officials concerning the way the government should handle the demonstrations; though he sent investigators into Chicago and maintained liaison with Mayor Daley, the government contended that he had no relevant testimony to offer, and the judge agreed. Again there is a huge gap between Ramsey Clark's politics and ours, but he was too liberal (or was it too honest?) to be allowed to testify.

Again the arguments and decision outside the presence of the jury. Again, orders from the court prohibiting the defendants and their lawyers from mentioning his name or in any way letting the jury know that he had come to Chicago to testify as a defense witness, but had been banned. Not surprisingly the order was subsequently violated: two defendants and one lawyer received contempt sentences for making references to the former Attorney General in front of the jury. Two spectators were ejected for making similar references. Of such nature were most of our "outbursts," our unseemly "antic," our assaults upon the so-called integrity of the courts.

As I write this, someone brings the news that Judge Hoffman has been rewarded for his courtroom performance by being granted an audience with Billy Graham and the President. The judge also had an opportunity to visit with Federal Judge Clement Haynsworth in the friendly atmosphere of the White House, to embrace Secretary of the Treasury, David Kennedy (one of the richest men in the United States, whom he described as "my banker") and to be introduced to the chairman of the Federal Reserve Board, Arthur Burns. Since the judge is intimately connected with the wealthy Brunswick Corporation (a war-contractor manufacturer) as stockholder, former secretary of the corporation, and husband of the heiress of the controlling Bensinger family, his intimacy with Judge Haynsworth (an investor in Brunswick stock and a man with a keen eye for capital gains) and with the two government bankers should do him no harm. If nothing else, they can swap anti-Yippie stories.

Clearly the courts do not operate in a vacuum. Behind every courthouse stands a jail—and near it a bank. Together these institutions reflect and protect the primary attitudes of the society toward life, property, truth, race and class privilege. On the most fundamental level the courts supplement the banker's money, the owner's title, the policeman's authority and the assassin's bullet in repulsing the drives of the poor and the dreams of the egalitarian revolutionist. On another level they are engaged in playing catch-up with history. At this late date

they are still facilitating the slow transition from the attitudes and customs of feudalism and chattel slavery to the more modern—but still inegalitarian and exploitative—relationships of capitalism.

Courts dole out the concessions, approve the structural adjustments, and make the all-important steelements of intra-capitalist disputes that are necessary to keep our form of class society functioning. In the process, they occasionally overrule ill-considered laws, frustrate over-eager prosecuters or rule in favor of a poor man or a black. These safety-valve functions are most dramatically carried out by the Supreme Court, which traditionally is entrusted with a large share of the task for keeping the long run viability of the system in perspective.

From all this there emerges an illusion, which is carefully cultivated by the courts and is indirectly fostered by the complaints of those who have to be dragged kicking and screaming into the Twentieth Century. It is the illusion that the courts are "impartial," "above the battle," concerned with the administration of (real) justice and the defense of human rights. Not untypically, a current news analysis by Paul A. Freund,

who is described as "Carl M. Loeb, University professor at Harvard and editor-in-chief of the multi-volume History of the Supreme Court," says:

> It is ironic and self defeating that the assault on authority should now focus on the courts, which have been the special shield of the liberties of the dissident and the despised. (Miami *Herald*, March 19)

Perhaps Professor Freund should spend a month in Cook County Jail in order to observe at first hand what happens to the dissident and the despised who are delivered over in the courts. In a celebrated case like ours, there is some partial recourse from the tyranny of a Judge Hoffman, because of the publicity and our middle- and upper-class connections. But the men in Cook County Jail had received the same atrocious treatment and mostly lacked such recourse. Actually they were double victims, of the courts, since, with rare exceptions, they grew up in the poverty which the courts help perpetuate by their defense of the property relationships of capitalism. Ninety percent of the prisoners were black; does anyone believe that there is no racism (however, unconscious) in the courts or that "crime" is not a by-product of poverty and oppression?

Already the fact that we got out on bail (after 26 days in jail for me, two weeks for the others) and the fact that we can appeal our sentences (after 5 months in court fighting the prosecution instead of going about our normal lives and work) are being used as arguments to show the ultimate fairness of the courts. Thus, Freund writes:

> The judicial process can commit blunders, but it has built-in correctives. If a jury convicts, an appeal can challenge the statute, the sufficiency of the evidence, and the rulings of the trial judge.

He neglects to state that appeals are the exclusive prerogative of the rich and the well-connected. Our lawyers estimate that the cost of our appeal may run as high as a quarter of a million dollars.

Incidentally, when word came through in the jail that the appeals court had overruled the trial judge's refusal to allow bail, a jail friend who is accused of being a member of the Mafia offered to put up my bail for me. He did it out of the kindness of his heart, because he didn't think I belonged in jail. But this little incident indicates one of the ways in which

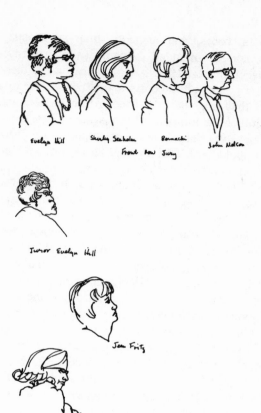

Evelyn Hill   Shirley Stenholm   Bonnacchi   John Nelson
Front Row Jury

Juror Evelyn Hill

Jean Fritz

Juror Kay Richards

"crime" and "criminal" connections are fostered by the bail system, as by prisons generally. (Why should the amount of money a man can pay determine whether or not he stays in jail?) I know of two or three instances in which members of the Mafia paid bail or hired a lawyer for a bewildered or dejected poor man. As with all investments under capitalism, I imagine that the investor (whether his original mpulses were fraternal or self-serving) will get a future return. Certainly the men who were enabled to get out on bail had driven home to them who were their friends and who were their enemies. Remember that in addition to experiencing the indignity of prison, an imprisoned man cannot gather witnesses or otherwise prepare an adequate defense.

The courts typically try to camouflage their true nature by

means of titles, robes, and ancient rituals of language and procedure, which are intended to convey the impression that they are above frailty and partisanship. In reality, these trappings unwittingly betray the courts actual nature, making clear that although they may have assisted in the modernization of some of the other institutions of our society, they have failed to update themselves. The content of some of the judges' decisions may uphold 20th century capitalism but their methods and their power over the hapless defendant are still feudal.

In our trial, Chief Prosecutor Thomas Foran frequently made a fuss over the fact that we were violating court procedures and contesting rules of evidence that had their roots in "over 500 years of Anglo-Saxon jurisprudence." Sometimes he varied the routine by referring to "two hundred years of American justice." From observing the court's methods and prejudices I couldn't help thinking that his characterization of the proceedings was accurate—but this did not make me any more enthusiastic about being treated in a manner reminiscent of the way British kings and barons treated their serfs in the 15th century. And one time I got a contempt citation for pointing out that under 200 years of American justice the blacks had been kept in slavery for half the time and in ghettos the other half, the native Indians had been systematically exterminated, and the poor had not escaped from their poverty, not even in midst of technological abundance.

One of the colloquies between Judge Hoffman and Bobby Seale made the underlying conflict in values and perspective clear—at the expense of a 3-month contempt sentence for Bobby. Behind the judge's chair hung pictures of the American founding fathers. (My co-defendants were not the only longhairs in the room.) After the Judge complained one day that he was "one of the best friends of your race," and shouldn't have been called a racist, Bobby responded by pointing to the pictures of George Washington and Benjamin Franklin and saying that they were slave owners. Without a trace of self-consciousness, in fact with complete self-assurance and self-righteousness, the judge leaned forward and said: "But George Washington was the father of your country."

Judge Hoffman was not untypical. Many judges convince themselves of the nobility of their role and act it out with great self-confidence, blind to its real social implications. Unfortunately, "nobility" is indeed an accurate term to describe the judge's behavior at its best, denoting as it does the sometimes attractive but always paternalistic qualities of people who hold aristocratic power over the lives of common people. (Our language is filled with give-away terms that reveal how little democratized we are.)

The normal bias of the court is perhaps suggested by the fact that one of the surest ways to a judgeship is through the prosecutor's office, by building a record of convictions. Another is to make a substantial financial contribution to the campaign of a successful political candidate, or do him some other favor (often shady). Sherman Skolnik, Chicago legal researcher whose investigations and public disclosures have led to the hasty resignations of several Illinois judges, tells me that Julius Hoffman was appointed to the federal bench as a reward for a $50,000 campaign contribution to the late Senator Everett Dirksen. In Hoffman's case, this was not considered unusual or unethical enough to cause him serious trouble. A third avenue to the bench is to be an unsuccessful candidate for high office. In New York City, for example, former mayors and mayoralty candidates who were selected by the machine but rejected by the voters are usually appointed to the bench (if they so desire). Someone has pointed out that this is real "contempt" of the courts.

Even the defense lawyers must be part of the club in order to stay on the right side of the judge's tremendous power—and to maintain satisfactory relationship with the prosecutor's office as well. As one of my friends in Cook County Jail described it, from his long experience in the courts, lawyers sit down together and say: we'll plead this one guilty if you drop the charges on that one. Another prisoner surprised me by pleading guilty and then explained that at the last minute his lawyer had told him to do so because the judge owed the lawyer a favor and would let his client off with a suspended sentence. There isn't usually as much honor among judges and lawyers as among thieves. Something went wrong and he got four years to be served consecutively with a previous sentence. Inspired in his own way by the manner in which we had handled our own case, he told the lawyer that he would file a public writ, detailing in open court what had happened. The lawyer responded by saying that he thought he could straighten things out with the judge.

Having undergone a rigorous conditioning in elitist universities, law schools and law offices, it comes naturally to most lawyers to fit in with the established way of doing things. Judge Hoffman was shocked by the persistence with which Bill Kunstler and Lenny Weinglass tried to get elementary fairness for their clients. He kept reminding them that they were "officers of the court." The prosecution kept jumping up and characterizing their conduct as "unprofessional." Grotesque as the charge seemed at first, it gradually became clear to me that by the ordinary standards of the profession, the prosecution was right. Once the king had smiled or frowned, the lawyers were expected to take the hint. He could interrupt them whenever he wished—and could rule on motions before they had completed their argument (often before they had begun it). No matter, once he had ruled, they were not allowed to continue, and got contempt citations when they did.

Like so many other aspects of the Chicago trial, the contempt sentences imposed on the attorneys represented only a slightly more dramatic exercise of the court's normal arbitrary power. Ordinarily contempt does not need to be imposed because the lawyers knuckle under in time. The lawyer who goes a little too far in defense of his client's right quickly becomes a marked man, like the suburbanite who entertains black people in his home or the university professor who sits in with the students demanding an end to R.O.T.C. After only a couple of days of our trial, before Lenny Weinglass had stepped out of line enough for his clients to notice it, Judge Hoffman was overheard in an elevator, telling a fellow judge, "Now I'm going up to hear that wild man, Weinglass." In a few very exceptional cases, the maverick's singularity helps him—he becomes too notorious, too powerful in his contacts with the press and the public to be routinely fucked over. But still he has to make the feudal gestures. I have seen some pretty radical lawyers, with reputations as mavericks, even revolutionists outside the court, bow and scrape obsequiously before the judge. In any event, ordinary lawyers who go a little too far are rewarded with a string of lost cases or unusually heavy sentences for their clients.

Subservience to the court's power usually begins with the plea. When I was in Cook County Jail while the trial was still going on, I traveled in the paddy wagon and waited for hours in bullpens with men who were being taken to the courthouse to approve the deals being worked out between the defense, the prosecution, and, according to them, the judges. Often the judge does not have to be in on this stage of the negotiations, because he will take his cue from the government later. For example, there was a theory held by a number of Chicago reporters that Abbie Hoffman got only a relatively light contempt sentence (though he more than upheld his share of our challenges to the court's pompous asininity) because the citations and sentences were drawn up by the prosecution, who like him. I knew that when several times a week he handed them his written travel plans, as we were all required to do, Foran and Schultz would grin broadly at his humorous documents and pass them approvingly around the table for everyone to enjoy.

Be that as it may, during the luncheon break in our trial, when I shared a courthouse bullpen with other prisoners, one or two of them would be called out and return a few minutes later to report: "My lawyer says that if I plead guilty to two counts, the government will drop the other charges and give me a dime (ten years), but if I fight the case, the judge will give

Sharon Avery

me 20." Always there were separate cells for the men who had turned states evidence against their pals and would end up with suspended sentences or with the charges dropped, as a reward. So much for even the crude idea of punishment that fits the crime. So much for the sentence as rehabilitation, unless rehabilitation means learning to fit opportunistically into established power relationships, without regard for the truth or elementary human solidarity. The public may possibly believe that the informer has seen the evil of his ways and is choosing reform and rehabilitation, but the prosecutors, who level the threats and offer the bribes, know better. There are few people in the world as synically corrupt as prosecutors.

The most flagrant case of extra punishment for not copping a plea that occurred during my stay in Cook County Jail was that of a man accused of having kidnapped a girl. She had been released unhurt, (and I think unransomed) but minus seven dollars she had in her purse. He convinced me, at least, that he was probably innocent, though that is not central to the story of what happened.

"I've done a lot of wrong things in my life," he said to me, "but this wasn't one of them. I did ten years for the other kidnapping that I did do (a knapping he participated in when he was a teenager, and in which someone was killed) and you know how it is, they goes right after you in a new case. They has to get someone, and if they don't likes to have black men messing around with white girls. They don't have nothing on me for the girls, but they knows I was messing around."

The evidence against him on the kidnapping was so slight that the Federal government dropped charges on the Lindberg law, but the state of Illinois plowed ahead with charges of armed robbery (the missing seven dollars) and attempted rape (the girl testified that her kidnapper had grabbed her by the arm and thrown her into his car). He was offered a sentence of ten years if he pleaded guilty, but he refused. ("How can I plead guilty and take ten years for something I knows I didn't do?) The result (which was handed down the day before I walked out of Cook County Jail with a heavy heart) was two sentences to be served consecutively—75 to a hundred years for armed robbery, to be served the first, and 10-15 years for attempted rape.

It's not hard to imagine the prosecutor—who has probably slipped a few bills to a pimp or two on his own out-of-town trips—saying to the judge in chambers: "The evidence is a little shaky, but we're pretty sure he did it. Besides he's a no-good sonofabitch who had a string of white girls in the Hilton. And he killed someone once and only served ten years for it."

By contrast, a white man of my acquaintance, a safecracker, had been caught many times but had never gotten a sentence of more than 15 months. "You can make plenty of money and as long as you're smart enough not to carry a gun, they never give you much time." The main fact, though, was that he had good connections and "plenty of money"—for the right kind of lawyer and judge. "I never fight the case in court. It's all worked out ahead of time. I say to my lawyer, How much do you need? and he works it out with the judge."

Those with plenty of money also had special privileges in jail, a subject which discretion forbids me to elaborate on. However, because it was so annoying not to be allowed access to decent razors, blades or a mirror (for some reason mirrors were forbidden) I will say that with the right kind of money you could have a contraband razor, fresh blades and a mirror. Because the convicts all enthusiastically supported our struggle against the hypocrisy of the courts, I had access to the normal contraband items free.

To be fair to Cook County Jail, which in other respects was atrocious, my impression was that bribery had been reduced to a minimum, though it will never be totally eliminated from any jail situation, simply because of the ordinary humiliations are so great that wealthy convicts will pay a lot for small favors, and guards and officials are at least as venal as other public officials. When I entered Cook County Jail, Warden Winston Moore pulled me out of line and gave me a private lecture on how to act and what to expect, somewhat dramatically: "If you get out of line, you will die the hard way." But he does appear to have reduced monetary corruption to a manageable level, below that of the Illinois courts.

After my co-conspirators had been sentenced to jail for contempt, Tom Hayden, with typical sensitivity, apologized to me for the fact that he had not shown sufficient sympathy for what I had been going through. "We just couldn't realize what it was like," he said. "We saw you sitting at the table every day and couldn't understand what you were undergoing." As Tom and the others quickly learned, it wasn't as bad as it seemed to them at first, simply because the revolutionary spirit can survive the most degrading conditions. But let me tell one of the things he was referring to—the daily trip from one's cell to court and back.

Court-call prisoners are awakened between 3:30 and 4:00 a.m., depending on the whim of the guard—in order to stand in line for a shave with a rusty blade and wait for the regular, 5 a.m. breakfast. From then till the time they enter the courtroom at ten, they proceed through seven stages of Cook County Jail, waiting at each one (usually standing) for anything from five minutes to an hour or more. First they are let out of the cell, then out of the cell block, then into a stairwell, then through the door and into the "pump room," (a narrow room so airless and overcrowded with prisoners—somewhat like a New York subway at rush hour—that the first couple of days I wondered why no one passed out from suffocation and wondered if I might be the first to do so). Then into the boulevard. On the boulevard, the prisoner strips, stands facing the wall, with his arms raised high, lifts his left foot, lifts his right foot, drops his arms, and spread his buttocks, turns around, opens his mouth and sticks his tongue out, jumps up and down with his arms raised, lets the guard run his hands through his hair, then retrieves his clothes and belongings (minus his comb, if he made the mistake of bringing one). Then to another door, then to a bullpen, where he waits till eight-thirty. He is let out, has a chain locked around his waist and his hands handcuffed to the chain, is let out of the gate, and climbs into the paddywagon, where he is buffeted around by the starts and stops, the bumps and the turns, until he gets to the courthouse. There procedures are more civilized (at least in the Federal courthouse) though only slightly.

The routine and stopping off places on the return trip are slightly different, but the prisoner is stripped and has his pockets searched twice, instead of once. It's a strange proceeding to strip, be examined, dress, walk through a single gate and then go through the boulevard striptease once again. Most of the time when I was on trial I did not get back to the cell block until 8 p.m. at the earliest, often until 10 or 10:30. (The lateness of my own return was a little unusual due to the fact that Judge Hoffman held court till 5:30 or quarter to six, six days a week, and I missed the first trip back.) When I got to the cell block, for the first four nights I had no bed, but slept on the floor, on a mattress. In my cell block there were always six or twelve prisoners who had no cell and slept in the narrow corridor or "day room," with the other prisoners having to step over or around them to pass.

On the day that we got bail, we went from our cells to the last bullpen much more quickly, except for a delay at the office, where we went through various discharge routines, including fingerprinting and receipt of some of our belongings, though not all of them, because the safe was locked on a Saturday. In the last bullpen, we stripped, showed our assholes a final time and had our belongs examined. Abbie Hoffman was standing next to me, and I remarked: "I guess we won't be able to get those reefers out, after all." "Quiet," said the guard. "No talking." Eventually we walked through the gate and into the paddy-wagon, handcuffed as usual. They were taking no chances on our escaping before we got to the Federal Building and were legally released. Finally, the Commissioner read us the conditions, as laid down by the appeals court. We must give advance notification anytime we left the state of our residence, supplying the Marshal's office with travel plans and local contacts. We could not leave the continental United States without securing permission of the court. We were ordered not to make any subversive speeches—in addition by the Commissioner, which was interpreted as a final threat by the Daley machine, which was headlined in the Chicago press, as a face saver to cover its embarrassment at having the Court of Appeads overrule the Foran-Hoffman contention that we were too dangerous to be allowed on the streets (a rare compliment, indeed).

After about a week, I filed a motion asking permission to go to Mexico. The government filed an objection, and the decision was delayed, but in the end I got it. If I travel in Mexico, I must send a telegram to the U.S. Marshal, informing him of each change of address. It's a good start in a small town to find the local telegraph office or ask the hotel clerk to send a telegram to the U.S. Marshal, informing him of your whereabouts. Everyday at meals, my young daughter tries to figure out whether some man or other is an F.B.I. agent.

I've been trying to write about the court system and I have ended by writing about Cook County Jail. This is not surprising, because jail is where you are apt to end up if you get delivered over to the court. Neither institution could exist, in the present society, without the other. Ultimately the courts can only be evaluated properly if one remembers that they assign people to prison. A few of those who are dropped into the court's meatgrinder manage to escape, as a few Jews escaped under Hitler and as a few black people manage to escape from the ghetto. But in the end the courts must be judged by what

Norman Mailer

they do to the losers and what they threaten everyone who violates the moral code and property relationships they hold. They must be judged by the fact that they are instruments for making imprisonment—and even execution—appear to be reasonable and just methods of dealing with existential dissenters and misfits.

Anita
Hoffman

The courts must be condemned for sapping the moral fiber and subverting the fraternal instincts of the citizenry. In a confused and ambivalent society, where nearly everyone feels strong pulls toward the ideals of love, mutual forgiveness, communal sharing and a classless society, the courts have the function of fooling the public into accepting the criminal notion that imprisonment and executions are civilized responses to theft (though property is institutionalized theft); disorder (though "order" is the unchallenged perpetuation of the status quo); and to violence—though the inexcusable inequalities and injustices of our society could not last a month without the overwhelming violence of armies, money, police, courts and jails.

Police Crush
Freedom House

Elizabeth Tornquist

GREENVILLE, N.C.—In eastern Carolina the corn is two feet high and the peanuts and tobacco stretch green to the horizon. Along country roads the fields come up close to the farmhouses, as if the tractor begrudged the house its yard with no crops: everything must be green and fertile; it is a time for growing.

In the midst of the early summer lushness an old farmhouse outside Greenville stands deserted, its spring garden already overgrown with weeds, the padlocked front door kicked in, and across the second story front, a painted sign: "They won the battle, we'll win the war." Below it a forlorn addition reads, "We tried." Inside, the house is empty except for a couple of chairs, a broken bed, and a shambles of broken boards and glass.

Until May 6 this was a commune, run by several young men from Greenville and neighboring towns. In the front yard they built a cross and madonna and planted flowers at the feet; on the porch they painted a peace symbol; and across the second story front they wrote "Freedom House." They had puppies, goats, a garden and long hair. Now three of them are awaiting trial, along with a girl friend who was there the day the police arrived. There are warrants out against the others.

One warrant against the boys reads: "keeps a disorderly and bawdy house and permits said house to be used as a bawdy house and used in such a way as to make it a disorderly and a common nuisance"; and the other reads, "received and have three markers from Brook Valley Country Club, the personal property of the owner . . . valued at $6.85, knowing the property had been feloniously stolen, taken and carried away." One boy and the girl are also charged with warrants reading "not being married to each other, did lewdly and lasciviously associate, bed and cohabitate together." In sum,

Schism v.1, no.4 (Fall 1970)

the boys are charged with running a house of prostitution and receiving stolen goods; and one boy and girl are charged with adultery and fornication. Another boy is also charged with obstructing an officer.

Freedom House opened on Feb. 15 and the boys let anybody in, with a policy of "all are welcome." One of the visitors was a drunk off-duty cop who came in and grabbed a girl standing in the living room; when he left he called one of the boys outside and asked if they wanted to sell any of their girls for the night because he "wanted a piece." At that point he was told to shove off.

It wasn't long before two TV newscasters came and wanted to do a "human interest" story on the house. The day after their show a deputy sheriff arrived in the yard to ask the boys what they were doing. And from then there was no peace. First they were subjected to a series of inspections—fire, electricity, and health. The SBI rode by every day, the police from a small town near Greenville rode by yelling at them, and sheriff's deputies stopped constantly. They'd come in and say, "What are you doing?" and when the boys would answer, "We're eating supper," or "We were sleeping until you woke us up," they'd go away saying, "We're going to be here so often you'll think we live here." The inspections didn't lead to any arrests, so the visitations continued, while people living up and down the road went by shouting obscenities. Finally on May 6, four sheriff's deputies came in, read no warrant, showed no identification, advised no one of his rights, and took everybody's names. Then they left. The next day four deputies, two SBI men, one man from the mobile crime unit, two TV newsmen, and the sheriff walked in reading a warrant for narcotics. They searched the house and found none. Then they arrested all the boys present for running a bawdy house and receiving stolen goods, and charged one boy and girl with fornication. All were taken to jail on $1700 bonds. That night a friend was at the house watching over their belongings when the sheriff came back. When the boy asked the sheriff about his warrant, he was arrested for obstructing an officer in the line of duty. One boys remains in jail because he has not been able to raise bond. ACLU attorney Jerry Paul, who is representing most of the defendants, has gotten the bond reduced to $250, but unless the boy raises $25 he will still be in jail when the trial comes up on June 30.

The girl charged with fornication was examined by a doctor afterwards and found to be a virgin. The "stolen goods"— two golf course markers worth $6.85—were brought to the house the day it opened, when some 25 or 30 friends and acquaintances just brought along anything they had for "decoration." The Freedom House occupants do not know who brought them and do not know where they came from. The charge of running a bawdy house does not seem even to be understood by the police who mean by it "something which annoys people living up and down the road."

After the boys were arrested, those people up and down the road came to the house and destroyed everything inside they could not steal. Some friends who went back to the house and slept upstairs for a couple of days watched them; they'd drive up and take everything movable, then tear up anything else in sight. One minister came and brought his Sunday School class to teach them a lesson about the sinful life, while he took away bits and pieces of the boys' property. And that is how the house came to be a shambles.

Students at East Carolina University demonstrated one day against the arrests, first at the Post Office, then at the jail. When they went to the jail they said they weren't going to leave until they were told why the boys had been arrested. And they sat down on either side of the steps leading into the jail. While they were there a magistrate came down the steps and said, "Get out of my way boy." One of the demonstrators replied, "Who are you calling 'boy,' boy?" And the magistrate said, "I'd hit you but you aren't worth hitting." The "boy," a crippled Vietnam veteran, said "Go on, hit a cripple," and after a couple more exchanges, the magistrate grabbed him around the neck. Some sheriff's deputies pulled him off and he went back inside. The door was kept locked and the demonstrators were told they'd get no information. But one was allowed to go inside at a time. A girl who went in and asked to see the warrants was told the charges were none of her business unless she was a member of the family; then she was told to leave. Shortly afterwards the demonstrators went back to the university, since their allotted time for the demonstration was up, the police said.

Two further demonstrations were planned, but the first had had to be called off because the person with the permit was sick and no demonstration could be held unless that person was present. By the time of the second, apathy had set in and too few people showed up to march. Some of the Freedom House residents said, "We're holding demonstrations not for ourselves, but for you—you're going to get it too." But apathy, fear (the SBI takes pictures of everybody who goes to any demonstrations in Greenville), and a terrible sense that demonstrations don't do any good were too strong to be overcome, at least for the moment. There were no further protests. Since then, a man and his wife and family who've moved into another country house have been visited by the sheriff and told not to "bed anybody down."

And when I went to Greenville and talked to the young people and their lawyer Jerry Paul, he said, "The disturbing thing is that people will read an article and shake their heads and say that's too bad; but how much is it going to take to make them act?"

Economics

Reprinted in *Schism* v.1, no.3 (Summer 1970) from *Life Lines*, v.12, no.8 (Jan. 17, 1970).

Toward a Critique
of Economics

Paul M. Sweezy

Orthodox economics takes the existing social system for granted, much as though it were part of the natural order of things. Within this framework it searches for harmonies of interest among individuals, groups, classes, and nations; it investigates tendencies toward equilibrium; and it assumes that change is gradual and non-disruptive. I don't think I need to illustrate or support these propositions beyond reminding you that the foundation of all orthodox economics is general and/or partial equilibrium (the two, far from being incompatible, really imply each other). And as for the point about gradualism, I need only recall that printed on the title page of Alfred Marshall's *magnus opus*, the *Principles of Economics*, is the motto *Natura non facit saltum*—nature makes no leaps.

It might perhaps be plausibly argued that equilibrium and gradualism provided a workable axiomatic base for a real social science at a certain time and place—the time being roughly the half century before the First World War, and the place Britain and a few other countries of advanced capitalism. For my part, I do not believe this was true even then. I think economics by the time of what may be called the "marginalist revolution" of the 1870s had already practically ceased to be a science and had become mainly an apologetic ideology. Putting harmony, equilibrium, and gradualism at the center of the

Schism v.1, no.3 (Summer 1970).

This article is the slightly revised text of a talk given at the New England regional meeting of the Union for Radical Political Economics (URPE) held at MIT, November 1-2, 1969.

stage was dictated not by the scientific requirement of fidelity to reality, but by the bourgeois need to prettify and justify a system which was anything but harmonious, equilibrated, and gradualistic.

It was almost at the same time as the marginalist revolution, when economics (as distinct from classical political economy) was being born as an apologetic ideology, that Karl Marx put forward a radically different and opposed mode of analyzing the dominant economic systems. In place of harmony he put conflict. In place of forces tending to disrupt and transform the status quo. In place of gradualism he found qualitative discontinuity. *Natura facit salta* could well have been imprinted on the title page of *Das Kapital*.

It seems to me that from a scientific point of view the question of choosing between these two approaches—the orthodox or the Marxian—can be answered quite simply. Which more accurately reflects the fundamental characteristics of the social reality which is under analysis? I have already indicated my own view that orthodox economics does not reflect that reality but rather serves as an apologetic rationalization for it. Similarly it seems to me that Marxism does reflect capitalist reality. Or, to put the matter in other terms, the world we live in is not one of harmonies of interest, tendencies to equilibrium, and gradual change. Rather, it is a world dominated by conflicts of interest, tendencies to disequilibrium, and recurring breaks in the continuity of development. A would-be science which starts with a false or irrelevant conception of reality cannot yield very significant results, no matter how refined and sophisticated its methods may be. The answers a scientist get depend, first and foremost, not on the methods he uses by on the questions he asks.

This is of course not to denigrate the importance of methods and techniques of investigation. In the development of science they have probably played as important a role as basic theory. The two are in fact intimately interrelated: theory poses questions, methods are devised to answer them, the answers or lack of answers make more theory necessary, and so on *ad infinitum*.

But the scientific endeavor is really not quite so simple and straightforward as this would suggest. Some of you may be familiar with the little book by Thomas S. Kuhn, entitled *The*

Structure of Scientific Revolutions,* which I think is very helpful in this connection. Kuhn argues that every scientific theory
rests on what he calls a paradigm, which I think is very close
to what I have been referring to as a conception of reality (or
of some aspect of reality). Ptolemaic astronomy, for example,
rested on a geocentric conception of the cosmos. The questions
any science asks are fundamentally limited and conditioned by
its underlying paradigm, which in time thus tends to become
a hindrance rather than a stimulus to further advance. When
this happens, the science in question enters into a period of
crisis. The previously existing consensus among its practitioners
crumbles. What is now needed is a new paradigm or, in my
terminology, a new conception of reality which will once again
form the basis for advance. This is often provided, as Kuhn
shows in a most interesting way, by outsiders, i.e., men coming to the science from some other field where they have never
learned to accept and venerate the conventional wisdom of the
science with whose problems they are now concerning themselves. Moreover, as a rule the older scientists are unable to
free themselves from their training and preconceptions, while
the younger ones find it much easier to accept the new approaches. Gradually a new paradigm emerges and once again
provides the basis for theoretical advance and for the unity of
the science. In the new phase what Kuhn calls "normal science"
becomes the order of the day, normal science being the posing
and answering of the questions which are explicity or implicitly
allowed by the new paradigm or conception of reality.

In Kuhn's view, then, scientific advance takes place not in
a straight-line, cumulative manner, starting from small beginnings and building up step-by-step and brick-by-brick to the
imposing scientific edifices of today. This, incidentally, is the
false idea which not only the lay public but the scientists themselves have of the process of scientific advance, a fact which
Kuhn attributes in large part to the role of textbooks in the
training of scientists. There are also other reasons, of course,
among which I would rate as very important the tendency of
scientists, in common with other bourgeois thinkers, to view
all of history, and not only the history of science, in an un-

*Paperback edition, University of Chicago Press, 1962.

dialetical way. The pattern of scientific advance, in Kuhn's view, is rather through the exhaustion and breakdown of paradigms, leading in sequence to crisis, revolution via the construction of a new paradigm and advance through normal science until a new period of breakdown and crisis is reached.

It would be interesting, and very likely fruitful, to try to apply this schema to the interpretation of the history of the social sciences. But certain obvious complications come to mind. For one thing it is clear that in the social sciences a paradigm can break down not only for what may be called internal reasons—i.e., the exhaustion of the questions it permits to be asked—but also because the social reality which the paradigm reflects undergoes fundamental changes. The crisis of Ptolemaic astronomy did not arise from any change in the functioning of the heavenly bodies, but rather because the geocentric paradigm became increasingly unsatisfactory as a basis for explaining observed phenomena. In the case of social science a new dimension is added: not only the observation of phenomena but the phenomena themselves are subject to change.

Another complicating factor is that the social world involves the *interests* of individuals, groups, classes, nations, in a way that is obviously not the case with the natural world. The resistance to the abandonment of old paradigms and the adoption of new ones is therefore much more complicated and is likely to be much more stubborn in the social sciences than in the natural sciences. I believe it could be shown that one consequence of this is that revolutions in the social sciences are always associated in one way or another with political and social revolutions.

Let us now turn to a consideration of the case of orthodox economics. Here it seems to me that the underlying paradigm, along with the normal science to which it gives rise, can and should be subjected to critical attack on several grounds. As I have already suggested, this paradigm take the existing social order for granted, which means that it assumes, implicitly, if not explicitly that the capitalist system is permanent. Further, it assumes that within this system (a) the interests of individuals, groups, and classes are harmonious (or, if not harmonious, at least reconcilable); (b) tendencies to equilibrium exist and assert themselves in the long run; and (c) change is and will continue to be gradual and adaptive.

One line of attack would be that this paradigm is about a century old and that most of the basic questions it allows to be asked have long since been posed and explored by the great economists of the first and second generations—men like Menger, Wieser, Bohm-Bawerk, and Wicksell in one tradition; Walras, Pareto, and the early mathematical economists in another tradition; and Marshall, Pigou, and Keynes in still another. (The list is of course intended to be illustrative rather than exhaustive.) More recent orthodox economics, remaining within the same fundamental limits, has therefore tended, so to speak, to yield diminishing returns. It has concerned itself with smaller and decreasingly significant questions, even judging magnitude and significance by its own standards. To compensate for this trivialization of content, it has paid increasing attention to elaborating and refining its techniques. The consequence is that today we often find a truly stupefying gap between the questions posed and the techniques employed to answer them. Let me cite, only partly for your amusement, one of the more extreme examples of this disparity that I happen to have run across:

> Given a set of economic agents and a set of coalitions, a nonempty family of subsets of the first set closed under the formation of countable unions and complements, an allocation is a countably additive function from the set of coalitions to the closed positive orthant of the commodity space. To describe preferences in this context, one can either introduce a positive, finite real measure defined on the set of coalitions and specify, for each agent, a relation of preference-or-indifference on the closed positive orthant of the commodity space, or specify, for each coalition, a relation of preference-or-indifference on the set of allocations. This article studies the extent to which these two approaches are equivalent.*

You will doubtless be glad to know that in his search for an answer to this momentous question the author enjoyed the sup-

---

*Gerard Debreu, "Preference Functions on Measure Spaces of Economics Agents," Center for Research in Management Science, University of California, Berkeley, January 1966 (mimeographed).

port of the National Science Foundation and the Office of Naval Research.

But a much more fundamental line of attack on orthodox economics proceeds from the proposition that, whatever relative validity its underlying paradigm may have had a hundred years ago has largely disappeared as a result of intervening changes in the global structure and functioning of the capitalist system. Conflicts of interest, disruptive forces, abrupt and often violent change—these are clearly the dominant characteristics of capitalism on a world-wide scale today. But they are outside the self-imposed limits of orthodox economics, which is therefore condemned to increasing irrelevance and impotence.

Before I turn in conclusion to the state of Marxian economics, let me add that what I have been saying applies to economics considered as a social science, as the modern successor to classical political economy, whose task is to comprehend the *modus operandi* of the socio-economic system. I quite realize that a great deal of what is actually taught in economics departments today and is called economics is something entirely different. It seeks not to understand a certain aspect of reality but rather to devise ways and means of manipulating given institutions and variables to achieve results which for one reason or another are considered desirable. How should a corporation allocate its resources to obtain maximum profits? How should a government department weigh costs and benefits in making its decisions? How can a centrally planned society achieve a distribution of goods and services and a rate of growth in conformity with the directives of its political authorities?

Naturally, I have no objection to asking and trying to answer questions of this kind, and I suppose it is no great matter that the work is carried out in economics departments (as well as in business schools, departments of public administration, and the like). What I do object to is calling this sort of thing "science." It is no more social science than engineering is physical science. The analogy may not be perfect, but I do not think it is basically misleading either. I will only add that I think a great deal of this social "engineering" is vitiated by taking its assumptions about how economic entities and institutions work from what I consider faulty social science. Here the analogy certainly does work: engineering isn't physics or chemistry, but its success depends on making use of the scientific laws of physics and chemistry. Social engineering is in the same state of dependence, and this explains why much of it is beside the point or worse. Try, for example, to prescribe a solution for a problem involving irreconcilable conflicts of interest on the assumption of underlying harmony. This, as it happens, is being done all the time in the United States today —with respect to such problems as the racial and urban crises, relations between the advanced and underdeveloped countries, and many others.

Now in conclusion a few words about Marxian economics. Here the underlying paradigm stressing conflict, disequilibrium, and discontinuity is also about a hundred years old. Since the knowledge which it yields is totally critical of the existing society, it was naturally unacceptable to the beneficiaries of that social order—in the first instance the propertied classes which are also the possessors of political power. Marxian economics was therefore banned from all the established instititions of society such as government, schools, colleges, and universities. As a result it became the social science of the individuals and classes in revolt against the existing social order. Three points need to be emphasized here.

1. The class character of Marxian economics in no way calls into question or impugns its scientific validity. That depends entirely on its ability to explain reality. And in this respect it seems clear, to me at any rate, that the record of Marxian economics is far better than that of orthodox economics.

2. But it also seems to me that the record is not anywhere near as good as it could have been. There are probably several reasons for this, only one of which will be mentioned here. This is that the practice of "normal science" within the framework of the Marxian paradigm has from the beginning been extremely difficult. Excluded from universities and research institutes, Marxian economists have generally lacked the facilities, the time, and the congenial environment available to other scientists. Most of them have had to make their living at other jobs, often in the nerve-racking and fatiguing area of political activism. In these circumstances what is perhaps remarkable is that so much rather than so little has been accomplished.

3. But why, it may be asked, have not the revolutions of the twentieth century, mostly espousing Marxism as their official ideology, not resulted in a flowering of Marxian economics (and other social sciences)? Here, I think, we meet a paradox which, however, can be explained by Marxian analysis. Revolutionary regimes so far this century have been largely preoccupied with retaining power against internal and external enemies. In these circumstances, their attitudes toward Marxism as a social science have been ambivalent for the simple reason that it is, or is always likely to become, critical of the new social order. It follows that under revolutionary regimes, as under the previous capitalist regimes, for Marxists the practice of normal science has been difficult and often practically impossible.

I do not want to end these remarks on such a negative note. Despite all the hindrances and difficulties, I think Marxian economics has indeed made notable progress and produced important contributions to our understanding of today's world. Let me cite just one area in which I think its superiority over orthodox economics is obvious and overwhelming—in explaining what has often been called the most important problem of the twentieth century, the growing gap between a handful of advanced capitalist countries and the so-called Third World.

Orthodox economics has nothing useful to say on this subject —largely, I would argue, because it is ruled out by the underlying paradigm. And the prescriptions of orthodox economics for overcoming the gap have been proving their impotence for many years now.

For Marxian economics, on the other hand, the explanation, if not simple, is at least perfectly clear in its main outlines. This explanation can be put schematically as follows:

(a) From the beginning, the development of today's advanced capitalist countries has been based on subjugation and exploitation of Third World countries. The latter's pre-existing societies were largely destroyed, and they were then reorganized to serve the purposes of the conquerors. The wealth transferred to the advanced countries was one of their chief sources of capital accumulation.

(b) The relations established between the two groups of countries—trade, investment, and more recently so-called aid

—have been such as to promote development in the one and underdevelopment in the other.

(c) There is therefore nothing at all mysterious about either the gap or its widening. Both are the inevitable consequence of the global structure of the capitalist system.

(d) It follows that the situation can be changed and real development can take place in the Third World only if the existing pattern of relations is decisively broken. The countries of the Third World must secure control over their own economic surplus and use it not for the enrichment of others but for their own development and their own people. This means thorough-going revolution to overthrow imperialism and its local allies and agents.

Marxian economists still have a tremendous amount of work to do to explain and elucidate the many complex facets of this global process. But I suggest that in the work of such outstanding Marxists as the late Paul Baran and Andre Gunder Frank great strides have been made in recent years, and that large numbers of dedicated young social scientists, not least in the Third World itself, are not only following in their footsteps but pushing on to new frontiers.

Can anything remotely comparable be said of the contribution of orthodox economists? I think the answer is obvious. And the thought I would leave you with is that the fault lies not in any lack of talent or dedication on the part of the practitioners of orthodox economics but rather in the fundamental falsity of the conception of reality which underlies all their theoretical and empirical work.

Hoax of Marxist Economics

Patricia Young

The basis of capitalism is the mass production of goods for consumption by the masses, created by public demand for a progressively higher standard of living.

Schism v.1, no.3 (Summer 1970)

The free enterprise system is based on the right of free men to compete with one another in an open market to provide these products and services, thereby giving the consumer a wide choice of products at varying quality and prices.

The common man as sovereign consumer, with his freedom of choice, determines not only what is produced, but in what quantity, quality and ultimately by whom. His avoidance of an inferior product determines who remains in business.

Under communism or State socialism, the consumer is forced to accept whatever products are put out by a single source —Government. This includes Government-controlled quantity, quality, variety, and price. The consumer, far from controlling production by way of his purchasing power, is held in economic bondage by a government monopoly which arbitrarily decides what the public may have and when.

Captalism has raised North America's standard of living to the highest level anywhere in the world. The gross national product of Red China is today at the same level it was in 1937. Economic growth in the USSR has increased since the days of the Tzar, partly because of a genuine technical advance, but largely because of the acquisition of millions of acres of territory plus the indigenous labor force composed of people who work for slave wages.

Following the Soviet take-over of the Baltic States, Hungary, Poland, Czechoslovakia, Rumania, and East Germany, huge quantities of material; including plants, factories, machinery, rolling stock, rails, etc., were shipped to the USSR.

Yet despite this seeming "economic expansion" and over 50 years of State ownership and control of the means of production, such items as clothing, shoes, radios, TV sets, automobiles, stoves, refrigerators, and washing machines are considered luxury items today. The Soviet consumer, far from creating the demand which controls the supply, is made subject to what the Government considers "priorities." Armaments, missiles, troop requirements and tanks are placed above the needs of the people.

To recognize the problem of communist economics, one must first recognize the basic flaw in Karl Marx's philosophy of "class struggle" as against cooperation between labor and management.

In the 1840's when Marx wrote *Das Kapital,* it must be admitted that working conditions in England were bad. Dickens, Ruskin, and Carlyle poured out volumes of protest and were considerably effective in bringing about change. Only Marx, rather than endeavoring to improve conditions, used the unhappy state of affairs to launch his doctrine of hatred and "class warfare" oblivious to economic realities and the nature of man. Indeed, from the outset, his design was a clever ploy to "use" the unhappy masses as a means of acquiring control and then further using them as pawns in a worldwide anthill.

On page 585 of *Das Kapital,* Marx writes, "The worker is cheated because his employer, instead of paying him the full value of his work, holds out on him profit, interest, and rent." He is oblivious to the fact that no one is prepared to rent tools without due remuneration (any more than the worker is prepared to work without wages.) Similarly overlooked by Marx are such basic realisms as the replacement of obsolescent equipment, the maintenance of tools or the expansion of plants and factories; that without such replacements and maintenance, any business ultimately goes out of business and robs men of their jobs.

The textile industry illustrates this. It is heavily taxed, making clothing exorbitantly expensive. Yet despite this system of robbing Peter to pay Paul, Soviet economy continues to fall behind because of a lack of "surplus value" needed for machinery replacement, factory expansion and the need to obtain new sources of raw material.

Most visitors to the USSR are made aware of this by their observation of obsolete machinery, ancient transportation and a shocking disregard for the replacement of such simple things as home, store and hotel fixtures, light bulbs, plumbing, automobile parts and even razor blades. Because of this obsolescence, ex-Prime Minister John Diefenbaker of Canada has observed that ten times as many men are often required to do a job which in Canada or the U. S. A. is done by two men.

This economic reality was made known to the Soviet people in a December 15, 1958, report by Premier Khrushchev who admitted that it was impossible to carry out Soviet agricultural theories without a thorough analysis of the cost of producing goods. Since then, the USSR has had to adopt many "capitalistic" economic theories, including incentives. Workers are more and more placed on a "piece work" system—getting paid, not by an hourly rate won for them by a Union bargaining agent, but strictly by the amount they are able to produce.

Despite trying to bury Karl Marx's economic boo boo's beneath a massive tax structure, the communist system still refuses to recognize the consumer as the "king" whose demands ultimately increase the supply and lower cost of production. For example, some 50 years ago in America, when radios first came on the market, a good set cost something like $300. Under the free enterprise system, radio manufacturers improved the design and method of production until today, the consumer can choose from an abundance of sets costing as little as $10.

Similarly, in 1830, an acre of wheat in the U. S. A. took 60 hours of labor to produce. Today, the same amount of wheat takes only two hours labor to produce in better quality.

Communist economics and disregard for the needs of the consumer have brought about a widespread black market in the USSR. This ranges from the factory owner and top-level communist leaders down through every strata of society. While the State sets levels of output which the factory may not drop below, most officials have worked out intricate systems of double bookkeeping which enables them to siphon off some of the cream, whether for personal gain or factory operation.

Self-interest, in conflict with State bureaucracy, has brought on widespread double-dealing by those in positions of authority. For instance, a factory manager may desire an extra vacation over and above that permitted by the State. The doctor in charge of caring for the factory workers' health is not allowed to let the level of absenteeism rise above a certain level. He can, however, grant the factory manager "sick leave" often by refusing those workers who genuinely need time off from work.

The State has set the number of square feet of living space permitted each individual, often making it necessary for four or five families to share one house. But top communist leaders still own large town houses as well as country estates. Most automobiles and other hard-to-get items first find their way to communist officials. Such morality is responsible for the cynicism of Soviet humor, not to mention its vast black market.

In short, the Soviet citizen has long since rejected Marx's

economics which fails to recognize human rights, motives, and desires. For even while they are forced to listen to hours of impossible Marxist ideology, they know that the system is forced to operate by way of lies and manipulation.

Today's "Ivory Tower" intellectuals and their misguided students fail, as Marx failed, simply because they refuse to face the reality of human nature.

Basic to man's nature is his self-interest, competitive spirit and knowledge of his God-given right to aspire and work to the limit of his desire and capability—with suitable remuneration for his effort. Nowhere in nature does the theory of "from each according to his ability and to each according to his need" work since the premise contravenes man's God-given right to acquire property and possessions through his own effort and to dispose of them as he desires. Any such economic system—which places people last instead of first—can only return man to the barbarism of the ancient world when a master class ruled a slave class.

Communism cannot work because it is a negation of these basic right, robotizing man, robbing him of his precious freedom.

Marxism-Leninism: The Star of Revolutionary Transition

Gus Hall

The stars in the galaxy of human thought are many but none quite so bright as the star of Marxism-Leninism. As is the case with bodies in the universe, bodies of thought also recede. Many are the "great" ideas that have faded into nothingness. But Marxism-Leninism grows in intensity and becomes an ever greater influence on the affairs of human society. In nature's

Schism v.1, no.3 (Summer 1970)

galaxy of endless bodies, only a select few have served mankind, as a dimensional point of reference, as a guide in unfamiliar terrain. In the universe of human thought Marxism-Leninism has emerged as the most trusted point of reference. It has become the compass in the struggle for social progress.

On this, the 100-year anniversary of the birth of one of its most illustrious advocates and moulders, Lenin, this science has emerged as the single most important influence on the thought patterns of human society. It is the unified field theory of human existence and the nature around it. It is the advanced outpost in mankind's endless search for the truth. It has given human thought an instrument, a science with which to probe ever deeper, to see the interrelationships within an ever-changing reality. It is a science of thought and action.

Marxism-Leninism is the greatest qualitative leap in human consciousness. It is truly the most significant turning point in the history of human thought. One cannot fully understand the significance of this contribution to human thought without seeing it in this broader historic setting.

Throughout history many have added something to the body of human thought, but only exceptions have in any basic sense influenced its overall direction. Before Marx and Engels many had interpreted or discussed one or another phase of social activity but only a few had unearthed connecting links and interrelationships, or understood the objective laws that propel and guide the processes of human affairs. Many had observed the unfolding of life's reality but very few had become a factor in changing it. Many had made one or another discovery about specific phenomena. Marx and Engels gave birth to a new science that encompassed and unified the best in all of human thought. Marxism-Leninism stands in a league by itself because it marked a qualitative leap in human thought.

It marks a new level of human consciousness. It marks the beginning of the end to human thought mainly based on subjective whims, conjectures, fancy, speculation abstracted from reality. It marks the beginning of a new level where the materialist scientific concept becomes the dominating factor influencing human thought.

This qualitative leap in human consciousness was not a thing in itself. It did not come out of the blue. This hurdle in human thought is a reflection of a corresponding shift in man's relationship to his environment. It marked a new era in human consciousness, when mankind becomes the master of environment. It marked a new era in human thought. Marxism-Leninism is the thought pattern of human consicousness, when mankind becomes the master of its own affairs and the environment around it. It is the dominant influence when mankind becomes a conscious factor determining the direction of its affairs. It is the guide not just for climbing the ladder but also for planning and building the edifice of social progress.

This qualitive leap in human consciousness is revolutionary because the turning point in human affairs is revolutionary. Let us place this projection in more concrete terms. A dominating factor in the history of human social existence has been man's exploitation of man. This produced classes of haves and have-nots; and thus the history of human affairs is a history of class struggle. Until the advent of socialism, social systems have been systems of oppression for the sole purpose of exploitation.

Thought patterns were largely moulded by the reality of exploitation. Most bodies of thought were geared to defending or justifying man's exploitation of man. When the systems of exploitation spilled over the national boundaries, the systems of thought followed to include the justification for the oppression and exploitation of other peoples and nations. Racism and chauvinism are the most vicious of these thought patterns.

All philosophical schools of thought accepted exploitation as if it was a natural phenomenon. Economic schools explained all economic deveopments as though exploitation for private profit of the few were the only possible kind of social structure.

History, theology, all social sciences were an extension of the concept of exploitation of man by man. Theologians defended the enslavement of man and promised its end only after death.

Even the newer philosophical concepts of idealism were thought patterns for a period when mankind was not the conscious determining factor influencing the direction of its affairs. They are expressions of hopes, of dreams and the human desire for a more just social order. But they are not assessments of reality—they are not instruments for changing reality. Marxism-Leninism is the qualitative break with all such concepts.

Civilization had reached a point where it was ready to end all concepts and systems based on man exploiting man. To become a force in this qualitative shift in human affairs, humankind had to know the laws of social development. It needed an advanced concept of what kind of a social order to build.

Marxism-Leninism is the accumulated wisdom—the science of this leap in social progress. For this task, a new class, a new human social breed was born: the working class, a class with a unique mission. The working class was born with the task of being the main force in the historic upheaval to put an end to all systems of exploitation of man by man. It was born with the mission to abolish all classes including itself. The mission is forced on the working class by objective forces, by the laws of social development. It is forced to become a conscious factor in the revolutionary transition. To become a force in this revolutionary change, it needed a revolutionary body of thought. A body of thought geared to changing reality.

Marx expressed this new relationship of thought to action in his now famous remark: "The philosophers have interpreted the world in various ways. The point however is to change it." This remark was not only an expression of new ideas but an expression of a new concept of thought as an instrument of changing reality. When applied to social affairs this was revolutionary. It expressed a new relationship between thinking and being. It closed the gap between theory and practice, thought and action. It introduced a new method of thought. Thus Marxism was moulded as a revolutionary theory of changing the reality of man exploiting man. It is the instrument through which man becomes the master of its social affairs. This was a bold and basic challenge to all schools of thought, because here was not just another interpretation; this was a new way of thinking—a leap in consciousness, corresponding to the new level of action.

The battle was on. The lion had been bearded in his den. The gauntlet was down. No body of thought has ever been under attack as has Marxism. The old schools of thought defending the ruling order did not give up. For them it was a matter of life or death. The new revolutionary patterns of thought challenged their way of life and their schools of thought. They saw the handwriting on the wall—ideas become a material revoltionary force when they are taken up by the masses. The attack has taken every possible form, direct and indirect. With time, the open, direct challenges failed to make headway. The main attack developed from within. A new breed of ideologists appeared on the world scene; they became known as the masters of revisionism, changing Marxism until it had nothing to do with the original. This breed came both from the left and right woodwork. It set out to emasculate the new revolutionary body of thought. Its open attack could not destroy Marxism so they set out to rob it of its revolutionary teeth. They set out to remake Marxism so it would revert to observing reality instead of changing it. They set out to remove the class concepts from Marxism. This was all done in the name of "bringing Marxism up to date."

This is where Lenin enters the historic and determining battle for the new revolutionary patterns of thought. His task was to rescue, to defend, and to further develop this scientific instrument of history's greatest revolutionary leap. Lenin undertook to scrape the barnacles of revisionism that had become attached to the body of Marxism. Lenin took up the battle against all forms of opportunism whose ideas had infected and poisoned the bloodstream of the revolutionary movement.

Lenin led the struggle that resulted in a qualitative shift in human consciousness. Lenin's contributions to Marxist thought are basic and fundamental. In a sense, Lenin's extension of Marxism expresses a further qualitative shift in human thought. This is a reflection of a new revolutionary explosion. Because now human society was ready to make the first breakthrough in establishing its first beachhead for the new system without exploitation. The birth of the first socialist state, the Soviet Union, was that event. This new level of consciousness developed in the form of a further development of Marxism. From this point on it is correctly referred to as Marxism-Leninism. In the process of applying this new science as the revolutionary instrument for changing reality, Lenin gave it new qualities. It now being not only the thought pattern for the historic transition but the guide for the breakthrough and the building of a new society. Marxism-Leninism became the unified field theory for the revolutionary explosion and for the building of a new life without exploitation, or war. Thanks to Lenin, the genius of thought; Lenin, the revolutionary leader of struggle; and Lenin, the builder of Socialism.

Lenin was the embodiment of the synthesis of thought and being. He unified theory and revolutionary practice. The building of the new social system of socialism-communism is accomplished with new qualitative shifts in human consciousness. The advanced concepts of this new consciousness constitute the science of Marxism-Leninism.

Mankind owes an everlasting debt of gratitude to Lenin. His contributions to human thought, his contributions to moulding the science of Marxism-Leninism as the instrument of revolutionary transition from the captalist system of exploitation and profits to socialism and communism, a system of exploitation and profits to socialism and communism, a system where the interest and welfare of human society is its only propellant. Thus Lenin has made the contribution that has changed the direction of social development. His contribution has made it possible for civilization to make a qualitative shift towards a social order where there will be no poverty, no racism, no bigotry and where there will be war no more. Lenin was certainly not a pacifist, yet he declared, "Socialists have always considered wars between nations as barbarous and brutal."

Marxism-Leninism is the guiding pattern of thought for the majority of the world's people. Because of Lenin it is the brightest star in the galaxy of human thought. It will forever be associated with the name of Lenin.

Compare the Results

Melvin Munn

If you are not convinced the American way is superior to totalitarian socialism, just compare the results. See how much more you would have to work to earn your food and how much less you would have in luxuries.

Schism v.1, no.3 (Summer 1970)

If you wanted to buy a car, it would take over two years of earnings in Russia—and then a long wait for delivery. After fifty-three years under communism, Russia offers a sharp contrast which favors our capitalist, free enterprise system.

When a new year of a new decade rolls around, many people are prone to set goals and analyze achievements, all of which may be good. National leaders, both in this nation and elsewhere, indulge in the same sort of thing. Predictions are made at certain points in time and history, and it becomes both interesting and revealing years later to look back and see how well those predictions have stood up.

Because predictions are always tricky, we would leave the job of making them to others as the world enters the decade of the 1970's. On the other hand, we find very interesting some comments regarding how some of the famous predictions made for Russia by her communist leaders have turned out. We should remember that the communism of which we are speaking is the same communism toward which some of our intellectuals and radical students are showing sympathy—some even favoring it for this country.

Back in 1961, early in the decade just closed, Nikita Khrushchev, who was at that time the dictator of communist Russia, made the public admission that the United Staes was "the most powerful and richest capitalist country," but he predicted boastfully that by 1970 workers in communist Russia would be producing more than the United States.

It is now nine years later—and what of his 1961 prediction? Well, Khrushchev was deposed several years ago, and it would appear that his boast has turned out to be no more than an idle wind.

Under its communist system, Russia is continually setting up "five-year plans" as an incentive to its workers to meet the goals established under each such plan. The current plan will expire this year. Delegates to the Supreme Soviet meeting near the end of 1969, were told that industrial and agricultural output had fallen below the goals set, that it had been necessary, therefore, to lower the expectations of the five-year plan.

The reality of the matter is that the Soviet economy under government planning is, as usual, lagging far, far behind that of capitalist America. Yet it is this very kind of government planning which many of our economic dreamers are supporting today.

That the Soviet economy is lagging in production is borne out by a recent study of prices in the Soviet Union made by Keith Bush for the Radio Liberty Committee. The principal point made by the study is that the Russian worker, after 53 years under communism, must still work much longer than his American counterpart to earn the money with which to buy food, clothing, the necessities of life. As for the luxuries, the Russian worker still obtains very few of these.

Besides working many more hours for what he purchases, the Russian worker winds up with much poorer quality in all these things than does the American. There is a reason why this is so, but in order to understand the reason why the Russian worker must be content with working longer hours for less in the way of a standard of living, one must know the basic differences between our freedom way and communism.

You say at once, "I dislike communism," but can you identify the things that go to make up communism if you encounter them without the communist label? Some of the elements and propaganda of communism can be very appealing to those who do not fully understand how it works. We need to be able to detect insidious movements and party lines when they appear without a communist tag on them.

Just what is communism and how does it operate? Basically, communism is a collectivist or socialist system, with the addition of a police state and dictatorship—by an individual or the party.

State socialism with "democratic tendencies" has proved time and again that it simply cannot do the job. Under state planning and with no profit motive, productivity just isn't possible that will compete with our free enterprise system. Thus, if those of the ruling class in a socialist state are to remain in power, they must turn their nation into a police state, and it becomes a dictatorship. The police state becomes essential if the collectivist idea is to be kept going.

Admittedly, our system is not without its faults and its inequities, but Americans would do well to make a comparison between their condition under capitalism and freedom and the Russian living and working under communism. The Radio Liberty Committee shows how in nearly every facet of life the American is faring better. Take food for example. Prices of food are worrying the conscientious American housewife—and rightly so. But we are ever so much better off than the Russians. As of last April, statistics showed that the average Russian family spends 50 per cent of its budget on food. The average American family spends about 17 per cent.

This is hardly the whole story for the Russians eat very heavily of bread and potatoes, while the quality of the American diet is much higher and the items in the diet far more varied. Just consider the bread and potatoes for a moment. A Russian must work twice as long to obtain money to buy a one-pound loaf of bread. He must work three and one-half times as long to buy a pound of potatoes.

Americans consider autos, refrigerators, and washing machines as necessities. They are still luxuries which few Russians can afford. In order to buy a small automobile, a Russian has to work two and one-half years—eight times the number of working hours it takes an American to buy a car. If the Russian happens to get enough money ahead for the car, he still has to wait three years to get delivery.

A small refrigerator requires 32 hours of work by an American, but 343 hours—or more than ten times the hours—by a Russian. The American works 53 hours to buy a washing machine; the Russian must work 204 hours.

Under communism, the Russian nation has repeatedly fallen short of the predictions made for it and the goals set under successive five-year plans. On the other hand, the free enterprise American economy, in spite of problems of inflation and high taxes, has proved to be far more productive in terms of a high standard of living for the American people than was ever envisioned or predicted.

The one falls short; the other exceeds expectations. There is the difference between communism and our freedom. Which will you support? Which will you choose?

The Anarchist Revolution

Dena Clamage, interview with
Murray Bookchin

Murray Bookchin is the editor of Anarchos magazine, a periodically appearing journal of anarchist thought published in New York City. Copies of his magazine and other writings are available from Anarchos, P.O. Box 466, Peter Stuyvesant Station, N.Y., N.Y. 10009.

This interview was conducted for the Fifth Estate by Dena Clamage.

Fifth Estate: What is meant by anarchism? Why talk about anarchism today?

Murray Bookchin: Most people associate anarchists with traditional bomb-throwers and nonsense like that. Anarchism is something much larger than a particular set or a particular school.

Some thousands of years ago men lived in some kind of totality with nature. They were dominated by the natural world, but they also lived in harmony with the natural world.

Then there was a tremendous cleavage. Man's attempts to free himself from the domination of the natural world, to gain some type of security, resulted in the domination of man by man. It split man from nature, it split man from man, it brought about class society. It not only split man from man, it split man internally. It split his mind from his body. It split the concept of subject from object. It produced a whole logic of domination.

During this whole period in which man dominated man there was a gradual development of the technological forces. Slowly, bit by bit, in the course of this class society, in the course of the propertied society, man began to develop his technology.

And for the first time over these thousands of years it's possible to see a unity restored again between man and nature, between man and man in which man will not so much domi-

Schism v.1, no.2 (Winter 1970)

nate nature but will be secure, will be able to shape the natural world consciously.

Anarchism has always been a libidinal movement on the part of mankind to go back to that unity.

During all periods of great transition of the masses of people have pressed against the system of domination that existed. They have seen it crumbling. They pressed against it and tried to restore this nonauthoritarian, free world. But they haven't had the material conditions, the technology, to consolidate this. There has always been scarcity, always want. And the technology has opened up an entirely new vista of human liberation.

We're sort of returning to the old communism now but with an entirely new level, an entirely new possibility, an entirely new potential for human freedom. This potential cannot only eliminate property, but might eliminate toil itself, might eliminate all those things which have kept man impoverished and divided between himself and the natural world. And this is what anarchism really means.

FE: What are the prospects of anarchy in the United States? How could anarchy come about?

MB: This is the country above all in which you have the highest development of this technology. What is happening right now is this: Throughout the course of history these classes, the systems of class domination, while they dominated mankind still played a certain social function. The city played a certain social function. It has also been said that the State played a certain social function.

Class domination, according to Marx in particular, was supposed to have made it possible for mankind to develop a culture, to develop the science necessary to free himself from the domination of nature over man. The theory here is that the ruling classes, despite all the crimes that they inflict on humanity, nonetheless, had the leisure time to develop a literature, to develop mathematics, to develop a technology.

The city also has been described as the arena in which human culture developed. Men were brought together, removed from the land and brought into close proximity with each other to communicate ideas.

The State, despite the fact that it's always been an instrument of class domination according to Marx, has played the role of maintaining a certain amount of social peace.

These institutions have played a progressive role. Whether they did or not, the most striking thing that has happened is that now they all play a totally regressive role.

The State mobilizes the means of production in order to enforce the system of domination at a time when this could be eliminated. The economy is being used to impose domination, and to preserve domination; in fact, to preserve scarcity today artificially. The armaments industry is the most striking case in point here.

We have a tremendous productive capacity, but this productive capacity does not return to the people, it is not used to support them or to emancipate them. It is used to preserve scarcity artificially so that people have to go to work even when work is unnecessary.

The city today plays a totally regressive role. It no longer unifies people or brings them together. On the contrary, in the large cities today people are more alienated than ever before. This is an entirely new development historically. The city is no longer conceived as the arena of culture but as the arena of deculturation.

The contradiction between town and country has produced an enormous ecological crisis today. The city crawls over the land in the most destructive fashion. It is the center of air pollution, the arena in which most of the poisons are introduced into the human environment. And here again you have a very striking departure from all of the past.

Technology which should free men from toil actually becomes a means of imprisoning man. We have technological developments which are entirely destructive, which are entirely coercive.

The result is that you have a total exhaustion of all institutions, of time-honored property society. They no longer play even the progressive role that Marx imputed to them.

What is happening in the United States? Here more than any place else in the world we sense this. We sense on the one hand the enormous technological possibilities even if we sense them unconsciously. We sense on the other hand a condition that exists, a prevailing condition which imprisons man. The tension between what-could-be and what-is is now becoming excruciating in the United States.

A whole generation has emerged which senses this tension almost intuitively, and some people sense this consciously. The result is that you have a tremendous polarization of the new generation which has not been able to justify in its own mind the dominating role, sexually, psychologically, politically, institutionally, of all those forces which men in the past accepted.

With this generation you have a genuine generational conflict which cuts across all class lines. A very significant fact is that the youth revolt came from the middle classes, from those classes which were most affluent. What this youth revolt essentially expresses is a hatred of the whole quality and banality of life. All the old institutions can no longer be justified in their minds. They no longer make any sense in the face of the new possibilities that exist, in the face of the patent hypocrisy that exists in terms of the roles that these institutions profess to perform and the reality of the oppression which they create.

FE: In what sense is this youth revolt revolutionary?

MB: In the profoundest sense imaginable, class youth. You don't simply have a class war; more significantly you have a struggle of young people in all classes outside of the bourgeoisie (and in some cases even within the bourgeoisie) who feel that the present society can no longer be justified. These young people will not be satisfied merely with reforms of society, such as wage improvements, changes in hours, or an increase in the standard of living. They have rejected the American Dream itself.

This is the biggest thing that is happening. Over the past one hundred years you had building up in the United States, an American Dream, which in the 1920's was expressed by men like Hoover with his "two chickens in every pot, two cars in every garage." This involved the idea that commodities would raise the standard of living and provide a new sense of American life. A new dream would be realized through the productive capacities of the United States.

What we have found now is that for millions of people who

had acquired this dream, life has become totally banal and meaningless. It has become senseless and pedestrian as well as vicious.

And the demand today gradually edges into a revolutionary dream, into a new sense of community to replace the exploitation of nature; into a new sense of sexual freedom to replace the patriarchal and even monogamous family; into a new sense of beauty of life itself, the idea that everyday life has to be liberated, that every moment has to be as marvelous as it possibly can.

These are entirely new conceptions. These notions which were once the property of a small handful of poets have now become increasingly general notions. And this represents an entirely new point of departure historically.

Nobody has brought forth this youth revolt. It has not been brought forth by a manifesto. It has not even been brought forth as such by the drug culture. It is something which rides on a new sense of technological possibility on the one hand and the absurdity of the whole past property culture on the other.

FE: Do you think this consciousness has an effect on the working class?

MB: I was personally a worker and I was even in the UAW, although not in Detroit. I remember the tradition of the working class at that time. The workers generally felt that they were anchored in the factories. They felt that the factory was their way of life, however much they disliked it. And young workers had a very fatalistic attitude about the job. This was, in a sense, their career and they took it awfully seriously. Bread and butter demands were the key demands of that period although union organization was also a very important demand.

Now what's happening is a young worker is beginning to emerge who does not regard the factory as his fate. This is the mentality of the most advanced sections of the workers today, particularly the young workers.

The feeling here is, in a sense, "What the hell am I doing here? I feel trapped." And there is a tendency to link up with the youth culture, to turn to dope, to turn to marijuana, to turn to rock music on an ever-increasing scale, to feel even intuitively, although there's still a very deep suspicion between young workers and hippies, a greater kinship when the chips are down than there is to the older workers who come to coun--sel moderation, be cool, stick by the rules, bureaucracy, etc.

There is also a stronger tendency to flip out, which manifests itself in the wild-cat strikes and in a gross mistrust of the union bureaucracy; in the feeling that whatever they're going to do as workers, be it in the factory, or outside the factory, they want to control and they don't want things controlled for them.

I remember as a worker it could be said very legitimately by a Marxist that workers respect their leaders. This was in fact true. There was a tremendous personality cult and the tremendous respect for the union leadership.

Today this has disappeared to a very great extent. The most advanced of the workers feel that they don't want any bureaucracy; they mistrust leaders rather than revere them.

I feel that these are all very great points of departure. They reflect the entirely new possibilities that are emerging today. They reflect the idea that men can begin to think of a society in which there will be no leaders, in which they, themselves, will completely control the conditions of their lives.

FE: You have written in Anarchos several articles on the question of ecology, the relationship between man and his environment. Could you run this down a little?

MB: We have now a tremendous crisis in man's reationship with nature. There's a very strong chance that if we manage to survive all the other crises, this crisis will become almost insurmountable at the present rate that it's going.

It is not my opinion, but the opinion of many ecologists that we may not be able to get out of the Twentieth Century intact at the rate that we're despoiling the natural world. Not only is this a social crisis, it's one that the so-called left should be giving a great deal of attention to. Because this crisis can only be solved by what would be called a kind of anarcho-communism.

This crisis arises not only from the exploitation of the natural world for profit. It also emerges from the split between town and country. We haven't developed merely an urban civilization; we've developed a particularly destructive form of urban civilization. The fact that nearly 60-70% of the American population begins to move into immense cities and urban belts has a devastating effect upon the atmophere.

We do not live in balance with the regions that we occupy. New York City or Detroit, for example, are no longer regional societies. They are really elements in a tremendous national division of labor in which vase areas such as the Mesabi range, such as certain farming districts, have to be despoiled, have to be exploited, in order to feed these immense populations.

The centralized nature of the societies today and the centralized natures of the cities today have turned the whole continent into a kind of factory. And this has had a destructive effect upon the natural ecology of every region in the United States, in fact, of every region in North America. The economy now organized on this centralized basis, organized on this national division of labor, has to override all the ecological distinctions, hydrological distinctions, atmospheric distinctions, climactic distinctions, differences in soil, differences in the ecology of animal and plant life to feed these immense giant centralized cities.

The results are likely to be catastrophic, if not in my generation, quite conceivably in yours or maybe in the generation shortly afterwards. At least we'll begin to feel the effects of it.

We have transportation systems today that are utterly destructive. The growth in the pollution of not simply the atmosphere but the soil, even up to the Greenland Ice Cap with lead deposits from our gasoline, is reaching appalling proportions. I think it's something we will have to contend with as a major health hazard in the not-to-distant future.

The spread of radioactivity, the spread of pesticides, not simply DDT, but a large spectrum of pesticides which are not receiving anywhere the attention that they should, are leading to massive pollution of the earth.

We are changing the whole carbon dioxide ratio in the atmosphere today, which may be leading to a warming up of the planet with all kinds of apocalyptic results in some distant future. We are polluting all the oceans on a massive scale, all the water-ways.

This is now becoming a problem, because what we are doing is undermining the complex biosphere, the complex world of life, on which an organism like man depends, not only for his health literally, but for his sanity. We are homogenizing the entire planet, we are turning it into a factory. And while man may be compelled to accept this kind of condition, nature will rebel against it.

We have to decentralize our cities now. This is an old and traditional anarchist demand and it was always seen as a dream. For the first time historically it has become not simply a dream but a necessity for human survival.

We have to eliminate the State which plays such a destructive role today not only in coercing people but in mobilizing the economy in the exploitation of resources. This is no longer merely a dream today, it has now become a necessity.

We have to eliminate property; we have to start using the earth as though it were a garden to satisfy human needs, material needs, instead of satisfying class interests. This today is no longer merely a dream. It, too, has become a necessity.

We have to start living in order to survive. That's the essence of the new situation which has arisen. In the past, everything was put this way: there is the dream, but we have to take care of survival first. The dream represented life, and survival represented economic necessity.

Now the whole question has been reversed. If we do not begin to live, we will be incapable of having any kind of reality at all.

For that reason the anarchist vision of a decentralized, propertyless, Stateless, communistic society, in which men will live not only in harmony with each other but in harmony with nature, are no longer really dreams. They have become preconditions, necessities for the survival of man on this planet.

Government by Science . . . or Chaos

Malcolm Christenson

America Has a Problem

As America progresses painfully into the last one-third of the 20th century more and more of its inhabitants are becoming aware of the fact that there is something radically wrong with their way of life.

Following the news media, we are told that our free enterprise system is the best possible way of life. Our national income is the highest in history. Unemployment is the lowest in many years and we have more money to spend per capita than ever before in the history of mankind.

However, the same news media tell other stories which do not add up to the same thing. Let us examine a few of them:

New York City, in January 1969, passed the one million mark of people on welfare, approximately 12½ % of that city's population. Los Angeles County in California had 550,000 on welfare, about 15% of its population. Over ten million Americans are on starvation diets, and suffering different stages of malnutrition. At least one-third of our population is ill-fed, ill-clothed and ill-housed.

Crime is increasing so rapidly it is recognized by the news media as a national scandal. Just one example will suffice, for now. The city of Houston, Texas, population 1,000,000, had more murders in 1967 than the entire continent of Europe with a population of 450,000,000.

In the last presidential election the people of this nation voted on a total of more than $9,000,000,000 worth of school bonds needed to keep our educational system going. Over $4,000,-000,000 were voted down; this action has already closed some schools, with many more in danger of being closed down due to lack of funds.

The total debt, public and private, has reached one trillion,

Schism v.1, no.2 (Winter 1970)

six hundred billion dollars. The interest on the national debt alone now runs over $16,000,000,000 annually, and it is going up every day. The news media tells us about a potential 'middle-class' income tax revolt. All indicators point to a nationwide tax revolt spreading to greater proportions in the very near future.

On January 11, 1969, President Johnson was making his farewell appearance before the Washington Press Club and his remarks were carried on a national television program. One reporter asked what he thought was the biggest failure of his administration. His answer should be very enlightening to all Americans. . . . He stated flatly that his inability to achieve an equitable distribution of goods and services to the American people, amidst the plenty available, was the biggest failure of his administration.

It is time for all Americans to realize that no social system using a medium of exchange based on human energy will ever distribute a technological abundance equitably. It makes no difference whether the administration is democratic, socialist, communist or fascist. They are all Price Systems designed in days of scarcity and are positively incapable of distributing an abundance in anything that even resembles a functional operation. All must maintain scarcity in order to maintain the price structure.

The Need for Change

It is obvious that our present political Price System cannot find the answers needed to survive. For example, with the impending tax revolt, already in motion, how can the people be taxed enough more to make even a small dent in the monies needed to properly feed our starving millions? More taxes only reduce the purchasing power of the nation which could throw the country into a sickening depression. There is only one answer: *Government by Science—or terrible chaos.*

How can a government by science cure the problem? Why will it cure the problem? How will it work? Let us examine the facts of the case.

Technological labor saving devices, displacing human energy and jobs, have grown to the point of giving every American the equivalent of 2,000 'technological slaves' for his individual use. Yet we still persist in the outmoded belief that the distribution of goods must be based on human energy, which is only 1.1% of the total. It is obvious that such a situation is entirely out of balance and that ways must be found to distribute our technological abundance through the medium of the 'technological slaves,' which represent 98.9% of the energy used.

Our present Price System has only been kept alive for many decades because of war and debt policies. We are supposed to be in 'boom-times' yet our per capita income is less than $3,300. With out presently installed technological equipment on this Continent, a government by science basing distribution on our 'technological slaves' would raise the per capita income to the equivalent of $40,000 annually.

The need for change is long overdue; the time is close.

Technocracy's Blueprint for Change

Fortunately for America, and in fact the whole world, men of some prominence began a study of the impact of technology on our economy in the winter of 1918-19 in New York. They called themselves the Technical Alliance and appointed Howard Scott as their Director. Their studies on the subject covered every possible phase of the situation, and at one time during that period one floor of the industrial engineering building of Columbia University was used by the organization to further its studies.

The conclusion of those studies indicated that an entirely new method of distribution would eventually have to be installed; it would have to include an entirely new form of government, a government by science to be called a Technate, replacing our present political government. Distribution of goods and services would have to be based on our 'technological slaves,' or technological energy, instead of diminishing human energy.

The group became a non-profit organization under the laws of the state of New York in 1933 and was called Technocracy Inc. Today Technocracy members cover almost every state in the union, as well as most provinces of Canada. Howard Scott became Director-in-Chief of the new organization, and remains in that position to this day.

Living in a Technate

It is, of course, impossible to cover a subject as important as this in one article. The only way the uninitiated could ever thoroughly understand the subject is to attend Technocracy's Study Courses, conducted in our Sections. All we can attempt to do here is to point out the great contrasts between what we now have and what a Technate would give us.

Because our presently installed scientific and technological equipment is capable of producing more than we could possibly consume, and would be the equivalent of the take home pay of $78,000 now paid President Nixon, every family on this Continent would have an income 'like a president.'

Crime would actually diminish by at least 95%. That percentage now represents what is called 'economic crimes.' There would be little need for jails and prisons in such a society. There would be no need to send our sons overseas to fight, and die in wars to keep our economy going. There would be no debts, no taxes, no murders for economic gain. Most racial strife would come to an immediate end.

The *Technocracy way* is the *Technological way* which must become the *American way*. It cannot be overemphasized that the Price System and political mode of social control in America is doomed completely and entirely, regardless of any and all efforts being made or anticipated in attempts to save it, and regardless of anyone's wishes or desires in the matter. The result is inevitable, regardless of any expressed approval or disapproval of the technological solution projected by Technocracy.

Join Technocracy now—and start building that *New America*.

What Is Property?

William W. Bayes

Private property has been the object of attack by socialists ever since the first nonproducer enviously viewed the fruit of the labors of the first producer. Property, like religion, has had ascribed to it all the evils arising out of the hearts of men. The institution of private property, some say, has perpetuated every manner of "social injustice." Karl Marx and Friedrich Engels called for the abolition of private property in the *Communist Manifesto*. Pierre Joseph Proudhon, a social-theorist contemporary of Marx, declared, "Property is theft!" He conveniently ignored the fact that theft has no meaning if there is no concept of property. Present-day proponents of the welfare state assert, in the name of "social justice," that "human rights are more precious than property rights." The inference one is expected to draw, presumably, is that rights belonging to humans are more important than rights belong to property—except that the human who owns the property is to be dropped from consideration.

These arguments for "social justice"[1] have a common denominator: an appeal to the emotions. Such an appeal is fraudulent. It would be fraudulent even if the unsupported assertions accompanying it were sound. It is fraudulent because it denies that one's listeners or readers are capable of interpreting a rational argument. If they are not, whatever action they may take in response to the appeal must be nonrational at best and perhaps even dangerous. Such emotional appeals, carried a bit further, have induced mobs to riot, loot, burn, and kill. One who desires to persuade others to accept a belief or to act in a rational manner ought to define his terms so that his listeners or readers will know exactly what he means when he uses those terms. To do else is to ask others to act on the basis of emotional stimulus, rather than on the basis of reason.

Largely by defining my terms I intend to show: (1) that property, far from being theft, is the result of a creative process; (2) that property so created benefits all, especially wage earners; (3) that property rights and human rights are identical; and (4) that such so-called human rights as "economic rights" are neither economical nor are they rights.

---

[1] The term "social justice" is one that needs to be analyzed. The modifier, the word *social,* implies that justice is divisible, which it is not. Since governments (which enforce justice) are instituted among men to secure the rights of life, liberty, and the pursuit of happiness, any violation of these rights in the name of "social justice" would deny elemental justice.

Human Rights Are Property Rights

I have said that the type of argument exemplified by the "human rights *versus* property rights" dicotomy is fraudulent. It is so because it does not define these terms about which it makes bold asseverations. If those who so argue should define these terms, it would appear that logic would compel them to change the relationship of the terms from one of opposition to one of identity: human rights *are* property rights. In order to demonstrate that this assertion is correct, we must first define the word *property*:

> . . . 3. Possessions irrespective of their ownership; wealth; goods; specif., a piece of real estate. 4. The exclusive right to possess, enjoy, and dispose of, a thing; owner-ship; . . . incorporeal rights, as patents, copyrights, rights of action, etc., . . . 5. That to which a person has legal title; thing owned; . . . anything, or those things collec-tively, in or to which a man has a right protected by law; . . .[2]

Property, then, is the *thing owned,* such as a material object or an incorporeal right. The above definition also mentions "rights of action." Actually, this *right to act* is the essence of property. If you doubt this, imagine "owning" a piece of prop-erty on the planet Jupiter, where you could not get to it or do antyhing with it. This view is not generally understood, be-cause many tend to think of property as static.

Let us for a moment envision a supposedly static property, such as a piece of land. Even when an owner of such land seems not to be using it, he is *acting*. Action is, of course, (or should be) determined by purpose. If the owner is holding the land to sell at a profit, he is using it; he is *acting*. His holding of the land is not hurting anyone else; rather, the taxes he pays support government functions. If it becomes essential to society that the land be productively used, at least two circumstances will concur: (1) he will be offered a price that will tempt him to sell the land; (2) the local government will raise his property

[2]*Webster's New International Dictionary* (Second Edition, Unabridged; Springfield, Mass.: G. & C. Merriam Company, 1950), p. 1984.

taxes to a level that will discourage his unproductive use of land while waiting for a higher price.

Either his land is *not* needed for production or living space by society, in which case its apparent disuse disturbs no one; or the land is needed by society for production or living space, in which case its owner will be motivated by circumstances to use it for production, rent it, or sell it. Whatever decision he makes, he will be *acting* for his own purposes; and his own purposes will not conflict with the good of society. Nature abhors a vacuum, and the economy abhors disuse of needed resources; nature will see to it that the vacuum is filled at the first opportunity, and the economy will see to it that needed resources are actively employed. Thus, we see that property always involves a *right to act*. And we have observed that apparent inaction is a form of action. That is why we speak of the right *to* property, rather than the right *of* property. Property, as the *thing owned*, has no rights. Only humans have rights: and these rights, all involving the *right to act*, are *property*.

The Right to One's Own Life

The fundamental right for any human is the right to his own life. He owns his own life, unless he is a slave. (Even if he is a slave, he has the natural right to his own life, but he is unable to enforce it or claim it.) His life does not belong to any other person or group. The *thing owned* is his body, and the related *right to act*, or property right, is the right to live. Now, matter is eternal, but human life is not; life must be sustained by procuring and consuming the means of subsistence. If we agree that man has a right to live, we must agree that man may use his mental and physical faculties to procure those means. Since the means (food, clothing, shelter, and the like) do not usually lie readily at hand, he must find or grow the food, manufacture the clothing, and build the shelter. In short, he must produce.

To produce is to *create* anything with exchangeable value.[3]

[3]*Britannica World Language Edition of Funk & Wagnall's Standard Dictionary* (Chicago: Encyclopedia Britannica, Inc., 1966), Vol. 1, p. 1006.

To create means, of course, to cause to come into existence what did not exist before. In the literal sense, of course, no man can create; he can only alter the form of things which already exist and discover laws which he can use as means to accomplish his ends. But the new form is something which did not exist before, and this is what we call creation. Thus, growing wheat, building a house, manufacturing clothes or automobiles, painting a picture, and providing such services as transportation, education, and legal advice, are all forms of *creation*. Those which do not involve originality are lower forms of creation, but they are still creation inasmuch as they bring into existence what did not exist before.

Creation vs. Expropriation

This creative aspect of capitalism is in sharp contrast to the *expropriative* aspects of socialism and the welfare state. Under capitalism, everyone is entitled to engage in free enterprise, must bear his own risks, and is entitled to receive whatever returns his creative enterprise will bring him. Under socialism, a man is not entitled to engage in free enterprise, he receives as a wage whatever the authorities decide to grant him, and he has no opportunity to earn more than a subsistence unless he is a high-ranking member of the bureaucracy. Under the welfare state, a man is entitled to engage in free enterprise, must bear his own risks, but is not entitled to receive whatever returns his creative enterprise will bring him. He finds that he is held responsible for those whose mental and physical faculties have been unused or misused. His returns are eroded by the effects of unfair labor laws and all manner of taxes, including the obviously inequitable progressive income tax. He is, in effect, penalized for his creativeness.

A corollary of the right to produce is the right to keep that which one has created. If one may keep this product, it follows that one may consume it, exchange it for goods or services offered by someone else, sell it, or give it away. He may do all these things because the right of the producer, or creator, is anterior to that of any other person or group. To assert that he does not have a primary right is, in effect, to deny him any right whatever. It is to say that he holds his property by sufferance of anyone (including a government) who is stronger than he, and that it is proper to plunder. But if it is proper to plunder from the producer, then it must, a fortiori, be proper to plunder from one who has himself plundered. It must then follow that only might can make right—one may take from another when one has the might, and one may keep only what one has the might to defend. Unless a person is prepared to accept the "might makes right" philosophy, he must respect another's right to live, to produce, and to consume, keep, exchange, sell, or give away that which he has produced. These property rights, it is important to remember, are dynamic, not static; they involve the right to *act*.

A man retains his property rights in any excess of his production over his personal consumption. It is important to remember, in this regard, that a man's production depends, not only upon his physical strength, but also upon his mental powers, his powers to create: to think, devise, plan, organize, coordinate, and so on. That which is physically performed by an employee is made possible by an employee is made possible by the producer's investment of his previously created capital and his managerial expertise. *No one else loses* anything by reason of such action by the producer, anymore than if he had produced only what he could personally consume. It must be remembered that he is *producing,* not expropriating the products of others.

Everyone Gains

But wait! While no one else loses, others *gain* as a result of this production in excess personal consumption. The producer may create an enterprise employing hundreds, possibly thousands, of persons. These jobs would not have existed without his creative efforts. Nor would the consumers have the benefit of the products this enterprise produces. In pursuing his own self-interest, producing the means for his own subsistence and achieving his own self-fulfillment, he becomes a benefactor of his community.

Remember Proudhon's dictum: "Property is theft!" We have seen that property is created although it is true that under socialism property is not free from the taint of stolen goods. Proudhon, who presumably had the interests of the poor at heart, could not have meant that nonproducers steal from producers (else he would have fought for property rights), nor that producers steal from other producers (which would have been a proper subject for criminal law, not for social legislation); therefore, he must have meant that producers steal from nonproducers or marginal producers. But, if the nonproducers do not create wealth, and if the marginal producers produce barely the means of subsistence, then they have little that may be stolen from them. (Mind, savings, and tools are the chief ingredients in the production of wealth—not manual labor.)

But property does not consist merely of real and personal possessions. Intangible, or incorporeal, rights which we Americans value as priceless, such as those guaranteed by the Constitution, being *things owned* and involving the *right to act,* are property. This means that such rights as the right to free speech, to worship, to peaceful assembly, and to due process, are all property. If they are property, then the rights involved are essentially property rights. There is no right which is not property, and there is no property which, if not a right in itself, is not a fruit of the exercise of a right. Thus the false polarization of human rights and property rights and the substitution of spurious rights to the property of others, as in the "right" to an education or to a guaranteed annual income, are but further links in the chain of violations of the real human rights, which are all property rights. A human without property rights is without rights.

Our Rights as Property

This view, that rights themselves are property, is a legitimate part of our political heritage. John Locke, from whose writings the Founding Fathers freely drew intellectual inspiration and guidance, asserted that we have property in our persons as well as in our possessions.[4] We have property in our life and in our mental and physical faculties. When these faculties are applied, as by mixing one's labor with nature's bounty, they create tangible property.

Both Thomas Jefferson and James Madison believed that ". . . government may not violate, directly or indirectly, 'the

[4]"John Locke," *Encyclopaedia Britannica* (Chicago, 1966), 14:192.

property which individuals have in their opinions, their religion, their persons and their faculties . . .'"[5]

It is interesting to note that many professors who do not share this traditional view of property pay it unwitting tribute when they insist upon "academic freedom." For so-called academic freedom is nothing more than the right (possessed by every free citizen and not merely by academicians) to hold (*i.e., to own*) opinions and to utter (to *use* and *enjoy* and dispose of, as property) those opinions. If they are paid for a speech, an article in a periodical, or a book, they are being paid for the articulate expression of their expert (or, perhaps, merely interesting) opinion. It is absurd to suppose that they should receive payment for something that was not theirs to sell, not their property. The property lies in their opinion which is fortified and given commercial value by their expert background knowledge and their ability to express that opinion clearly and interestingly.

In the case of professorial opinions expressed in the classroom, it should be noted, many writers have emphasized that other property rights than the professor's own are involved and that these deserve protection also.

Economic Rights Derivative

I have said that so-called economic rights are neither economical nor are they rights. There are no economic rights as such; all rights are political rights. The freedom to engage in any type of enterprise, to produce, to own and control property, to buy and sell on the free market, is derived from the rights to life, liberty, and property, together with the *pursuit* of happiness, which are stated in the Declaration of Independence as self-evident truths and are hypostatized and secured by the Constitution. When a government guarantees a "right" to an education or parity on farm products or a guaranteed annual income, it is staking a claim on the property of one group of citizens for the sake of another group. In short, it is violating one of the fundamental rights it was instituted to protect.

To the extent that one citizen must labor involuntarily for

[5]"Civil Liberties," *Encyclopaedia Britannica,* 4:837.

the benefit of another citizen, he has lost his liberty and has been subjected to involuntary servitude. To the extent that income which the producing citizen would otherwise invest in capital is diverted to the propping up of a nonproducing or marginally producing citizen, that money is wasted. It is spent rather than invested, and it teaches the citizen who receives the dubious benefit to be dependent upon government. Still worse, perhaps, is the fact that the recipient of largesse from an anonymous, monolithic, endlessly wealthy state loses sight of his real benefactor—the producing citizen. Neither that recipient nor the government is concerned about the use to which the producer would have put his money if allowed to keep it. One thing seems certain: he would have invested his money (whether by means of a bank, the stock market, or otherwise) in a capital pool, where it would have been used to create additional wealth.

The Corruption of Terms

One of the most important means used by the enemies of freedom to bring down our institutions is the corruption of the meanings of words and hence of the concepts for which those words are symbols. These institutions, including that of private property rights, are very dear to the American people and so they must be attacked by indirection. Instead of attacking property rights as here correctly defined and explained, the socialists and other statists use the word *property* in a diminished sense, although they are careful not to define it. Its meaning is thus attenuated, hedged, and qualified, until it seems to represent merely real and personal property of a considerable magnitude.

The mental image is created of a Croesus on the one hand, living in the lap of luxury with a train of servants at hand to attend to his every want; and of an indigent person on the other hand, probably living in a hovel and working in a sweatshop, if employed at all, for a mere subsistence. The mental image this created is meant to arouse our sympathy and to obscure questions as to *why* one is wealthy and another poor. It is also meant to obscure the fact that, unless wealth honestly gained is protected from confiscation, anything gained by the poor will be equally subject to confiscation; and equality will be achieved only in want and slavery.

Surely, those who say that "human rights are more precious than property rights" cannot mean by *property* a man's life or a mere subsistence, such as the food a man eats, the clothes on his back, and the hovel in which he may live. They must, therefore, mean that wealth which a producer has *created* in excess of his personal consumption. But it has been shown that such wealth comes into being only as a result of a particular producer's efforts, is not acquired at the expense of nonproducers or the marginal producers, and actually benefits the latter (who receive far more than their manual labor contributes to the product). Thus, the communists, socialists, and other statists set up a diminished idea of property, *i.e.,* great wealth, as a straw man by means of whose defeat they intend to destroy all property rights, which means all rights.

The communists, socialists, and other statists have been aided in this endeavor to corrupt the meanings of words by Americans who do not define their terms and do not insist that others define *their* terms. I do not imply that such Americans are communists or socialists or have impure motives. I cannot read motives. But I am able to see the effects of certain expressions and acts; it is acts, after all, which are able to injure and destroy, not motivations as such. I merely offer my opinion that those Americans who permit this corrupted idea of property to be foisted upon them make the task of the socialists much easier to accomplish. They are like the homeowner who leaves his house and does not lock his doors and windows to bar the entrance of burglars. They do not guard the doors to their minds by questioning the meanings of words and concepts and the logical structure of arguments. In so doing, they passively allow their minds to be filled with false concepts. Dupes are not always innocent. They are not innocent if they have not tried to protect themselves.

The Poor Stand to Lose Most from Attacks on Property

Preservation of the full meaning of the word *property* will do much to preserve liberty in this land and perhaps even restore that portion of liberty which has been lost. It will do little good to talk about property rights, unless listeners and speakers construe the word *property* in the same way. We must insist that those who talk about human rights and property rights define their terms, and we must not deceive our listeners by our use of the word *property*. If we permit the degradation of this word to mean nothing more than great wealth, we may as well speak no more of property rights; only the wealthy will listen. We need to show the inseparable link between the right to property, even to great wealth, and the rights to life and liberty. We must demonstrate that production is the *creation* of wealth and that the only expropriators are criminals and unlimited governments. An attack upon private property rights is not merely an attack upon material objects divorced from human owners; it is an attack upon the owners. It is an attack upon production and creativity. It is an attack upon the right to use one's mental and physical faculties (are you professors and reporters and artists listening?) It is an attack upon one's right to act. It is an attack upon the right of the propertyless to dream, plan, and work for a brighter day. It is an attack upon one's right to live—as a free man.

Poverty: A Libertarian View

Rod Manis

Government is the greatest enemy of the poor. Its taxes, regulations, and expenditures are the primary obstacles the poor face in trying to better their lot. Americans have, for too long, been convinced that any problem can be solved with government bureaucracy and tax money. Perhaps the bitter reality of the poor's plight will force us to give up this dangerous illusion.

A Tax Foundation study shows that national, state and local

Schism v.1, no.3 (Summer 1970)

taxes take 34 percent of the income of those who make less than $3,000 a year. (*U.S. News,* Dec. 9, 1968).

The government gives unions the power to exclude poor and minority workers from jobs. When white, middle-class union members go on strike demanding increases in their ten to twenty thousand dollar-a-year salaries (Philadelphia plumbers are guaranteed a minimum of $19,400 a year), seldom can employers legally hire poor blacks who desperately need the jobs.

"Only 4 percent of the building-tradesmen are Negroes and most of them are concentrated at the bottom of the industry's wage scale. Nationwide, despite years of pressure, government surveys indicate that currently only 5,000 of the 130,000 youths now in construction-industry apprenticeship programs are black." (*Newsweek,* Oct. 6, 1969, p. 105). Through government-granted monopoly powers, unions have become the primary bottleneck to the advancement of poor blacks in the cities.

Minimum wage laws sharply increase unemployment among the poor. If a man can only produce $1 worth of output in an hour, no one is going to pay him $1.60, the current national minimum.

Spot checks by civil rights workers in the South indicate that 100,000 farm workers have lost their jobs because the minimum wage law has been applied to them. (New York *Times,* Feb. 13, 1967).

Innumerable regulations by national regulatory agencies, state boards, and local governments keep the poor out of countless businesses, professions, and occupations. Blacks can't be Certified Public Accountants in Alabama. Big city governments run by political machines close down businesses for alleged violations of endless rules.

Most cities give service monopolies, (e.g. taxis, buses, parking garages) to a few companies—the poor need not apply. Unnecessary government educational and financial requirements keep the poor from being beauty parlor operators, real estate workers, butchers, and barbers (and many other occupations). In one city it takes a $150 license to move someone else's furniture for them—obviously to protect large movers from the competition of small operators.

Government expenditures offer little help to the poor. Of

the $100 billion we spend on programs that are supposed to help the poor, little gets to them. (If it all went directly to them, the poorest 10 per cent of the population would get $5,000 each.)

Welfare weakens incentives of recipients to find work when it reduces the welfare check by a dollar whenever a dollar is earned. It often breaks up families by offering money only when the father leaves. Welfare workers not only snoop into and often tightly control the lives of their clients, but they seem to provide little help. Recent studies find that trained social workers do not improve the functioning of families on relief or of potential high school age delinquents. (Gordon E. Brown, 1968.)

The government schools are failing to help the poor. "The sad truth is that American Schools, by and large, do not know how to teach—nor frequently want to teach." (Martin Luther King, *Where Do We Go From Here,* p. 226). Tragically, "in many underprivileged schools the IQ steadily falls the longer they go to school." (Paul Goodman, *Compulsory Mis-Education,* p. 26). "Teachers are not teaching, but trying to maintain order, to survive the classroom war from day to day." (Hemdon, *The Way It Spozed To Be*).

School "cannot be in both the jail and the education business." (John Holt, *The Underachieving School*).

Their failure cannot be blamed on a lack of funds. The famous Coleman Commission report showed no relationship between either expenditure or class size and student achievement.

Schools fail because they are a government monopoly. Without the pressure of competition they are neither progressive, efficient, nor competent. Government schools succeed only in destroying the students' curiosity, initiative, and originality.

The building-trades unions (with government monopoly power) have greatly increased the cost of housing for the poor "by rigidly controlling membership (as one example, the International Brotherhood of Electrical Workers in Pittsburgh has 1,000 members—the same membership it had 25 years ago) and creating a false labor shortage." (*Newsweek,* Oct. 6, 1969, p. 105). Building codes prevent the use of newer and cheaper materials. Property taxes add greatly to rents, and rent controls cause housing shortages and slums. The national urban renewal program has thrown more than two million people out of their homes, 60 per cent of whom are from minority groups. They had to crowd into poorer accommodations and pay higher rents. (Martin Anderson, *The Federal Bulldozer*.)

Farm subsidies are supposed to help poor farmers. In fact, 85 per cent goes to farms whose average sales exceed $10,000 while only 7 per cent is spread thinly among those selling less than $5,000 a year.

The national government has taken the responsibility of taking care of American Indians. The Bureau of Indian Affairs has one bureaucrat for every 25 Indians and spends over $700 per Indian. What has government beneficence wrought? The Indians' life expectancy is less than 45 years; their income is about one-third of that of all other Americans; only one-fourth are considered employable, and of these 40 per cent are unemployed. (See the Report of the Senate Interior Committee, 1966 and Los Angeles *Times,* Sept. 10, 1969, I-26).

Only a libertarian approach can help the poor. This requires an end to the taxes, expenditures, and regulations that hurt the poor. Despite popular myths, it is inherent in the nature of government that intervention be promoted by and for the rich and powerful. As Milton Friedman has written, "I do not know of a single example of a predominently collectivist or centrally planned society in which the ordinary citizen has achieved a major and substantial improvement in the condition of his everyday life or a real hope for the future of himself or his children."

When power is radically decentralized, people will be free to run their own lives. Different approaches could be tried and successes would be imitated. The systems that obtain the greatest individual freedom would be the most successful and would provide the greatest opportunities for the poor.

Our Tax Money Breeds Misery

The Dan Smoot Report

On June 4, 1970, the House, by a vote of 191 to 153, passed HR 17867, appropriating $2.2 billion for some aspects of foreign aid in fiscal 1971. President Nixon had requested $2.9 billion.[1] The Senate has not acted on this bill.

There was much moaning among foreign aiders about this "gutting" of the foreign aid program. There was much breast-beating about America's callous neglect of her responsibility to help less fortunate nations. There were warnings that calamity will overtake us if we do not open the spigots wider and drain off more of our wealth for poor nations.

Dr. John A. Hannah, Administrator of the Agency for International Development (AID—the current name for the foreign aid agency) says:

> The United States must help the people of the poorer nations to improve the quality of their lives if Americans expect to enjoy the stability and prosperity of a peaceful world . . .
>
> It is unrealistic to think that thirty years from now 300 million Americans can live comfortably here while across the continents of Asia, Africa, and Latin America, more than twice the present population—some seven billions of people—struggle to eke out an existence.[2]

They already outnumber us more than 15 to 1. In 30 years, they will outnumber us almost 25 to 1. They have natural resources more abundant and more varied than we have. We have already given them billions of dollars in aid to get started;

Schism v.2, no.1 (Winter 1971)

[1]*Congressional Quarterly Weekly Report,* June 14, 1970, pp. 1521-1523.

[2]AID press release, Oct. 30, 1970.

but, according to foreign aid lobbyists, the living standards of poor nations continue to fall further below ours.

AID director Hannah says that, although classrooms for school-age children in the poor nations have "tripled and quadrupled in number in the last 20 years," those countries soon "will be swamped in a tide of new illiterates" because the "school-age population . . . will double in the next decade."

In short, destitution worsens in many poor nations, despite all outside aid and whatever efforts they make themselves, because they breed people faster than they gain in any other activity.

We have spent billions on food to alleviate hunger in such places as India; but we have thereby probably caused more hunger than we have alleviated. American food given away abroad not only enriches a few foreign politicians (and possibly some Americans), but it also accelerates the reproductive activity of the undernourished millions. Our medical aid has increased the life-spans, and consequently the numbers of children, of the impoverished.

Today, throughout the "developing countries," there may be twice as many people suffering in squalid poverty from malnutrition and exposure as there would have been if our aid had not subsidized population growth. In the same way but on a much larger scale, our tax money is also subsidizing bastardy, idleness, and excessive population growth among welfare recipients here at home.

AID director Hannah tells of an AID measles-control and smallpox-eradication project which resulted in the innoculation of 100 million people against smallpox and 20 million chidren against measles in 19 nations of central of west Africa. He says:

> In those countries, almost 200 years after the beginning of vaccination against smallpox in this country, thousands of people were dying each year from smallpox, and tens of thousands of children were dying each year from measles. . . . In a little over two years, smallpox as a cause of death has practically disappeared.[3]

[3]AID press release, Dec. 29, 1969.

If this AID project did save the lives of millions of children, it did not "improve the quality of their lives." It will, however, make possible the breeding of tens of millions of other children who will spend their lives in grinding poverty, hodling on to existence just enough to breed more scores of millions to live and die in want.

Crowd diseases and filth diseases are the only real controllers of population among the illiterate masses of Asia, Africa, and Latin America. We may curtail or eliminate the disease; but we can do little about the resulting population explosion which, some say, already endangers all life on this planet.

Bert M. Tollefson, Jr., AID assistant administrator, says:

> Can we afford to assist international development at a time when the United States is confronted by pressing problems of domestic development? The answer is clear. We have already learned at home the price a society pays for ignoring the problems of the disadvantaged—of telling the poor and hungry that they must wait.[4]

There are three monumental fallacies in Mr. Tollefson's veiled threat that the poor nations, out of envy and hate, will some day rise up and strike us down if we do not give them all the aid they demand.

Fallacy One: Mr. Tollefson implies that poor nations have the capacity to fight major wars against advanced nations. They do not. They do not even have the capacity to initiate such wars, though they are often used as pawns in conflicts between advanced nations.

Fallacy Two: Mr. Tollefson implies that the violence which has scarred the face and soul of America during the past six years resulted from poor people revolting in righteous anger, demanding what is morally and legally theirs. The implication is a lie. Leaders of the worst U.S. riots since 1964 were well-financed revolutionaries. Many, if not most, participants in the riots were persons who had, or could have had, good jobs—or they were pampered brats from prosperous families.

Fallacy Three: Mr. Tollefson assumes that aid from govern-

[4]AID press release, Aug. 16, 1969.

ments of advanced nations can solve the interior problems of poor countries, but it cannot. What our foreign aiders see as problems in poor countries is a way of life. Our government can finance (and has been financing) social and political upheavals which deliver poor countries into the grip of communist dictators (or tighten the hold of existing dictatorships); but the U.S. government cannot force, bribe, induce, educate, or train other nations into a way of life satisfying to our political leaders; and it has no business trying.

If American individuals, private organizations, private businesses, or churches want to do business or missionary work (religious, educational, medical, agricultural, industrial, cultural) in poor nations, assuming whatever risks may be invovled, our government should not prohibit them. Over long stretches of time, such private aid can alter a poor nation's way of life and shape it into something more nearly resembling our own (though only God knows whether that should be done). But any kind of development aid from a foreign government (ours or any other) is indictable on many counts.

In any kind of government aid, selfish political interests dictate decisions that (if they are to help people in receiving nations) should be made solely for economic reasons. For example, among the "experts" we send abroad to give technical assistance to poor nations are men who teach the people how to organize and run American-style labor unions.

Ostensibly, poor nations want higher productivity so that they can support themselves and find foreign markets for some of their goods. But present-day, American-style unionism decreases, rather than increases, productivity. It stresses low productivity and high wages. It causes needless work stoppages and strikes. It requires costly payroll padding and cumbersome management procedures, intended only to enhance the power of union bosses. It discourages individual resourcefulness and initiative on the part of workers, and schools them in the attitude that the way to get ahead is to demand large return for little output, and to back their demands with force. Worst of all, American unionism impinges on the freedom of individual workers—forcing them to pay dues for political purposes they often dislike; forcing them to support an expensive and frequently corrupt union bureaucracy; eliminating their privilege of advancing as individuals on the basis of individual skill, energy, and diligence.

Why do Members of Congress tax us to send union organizers abroad, under the flimsy pretense that this will improve the economy of poor nations? They do it to get for themselves the political support of powerful U.S. union bosses.

Why has Congress wasted billions of our tax dollars on foreign aid harmful to poor nations because it provides them with sophisticated machinery and industrial installations which they must in part help finance and maintain, but do not have the capacity to utilize? Members of Congress have voted for such foreign aid because it provides lush contracts for important constituents back home.

Why do governments of receiving nations accept foreign aid that hurts rather than helps? Politicians in those nations can fatten their own pocketbooks, and also point to extravagant projects, equipment, and public works, boasting about what they have done for their people.

The foreign aid lobbyists' perennial wailing about congressional reductions in foreign aid is not only propagandistic, but also false.

The foreign aid appropriations bill for fiscal 1971 (already passed by the House, as mentioned before) was for the so-called "mutual security" part of our foreign aid program— always publicized as if it were the whole program; but our overall foreign aid program has more than a score of other parts, put elsewhere in the federal budget, and not labeled foreign aid.

Foreign aiders called President Nixon's $2.9 billion foreign aid appropriations request this year dangerously low, among the lowest requests in history. But the President actually reqested $12.1 billion for new foreign aid authorizations in fiscal 1971; $2.3 billion of it was in our Department of Defense budget (for foreign military assistance); $933 million of it was in our Department of Agriculture budget (for agricultural commodities to be given to other nations); $2.9 billion of it was to underwrite long-term credits issued by the Export-Import Bank; $1.1 billion of it was for the "regular operations" of the Export-Import Bank; $540 million of it was for "expanded multilateral assistance" (bureaucratic jargon for U.S. tax money donated to United Nations agencies to give away as they please, without the trouble of making any accounting to the American people or to Congress); and so on. In all, there are 27 "parts" to the foreign aid appropriations request this year.

There is also a total of $18.5 billion in accumulated, unexpended foreign aid funds—tax money which Congress authorized for foreign aid in previous years, which is still available for foreign aid spending, but which the foreign aiders have not yet managed to get rid of.

If Congress passed no foreign aid appropriations bill at all this year, the Nixon administration would still have $18.5 billion to spend on foreign aid. If Congress grants all of President Nixon's requests for fiscal 1971, more than $30 billion will be available for spending on foreign aid between now and June 30, 1971.

In our voting on November 3, we failed to improve the quality of Congress; but if enough of use care, and try hard, we can persuade the Congress we have to stop foreign aid.

Suggestion: Distribute this Report, and other recent issues on foreign aid, as widely as possible to inform and activate others.

We Took
What We Needed . . .

Rat

Early Thursday morning, Nov. 6, over forty mothers who went into Macy's to get school clothes for their children walked out of the store with armloads of clothes, without bothering to stop at the cash register. They are members of Welfare Rights Organization (a nationwide organization of people living on welfare who are committed to fighting the injustices of the welfare system). Ten of the women were arrested by security guards at the 34th St. entrance of Macy's. Before they were taken to a nearby precinct they insisted that Macy's wrap and package all the clothes. At the precinct police officials attempted to dismiss their case quickly by serving the women with summonses and sending them home. But the women had come prepared to make their point. They had all arranged for the care of their children so that they could stay to be heard in court. Police officers repeatedly tried to take the clothes from the women, but the women did not allow them to. They knew that the school clothes were important evidence. If they didn't have the clothes the police would charge them with stealing all sorts of things—which would lessen the political implications of their act.

In Night Court the ten mothers pleaded guilty to reduced charges of criminal trespass and were paroled by the judge, who dismissed the case saying that their action was "political." The D.A. and the arresting officer were mad that the women were getting away to easy. The singled out one woman, Jeanette Washington, a leader in the WRO, and charged her with non-cooperation with a police officer because she refused to have her picture taken when she was booked. These charges were also thrown out.

The Welfare Rights Organization has been waging a fight to get money for school clothes for children. Two years ago the N.Y. State legislature cut back the funds for "special allowances" which included money for clothing and furniture, the only time special allowances are now available are in cases of fire and flood. This leaves already hard pressed welfare mothers with no way of providing clothes for their children.

The WRO has centered its fight both in N.Y. and around the country on trying to obtain federal funds from local Boards of Education. Five years ago congress passed Title I, a bill designed to put funds into the education budget for the use of welfare and low income children. The money was primarily intended for school clothing and lunches. These funds have never been used to benefit the poor, they have been used to subsidize middle class oriented programs—a drum and bugle corps in one state, gym programs, swimming pools.

The Welfare Rights Organization has been demanding $100 per year per child for school clothing from Title I money. On

Sept. 17 a rally was held at City Hall and the 3,000 people who had gathered marched across the Brooklyn Bridge to present their demands at the Board of Education. About a week after representatives of Welfare Rights met with the mayor's office to discuss the issue. Another meeting with city officials followed that.

On Oct. 21 Welfare Rights mothers attended a public hearing of the Board of Education. They demanded time to talk about money for school clothing. They were told that they would be put last on the agenda. The women were unwilling to allow the Board to proceed with business as usual. After stating that poor people were tired of always being considered last.

Five borough rallies were held in the days following the disruption at the Board of Education. The feelings of the parents who attended were that more direct action was needed. With the weather getting colder there wasn't any time left for administrative bullshit. Five hundred mothers signed up to participate in "shop-ins." Two days later Macy's was hit.

New York City has received $125 million a year from Title I. Much of this money has been channeled into the More Effective Schools program, an "enrichment" program staffed largely by paraprofessionals. When the city threatened to fire The paraprofessionals because of "lack of funds," the United Federation of Teachers stepped in and negotiated a contract which would pay the paraprofessionals from Title I money. The same money that welfare mothers are trying to get for clothes for their children. This has pitted two groups of poor people against each other. It's the old divide and conquer tactic. Paraprofessionals, are paid very low salaries which are sometimes a supplement or a replacement of a welfare check—they are being forced by the city (which administers the More Effective Schools Program) and the UFT to fight welfare mothers.

Welfare and the Constitution

Dr. Thomas L. Johnson

All welfare legislation is unconstitutional, denying each citizen the rights guaranteed by the Ninth and Thirteenth Amendments of the Constitution of the United States.

The Ninth Amendment, which was ratified in 1791 as a part of the Bill of Rights, is the most important statement in the Constitution protecting individual rights. It reads: "The enumeration of the Constitution, of certain rights, shall not be construed to deny or disparge others retained by the people." By implication, this ("others") was to include the most fundamental rights of man which were not specifically stated in the Bill of Rights—i.e., the inalienable rights of life, liberty and the pursuit of happiness (property) which had been explicitly incorporated in the Declaration of Independence.

The Thirteenth Amendment, which was ratified in 1865, provides for the elimination of all forms of human bondage. It reads: "Neither slavery nor involuntary servitude, except as a punishment for crime whereof the party shall have been duly convicted, shall exist within the United States, or any place subject to their jurisdiction."

With the introduction of welfare legislation by the Congress in the 1930's, citizens lost the right to labor freely in the support of their lives (in contradiction to the Ninth Amendment) and, if they took employment, they became chattels (in contradiction of the Thirteenth Amendment) providing support for those citizens designated by the legislation. In support of this contention, consider the following arguments.

If a man chooses to work, he automatically becomes an involuntary servant, for a substantial portion of his income is expropriated by the government and used to provide income for those who cannot or do not choose to work. The only possible way to avoid involuntary servitude is not to work.

Schism v.2, no.1 (Winter 1971)

Reprinted with permission from *Freedom Magazine* v.15, no.3 (Autumn 1970).

Since a man must support his life by working, it must be assumed that each man must have the right to work—this would be guaranteed by the Ninth Amendment. Since each man is also guaranteed the right not to be subjected to involuntary servitude, he must have the right to work without having his earnings expropriated for the purpose of supporting others. Every taxpayer in this country is now working as slave labor, for if he chooses to work, he is required by law to work for the support of other men from whom he receives nothing in return (except demands for greater enslavement).

"One who acts through a power outside himself," says the philosopher (St. Thomas Aquinas—following Aristotle) "is a slave."

The entire welfare concept could be challenged in the courts based on the right of each man to life (guaranteed by the Ninth Amendment), and thus to the right to take the action necessary to support that life (this action being work).

'At present, a man's right to work, without involving involuntary servitude, is nonexistent.'

In 1911, the Supreme Court (Bailey vs. Alabama) held that: "While the immediate concern was with African slavery, the (Thirteenth) Amendment was not limited to that. It was a charter of universal freedom for all persons, of whatever race, color or estate, under the flag. The plain intention was to abolish slavery of whatever name and form and all its badges and incidents, to render impossible any state of bondage; to make labor free, by prohibiting that control by which the personal service of one man is disposed of or coerced for another's benefit which is the essence of involuntary servitude." (emphasis mine)

Today, labor is not free, for welfare legislation is the control by which the personal service of one man is disposed of or coerced for another's benefit. such legislation is thus unconstitutional.

Slavery was outlawed in this country in the 19th century, but the enslavement of the productive members of the American population, via legalized welfare, has rapidly accelerated in this century. The time has come to end slavery—"to abolish slavery of whatever name and form"—to forbid circumstances which require involuntary servitude—and this can only come about by the elimination of all forms of government welfare.

To restore the dignity of every citizen of this Nation, and to eliminate the working man's present status as a permanent indentured servant, action must be taken to enforce the Constitution and remove the welfare legislation which, by its nature imposes human bondage and destroys man's freedom to work.

The Liberty Amendment will enforce the Constitution, outlaw "welfare legislation" which violates it and enslaves men. It will reaffirm the Ninth and Tenth Amendments, and return all unauthorized activities, rights and properties to the states and people from whom they were taken.

This, in turn, will remove the need for—and repeal—the Sixteenth (income tax) amendment, ending the slavery of producers at one stroke, and restore the "blessings of liberty" to all people as it resolves a multitude of problems—national, state, local and personal.

Lessons from the Summer Work-in

Bob Siegal, Fred Kushner
and Carol Schik

Over the last few years SDS has changed a great deal. Not only is it growing in numbers, but it is also growing politically, seeing the need to go beyond the campus and ally with the other forces in this society in order to bring about real change. The question of what is the key force for change must be seen in terms of who really makes the society run (i.e., who produces all the wealth), are they benefiting from or being hurt by the system, and, as a result, do they have a real stake in changing things. The summer Work-In, a project in which SDSers took jobs in plants that produce steel, glass, clothing, telephones, magazines, etc., made us see much more concretely the fact that working people produce all the wealth of this society.

Schism v.1, no.2 (Winter 1970)

And we came to see something much more important, something that contradicted everything that we had been taught in our universities, and was told to us by the newspapers and TV: the fact that although workers produce everything, they really get nothing in return. Like in this printing plant where some of us worked, the workers took home about $110 a week (if they were there for a few years). Well, what does it mean to live on $110 a week for a family of four? It comes down to barely getting by. With skyrocketing prices, you spend $40 a week for your family just to eat, and then make payments on a car and other things (including credit), pay $125 a month in rent, pay increasing taxes for war in Viet Nam— you wind up treading water and still sinking. And you don't get that paycheck without sweating. There's a bundle of magazines coming down a conveyor belt continually. For three hours straight you put 35 pound bundles in sacks and throw them up on skids. So, comes a ten minute break, what happens? The boss doesn't let people on the line go all at once; no, you 'relieve' one another. That means that when the worker next to you goes for his break, you have to bundle twice as fast! The boss makes you pay for your fellow worker's break—not to mention your own!

Then there's speed-up. This printing company is making millions in profits but won't spend the dough to have safe machines; in fact, the conveyor one of us worked on was built in 1924. So they break down. But they never get really fixed: the boss makes more money by patching them up and then increasing the rate of speed than by having them repaired. And in the lunchroom the workers see a sign that says, 'Keep Our Company Growing!'

In the final analysis, the vast majority of this society (working people, men and women) work for 35 years, if they live that long, and in return get polluted lakes, deteriorating schools, and bad housing. They also have their sons drafted to fight in a war that's against their interest. All of this so that a very few can get richer and richer.

Well, you can say, 'What are they doing about it?: Do they really want to fight? There is a very deep lie we often hear in our sociology classes about the 'happy and contented' workers who have plenty and don't really care about anything but baseball and beer. (Kind of like the racist myths about the 'care-free' slaves on the plantation.) The fact is that there have been more wildcat strikes (strikes against not only the company but also the union leadership) in the last two years than in the fifteen years before that. We have seen the power of the workers' unity not only across the ocean in France, but right here in the U.S. Like at United Parcel Service here in Chicago; the men had to work compulsory overtime, up to seven extra hours a day; no time to see their wives and kids, either work the overtime or get bounced. They fought back! 250 of the workers wildcatted because the sell-out union leadership took the side of the company; even though the overtime was a violation of contract, the union misleaders told the men to go back and then it would be 'discussed.' For two weeks they stayed out with no strike fund, harassed every day by the cops (who made sure that trucks and scabs could get through the picket lines).

Another lie that we're taught in school is that workers are the most reactionary force in this society. But the increase in strikes and wildcats has come during the war in Viet Nam despite the squeals of bosses and politicians that they're against the 'national interest'—kind of funny for 'super-patriots'! While it's true that workers have many bad attitudes (like all of us in this society), the key question is who gains from these attitudes and who do they hurt. Our experience and the facts show that only the bosses benefit from racism, patriotism, etc., and all these attitudes and ideas hurt workers. Racism, for instance, is one of the bosses' main weapons to divide the working class, to prevent Black and white workers from uniting. The material basis of racism is the super-exploitation of black workers: bosses make $22 billion a year on the wage differential between Black and white workers. To maintain this situation they push the idea that Black people are inferior, lazy, the ones who are responsible for the miserable conditions faced by whites, etc. Racism—seeing Black people as the enemy—makes white workers ally with the same bosses who are putting the knife in them—it means that the boss can play one group off against the other, breaking strikes and all attempts to fight back. It's not workers who benefit from the oppression and exploitation of Black People—it's the same class that controls everything in this society! More and more, though, white workers are allying with and following the militant lead of Black workers. In the United Parcel strike, for example, the white workers followed the walk-out of the Black workers; this has been true of all the militant strikes in Chicago over the last two years.

The myth that we have been fed that all workers are innately racists has been demolished by our experience on the job. One Work-Inner was working in a giant department store. While she was on break, a rich white lady came over to be served. The lady refused to let one of the black salesgirls help her. When the Work-Inner returned from her break, she noticed the woman; since nobody was helping her, she took care of her. Afterwards, the women in her department explained that none of them (Black or white) would help this woman because of her racism, and told the Work-Inner that catering to racism could not be allowed.

All across the country, from militant battles at Newport News Shipyard in Virginia to the long struggle at the Figure Flattery Clothing factory in New York City, workers are struggling to gain a decent life. So what does all this mean? Is it just something to put in a muckraker's novel? We think it means a lot more. The exploitation of the working class is the basis of this society. The bosses maintain the armies, the cops, and the courts (the whole apparatus of the state) by stealing the value workers produce. The contradiction between Henry Ford's daughter's $500,000 coming-out party and a worker losing his hand making a Fairlane, between the billions GM makes each year while paying its workers a few thousand, makes clear the interest workers have in changing this system. With workers united against them, the whole class of corporation owners and all their front men (from politicians to university administrators) are very weak.

Students and working people have a common enemy. The bosses who screw workers in the plants are the same guys who run universities. This means that they not only oppress campus workers, but also students. They run the university in order to further the interests of their class, seeing to it that only ideas that help them are taught: racist ideas (like the idea that the problem with Black people is that they live in a matriarchal society and have to regain their manhood, not that they are super-exploited), anti-working class ideas that make students think there is no working class, or that it is below their super-sensitive beings, etc., and every other idea that divides people in this society, especially students from working people. The university also performs many other concrete tasks for imperialism: counter-insurgency research, ROTC, etc. Intellectually the ideas that are taught in the university oppress students—they are deliberately mis-educated as to the nature of this society, as to who their real friends and who their real enemies are. They also suffer material oppression: most students who graduate (50% of all entering freshmen flunk out or drop out) become mental workers in some form—teachers, social workers, etc. As such, they face terrible working conditions, lousy wages, etc.—not to mention getting drafted for wars like Viet Nam. The only way this oppression can be fought is by allying with the key force—the working class.

Will the Workers Revolt?

Dean Clarence E. Manion

One of the Marxism's basic planks is that the revolution must come from within the working class—the proletariat. The workers, protesting the use of their labor by "capitalist" owners and managers, are supposed to rise up and destroy the system that "exploits" the laboring man. One of the most vital tasks of the Communist underground in a non-Communist country, therefore, is to "educate" the workers. They will not revolt until they are convinced that they *are* being exploited, used, and abused by the owners of the plants and factories in which they work.

The Communist Party in the United States has been trying for many years to brainwash the working man and to infiltrate organized labor. Their efforts have not met with wholesale success. While U.S. Reds have made some inroads into organized labor—as they have in all segments of society—they have never been able to capture the "working class." For one thing, the average working man in this country is not poor and downtrodden. More typically, he is middle class, with all of the aspirations and connotations that the label implies. Instead of desiring to destroy the free enterprise system, he is eager to gain more of its fruits. One American radical, 30-year-old Richard L. Greeman, expresses his frustration in this way: "Mao tells us to build from peasants, but we have no peasants."

Lacking peasants, the Communists and other radicals and revolutionaries have turned to the campus. There, amongst affluent and restless youths, they have reaped a sizeable harvest. But students are not the proletariat by anybody's definition, and although they have managed to revolutionize much of the academic world, they have not conquered the real world outside, where men work for a living and have little time or inclination to disrupt society. Having failed to take over the unions, the radicals now propose to woo individual workers with the ultimate aim of a student-worker coalition. The Students for a Democratic Society, as we have pointed out in the past, are attempting to build such a coalition through summer "work-ins."

Writing in a recent issue of the Wall Street Journal, Alan Adelson describes some aspects of this ambitious summer project:

> . . . many student militants are convinced their movement eventually will succeed among workers. They say that the antiwar sentiment that now pervades university campuses started with a relatively small number of activists.
>
> Some even see the time when a student-worker alliance will wrest control over American factories from management. According to this view, shareholders and executives would be compelled to surrender their rights and money just to keep the system going. "If things happen here the way they did in France," says one militant, "The army and the police will be unhappy too, and will flatly refuse to move against their class brothers (the workers)" . . .

Will this radical prediction come true? If it does, we shall not have been unwarned.

"Middle Class" Workers
and the New Politics

Brendan Sexton

Much of my life has been split between two worlds: blue-collar unions and the intellectual-academic arena—a sort of long-haired working stiff, or at least an uncommon marginal man.

Born in a tough Irish working-class neighborhood and reared on Catholicism, Irish rebellion, and their socialism, I fell into the life of an organizer during the great depression and the early days of the CIO. As a reader of everything in reach, I have followed with great regret the growing schism between organized labor and middle-class liberals during the past decade. Like others, I was stunned to see the old liberal coalition finally fragment during the Presidential election under the separate discontents of workers (out of sight and mind to most observers, but not, alas, to George Wallace) and the middle-class liberal antagonists of LBJ. What the consequences of the fragmentation will be only Nixon and Agnew may know.

Yet I continue to believe, in my old-fashioned, radical-populist way, that a broad alliance between these two groups at their center remains the best hope for reconstructing our society along democratic-humanist lines.

Most issues need clarifying if we are to halt a national move to the Right. I wish to explore only one here: the assumption that blue-collar workers are "middle-class" and sitting pretty. I'd also like to suggest some of the political consequences of both the assumption and the reality of workers' lives.

In December of 1967 the "average producton worker" with three dependents took home $90.89 for a full week's work. Measured against the previous year, his dollar income rose about $2.34 a week. In fact, however, his actual purchasing power *declined by about 6 cents per week*. He was worse off in 1967 than in 1966, and probably even more so in 1968.

Now $90.89 take-home is not "middle-class," especially if you are an "average" family head with three dependents. If such a man puts aside $25 a week for house or rent payments (a modest enough sum), he's left with less than $66 a week to pay for food, clothing, medicines, school supplies, etc. for two adults and two children. That comes roughly to $2.37 per day, per person, for a family of four—about the amount a big-city newspaper reporter (or any of us in the real middle class) is likely to spend for lunch.

These figures are distorted a bit by the inclusion of Southern, and largely unorganized, workers. But in 1967, *manufacturing* workers (most of whom are organized) with three dependents averaged only $101.26 in take-home pay. As against the previous year, they also experienced a slight dip in real income and purchasing power.

In New York, the locale of many observers who write so expertly about "middle-class" workers, manufacturing workers averaged a gross income of $114.44. Only in Michigan, among all continental states, where the weekly gross was $145.78, could an average manufacturing worker come close to the national family median (about $8,000) with a full year of work.

At the other end of the scale, retail workers averaged just slightly less than $71 per week during 1967. The retail worker, if he worked a full year, earned a gross income high enough to lift him barely above the "poverty line" of $3,000, but low enough to leave him with less than half the national family median income. This is the extreme example. Still, there are more than 8 million workers in retail trade. Even when they wear white collars, they can't, at this rate, be factored into the middle class.

Skilled workers are the aristocrats of labor, yet the median earnings of male craftsmen who were employed full-time in 1966 was only $6,981.* Of course, a good many of the elite and highly organized urban craftsmen—electricians, typographers, lithographers, etc.—rise to and above $10,000 a year. For a blue-collar worker, this is really "making it." For the new college professor, fresh out of graduate school, it's just so-so.

Where affluence begins and ends no one knows, but it must be above the levels cited. In late 1966, the U.S. Department

---

*Gaps of a year or more sometimes occur in government statistics. In all cases, I have used the most recent annual reports available.

of Labor said that an ncome of $9,191 would enable a city family of four to maintain "a moderate standard of living." Only about one-third of *all* American families reach that now dated standard. Certainly, the typical production worker is much better off than a Mississippi farm tractor driver or a city mother living on welfare, but he hardly lives opulently. He treads water financially and psychically.

The myth of the "midde-class" worker is kin to the Negro of folklore who "lives in the slums but drives a big new Cadillac." He's there, alright, but his numbers are grossly exaggerated.

Workers with small families and two or more paychecks coming in each week may be able to make it. Among all American families with incomes of $10,000, the multi-incomes are twice as numerous as the single income. Still, millions of families combine two or even three paychecks and yet earn less than $5,000 a year.

The young worker is hardest hit and hence most discontented. He often holds down the lower paid and more onerous job. He is somewhat less likely to work overtime at premium rates and more likely to be caught in temporary layoffs, though in some union contracts he is now protected against loss from the latter.

No less than others of his generation, the young worker expects more. Why not? He belongs to a generation with rapidly rising expectations. As long as he's single, his first paychecks may give him more money than he's ever seen before. He dresses well, owns a new car, and generally lives it up.

But once married, his problems multiply. He furnishes a home, perhaps buys it. He does it "on time." He pays more for furniture and appliances than anyone ever did before. The house that cost his father $12,000, with a mortgage at 5 per cent, now may sell for twice that and be financed at 7 per cent. The young married worker age 25 or 30 will probably carry twice the burden of debt as the worker age 40 to 45. When children come, the wife of the young worker will probably drop out of the labor market leaving him as sole support for perhaps 15 or 20 years. In these years his financial needs increase wtih the size of his family, but his paycheck does not respond to need.

These economic realities confront workers with a long list of harrowing problems. How, for example, do they shelter them against the draft for four years when the cost of sending a son to the state university now averages nearly $2,000 a year? *Perhaps less than a quarter of all high school graduates who are children of factory workers enter college.* (The myth that something like half of all young Americans go to college is very nearly unshatterable. Actually, 46.3 per cent of the 18- and 19-year-olds, but only 19 per cent in the age group of 20-24 are "in school." U.S. Office of Education reports are so unclear here that I suspect the agency of misleading us regarding the accessibility of college opportunities.)

Children of workers are overrepresented in the mass of those excluded from college. Working-class kids make their trips abroad as members of the armed forces, while some middle-class youths, student deferments in hand, spend a junior year at European universities. While the college boy steps on an escalator that moves rapidly upward, the worker's son may step on his father's assembly line and into a job without much promise.

Relatively few colleges, social agencies, schools, or other public institutions mount programs to meet special needs of workers. In many places, even the services provided by "Red Feather" agencies seem more closely geared to middle than working-class needs.

Inevitably, many workers come to feel they are being dunned and taxed for the benefit of others. Considering the notrious imbalance of our tax structure, they have a point. *In general, the rate of taxation declines as income rises.* This is most obviously true of the state sales taxes. It is almost as true of the federal income tax, under which, in the most extreme cases, some individuals and corporations pay little or no tax at all, though their incomes may exceed $5 million annually. Estimates of total tax loads indicate that 33 per cent of the incomes of those earning $3,000 to $5,000 goes to taxes, and only 28 per cent of those earning $15,000 or more.

So we have the case of the "invisible" and aggrieved worker. Many of his breed are even found among Mike Harrington's invisible poor. In fact, about one-third of all heads of impoverished families hold down full-time jobs. They are generally not organized, but they are workers. While millions of workers live in poverty, millions more barely escape it. Most are in income brackets between $3,000 and $10,000 (which includes some 56 per cent of all American families), with probably more workers near the bottom than the top.

Reporters often talk about the sweeper who "makes more than a teacher." True, a sweeper in an auto plant in Michigan or New Jersey probably earns more than a teacher in a backwoods school in Mississippi, but his pay is hardly a pot of gold. The sweeper seems to fit a set of hidden assumptions according to which the society is divided, at a magical line, between rich and poor. The premise of this stereotype is that our class structure is a dualism—rich and poor. In this simplified pseudo-Marxian schema, organized workers are seen as part of the richer half, along with bankers, businessmen, professionals. They are, it is assumed, well-fed, well cared for, up to their hips in "things," and all-around partners in an open and affluent society.

According to this hidden assumption, all or nearly all the poor are black. They are mostly mothers of large families living on welfare in big city ghettos. The rest (except for a few Appalachian whites) are young blacks who can't find jobs because they are school dropouts or because they are excluded from unions by corpulent and corrupt union bosses. So goes this version of things, especially popular in some college circles. But in fact about 80 per cent of the poor are white, and a startling proportion of them work full-time.

In real life the typical worker has lived on a treadmill, except where union contracts have protected him from rises in the cost of living. Everyone else—including the poor and the militant blacks (at least as their image was cast by the media) —*seemed* to be moving forward, while only *they* stood still, waiting in a twilight zone somewhere between hunger and plenty. Some comforts came to them through expanded consumer credit, but the credit exacted high costs in tension, insecurity, and interest rates. They gave increasing taxes to the government, their sons to the army. They seemed to get little in return: only conflict and sometimes mortal combat with the emerging black poor over jobs, neighborhoods and schools.

Here is fertile soil for the growth of resentment. For a time, it grew like a weed under the cultivation of George Wallace.

A turning point in the Presidential campaign may have come when Hubert Humphrey began to see something Wallace always understood: that while many "experts" said the "old issues" were dead, millions of American workers angrily disagreed and wanted a better life. Many workers were ready, in short, for a campaign resembling Harry Truman's historical effort of 1948, a hell-raising campaign about the "old" economic issues (social justice, more and better jobs, more opportunity, good schools, health care, etc.).

The trap almost sprung by Wallace was set by those "opinion-makers" who dismissed all Wallace supporters as red-necked bigots and opponents of Negro aspirations. Fortunately, they were mistaken. While many workers have no doubt been shook up quite a bit by the black revolt, they have been even more shaken by their own failure to get on in life. Being far wiser than we think, they knew this was not the fault of blacks.

Sadly, some of the Wallaceite resentment was, of course, turned against the poor and the black. Yet it is possible that Wallace's exposed bigotry finally did him in among Northern workers. Industrial workers generally have closer relations with Negroes than any other class, and the big factories in steel, auto, rubber, glass, etc., are probably the most integrated work places in the society. Most workers who were drawn to Wallace because he spoke their economic language must have had problems of conscience about blacks with whom they worked and had friendly relations. As Wallace's campaign became more violent in tone, many of them probably grew uneasy and fell away from his camp.

When "opinion-makers" bothered to talk with workers, they found to their surprise that not all were racists. After talking with Wallace supporters in Flint, Michigan (said to be a hotbed of Wallace sentiment), Mike Hubbard, a student editor of the University of Michigan *Daily*, wrote:

> Certainly these Americans do not identify with red-necked racism. . . . No one ever taught them Negro History, but they grew up with blacks. . . . They don't dislike blacks, they just feel black men shouldn't be given a bigger break than anyone else. The white UAW members as a whole do not believe Wallace is a racist. All they know is what

he told them, and he never said he hated blacks. Even the most militant Negro workers I talked to didn't feel there was large-scale prejudice in the Union. They dislike Wallace, but not the men who are voting, for him.

Others found many Wallace supporters who would have preferred Robert Kennedy, and some even Eugene McCarthy. *Time* found many such in its 150 interviews across the country, and Haynes Johnson of the *Washington Star* reported this comment from a leader of the Wallace movement in Duluth, Minnesota: "The reason I got into this actually was when Robert Kennedy was shot. . . . That assassination—plus that of Martin Luther King—pointed up for me just how sick it was in this country, and I decided to do something for my country."

The "new issues"—the war on poverty and bureaucracy, the struggles for racial justice and world peace—can be lost unless they are paralleled by campaigns on issues that are important to those millions who are often ignored except by demagogues.

The mythology that obscures the realities of working-class life derives in large part from the success story of unions and what various observers have made of that story. Unions have made great gains in wages, working conditions, fringe benefits, politics; but they started from very far back, and they are still very far from the millennium. Since our society has been late and miserly in providing social insurance, unions have had to push hard in collective bargaining for benefits that don't show up in pay checks. Their focus on such goals has had some negative side effects. Fringe benefits mean more to older than to younger workers—and it is the young who are drawn to men like George Wallace.

Unless unions were to act irresponsibly toward the aging (one of the most impoverished and helpless groups among us), pensions had to be won. Pensions cost money, and that money was subtracted from the wage package won at the bargaining table. Also, older workers need and make more use of hospitalization, medical and sickness insurance. These too came out of the total package, leaving less for wages. It was humane to help the older worker, and it helped him retire and make way for the younger workers. But it was costly. *In the UAW* *alone, more than 200,000 members have retired and received pension benefits of over $1.5 billion.* Unions sometimes may have overresponded to the older workers, as in seniority and vacation benefits, etc., but one can hardly look at the life of the aging worker and say he has too much.

Unions need to make a new beginning, paying more attention to the needs of the young. An aging and sometimes feeble union leadership needs to refresh itself with activists and new leadership recruited among younger generations. Unless the young become partners in the union movement, they may end up wrecking it. The dramatic rise in the rate of rank-and-file rejection of union contract settlements is a clear signal of distress among workers. Usually, veteran unionists report, the increased rejections result from organized opposition among young workers.

Unions need to do a lot of things, far more than I can mention in this brief space. I come from a union that has split from the AFL over some of these issues, including foreign policy, interest in the poor and minorities, and general militancy. I have opposed the Vietnam War, and I think labor should have. I have been involved in the war on poverty, along with many other unionists though it is remote from many others. Still, one observer says, "If the labor movement in this country moves to the Right, it's not least the fault of those, like Sexton, who will not say a word of criticism of its policies." I leave nothing to the imagination of readers, for we are all deeply aware of the shortcomings of unions. I do not dwell on these flaws for another reason: whatever their blemishes, unions have given workers the only support and attention they have had—and they needed a lot.

Unions are, however, limited in what they can do for members. They are limited by their own willingness and that of their members to go into battle, to strike. They are limited by the public's willingness to accept strikes. The middle-class liberal himself is often offended, sometimes outraged, by strikers. He may say, "They're selfish and out for themselves." When the desperately poor hospital worker strikes, the liberal will see only the patient as victim; but he will offer no clues as to how else the hospital worker can win a measure of justice. When subway and sanitation workers in New York strike for a modest $3.50 or so an hour (to perform some of the most disagreeable jobs known to man), many middle-class liberals complain bitterly, without also noting that New York's affluent can afford to pay men decent wages to do hard, often danger-ous, aways unpleasant work.

Many liberals dismiss as unimportant, if not irrelevant, every claim workers make for their attention and support. In few cases do they distinguish workers from union leaders, from some of whom their contempt may be warranted. It is not sur-prising, considering their mentors, that so much of the young New Left seems to despise the working class.

Not since the early and dramatic days of the CIO have lib-erals and intellectuals (with some honorable exceptions) shown much sympathetic interest in workers or unions. Now workers come sharply to their view only when they threaten to make life inconvenient or dangerous. A subway strike, shutdown at *The New York Times*, a large vote for Wallace may do the trick—momentarily.

I believe that liberals and moderate leftists—in whose circle opinion-makers are heavily represented—are out of touch with the reality of American working-class life. Many of them live at rarified levels where almost everyone's income is at least $15,000 a year. *Less than ten per cent of the nation's families earn that much;* still they form a mass of between 18 and 20 million people. Those who live within it can easily come to think that all Americans, except the poor, are living just about as they and their colleagues and neighbors do. Having little contact outside their own circles, and having heard so much about the great gains of unions, they may naturally assume that workers have made it too.

Many of these opinion-makers are men of my generation or near it. Forgetting the ravages of inflation, they may think of $6,000 a year as a fairly substantial income. They may remem-ber a modest existence on even less. I recall that I was 35 years old when I first earned $5,000 a year as president of the nation's second largest local union. Now when I hear that auto workers gross more than $8,000, I too sometimes forget the dollar's decline and assume they've got it made. Relative to most other workers, they have; but they are still far from well-off. These opinion-makers greatly influence what appears in periodicals and dailies, and what is said on TV and radio. They often draft political platforms and write candidates' speeches. When they don't, their readers do. They think of themselves as open-minded and sensitive, and sometimes they are. But too often their politics are introspective—concentrated only on issues that touch them, plus a now fashionable interest in the poor.

Their political attitudes are sometimes expressed in the kind of thin-lipped and vinegary liberalism that found its ultimate expression in Senator McCarthy's endorsement of Hubert Humphrey. To the dismay of at least one early supporter—me—McCarthy urged in that endorsement that the rights of honest draft dissenters be protected but said nothing about the draft's discrimination against Negroes, the poor, and the working class, and made no significant comments about other social and economic issues. The Senator's failure to ignite fires outside the midle class can easily be understood in the light of that arid statement. In the primary campaign his speeches (at least in the printed text) were often unexceptionable; but, notoriously, he often left unsaid what decent liberals and radicals on his staff wrote into those speeches. Later in the campaign, and in the Senate leadership fight, the warts on that handsome liberal facade grew larger.

Senator McCarthy, like some who supported him, had to subdue his conscience before endorsing Hubert Humphrey, yet he has always seemed comfortable with Senator William Fulbright, a man whose record on civil rights almost duplicates George Wallace's except for greater gentility of expression.* (A friend explained to me that he could support Fulbright because the Senator had "style," a matter of overriding merit to many liberals.) Finally, petulance and spleen seemed to consume this hero of the middle-class liberals when he chose Long over Kennedy.

The chemistry of the Kennedys has been different. The contrast is highlighted in Senator Edward Kennedy's appeal to

---

*I don't wish to downgrade Senator Fulbright's obvious courage. We are all in his debt. Some young Americans may owe him their lives. I do wish to point out that liberal and radical intellectuals of principle are also capable of compromise, though their evaluation of issues may differ from the trade unionists or even the black militants.

supporters of his two slain brothers to reject the "dark" and "extremist" movement of George Wallace.

> Most of these people [Kennedy said of Wallace supporters] are not motivated by racial hostilty or prejudice. They feel that their needs and their problems have been passed over by the tide of recent events. They bear the burden of the unfair system of Selective Service. They lose out because higher education costs so much. They are the ones who feel most threatened at the security of their jobs, the safety of their families, the value of their property and the burden of their taxes. They feel the established system has not been sympathetic to them in their problems of everyday life and in a large measure they are right.

If a meaningful New Politics is to work in this country it must be based on the kind of empathy expressed in these words.

Too few liberals realize that millions of workers and voters fit Ted Kennedy's description. Young workers outnumber all college students, and there are perhaps 15 or 20 of them for every one disaffected youth upon whom various advocates of a New Politics are counting. The big three in auto alone employ about 250,000 workers who are 30 or under. Total UAW membership of that age group may reach 600,000, with perhaps half of these under 25. Among organized workers, possibly 5 million are young people under 30.

Young workers seem to be tougher and to have more staying power than students. Their stake in social change may turn out to be greater and more compelling. Most will never experience the softening effects of well-paid, high-status jobs in the professional, academic, artistic, or business worlds—jobs to which most student rebels are on their way. Knowing they're unlikely to escape individually, workers can grow desperate when denied political hope.

One pollster puts many workers in the "no change" coalition. He misunderstands. Workers simply oppose changes that benefit or seem to benefit others while increasing their own burdens.

The auto industry average wage of $3.80 per hour, though

the highest in manufacturing, still does not mean affluence. The UAW (like many other unions) has won comprehensive medical protection, including coverage for psychiatric care of a million members. Its contracts now provide tuition remission plans for members who wish to take classes that may help them escape from dead-end factory jobs. In December of 1968, the hourly wage system came close to ending for perhaps a million UAW members; thus, in one industry, workers have almost scaled an important barrier between them and the middle class; they will be salaried rather than hourly workers. UAW contracts have moved toward the guaranteed annual income and retirement with decent security. Gains have been made, yes; but even auto workers still have far to go.

One friend tells me, "intellectuals still cling to a hopeful and perhaps incorrect view, idealizing the union members as an instrument of class struggle." What members and their unions try to do, at best, is not class struggle in any classic sense. Their conscious antagonists are the employer and the conservative legislator, not the "capitalist system." Yet their efforts have profoundly influenced American life. And unionists have tasted enough of victory so that they generally do not believe in the "final conflict" for which the "prisoners of starvation" must arise.

Those publicists who seek such an apocalypse will not find unionists mounting the barricades with the swiftness and pleasure of student rebels or black militants. Unionists have learned a hard lesson after almost a century of fierce blood-letting on the picket line: *that combat is the last, not the first, resort.* Unionists have possibly been too moderate in this respect, for open conflict sometimes is the only way to rally people and get what you want. But they have learned many other good ways to get on with it. They will not be found burning down their own neighborhoods to prove a point, or otherwise sacrificing their own ranks in unproductive, self-destructive conflict. In this respect, interestingly, some black militants seem to be taking a rather active interest in labor studies. Most militants, coming from poor families, are interested in the "old issues" (opportunity, jobs, etc.) and in ways of organizing people for effective action. A similar interest in unions has not come to the campus, thanks to the myth of the middle-class worker and other academic folklore. (My wife and I taught a graduate sociology course at NYU last year in Labor and Society. So far as I know—outside the narrow limits of labor-and-industrial programs—it is the *only* such course taught in the country.)

Workers and their unions have many problems and they need lots of help. On the other side, the middle-class Left may find itself isolated if it accepts the standard mythology about workers. If they are to create a New Society, liberals and radicals need to become aware of socially excluded workers and find avenues of communication with them, as well as with Negroes, Latin Americans, and the oppressed poor generally.

The Grape Boycott Farce

Melvin Munn

My family and I took a brief vacation in the summer of 1968, and elected to go to Southern California, among other points to the west.

I had heard a great deal about suppression in the vineyards of California, so I did some investgating. After that, I compiled much information from both sides of what has been a long and senseless struggle.

From the first it was obvious that the public in general has a mistaken idea of what is actually taking place in the grape growing areas of California.

According to Cesar Chavez, director of the "United Farm Workers Organizing Committee," grape workers in the Delano, California, area are miserably paid, poorly housed, and variously abused. He goes about the country urging Americans to help feed hungry children who are the victims of a system that he claims, denies men a living wage.

The typical Chavez "handout" is a printed pamphlet that claims: "At present rates a farm worker who is fortunate enough to work 40 hours a week, 52 weeks a year, would earn $2,386."

This is sheer nonsense. Any reporter taking the time to check payrolls, walk into the fields, visit with the workers, step into their homes, and inspect the labor camps gets a totally different picture. Even today the base wage for grape workers is $1.65 an hour. At 40 hours a week, 52 weeks a year, his earnings would be $3,432. That is $1,100 more than Chavez claimed. Even so, this example has no illustration in practice. Grape workers do not work in this fashion.

Were you to go to Delano, or any grape growing area in California that has not yet surrendered to Chavez, you would discover that the average grape picker is a middle-class Mexican-American, with little formal education and few skills beyond those of the grape and vegetable culture. He will have a wife and two or three teenaged children. He will have up to a dozen different employers during the year. A normal bargaining unit is out of the question since the workers move around from one vineyard to another.

Picking grapes is tough work. In the summer it is hot and hard. At other times it can be pleasant, more like a picnic. Families do take their lunches to the fields. A family of four earns about $325 a week, including base wage and incentive supplements. At harvest time, this amount can double. One such family drives a 1968 station wagon and has a son in college. They are not the exception, but rather the rule.

Cesar Chavez wants to control the table grape business in Southern California. His efforts to recruit union labor have been a flop. His publicity efforts, on the other hand, have had remarkable success. Chavez has enlisted hippies, priests, professors, political figures, Yippies, and housewives all across the country in support of the nonexistent "downtrodden grape pickers" of Kern County, California.

The workers have informal organizations, and their spokesmen are trying their best to "tell it like it is.' Grape pickers do not get rich, but they are far from starving. When housewives in New York City refuse to buy james and jellies made from Southern California grapes, they are promoting a one-man power grab effort almost without parallel in the history of farming.

The workers themselves speak of Chavez with fear and contempt. They tell of threatening telephone calls at night, of repeated acts of vandalism and intimidation. They are afraid that growers, in an attempt to end the nationwide boycott, may sell out to Chavez, who would then control them and their jobs.

Cesar Chavez is trying to secure press-gang power over the grape workers. He wants his organization to become the sole source of agricultural workers, under contracts that would forbid the growers to hire any nonunion men. That, my friends is precisely what the fight is all about. It is amazing that liberals, professing a love for the little man, would give active support to a movement designed to ensnare and trap free Americans who have not asked Cesar Chavez or anybody else to run their lives for them.

The Union has called on members and friends of the Union to write to their Congressmen and Senators protesting this flagrant Union-busting with tax payers' money. And it is more important than ever to continue and to expand the grape boycott in the U.S. and Canada to counter the military's insidious strike-breaking plot.

The Army Buys Up Grapes . . . to Defend the American Way of Life?

El Malcriado

The end of the government's fiscal year, 1969, on June 30 closed the books on the Federal government's most blatant attempt in recorded history to break a labor Union through massive purchases of scab products.

The United Farm Workers Organizing Committee has repeatedly charged over the last two years that the Federal government, and especially the U.S. Defense Department, have

Schism v.1, no.2 (Winter 1970)

sought to bust the Union's boycott of table grapes by huge purchases of the grapes for distribution to the armed forces.

On June 6, 1969, the Department of Defense released information to the Los Angeles Times and other newspapers which tragically confirm the worst of the Union's accusations.

• The Department of Defense says it is now shipping eight times more grapes to U.S. Troops in Vietnam than in any previous year. "There is no record of any grapes shipped to Vietnam prior to fiscal year 1967," the Department of Defense admits. In the fiscal year ending June 30, 1967, U.S. taxpayers payed for 468,000 pounds of grapes shipped to Vietnam. The following year (which was the first of the all-out grape boycott effort) purchases of scab grapes jumped to 555,000. For the first half of this year purchases topped 2,000,000 pounds. Defense Department officials admitted that purchases of the scab grapes were expected to top 4,000,000 pounds for the year, when all figures were in and recorded for the fiscal year ending June 30.

• The Department of Defense admits that overall purchases of grapes, for armed forces in this country, Vietnam, Europe, and elsewhere, were expected to top 16 million pounds this year, compared to 7.5 million pounds in 1967.

• Civilian purchases of grapes in Vietnam jumped from 350,000 two years ago to 2,800,000 last year. Most of these purchases are by the Government (Departments of State, Agriculture, etc.) for consumption by their "advisors" in that war-torn country.

The Defense Department says that the increases are due to increased "Troop acceptance." The Department also states in a "fact sheet" whch it distributes, "The Department of Defense does not purchase grapes merely because they have been made more available and less expensive due to the effects of the boycott. . . . In the interests of objectve and systematic management, menu planners . . . should not be required to consider whether a labor dispute exists when making these decisions."

Spokesmen for the UFWOC charge that, on the contrary, the tremendous increase in grape purchases can only be explained by the fact that purchasers for the Department of Defense and other Federal Agencies knew about the boycott and *were under orders to help the grape growers defeat the union.* "The military has been buying up dumped California grapes as a market of last resort for the struck grape growers," charged UFWOC research director Jerry Brown. "Giumarra and Bozich and the other 93% of the grape growers who have refused to negotiate with the Union are counting on the Federal Government's spending tax-payers' money to bail them out from the effects of the international boycott of table grapes."

The Union has called on members and friends of the Union to write to their Congressmen and Senators protesting this flagrant Union-busting with taxpayers' money. And it is more important than ever to continue and to expand the grape boycott in the U.S. and Canada to counter the military's insidious strike-breaking plot.

Race Relations

"PROWL CAR 39 THINKS HE JUST SEEN A SUSPECTED BLACK PANTHER CARRYIN' WHAT HE IMAGINES COULD BE A CONCEALED LETHAL WEAPON!"

Reprinted in *Schism* v.1, no.2 (Winter 1970) from *Heterodoxical Voice* v.1, no.16 (Oct. 1970).

State vs. Racial Nationalism

Peter the Hermit

It is generally agreed by most right-thinking individuals that internationalism is basically a crock of warmed-up, left-over crap for the slobs and boobs called the people, pushed by fat-cat businessmen, illuminated bankers, cretinous educators and the tribal descendants of King Bulan.

Most of us agree that internationalism seeks to mongrelize the races, to compress all of us into soulless, amorphous, opaque beings of "diversified greatness," if we may quote the glorious Harry Golden.

But what about nationalism? Is that healthy? Isn't nationalism the direct opposite of the hated internationalism? Isn't a nationalist someone who puts country first? . . . a patriot? . . . a man whose eyes glisten whenever the flag passes before him and he hears his national anthem being played? We can be sure that this is a form of nationalism known as *state nationalism,* or love of state, the type most thrilling to conservatives.

A provincial, narrow, state nationalism of flag waving has been the nationalism that has been promoted for years by the war merchants and political profiteers. The hideous fiasco in Vietnam is the most current example of how the cream of our White youth can be convinced to spill their blood fighting Bolshevist Asiatics on behalf of non-Bolshevist Asiatics, for a milk-sopped ideal known as democracy or "The American Way of Life."

State nationalism brought about the Peloponnesian Wars which resulted in the destruction of Greece in its golden age of Nordic Culture. State nationalism helped bring about the

Schism v.1, no.2 (Winter 1970)

Thirty Years War and sucessfully wiped out some of the best stock in Germany. State nationalism, inspired by mercantile imperialism, brought about the monstrous fratricidal war in 1914, leaving Europe's White population stock greatly depleted. And let us not forget the great bloodletting of the American Civil War—international interests promoting a perverse "nationalism" north and south, resulting in hundreds of thousands of our finest Whitemen of that era being ground into the dust of untold battlefields. In 1941, using a racial war with Japan and the secret reason of saving Bolshevism in Russia, America rushed into the Euorpean meatgrinder to join the slaughter of the White Race, Roosevelt, of course, was a big flag-waving promoter of state nationalism, while at the same time organized the U.N. behind our backs!

The raceless conception of the basis of nationality, officially sanctioned and promoted by the American state was codified at Columbia University by the Jew, Franz Boaz: "A nationality is any group of people who speak a common language, share common historical tradition and share common geographical circumstances."

Thus, we use geographical criteria and not racial to describe the "nationality" of a man. This induces xenophobia, or fear or hatred of strangers or foreign persons. Just witness the endless bickering and petty arguments at some of the so-called "anti-Bolshevist" groups. The Poles hate the Germans, the Germans hate the French, the French hate the English, the English hate the Russians, the Russians hate the Italians, etc., etc. ad nauseaum. If they would only stop and recognize that they are all descended from a long and complicated line of Franks, Jutes, Angles, Saxons, Burgundians, Norsemen, Goths, Lombards and Swabians, and that finally, they are merely representatives of formations which have grown out of the great Aryan migrations.

Because of the different linguistic and geographical considerations, xenophobia within the White Family is multiplied. This is certainly not the case with the negroid. He is calling for an all-out race war and is ready for it. He has no past cultural differences with other negroids to cause disunity. When the time comes, he will paint *"soul"* on his shop windows and grab his machete.

The Oriental man, with his infinite patience, bides his time and plays the waiting game. He waits for the dying gasp of the White People before he makes his decisive move. Either way, militarily under Red China or economically under Japan, the Oriental man stands united.

Meanwhile, back in the States . . . your favorite hero, *Whiteman,* won't unite because he's too stupid.

Whiteman, you are indeed a difficult student! When you burn your fingers a hundred times on the stove, one would think you would keep your hands away . . . so why do you insist on putting them on the stove again?

Remember these words spoken many years ago: "We must not allow the greater racial community to be torn apart by the divergencies of the individual peoples. A culture which spans millenia and embraces Hellenism and Teutonism is fighting for its existence."

The Fallacy of Race and the Arab-Israeli Conflict

Ray L. Cleveland

Nationalism, as based on racism, has contributed grievously to international conflicts, and there is no major world problem more confused by the mingled concepts of race and nation than the one which boils around the state of Israel. Discussion of the Arab-Israeli conflict—and unfortunately not only that which is partisan and propagandistic—is literally drenched in the fallacy of race. Nearly every facet of the endless literature on the subject, written from nearly every emotional standpoint, exhibits aspects of the racial mythology which plagues

Schism v.1, no.2 (Winter 1970)

This article, reprinted with permission from *Issues* (Winter 1969), is not fully representative of the viewpoints of The American Council for Judaism.

mankind like an incurable disease. While God is not represented as being a respecter of persons either by reason of social status or communal identity, it seems that man is determined to remain so.

An all-embracing definition of the fallacy of race would be
lengthy and intricate, for there are a number of false notions
involved in the popular concept of race, and these erroneous
ideas support various types of racism. Perhaps the most widespread and injurious racism is that which assumes a necessary
connection between external physical characteristics (such as
skin pigmentation) and personality. One aspect of the fallacy
of race which lies behind this type of racism is defined by
Ashley Montague (*Man's Most Dangerous Myth*) as "the belief that physical and mental traits are linked, that the physical
differences are associated with rather pronounced differences
in mental capacities, and that these differences are measurable
by IQ tests and the cultural achievements of these populations." Most other manifestations of the fallacy of race are
based on this idea or are complementary to it.

A second widespread and unscientific assumption about race
is that clearly definable races or peoples exist and that these
constitute national groups—if not actually, then potentially.
This racial basis for nationalism is not regarded merely as
existing at present, but as having a historical dimension. In the
conceptual world of those who think in terms of the proposition race-nation there are no problems in determining who is
and who is not, e.g., an Italian, and furthermore, there is no
doubt about all Italians being descendants of ancient Romans.
Critical poeple know this attitude lacks objective validity; yet
the tendency to racial categorizing continues to influence and
even dominate the thinking of most people, often the thinking
of those who have presumably been educated to a high degree
of critical sophistication.

What are the forms in which the fallacy of race appears in
the Arab-Israeli conflict? Well, indeed, the very use of the
parallel terms *Jews* and *Arabs* is fraught with racial implications. These are exacerbated by statements, conciliatory in intent, to the effect that Arabs and Jews are fellow-Semites. The
historical dimension is rendered more explicit through references to Ishmael and Isaac as the respective ancestors of the
two "peoples," while the present conflict is traced back to such

events as the raids of Midianites on the Hebrews in the time of the Judges. Finally, the race-nation fallacy is sealed by the identification of Jews with the state of Israel and Arabs with the nation-states of the Arab League.

Thus the current conflict is viewed as the only most recent stage of relations between two races of people, relations which began with Isaac and Ishmael. A long history is then traced in the relations between the descendants of the two sons of Abraham. The most elaborate treatment along the lines of the contacts and conflicts of the two groups is found in the book *Jews and Arabs,* which was written in scholarly terms by S. Goitein more than a decade ago. However, many of the assumptions underlying this historical interpretation lack any kind of validating data, and the widespread acceptance of this racial approach has obscured the real nature of the present conflict.

In discussing the elements of this racial interpretation of the conflict, one may begin with the present and point out that there is neither an Arab nor a Jewish race in any meaningful scientific sense, i.e., neither grouping has pervasive physical characteristics which distinguish it from other groups.

The case of "Arabs" may be considered first, and we discover immediately that there is no universally accepted definition of who an Arab is. Is an Arab anyone who is a citizen of a nation which is a member of the Arab League? Or is it anyone who speaks Arabic as his native tongue: (In view of the many Arabic-speaking Jews, this raises some very interesting considerations.) Or perhaps anyone who belongs to Arab culture? Or is being an Arab an entirely subjective matter— anyone who regards himself as being an Arab is Arab? Even excluding all those who do not meet the narrowest of definitions, it is, next, quite obvious that the range of physical characteristics and societal habits is so broad that it is difficult to think of all those identified as Arab as being one people. Certainly they cannot be regarded as a single race. In skin color alone, individual Arabs vary from blond to Negroid, while there are likewise great variations in such old-time anthropometric standbys as cranial measurements. It is, in fact, totally impossible to isolate an Arab type.

Nevertheless, the popular notion still being propagated is that Arabs are in some way a race of people with particular traits both physical and cultural. Then, by parallel use of the

terms *Jews*, the same category is implied for that identification, although the only definition for *Jews* which has any positive relevance is essentially religious. A Jew is one associated
with the faith of Judaism either through personal commitment
or birth. A visit to Israel and a few days observation of "in-
gathered" Jews is sufficient to convince any intelligent and
open-minded person that there is neither a Jewish physical nor
cultural type. There is no distinguishing pattern in the variety
of physical characteristics, and the social behavior of Jews from
Asia and Africa is as different from that of European Jews
as the cultural patterns of any Europeans from those of Afro-
Asians. Cultural assimilation in Israel, as well as social discrimination, is an enormous problem which has remained muted
only because of the feeling of common outside danger.

The dichotomy which exists in thinking about the question
of Jewish identity is reflected in *Race and Science* (published
by the Columbia University Press for UNESCO). While one
anthropologist dispatches the myth of a Jewish race, another
writer in the same volume uses the word *people* with all the
connotations of *race*, even after admitting that there is no
biological Jewish race. This is an example of how objective
knowledge may be overridden by subjective factors; thought
patterns may follow old habits or may conform to precon-
ceived ideology without regard to the most significant data.

The terms *Semite* and *Semitic* were first used in English in
the nineteenth century when not so incidentally racist anthropology was flourishing. The earlier form *Shemite* reveals the
origin of the words Shemites were the supposed descendants
of Shem, one of the sons of Noah. In those days, before
anthropology had emerged as the science it is now, contemporary Jews were regarded as the principal Shemites. The Old
Testament account of Noah and his offspring, however, does
not in any way justify the nineteenth-century concept. While
descendants of Shem in the early generations may have been
accurately informed of their genealogies, moderns have no data
whatever in this matter. Just as it is improper to base slavery
on the concept that Africans are the descendants of Noah's son
Ham, it is also erroneous to base racial attitudes on the assumption that Shem's descendants can be identified with any
modern division of the human race.

The only scientific use of the term *Semitic* is as a description of a family of languages and even there the term is arbitrary. In the nineteenth century linguists worked out the relationships of such languages as Accadian, Aramaic, Hebrew, Ethiopic and Arabic; scholars began describing them as Semitic languages, because in the Bible people using these languages were listed as descendants of Shem. The people who used Semitic languages in ancient times or who now use them are not all members of a single race which can be differentiated from other races. The idea that language is of necessity linked to race is a myth. For instance: the majority of English-speaking people in North America today are not the descendants of people who were English. Anthropologically speaking, language is a part of non-material culture, and all such cuture may be transferred quite independently of biological generation. The overall effect is that the use of the term *Semite* is misleading; it can properly refer only to a person who uses a language belonging to a certain racial group, characterized in one respect by language. As a consequence, *Semite* is a word which could be happily dropped from the language entirely.

To assert that Jews and Arabs are fellow-Semites, as is frequently done, assumes that there is a race of Semites, a people with some common traits and ancestry, and that both Jews and Arabs belong to this race. (The well-known scholar Philip Hitti makes this error in his book, *The Arabs: A Short History*.) There is not in the first place sufficient uniformity among individuals collectively labeled either as Jews or Arabs to justify regarding them as races separately; any attempt to justify the concept of a broader Semitic race fails on the same grounds. The total lack of realism in this view should be manifest when one compares a blond Israeli with a Negro of Ethiopia, where the major tongue is as fully Semitic as Hebrew or Arabic.

Whatever the proper theological interpretation of the Biblical account of Isaac and Ishmael may be, it has no relationship in any objective way with the people who are presently labeled as Jews and Arabs. That is to say, there is no historical or anthropological basis for identifying or equating modern people bearing these names with ancient people to whom the same labels are affixed.

There has been so much movement of people into and out

of the Arab area that modern Arabs cannot even be identified with Arab's of Mohammed's time. The Arabs of the early seventh century A.D. nearly all lived in the Arabian Peninsula. Those known as Arabs today live in an area many times as large; religion, language and some other aspects of culture spread to a large geographical area from Arabia, but these were carried by relatively few people. The native populations of countries in the Syrian region and in North Africa were Arabized; they were not driven out and replaced by newcomers from Arabia. Then in subsequent centuries there were invasions by Mongols, Turks, European Crusaders and others, as well as peaceful immigrants. Each group left its demographic imprint, so that the composition of the people known as Arabs gradually changed.

A similar process affected those who followed the religion of Judaism. Many ancient Judaeans did not leave their homeland, but remained to be Hellenized, Christianized and then Islamized and Arabized. Those who went into the diaspora generally took on the biological, as well as the cultural characteristics of the various communities in which they lived, even when they were prevented from assimilating fully. There were converts from paganism and Christianity to Judaism, while some Jews converted to Christianity and thus dropped out of Jewish history, biologically as well as culturally. No reasonable claim for a unilinear racial continuity from ancient Hebrews and Judeans to modern Jews can be advanced. Yet this very concept underlies most thinking about the history of the Jews and their "return" to Israel. The subtlety of this and other assumed ideas is deceptive, and many readers may deny the extent to which false racial attitudes affect their view.

Many speakers and writers have in all good faith advanced many of these mistaken ideas in the interest of conciliation; yet the general effect of the racial outlook has been divisive. Those directly involved in the Arab-Israeli struggle have this in common: they are members of the same race, the single human race which is universal and to which we all belong. The differences within the species are minor when compared with the similarities. Regional and world peace can be guaranteed only when this is globally recognized. The selfish interests of one party or the other in any dispute too often overlook the proposition that in the broadest sense we all share in a common destiny in terms of the world's history. The elimination of the myth of race from our thinking about human conflicts, such as that which bedevils Palestine, is essential. In this particular problem, to dispel the fallacy of race could produce more flexibility on the part of the partisans and more intelligent help from the outside world.

Is the Concept of Race Evil?

James H. Madole

The chief exponents and political theorists of both Marxism and Capitalism are united in their mutual hatred of those courageous souls who dare to proclaim that *race* and not *economic factors* determines the capacity of a nation to survive and erect pillars for a mighty civilization. The National Renaissance Party believes that *quality* is more essential than *quantity* in building the edifice of a Racial National State on the North American Continent hence we are slowly but surely creating a *leadership cadre* that can withstand both success and defeat yet always return undaunted to the battle for our race and nation. Some few will fall by the wayside because they were fundamentally too weak for this kind of struggle but those who remain after passing through every form of adversity will *be as gods among mortal men!* To these men I look to create an Aryan Empire greater than Imperial Rome under the Caesars or Egypt under the Pharaohs.

The racial philosophy of the NRP dictates that humanity, like all other forms of life, must live in accordance with the immutable Laws of Nature which govern the universe and not seek to develop humanistic, man-made creeds which attempt to nurture and protect those racial elements whose capacity

Schism v.1, no.3 (Summer 1970)

for civilization and progress is absolutely nil. These un-natural credos, largely promulgated by Jews and Christian religious fanatics, have flagrantly violated *cosmic law* with the result that America is rapidly degenerating into a "Welfare State" overflowing with non-productive, illiterate Negroid-White, Negroid-Indian, and Negroid-Asian hybrids whom the productive Aryan remnant of our population must support through excessive taxation. A mixed race can never form a sufficiently powerful base to support the pyramid of civilization as any tourist who has travelled in Brazil, Central America, the Caribbean Islands or the sub continent of India can tell you from bitter personal experience. Because the NRP places the concept of *race* foremost in its program for the resurrection of White Civilization in the United States both Marxists and Conservatives have reviled us in their periodicals. Both of these fallacious economic dogmas glorify the "mass-man" although both Russian Communism and American Capitalism are confronted with the irrevocable Natural Law which dictates that *quality* will rise above *quantity* through the process of Natural Selection of competition between individuals, nations or races. This holds true whether in a primitive jungle environment or in the steel, glass, and concrete metropolis of modern industrial society. Sometimes when puny humanity becomes "over-civilized" they sink into decadence and make vain efforts to overcome the Laws of the Universe (which are the Laws of the Cosmic Architect or Creator) by encouraging the survival of the weakling and the mindless primitive but those fools who dare to transgress against Nature are ever doomed to retribution through extinction of their species.

The NRP is not concerned with flattering subhumans in order to assure American Capitalist consumer markets in Africa or amongst Afro-Americans and half-castes. Fitness to survive in this universe is determined solely by struggle hence men with high intelligence encased in strong bodies and Aryan women whose beauty, inner strength, and femininity will make them fit mothers and devoted wives. A new humanity, not Capitalist consumer markets, will assure the future mastery of this globe by *Aryan man*. Our leaders will not be "mass-men" or political hacks produced from a ballot box as were Nixon, Johnson, Eisenhower, Truman ad nauseam but rather men who embody the collective will and genius of our race; the philosopher-kings of Plato incarnated within a God-like personality. These leaders will not be motivated by false humanist considerations but solely by the current needs of the Aryan Race whose collective will they physically embody. The early ancestors of present-day humanity, the Cro-Magnards and Grimaldi men, expressed by instinct their obedience to Natural Law when they first came into physical contact with the bestial Neanderthal species of submen. There was no hue and cry for "civil rights" by our more sensible ancestors. We quote from *Outline of History* by the renowned historian, H. G. Wells: "The appearance of these truly human post-glacial Palaeolithic peoples was certainly an enormous leap forward in the history of mankind. Both of these main races had a human forebrain, a human hand, an intelligence very like our own. They dispossessed the Neanderthal from his caverns and his stone quarries. And they agreed with modern ethnologists, (students of race) it would seem, in regarding him as a different species. Unlike most savage conquerors, who take the women of the defeated side for their own and interbreed with them, it would seem that the true men would have nothing to do with the Neanderthal race, women or men. There is no trace of any intermixture between the races, in spite of the fact that the newcomers, being also flint users, were establishing themselves in the very same spots that their predecessors had occupied."

We know nothing of the appearance of the Neanderthal man, but this absence of intermixture seems to suggest an extreme hairiness, an ugliness, or a repulsive strangeness over and above his low forehead, his beetle brows his ape neck, and his inferior stature. Or he—and she—may have been too fierce to tame. Says Sir Harry Johnston in a survey of the rise of modern man in his *Views and Reviews*: "The dim racial remembrance of such gorilla-like monsters, with cunning brains, shambling gait, hairy bodies, strong teeth, and possibly cannibalistic tendencies, may be the germ of the ogre in folklore." Life has been a constant struggle between opposing species, races, and nations for living space, sustenance, the right to procreate, and the right to dominate lesser species. Every species of living creature, whether plant or animal, struggles for survival against those who seek to supplant it and Nature and the *Cosmic Deity* through the process of evolution (both mental and physical) will ever develop new, more adaptable, mentally superior organisms. This struggle amongst life forms has been going on for at least 500 million years on this planet alone. The procession of life over this vast time period was beautifully portrayed by A. Merritt in his book: *The Metal Monster,* as follows:

> Nor is Jehovah the God of myriads of millions who through those same centuries, and centuries upon centuries before them, found earth a garden and a grave— and all these countless gods and goddesses only phantom barriers by man to stand between him and the eternal forces man's instinct has always warned him are ever in readiness to destroy. That do destroy him as soon as his vigilance relaxes, his resistance weakens—the eternal, ruthless law that will annihilate humanity the instant it runs counter to that law and turns its will and strength against itself . . .
>
> Weaklings praying for miracles to make easy the path their own wills should clear. Beggars who whine for alms from dreams. Shirkers each struggling to place upon his God the burden whose carrying and whose carrying alone can give him strength to walk free and unafraid, himself godlike among the stars . . . Dominion over all the earth? Yes—as long as man is fit to rule; no longer. Science has warned us. Where was the mamal when the giant reptiles reigned? Slinking hidden and afraid in the dark and secret places. Yet man sprang from these skulking beasts . . . For how long a time in the history of the earth has man been master of it? For a breath— for a cloud's passing. And will remain master only until something grown stronger wrests mastery from him even as he wrested it from his ravening kind—as they took it from the reptiles as did the reptiles from the giant saurians—which snatched it from the nightmare rulers of the Triassic—and so down to whatever held sway in the murk of earth dawn. Life! Life! Life everywhere struggling for completion! Life crowding other life aside, bat-

tling for its moment of supremacy, gaining it, holding it
for one rise and fall of the wings of time beating though
eternity—and then—hurled down, trampled under the
feet of another straining life whose hour has struck . . .
Life crowding outside every barred threshold in a million
circling worlds, yes, in a million rushing universes; pressing against the doors, bursting them down, overwhelming,
forcing out those dwellers who had thought themselves so
secure.

You can see that Natural Law which governs this universe
has no use for cliches about tolerance and "brotherly love."
This liberal democratic nonsense is purely a self-destructive
impulse on the part of weaklings and misfits to rationalize
their failure in the competition of life. Such human failures
and freaks of nature as sex perverts, nihilists, religious crack-
pots seeking utopian phantasms in which the weak always
supplant the strong and healthy; these are the sub-humans in
our Western Society who combine with racial inferiors to overthrow Western Civilization. We quote from an article entitled,
"Der Untermensch," or "Sub-Man," published by the education division of the Nazi SS in 1942. "As night rises against
day, as light and shade are each other's eternal enemies, so
the greatest enemy of man—of man, the master of this universe—is man himself. Sub-man, the biologically apparently
quite similar creation of nature, with hands, feet, and a sort
of brain. But it is a very different sort of creature, a terrifying
creature—a mere projection of a man. His features may re-
semble man, but intellectually, spiritually, he is lower than
any animal. His inmost being is a cruel chaos of wild, unbridled passions—an unbounded will to destruction, the most
primitive desires, undisguised baseness. Sub-man, nothing else!
For not all is equal that bears the human face. Woe to him
who forgets that! Whatever this earth has produced by way
of great works, thoughts, and arts, man has thought of it, created it, completed it. Man contemplated, man invented. Man
had but one aim: to work his way up to a high existence, to
complete the incomplete, to replace the imperfect with the better. Thus culture grew. Thus the plough came into existence,
thus tools, thus the house. Thus man became social. Thus the

family was created, and the nation, and the state. Thus man became good and great. Thus he excelled all other living creatures. Thus he became God's neighbor! But sub-man lived, too. He hated the work of the other. He raged against it—secretly, as a thief; publicly, as a slanderer, as a murderer. Like found like. Beast called to beast. Never did sub-man give peace. For what he needed was semi-darkness, was chaos. He shunned the light of cultural progress. What he needed for his selfpreservation was the morass, was hell, not the sun. And this sub-world of sub-man found its leader: *the eternal Jew! . . ."*

Lessons from Mein Kampf:
White Racial Solidarity

White Power

The building of Aryan racial solidarity is not only the goal of the National Socialist White People's Party in its struggle in North America; it has been the goal of the entire National Socialist movement since its inception.

There are two aspects to our struggle toward this goal: one, which applies principally to North America, is the development of a militant White solidarity specifically to combat the rising Black menace here; the other is the much longer-range development of a strong sense of racial identity and racial idealism in all the healthy and sound elements of our race throughout the world.

In striving toward this long range goal, perhaps the greatest obstacle which stands in our way is parochial state-nationalism —that is, the identification of the individual's interests with those of some geographically defined political entity rather than with those of his race.

The rise of widespread state-nationalism may have been a reasonable and natural historical phenomenon—that is, it may have served a real need in the history of our race. But for quite a number of years now it has played a purely negative role.

In partciular it has given our racial enemy, the Jew, an enormous advantage in his never ending war against us: state nationalism was the means used to engage our race in two great and senseless acts of fratricide in the last half-century.

Beyond the need to eliminate the threat of further fratricide by replacing national parochialism with a sense of Aryan racial brotherhood throughout the world, we should understand that we can have a full realization of the National Socialist idea only when our Movement has embraced all the Aryan nations of the world. For the success of the Movement in any one nation can be only a partial success.

This pan-Aryan aspect of National Socialism is one of the things the Leader brought out in *Mein Kampf*. It is important to call attention to this point in combatting the erroneous notion that National Socialism is tied specifically to German state-nationalism.

In the chapter of *Mein Kampf* titled "The State," Adolf Hitler says:

> We must not allow the greater racial community to be torn apart by the differences of the individual peoples. The struggle that rages today is for very great stakes. A culture spanning thousands of years and embracing Hellenism and Teutonism is fighting for its existence.

And in the 13th chapter of the second volume of *Mein Kampf*, he says:

> And again the National Socialist movement has the mightiest task to fulfill. It must open the eyes of the people where foreign nations are concerned . . . Instead of hatred against Aryans—from whom nearly everything may separate us, but with whom we are bound by common blood or the great line of a kindred culture—it must call universal wrath upon the foul enemy of mankind . . . It must make certain that in our country, at least, the deadly enemy is recognized and that the fight against him becomes a gleaming symbol of a brighter time, to

show other nations the way to the salvation of an embattled Aryan mankind.

That the Leader regarded Germany not as a complete end in itself but only as a part of a greater racial whole is also emphasized by many of his public statements. At Braunschweig in his speech of October 18, 1931, for example, he said: "Today we fight for the future of the German people, tomorrow for the future of our race."

Tomorrow is here.

No Justice for Black People

Ronald Stevenson

On the night of November 7, 1968, Shirley Anderson was home alone. She was suffering from an acute nervous condition and called the police and asked to be taken to the hospital. No ambulance came, but the police did. The results: Mrs. Anderson was pushed around, dragged down her front steps and thrown to the ground. She was then arrested, and later tried and convicted for disturbing the peace and resisting arrest.

Shirley Anderson does not talk about that night very much. Now she mostly sits and stares, and occasionally speaks of revenge.

For nearly a year James Anderson tried to do something about the brutal and unprovoked attack on his wife. He contacted three different newspapers in the Bay Area, a television station, the Police Internal Affairs office, the San Francisco Community Relations office of the Justice Department and the Federal Bureau of Investigation. None of them were interested in his problem. Then Anderson told me his story.

Schism v.1, no.2 (Winter 1970)

James and Shirley Anderson have been married for five years and have four children. He is 45 years old, she 29. Anderson is a World War II veteran, receiving a total disability pension. For some time, Mrs. Anderson has suffered a nervous condition and has needed occasional psychiatric treatment. In 1967, they started buying a home.

Before that night last November the Andersons were mild-mannered black people. By their own admission, they were apathetic when it came to struggles and were usually willing to accept the lesser evil. Neither had ever had any encounter with the Oakland police.

Louisiana-born Anderson had worked as a sandblaster in his home state. In Los Angeles he had been a special cop and, for a time, a salesman in a record shop.

"Until this happened to us at our home in Oakland, I did not believe that the police were as brutal as they are. I did not honestly believe there was any such thing as police brutality," Anderson told me.

Two cops answered Mrs. Anderson's call—one was Negro and the other white. Anderson returned home as his wife was letting the police in.

He asked them what they wanted and was told: "We don't want to talk to you."

"Our .38 caliber pistol was on the kitchen table," Anderson said, "and when the cop spied it, he wanted to know what we were doing with a gun. My wife told them there had been a lot of house breaking and robberies in the neighborhood. She said I hadn't been home and that she was afraid. The cop took the gun and kept it." Anderson again tried to question the police, but was told "we want to talk to Mrs. Anderson."

"At this time the white officer took my wife out to his car to talk with him but the Negro officer wouldn't let me go with her," Anderson said.

"We sat for five or ten minutes, and finally he told me he was on my side. I told him, 'brother if you was on my side, you wouldn't let the white man take my wife outside in the dark to talk to her. You'd go out and talk to her and let him stay in here with me.' He told me to just set down, and I just sat at the kitchen table."

Anderson said he then told the officer: "If you was in Piedmont, (a wealthy suburb) you could not take no white woman out of her home and talk to her alone in a car and let the white man stay inside and talk to her husband."

The tall thin, dark-complexioned Anderson seemed to be struggling with something and when his eyes met mine again he said: "Don't ever fool yourself. Black policemen are just as bad as the white police." Then he continued: "After a while the other officer blew the horn. The Negro officer and I went outside. When my wife saw me, she asked to talk to me and was refused.

"About this time, my father-in-law and his friend, who is white, walked up. When my wife saw her father she got out of the police car. Just then four police cars arrived on the scene. There were no fights, no arguments, no nothing. When my wife started towards her father the police grabbed him. She was thrown on the ground and he was pushed up against a car and handcuffed.

"The friend of the father-in-law said, 'That is no way to treat a lady. A police sergeant came up behind him and hit him on the back of the head."

Anderson then added: "What's so bad, and people know it, is that there is not only police brutality against black people but against white people also. The police hit the white man because he spoke up for my wife.

"My father-in-law and his friend were taken to jail. My wife was then taken to Highland Hospital, to the insane ward. I followed the car she was take in. I asked to see her at the hospital. I wanted to talk to her. But the police said to me, 'Nigger you can't talk to your wife.'

"Is asked what they were going to do with her. They told me, if the doctor turned her loose, they were going to arrest her for disturbing the peace. I asked them what peace, and told them we were at home. They walked out of the hospital. In about five minutes the doctor called me in and told me to take my wife home, that there was nothing wrong with her. That she was not crazy."

Two weeks later two more Oakland cops came to the Anderson home.

"My wife had just taken a bath. She had on a bathrobe, no panties, no bra, no nothing. She answered the door and asked them what they wanted. One policeman said he had a warrant for her arrest for disturbing the peace and resisting arrest.

"They would not listen to any arguments. I tried to get them to let my wife put some clothes on. They refused. This time they drug her down the steps with nothing on but her bathrobe. They put her in their car and called the paddy wagon.

"In the meantime, I started down the street to the home of Mr. Williams who is a bailsbonds man," Anderson said. "I heard an officer say, 'Stop.' I thought they were going to shoot me. I turned around and walked back to my car. I said to the officer then—he had his hand on his gun—since the last time you arrested my wife, I met a Negro officer downtown. He told me, that if anything else happened on this case, to let him know. I want to talk to him. His name is Captain Sylvester.'

"When I mentioned that name, the officer immediately pulled his gun and put it up to my forehead. Then he said, 'Nigger if you mention Captain Sylvester's name one more time I'll blow your damned brains out.' "

Anderson went downtown and made arrangements to bail his wife out. By the time he reached jail, a parking violation had been added to his wife's charges.

"We had an old car that we never drove, and they said there was a red sticker on it. We didn't know anything about it. When they got through, her bail was $750. She had been in jail three and a half or four hours, with nothing on but her bathrobe."

Anderson, used to letting things "kinda slide," now wants to do something about what has happened to him. The frustration of not knowing what to do, or who to turn to, is getting next to him. His voice gave him away. He sounded cold. His burning anger was buried deep inside and his voice was very cold.

"Before all this happened, my wife was going to the psychiatrist once in a while," he said. "Now she has to go every week and they put her on two years probation. She didn't do anything, but the jury found her guilty of resisting arrest."

This was at her trial in March. "The judge gave her a lecture that was uncalled for," Anderson said, shaking his head from side to side. "Now she can't stand being around anybody, not even me. She just lays around on the couch at her mother's house."

"We had filed charges against the police," Anderson said. "During the trial the police came to the house. They asked me if I would drop the charges against them, and said they would drop the charge of resisting arrest against her and just charge her with disturbing the peace. I refused, because she wasn't guilty. But I found out that if you move your shoulders around or say anything the man don't like, he'll charge you with resisting arrest."

Now Anderson believes in the Community Control of the police. "I believe the police think, just like black people say they think. I believe they react to black people, just like black people say they react to them. There is no such thing as justice for black people."

A telephone check with the Justice Department showed, that the Anderson case is well known to them. But there is no comment they can make, they say, even after eight months.

White Reply to the Black Manifesto

The New Right

Brothers & Sisters

We have come from all over the land, and are fed up with black demands and chicken hearted white church, school and government leaders. There will be no further accommodation to black or white anarchists and traitors. Either we destroy their power, or they will truly overcome our land.

We ask nothing from these forces of evil. These are the anti-Christ—the beasts with the mark foretold in the bible.

Our country is but an adolescent in history's family of nations. Our mother and father were Europe—not Africa. Our values are of Europe—not the Congo. Tribal concepts are communal, not individualistic. Black Nationalism means tribal concepts, which are rooted in communalism. Our forefathers rejected the theory of mass subjugation by their own race—why would we now voluntarily accept it at the hands of an alien racially mutated group, whose goal is destruction of the individual to benefit this faceless mass?

White and Christian America must cease its self searching, its willingness to listen to voices of defeat, of confusion and of evil. It is a simple choice, either we conquer them—or they conquer us. No other alternative is left. Tribalism, sensualism and animalistic worship versus an orderly, family oriented and self disciplined Christian society. We have no choice. We, who have children, who believe in the faith of our fathers which made this land as bounteous as it is, must stand and fight.

What was done 100 or 200 years ago is past. Who was guilty of what is of no importance. It is a black guilt as well as a white. Black men sold their black brethren into slavery. Black overseers kept black men in chains. Black women crossed the color line as fast as they could desert their race. Black exploited black as continuously as did white. Black guilt matches white—indeed surpasses it in that it represented betrayal of its own race for gold in the very beginning.

Any church leader who accepts the responsibility for permitting black traitors to enter the solemn sanctuary of God; permits them to read the threatening, extortionist words of the Black Manifesto; has desecrated the House of Worship. Such a leader is beyond the pale. He is to be charged with treason by his congregation. He has permitted his own flock to be destroyed by the wolves when, as shepherd, he should have been strong enough to have guided them away.

Each of you must stand up and denounce this manifesto for what it is—a declaration of a race and class war. If their spokesmen appear in your church, the spokesman should be ejected as promptly as his doctrines are rejected. He should leave the church knowing that the wrath of a white man is still terrible to behold; that the white fury bites sharper than his memory could visualize. If they will not respect our institutions and our leaders, then let them fear our people.

We were inclined to charity but their savagery has turned

this to stone. We were willing to compromise, but their greed has changed this to unflinching resistance to any further concessions. We looked to a new day together but their view of a black America blinded our vision and turned our eyes to the true light. We are changing—we are frustrated and are angry. We are white America in rebellion against the black tribalists who would destroy our government.

We, therefore, reject the monetary demands of the blacks. If they call for payment of debts to them, we answer by reciting their debts to us.

1. $225,000 in riot damages since 1966—UNPAID.
2. $400,500,000 in social experimentation costs since 1952 in welfare, integration and similar ill fated Federal projects—UNPAID.
3. $800,000,000 for some 2,000,000 blacks' boat passages from Africa to America in the 19th century at today's prices—UNPAID.
4. $100,000,000 for original purchase price paid to black slave salesmen for black slaves—UNPAID.
5. $600,000,000 in indemnities to all participants in the Civil War—North and South—who suffered due to black presence in North America—with interest—UNPAID.

$2,125,000,000—Blacks OWE Whites

Further we demand that:

1. All blacks cease supporting leaders of their race who are financed by Communist China, Cuba or Russia.
2. All blacks denounce those black leaders as hypocrites where such black leaders have betrayed their own race, by insulting black women, and have taken white wives as mates.
3. All blacks denounce the church leaders in their race who, while owning Cadillacs, $200 suits and living in high fashion, march in poverty parades and urge strikers to continue to forfeit wages in states far removed from their own congregations.
4. All blacks sincerely interested in community control cease symbolic fights for forced housing and concentrate on im-

proving the relatively new areas which they have just penetrated.

5. All blacks join together to encourage a return to Africa of their youth so that a true Zionist type awakening of their people be promoted.

6. All blacks exert as much effort in trying to have a "quiet summer" as they do in threatening whites with a "hot summer."

7. All whites stop feeling guilty about a group of people openly dedicated to destroying our society.

8. All whites recognize that God made separate races to enhance the beauty of the differences, and never intended mankind to destroy his work.

We are at the point in history where we either are honest enough to face our problem or are dishonest enough to turn our back on it while it smites us. Race war is not of tomorrow. It started when blacks were permitted to lose respect for a white society which protected them. It will not end by wishful thinking—by hopes that all will have a change of heart some day. It will end by one race conquering the other—once and for always!

If this land, your faith, your family and your traditions mean as much to you as they did to your forefathers—there is no question as to the outcome. We shall maintain the order. We shall conquer. We shall remain white, free and a Republic forever!

Are the Black Panthers Being Persecuted?

Christian Anti-Communism Crusade

Gun battles between the Black Panthers and the police are now almost commonplace. Most of the known leaders of the

Schism v.1, no.3 (Summer 1970)

Black Panthers are in prison or in exile. Their chairman, Bobby Seale, received national publicity and considerable public sympathy when he was chained and gagged in the courtroom presided over by Judge Hoffman in Chicago. They are reported to torture and kill defectors from their own ranks and to terrorize the black community.

The Black Panthers are claiming that they are the victims of a conspiracy to destroy them. This claim has the support of the radical press and community throughout the country. These unite in proclaiming that the Panthers are the vanguard of the revolution and that they are black patriots, not criminals. Those in jail are called political prisoners, and police frameup is charged.

The Black Panthers are truly victims of their false doctrines and of such white advisers as attorney William Kunstler. It appears that the Black Panthers have heeded the advice that he gave during his speech at the Conference for the United Front Against Fascism on Saturday, July 19, 1969. During this speech he told them they had a political right to shoot white policemen who entered the territory of the ghettos since these policemen were armed foreign invaders. Since he made that speech, there have been numerous cases of Black Panthers shooting at policemen when they were called to duty in the ghetto. This has resulted in the death of a number of policemen and Black Panthers.

The doctrines of the Black Panthers are expressed by Eldridge Cleaver, their Minister of Information. He delivered a speech to the International Conference on Tasks of Journalists of the Whole World in Their Fight Against U.S. Imperialist Aggression on September 22, 1969, in North Korea. His full speech was published in the *Black Panther* of October 25, 1969. Here are extracts from that speech:

> To the International Conference on Tasks of Journalists of the Whole World in Their Fight Against U. S. Imperialist Aggression.
>
> In our era of class war and revolution against capitalism, racism, imperialism, colonialism and neo-colonialism, we are able to zero in on the very geographical location of the hiding places of the enemy. Standing dead-center

on the bullseye, we find the United States of America—
U.S. fascism and imperialism—to be the No. 1 enemy of
all humanity, the arsenal and banker of exploitation and
oppression, and chief purveyor of death and destruction
all over the the planet earth.

The United States of America is not a democratic country. It is a cruel fascist country. It is a democracy for the
bloodsucking capitalist vultures and the bloodletting warmongers who control the U.S. government and benefit
from its barbaric policies. It is a prison for everyone else
and President Nixon is nothing but the Warden of the
prison. Indeed, U.S. imperialism seeks to turn the entire
world into a huge prison under its bloody thumb and under the boots of its troops and puppets.

The American flag and the American Eagle are the
true symbols of fascism, and they should elicit from the
people the same outraged repugnance elicited by the
swastika of nazi Germany and the flag of the rising sun
of the Japanese imperialists.

The truth is that there is a sound revolutionary movement inside the United States that has already tasted the
blood of the hated class enemy and is delivering deathblows
to its system and is locked irretrievably in a battle to the
death against the U.S. fascist imperialist regime.

The revolutionary forces inside the United States must
be supported by the revolutionary peoples of the whole
world, because whereas the people outside of the United
States will slice off the tentacles of the hideous octopus
of U.S. oppression, the revolutionaries inside the United
States will cut its wicked heart and give the decisive death
blow to U.S. fascism and imperialism.

We fully agree with the theme of this conference, that
the task before us is the total annihilation of imperialism,
particularly U.S. imperialism, because for us this will mean
the victory of socialism and the end to the fascist state
under which we now suffer.

It is time for the revolution to explode inside the imperialist nations themselves.

The U.S. imperialist aggressors must cease their role of
merchants of death and destruction who are guilty of fi-

nancing and arming and protecting the arrogant, nazi-like, Zionist landgrabbers who have usurped and plundered the Fatherland of the Palestinian people.

The so-called President of the United States, Richard PIG Nixon, is the spokesman and frontman for U.S. fascism and the arch enemy of oppressed black people, poor white people, Mexican-American people, Indians, Puerto Ricans, and Eskimos inside the United States. We want the people around the world to throw rocks, and bottles, and spit, and hand-grenades, and bullets, and bombs, and curses at Nixon if he dares to visit their country.

Let us lift up our pens, our voices, and our guns, with all our revolutionary fervor to defeat the freaks of mankind who hatch such dismal schemes and strive diligently to put an end, once and forever, to the monster of U.S. imperialism.

We need articles, essays, poems, and books that will make men pick up guns and enter onto the field of battle against the enemy; we need words that will make the soldiers, sailors, marines and special forces of the U.S. imperialists turn their guns against their commanding officers . . . We need words that will return the U.S. troops to the United States with their guns still in hand, there to put before firing squads President Nixon, ex-President Johnson, all the generals of the U.S. Armed Forces, all warmongers and exploiters.

We need articles by journalists that will inflame the masses, that will spur on the revolutionary temptation to kidnap American ambassadors, hijack American airplanes, blow up American pipelines and buildings, and to shoot anyone who uses guns or weapons or causes others, directly or indirectly to use guns and other weapons in the blood-stained service of imperialism against the people.

The police merit all our understanding and support. Try to imagine facing the task of arresting a group of fanatics who believe this philosophy and who have heavily armed and located in a fortified building.

Mendenhall: Old-Time Violence

Jan Hillegas

Editor's note: In February, many people across the country became upset by sporadic outbreaks of violence among young people protesting the conviction of anti-war leaders in Chicago. During the same month, a group of blacks (and a white supporter) were brutally beaten by Mississippi Highway Patrolmen. Few people protested; the nation's press hardly noticed.

It was the kind of sadistic violence by which a tiny minority of Southerners kept control back through the years. It was the kind of violence that was temporarily restrained and mitigated while the world watched in the 1960's. It is now on the rise again—as the world looks the other way.

In this time of increasing concern and talk about the violence in our country it is time we took some hard looks at the sources of violence: the efforts of those in control to crush the people who demand their rights. This is what happened in Mendenhall, Miss., in February, 1970.

MENDENHALL, Miss.—Saturday marches continue in this central Mississippi town in spite of severe beatings of leaders in early February.

The marches began in late December to support a selective-buying campaign to press demands to end police brutality, job disrcrimination, and other inequities.

On January 24, about a dozen students from Tougaloo College and a comparable number of whites from Jackson began joining the marches, at the request of local leaders.

While Tugaloo students were being driven home on February 5, the vehicle was stopped just across the line in Rankin County. The driver, Doug Huemmer, is white and works at Mendenhall Bible Institute in the black community.

He describes what happened: "We were stopped by a Highway Patrol who ordered me out of the truck and sit in his car and he told me if I made one move he was going to put a bullet in my head. He took my driver's license and then he got on his microphone and called other units. And you see the truck that I was driving was full of students and they just stayed in the truck. . . .

"Then about 6 to 8 minutes went by and we were surrounded by 5 or 6 Highway Patrol cars and the guys poured out of the cars and ordered all of the students out of the cars and frisked them . . . And I was put in the back seat of a car and I was beaten all the way to the jail . . . And then when we got to the jail . . . they kept me out in the patrol car and beat me every few minutes for about 40 minutes."

The Rev. Curry Brown of Mendenhall continues: "We got a phone call that some of the Tougaloo students had been arrested . . . So as president of NAACP in Simpson County (Mendenhall) I felt responsible, Rev. John Perkins and I, for them . . . We got out of our little red Volkswagen (at the courthouse) and we were standing waiting for the chief of police to come out. And pretty soon a whole bunch of Highway Patrolmen came out of the jail with their flashlights and guns and walked over to us and said to Rev. Perkins and said Alright you're first . . . The patrolman that took me beat me and kicked me in the groin and everywhere on the way to the jail before we got even into the office.

"And after we were in the office, then they began to beat Rev. Perkins and Doug and everyone else who was in there. And they told Rev. Perkins that this was a whole new ballgame, that we weren't in Simpson County, that we were in Brandon (Rankin County) . . .

"And a patrolman came over to me and said, this is what you wanted, this is what you've been wanting. He began to beat me. And then they cut off Doug Huemmer's hair . . . They slapped me until I couldn't hardly see or hear what was going on. And then they cut my hair off, my mustache and sideburns and stole my NAACP card . . . They all got around Rev. Perkins and took the demands for the boycott and told him to read them . . .

"While we was arrested they never said we were under arrest at all and never informed us of any constitutional rights or anything like this.

"And the amazing thing that frightened me was that these

were men that were supposed to enforce the law, men who you're supposed to respect, men who should protect you from violence and who when you turn yourself over to them, there should be some rights to protect you from violence. And yet these men beat us unmercifully and I thought I was going to die and I was not in America."

Mr. Perkins is Mississippi organizer for the Federation of Southern Cooperatives and a resident of Mendenhall. He stated: "They began to say that this was that smart nigger and they began to just beat me and beat me and beat me on the ground, on the floor, then they stomped me and beat me and then in the midst of the beating and the blood from my head and from Rev. Brown's head and the others had just smeared the floor with blood. And in the meantime they got a call over the radio that the FBI was coming and so they took and had me to mop up all of the blood off of the floor and when I got through mopping the blood they had me go into the back room and wash my head . . .

"And there were big officers knocked me down, knocked me out and unconscious for just a little bit and then they jumped on me and they stepped on me . . . One of them took a fork and bent down the two inside prongs of the fork and ran it up in my nose until blood came out, and then took, then into my throat here . . . And they beat me for about 2 hours . . . They kicked me into the jail and I fell and the students from Tougaloo came and got me and put me in the bed, began to put towels and water around my head and just kept me, just sort of kept me alive, kept me conscious while I was there."

After interviews with Mr. Perkins, Mr. Brown, and Huemmer were aired on Jackson television, one reporter said the phone calls the station got were the worst since 1965.

Lawyers have filed a petition for removal to federal court of the charges against the 23 persons arrested.

Public requests were made by Owen Brooks of the Delta Ministry and Mayor Charles Evers of Fayette for federal and state investigations of the beatings.

Civil rights attorneys report that police brutality has increased in many parts of the state in recent weeks, and the feeling is that it is related to what whites call the "crisis" caused by school integration.

The boycott is continuing in Mendenhall, and one has begun

in Rankin County, under the leadership of the movement there.

U.S. District Judge Harold Cox prohibited a march in Mendenhall on February 21, ostensibly for a cooling-off period. Then he ordered Menderhall officials to issue permits for future peaceful marches, but also ruled that "No person shall participate in any march held pursuant to this order unless he resides within a 25-mile radius of the Town of Mendenhall." His order is being appealed.

On Police Murder

Black Politics

Tired of reading about violence? No longer news to you? Does it bore you to read or hear about it?

Many of us now feel this way and can't even feel rage when we read of a beating or a killing of a black person or any ethnic minority person in the United States by the police. To be sure, rage is by no means an automatic reaction to an injustice. We show raving fury only when we are sure that conditions can be changed. It follows then that *black Americans don't feel that anything can be done to stop the murder of their leaders or the boy next door by the police— because the black community has shown no rage since the abortive insurrections following the death of Martin Luther King!*

As far as the general public knows there have been no giant street demonstrations of 25,000 enraged people, no police commissioner's home has been firebombed, no police chief has been shot at, no flatfoot who actually squeezed the trigger has been physically assaulted, no defense attorney for a cop found "not guilty" has been placed in jeopardy—no member of the government involved in any way with the continuing direct physical violence against the Afro-American citizens of this country has a damn thing to worry about.

The number of black people, Latin-Americans and other minority groups, murdered by "officers of the law" during the past two months is too numerous to go into in any detail. Each case ends in the same final verdict whether it be handed down by a court trial, a police department "investigation," or a coroner's jury.

The witness to these crimes, whatever their number, have no affect on the final outcome. No one knows how many people saw San Francisco pig Michael R. O'Brien shoot George Baskett, but O'Brien played cat and mouse with his victim long enough for a sizable crowd to gather. His defense attorney, the noted J. W. Erlich, claimed that the black neighborhood in which the murder took place was "a hellhole with some 200 hyenas in there" and that the neighborhood's witnesses who testified in court had absolutely no respect for an oath, the truth, or for common decency."

In the case of the cold-blooded murder of 19-year-old Albert Joe Linthcome by San Francisco pig, Gerald Roberts, there had been no argument between the two and no cat and mouse game on the part of pig Roberts. It was simple. Mr. Linthcome ran into a record shop and stopped because there was no exit. Pig Roberts ran to the door, saw his victim, took a few steps forward to help his aim, and then coldly and deliberately fired his revolver in spite of the witnesses in the room and on the sidewalk screaming, "Don't shoot him!"

The Coroner's jury verdict was "justifiable homicide" because pig Roberts was acting "in the performance of his duty."

This is true! The duty of every cop in the United States now is to kill every member of every racial minority group they see violate *any* law, or suspect of violating a law, or anyone who "talks back" to any cop. Their duty was made clear to them by their respective police departments during the past three years and now they have engaged in enough actions for the public to be aware of it.

It is true that there are laws against murder, but how can you expect a government to enforce these laws if it is engaged in the wholesale murder of hundreds and sometimes thousands of men, women, and children in Vietnam every day? A government that uses violence to control any country in the world will use it to control its own people.

George Wallace may be the best example we have of an individual achieving success through defying the law. He became nationally prominent by refusing, as Governor of Alabama, to obey federal laws. He forced the government to bring in U. S. marshals and soldiers to enforce the law in Alabama. He made his name breaking and defying the law, and now poses as the leader of the forces of law and order at any price.

Despite many demonstrations, speeches, and other efforts over the years it took the death of Martin Luther King and the insurrections that followed to convince Congress to adopt open housing legislation.

Almost all of our so-called civil rights legislation grew out of civil disobedience—some peaceful, but some very violent.

No steps at all are taken to alleviate the horrors of Ghetto life until the Ghetto erupts in a "riot."

It is regrettably true that, with rare exceptions, violence has been the only way to convince the legislators that serious problems exist and that something must be done about it.

The victims of police violence are placed inside boxes for convenient disposal and everyone of us are in there with them. The bolts are being tightened down which makes it darker and its crowded. It has a leaky roof and a clogged up toilet in the hall. It has rats and roaches. The leaky sewer lines stink. We're locked in and we've lost the key.

Do we editors of *Black Politics* know what to do about this situation? Yes, but—if we begin to spell it out for you our fate would soon be sealed like that of Malcolm X's because *we know now that the power structure of Babylon will not permit anyone to march far ahead of the people anymore to show the people the way to take power*. Therefore, we can only talk in parables in both our editorials and articles and urge "those who have ears to hear, let them hear."

Why Some Whites Are Arming

The White Sentinel

According to a young tunnel worker in San Francisco, the biggest race war of them all may have already started. "I think you have one of the biggest race riots in the world coming," he says. "and they'll call it the black-White civil war. I'd say it started already, only on a real small scale. It will start out like it's happening in Oakland right now. I know for a fact that Friday nights, you got the backs and Whites going at it all the time. Whitey's getting tired of being pushed around. I can see fighting on the streets, from house to house, starting with the black militants and the police force, or in some high school. The first thing you know, a couple of cops are going to go out, and about forty or fifty White guys are going to go out and back them up and the next time, maybe there will be a hundred colored guys and two hundred White guys, and the first thing you know, there will be swarms.

"I have several guns at home," he says, "I also have a German Shepard, primarily to protect my wife. I made damn sure the wife is a crack shot. In the event someone ever comes into the house, it's shoot first and ask questions later. If somebody breaks in, he isn't coming in to shake your hand, is he? I know for a fact that people are arming themselves. Friends ask me to teach them how to use a gun. They want it for self-protection because they're scared. I also know a man who owned a gun shop over in Oakland and sold out lock, stock, and barrel because he got to the point where even he got scared. Most people you talk to today, they feel it. I hope trouble never comes— there's got to be drastic changes made."

A gun shop owner in Orange County, Calif., says, "If a story were to be made to really shock people, who think this gun law did any good, they ought to find out how much is being stolen from these military posts. One post up here reported a theft, over a three month period, of a hundred thousand rounds of small arms ammunition."

A conversation between two automobile salesmen fits the same pattern as in the rest of the country. Fear, Guns. "We're going to leave them alone as long as they leave us alone," says one, "There are very few colored in Orange County, but in case of rioting, I'd use my gun for self-protection. Most people would protect their property, same as I would. Ninety-five percent of my friends would do the same thing, and they almost all have guns."

"What are the Whites doing about all this violence? We make sure that we're protected with bats and guns. I have an unregistered gun, and I'd use it—I'd do anything to protect my life, legal or otherwise. I wouldn't stop at anything. I carry a gun all the time. I have it in the trunk of my car, brand new .38. I would rather take the chance of going to jail than being dead. All my friends have guns. I think the average White is carrying a gun for the same reason I'm carrying one—to protect myself from the extremist black man, 'cause that's who's causing all the trouble."

The speaker is a Brooklyn welfare worker. He is one of a rising number of angry Whites growing impatient with politicians and violence in the streets.

"Just watch how blacks operate. They live by violence, that's their code, that's what they love. What the hell did the other nationalities do? Did we go and burn down stores on Pitkin Avenue when we wanted better things for the Italian and the Irish? We didn't do that. I'd like to move them all out of the country, that's what I would like. Give them an island. They're only ten percent in America. Why do ten percent have so much to say about ninety percent?

"If you want to be a millionaire today, the easiest way is to be black. The administration will give you five, ten thousand dollars, and I couldn't get it when a business I had folded. They wouldn't give it to me.

"You know what I see happening? The black man is going to continue what he's doing, and the White man is going to end up using force to beat force. I mean White middle-income people. They're going to organize politically, socially and violently. I can show you a neighborhood in south Brooklyn where I know, for a fact, there are organizations that will not allow a negro family to move in that neighborhood. I know they're doing it 'cause I'm part of the movement. By now, a hundred guns could be brought here in five minutes—in case of a confrontation between blacks and White wives or daughters. These people will not move out—they're going to stay and fight. They're not moving—a line has been drawn."

During a lunch break at a Brooklyn restaurant, two more welfare workers told of their reasons for the growing tensions of the Whites, many of whom now call themselves the forgotten majority, rather than the silent majority. "It's becoming annoying," said one worker, "The White man doesn't mind competing with the black man for a job—they're annoyed because they feel it's not a fair competition when they compete with someone of lower intelligence and lower educational background and then lose out to the black. Friends of mine who work for utility companies see negroes with less capability, less seniority, getting higher positions, and they don't like it."

The other worker said: "Everybody's afraid of what's happening. I'll admit that one of my fears is inter-marriage. The last place to integrate is in the bedroom. Sooner or later, you're to have the all-time race riot. Whites are getting ready to organize. I've even been approached. And it won't be long before they start building up in Brooklyn. They won't attack anybody, the plans are for home or area defense. I have three guns at home, and I taught my wife how to use them—just in case."

More talk about black militants is heard in a neatly paneled tavern in the Bay Ridge area of Brooklyn. The men are mostly construction workers. "Who built this country? asks one iron worker, "The immigrants—that's who! Organize politically? We have Democratic and Republican clubs and vote for this guy or that guy. It's like a friend told me, "Thank God they both can't get in, 'cause they all cater to the minority groups.' What do we do? Take off and storm City Hall 'cause the negroes are doing it? Two wrongs don't make a right. I wish I was mayor for one day. I wouldn't tie no policeman's hands. I'd give him back clubs, guns and the whole works. It's all political. Who gives the authority? Who holds the cops back? Who doubled the water rates two years ago in this community? We don't turn the hydrants on. In Harlem, all the hydrants are causing the water shortage, and all the little kids turn them on. We had a water shortage here, and you couldn't turn the air conditioners on in a place where you're paying taxes. But they threw water all over the streets. Who's paying the taxes? How many taxes come out of Bedford-Stuyvesant? We're only paying for the bums that don't want to work. We're not paying for the good people. We're paying for the guys that don't work. It's not that bad for me personally, as far as living with them goes. Bay Ridge is a White neighborhood. But if I get an influx of negroes here, well, I've got an unregistered gun at home."

A dock worker is worried about black demonstrations. He is alarmed at the threat of violence in White communities. "Look at those demonstrations," he said, "they don't do it on their own hook. They're led by somebody. Somebody's running them—financing them. How do you get a hundred thousand leaflets printed up in a matter of hours? I can't get it done, but they can make it. My kid came home from school one day with a leaflet from some kind of student organization. It had a big black hand sticking up, and it said, 'get rid of the pigs—the pigs will be there—don't attend school—go to this other school 'cause there's going to be a demonstration there.' What the hell is this coming to? You've got to have law and order in this town before you can do anything. These people, they do just what they please. They just get a bunch of jerks together and go down and shoot somebody. There are demonstrations and demonstrations—two different things, and when they become violent, then it's not a demonstration any more, it's a civil war. The police should have the power to knock 'em off. Give them machine guns, I don't care. If you don't get that done, you can talk and talk—the politicians can talk and talk—and you never get anything done."

White anger smolders in South Bend, Ind. A west side store owner receives visitors at the back door of a boarded up home. "I've pulled this gun out about ten or fifteen times in the past five years," he says, "and I can show you case upon case where the gun saved me." He tells about robberies in his store, and about the night he waited until after closing and caught three men breaking in and running up the aisle and how he shot one black, with a .22 rifle.

His stories of subsequent fire-bombings at home and the

store, telephone threats and confrontations with angry black people have etched deep lines of terror on his face.

"This neighborhood is headquarters for all the goons. My God, they burned a couple of garages here recently, a block away. And of course there's a problem of purse-snatching and window-breaking. One day when I was riding my bike, they wanted to beat me up with bricks, these three big negroes. I jumped off my bike and reached for this .38 and told them, "If you fellows throw that, you're dead.'

"There's two things these people respect—a dog and a gun. There's only one thing to do—lock up all your militants. If you could just get them off the street. White people are running. They're running to the suburbs. Where are they going to run from there? They think they can run away from this, but it's impossible. We're just heading for a lot of trouble in this country."

Eldridge Cleaver: A Man to Believe

Stephan Bodian

On November 27, 1968, Eldridge Cleaver was to turn himself over to the California Adult Authority for violating his parole. Though Cleaver knew his own innocence, he also knew that the California political establishment, intimidated by his brilliant political activity, was bent on "putting him out of action." So Cleaver never appeared that November day, turned up subsequently as the guest of various African nations and of Cuba. But in early December Cleaver applied for a passport to return to the U.S. He had vowed to friends and to himself that he would be back. For the land he has come to call Babylon is very much his own.

Cleaver is one of the most honest of radical writers, one of the least prone to rhetoric and sophistry, and has one of the

Schism v.1, no.3 (Summer 1970)

clearest, most forceful prose styles in America, as his articles in recent issues of *Ramparts* have shown. But many a liberal reader feels a gulf separating him from Cleaver, a gulf, interestingly, not so much of sensibility as of credibility. What brings the spokesman for a much-oppressed, armed black revolutionary cadre to make an admission like, "I also came to see that the price of hating other human beings is loving oneself less?" Why should he be so candid about himself, about the Panthers, about other blacks? That is, why should we believe what he tells us?

Well then, why do we believe any man? Why did we believe Johnson in '64? What did we really know of the man's *Honesty?* or Nixon in '68? I press this point because I want you to believe Cleaver, I want you to lay aside the biased news accounts and your own fears and realize for yourself the essential honesty and integrity of the man. For it seems to me, if not Cleaver, WHO?

While writing *Soul On Ice* in prison, Cleaver had evolved no ideology, no dogma; he had no preestablished, sympathetic audience. He was simply a man in search of himself—testing ideas, developing a talent. "I write to save myself." The book is a mind's testament of itself. It clears the air, it purges the anger, it replaces a black man's hatred for the white man, essentially negative, with positive symbols, allegories, ideas. Not Cleaver the public figure, the revolutionary, but Cleaver the man, speaks here. *Soul On Ice* sets the stage for a radical ideology by clearing away some of the props. Now, in *Post Prison Writings and Speeches,* a compilation of the essential works from prison to exile, Cleaver, continuing to probe, analyze, deflate, emerges completely as political man.

Of the writings, only two pieces deal at length with Cleaver's radical political views, but they really exhaust that topic. The first, "The Land Question and Black Liberation," analyzes the desire for land among black organizations in the context of Black America's status as colony within the mother country. Integration is at once the ploy of an imperialist government to maintain its image abroad, and the possible design of liberals intent on absorbing the colony and thus completing at last the American dream. What black people really want, Cleaver maintains, is land, self-determination, an end to colonial status. First he traces the "land-hunger" of Afro-Americans from the (un-fulfilled) Reconstruction promise of forty acres and a mule, through Marcus Garvey's "Back to Africa" movement to the modern national consciousness of Malcolm X:

> The point is that Malcolm X had begun to call for Black National consciousness. And moved this conscious-ness into the broadest possible arena, operating with it as of now. We do not want a Nation, we are a Nation. We must strengthen and formalize, and play the world's game with what we have, from where we are, as a truly separate people.

Moving from this premise, Cleaver introduces the Panther proposal that the United Nations conduct a plebiscite among black Americans:

> The purpose of the plebiscite if to answer the question, once and for all: just what the masses of black people want. Do the masses of black people consider themseves a nation? Do they want U.N. membership? . . . Domes-tically, America will be placed in the peculiar position or arguing to black people that they do not need U.N. membership because they are American citizens. The blacks in the ghetto will respond with, Oh yeah. Well, if I'm an American citizen, why am I treated like a dog? The entire problem will be decisively internationalized and raised to a higher level of debate.

What could be more just than this proposal? This sense of justice, and an equally strong sense of humanity, of *LOVE,* per-vade all of Cleaver's writings.

The second political essay is a reprint of an interview with Cleaver by Nat Hentoff, who asked some very pointed ques-tions. Cleaver's answers are remarkable. Concise, comprehen-sive, clear, never evasive, painstakingly factual. And convinc-ing. So convicing. Let Cleaver speak for himself:

> Let me make myself clear. I don't dig violence. Guns are ugly. People are what's beautiful; and when you use a

gun to kill someone, you're doing something ugly. But there are two forms of violence: violence directed at you to keep you in your place and violence to defend yourself against that suppression and to win your freedom. If our demands are not met, we will sooner or later have to make a choice between continuing to be victims or deciding to seize our freedom. . . We are demanding structural changes in society, and that means a real redistribution of power, so that we have control over our own lives . . . It's by coalition (with white radicals) that we intend to bring together all the elements for liberation—by force, if all the alternatives are exhausted.

We have the courage—and the good sense—to defend ourselves, but we are not about to engage in the kind of random violence that will give the pigs an opportunity to destroy us. We are revolutionary, but that means we're disciplined, that we're working out programs, that we intend to create a radical political machinery in coalition with whites that will uproot this decadent society, transform its politics and economics and build a structure fit to exist on a civilized planet inhabited by *HUMANIZED* beings . . .

We've got to rid ourselves of this dreadful and all-consuming hunger for *THINGS,* this mindless substitution of the ratrace for a human life. Only then will people become capable of relating to other people on the basis of individual merit, rather than on the basis of status, property, and wealth. The values I'm for are really quite traditional and simple—like respecting your fellow man, respecting your parents, respecting your leaders if they're true leaders. These revolutionary goals are as old as time itself: Let people be. Let them fulfill their capacities.

As these essays show, Cleaver is quite consciously caught up in the paradox of the revolutionary, a paradox irresoluble save through action. For the vision of a gentle, humane society we take up arms. In theory the ends may not justify the means, but then, the call of supremely human values drowns the whisper of theory. As Marx, so Cleaver: "The philosophers have only interpreted the world in various ways; the point, however, is to change it."

Too, Cleaver is clearly an Afro-American, for his people's revolution, of whatever kind, will be here! Most of the other pieces in the book describe episodes in that incipient revolution. Cleaver presents the facts as he has seen them, and it is here you are asked to trust the man. He describes police harassment of Black Panthers:

On February 22, 1968, a posse of Berkeley police kicked down Bobby's (Bobby Seale) door, dragging him and his wife, Artie, from bed and arresting them on a sensational charge of conspiracy to commit murder. The same night, six other members of the party were arrested on the same charge. The ridiculous charge of conspiracy to commit murder was quickly dropped, but all arrested were held to answer various gun-law violations, all of which were unfounded.

He describes how his parole officers interferred with his political activity:

Even though I had a perfect right to free speech, Mr. Rivers and Mr. Bilideau said there were those in the State Capital who, for political purposes, were clamoring to have my parole revoked and me returned to prison. They advised me to cool it and forsake my rights in the interest of not antagonizing those in Sacramento who did not like my politics.

And he describes how police, without cause, shot seventeen-year-old Black Panther Bobby Hutton in the back:

The pigs told us to stand up. Little Bobby helped me to my feet. The pigs pointed to a squad car parked in the middle of the street and told us to run to it. I told them that I couldn't run. Then they snatched Little Bobby away from me and shoved him forward, telling him to run to the car. It was a sickening sight. Little Bobby, coughing and choking on the night air that was burning his lungs as my own were burning from the tear gas, stumbled forward as best he could, and after he had traveled about ten yards the pigs cut loose on him with their guns, and then they turned to me.

Cleaver survived this incident, unscathed but deeply embittered. Soon after he left Babylon, but he will return soon—to his people, his movement, his ethos, his world. For whether or not you are listening, Eldridge Cleaver is irrepressible—and he has cast thousands of young black men in his image.

"Wherever death may surprise us, let it be welcome, provided that this, our battle-cry, may have reached some receptive ear and another hand may be extended to wield our weapons."— Che Guevara

Quality Education or Craven Accommodation

Counterattack

Americans may now look back with some nostalgial to the good old days when our main educational concern was a simplistic suspicion that our little red school house was becoming a little Red school house. Growing racial tensions, disruptions and racial polarization that oftentimes explode into violence now plague both our law enforcement officers and our school administrators in virtually every part of the country where schools have substantial black enrollments. Ever since the social revolution which had its great impetus in Brown v. The Board of Education, relations between white teachers and administrators and black students have been steadily eroding. In some areas the erosion has begun to create conditions of paralyzing anarchy necessitating the marshalling of large police detachments to keep schools functioning and to put down outbursts of violence of incorrigible and rebellious students.

The same type of disruptions and clashes that have occurred in the major cities of the North are now occurring increasingly in our smaller towns and cities. A definite pattern of school-oriented racial protest and tension is becoming more apparent in the South as schools there begin to embrace the blessings of integration. Our educators now tell us that racial tensions seem to be moving downward in grade levels as black dissent is becoming apparent at lower scholastic levels.

Many urban sociologists and educators directly involved in school racial problems are becoming outspoken on the subject of integration. They have made a 180 degree change in their attitude as they inform us that an evenhanded color blind approach will not work. School administrators are becoming color conscious as they forthrightly meet the problems head on by making all kinds of accommodations to placate the young delinquents. No section of the country seems to be free of serious racial problems in secondary schools. In fact, the widening gulf between the whites and blacks in our schools is convincing increasing numbers of educators that the fading promise of school integration can never be more than a hollow piety.

We are told by human relations directors involved with school racial problems that polarization between the races is traceable more to a quest for black identity and unity than to racial animosities. Black students demand greater hiring of black school personnel and the revamping of school curriculums to include "black studies." Black students demand the serving of "soul food" in school cafeterias and the placing of portraits of black heroes, such as Malcolm X, Eldridge Cleaver and Huey Newton in school buildings. Some blacks believe they are flaunting their heritage validly in donning African shirts called dashikis and wearing talismans, or by attaching the emblems of black power movements to Army combat jackets as they truculently mouth the patois of hard-core militants.

The tragedy of educational accommodation to militant blacks in our secondary schools is the fact that the watered-down modified courses lead nowhere beyond giving a student a meaningless diploma. In the controversy over whether it is the schools that are failing to teach blacks or the students themselves who are failing to learn, it is undisputed that the resulting illiteracy is catastrophic. Unfortunately the masses of undisciplined students, including dropouts, truants and drug users never achieve a sixth grade level of reading.

We live in a language society. The effective use of it is a primary essential to achievement. The one important consideration in educating our masses is the ability to read and write effectively. Unless the blacks and the poor are provided opportunities for quality education and gainful employment, the pious platitudes about integration and social equality are shoddy political rhetoric which will not eliminate abysmal ignorance. The greatest danger to the achievement of equality in our society comes from two sources, the New Leftists and patronizing demogogic politicians. The latter grovel at the feet of the pot and protest set and curry the favor of the draft doggers, the campus militants and the masses of hippies who sport Old Testament beards to embellish their acute reversion to stone age manners and personal hygiene. The political charlatans loudly demand due process for muggers and rioters but don't give a damn about the victims of crime. The New Leftists, including the Students for a Democratic Society, the Black Panther Party, and the Black Radicals Onward aid and abet revolution, anarchy, racial hatred and incite a complete abhorrence of peace officers, referring to them as "pigs."

The following excerpts from a pamphlet of Black Radicals Onward appeared as an exhibit of a hearing, "Extent of Subversion in Campus Disorders" released on January 29, 1970 by the Subcommittee to Investigate the Administration of the Internal Security Act and Other Internal Security Laws of the Committee on the Judiciary United States Senate: (The excerpts from this pamphlet, purportedly written by an ivy league alumnus, are printed verbatim in its unique neologistic dialect.)

"The churches takes up collection from the people to benefit the churches, now the community makes them a part of the capitalistic system, which means money, money, for me, me, me, and not for the betterment of the community. The only thing the churches have done were to keep our people mentally dead; for example, dig how the pig mother lovers tells the churches to be nonviolent and then tells you to send your sons to war in the name of God.

"Pope Pocket-Pickin Paul has the nerve to oink at the people from the Cathedral's balcony, saying oink, son of the world with my blessings I send you to oppress other oppressed people of the world. Our Vietnamese Brothers. How can we relate this to the $50,000 churches in the 10¢ ghetto? Bethesda, which is capitalistic exploitation, can see that the churches are in cahoots with the White power structure which is a device to keep the people oppressed . . .

"By keeping you mentally dead, we mean, all the money you make goes into that mother-loving plate, and you can't afford luxuries yourselves . . . The church is just a justification for promoting poverty. ALL POWER TO THE PEOPLE."

Karl Marx said it more simply, "Religion is the opiate of the masses."

The following excerpt from an SDS training pamphlet disseminated among black students is reprinted from the same source as the foregoing diatribe on religion:

EQUIPMENT FOR RALLIES AND OTHER BATTLES WITH THE PIGS (Confidential)

Basic Equipment: 1. Crash helmet, 2. Safety Crotch protection cap, 6. Tightly fitting gloves, 7. Heavy Duty Picket Sign, 8. Heavy Duty or Construction Boots, 9. Improvise from the above.

Optional List: a. Army helmet, b. Football helmet, c. Gas mark, d. Ski mask, e. Chap stick, f. School bag, g. Attache case, h. Disguise kit, i. Fake make up, j. Tennis shoes, k. Track flats, l. Padding, m. Brass knuckles, n. Extra rings.

Supplies, ordnance and logistics

A. Rocks and bottles—Before rallies, rocks or bottles should be brought to campus by as many people as possible. Students should fill purses, lunch bags, pockets and attache cases full of rocks and while strolling around the campus grounds, he/she can casually drop rocks or bottles in strategic locations; e.g. (1) rally area; (2) streets; (3) walk ways; (4) off campus near intersections.

2. Throwing rocks or bottles—(a) Before you throw any rocks or bottles, observe if there are any pig cameramen on top of buildings. If there are any on the roofs, throw at them first. No pictures will be taken if they are driven off. (b) During any disruption, the scabs always are at the windows watching the pigs beating the ——out of the people. They, the pig scabs, are also good targets.

(c) When throwing at the pigs, aim at their midsection or necks. They all wear helmets. (d) If you can identify scab cars, throw at them when no other prime targets are available.

B. 1. Red pepper: Can be very effective against mounted pigs. Always try to position yourself so you throw the pepper downwind into the horses faces.

2. Darts: Should be thrown at the horses body, not the pig, because the horse is an easier target.

3. Water guns: Fill guns with regular household ammonia (H3) and squirt in horses' eyes and face. If all goes well, the pig again will end up on his fat ———.

4. Cherry bombs: To be effective, they must have BB's and tacks glued into the cherry bomb's surface. Those horses are trained against noise but not against pain.

C. Ice picks, leather punches, and can openers can be used to best advantage on car tires of scab teachers, students and administrators. Scratches paint jobs. Very good on plain clothes pigs too.

D. Sling shots: Buy a 'Wham-O' sling shot at your sports store and a package of marbles. Sling shots can be used at long range and with great power and can do great damage to the pigs. Highly recommended.

E. Picket signs: A 1"x2" or larger broom or axe handle make very good clubs or at least defensive weapons to block clubbing pigs. You may want to sharpen the end of the club. You may use the spear to stab or throw at the oncoming pigs . . .

J. Cigarette lighter: This little device has been very successfully used by our enemies in Vietnam (the U.S. military). We can ignite curtains, waste baskets, bulletin boards, paper towels in bathrooms . . .

M. Bombs: A. Cherry bomb with armament. Take bomb and dip in a pot of glue. While still wet with glue, dip into pot of tacks or BB's. Repeat gluing and coating process so that you have several layers of tacks and BB's and let dry . . .

C. Molotov cocktails: Named after Hon. V. M. Molotov, a bottle filled with gasoline and wrapped in a saturated rag, ignited and hurled as an anti-tank grenade. Best used on hit and run operations (window near street, ex. Science Bldg.) The principle involved here is that when the bottle crashes through the chosen window and breaks when it hits the floor the burning rag (fuse) ignites the gasoline, thus setting off the explosion . . .

The pamphlet gives explicit details on the manufacture and operation of a semi-sophisticated pipe bomb using gunpowder as the explosive and a king size cigarette as the fuse. Space limitation precludes our printing the instructions verbatim.

While his white counterpart enjoys conspicuous prosperity, the American black revolutionary has a driving desire to improve his people's economic condition. What the young revolutionary of today has to offer, apart from instant violence and obscene graffiti, is unfortunately obscured. When one rejects reason, he loses his perspective.

The rise of black nationalism has thus far achieved only a bitterness of factionalism between the races. The militants cannot awaken the intelligence of a minority by inciting violent behavior. Violence, once started against the "pigs," will inevitably be turned against the blacks. The polarization of the races in America is part of the fall-out syndrome of a thwarted instant integration which only quality education for all, equality of economic opportunity and bilateral compassion can improve. With generation now pitted against generation and race against race, there is no way to bring opposing forces together except by a better understanding of the past, a better analysis of the present and a better view of the future.

The groveling political hacks still believe in touching all bases. While expressing concern over the "upright hangups of violence and anarchy," they cheerfully tell us they "trust the fate of our nation to our callow youth who are experiencing growing pains." The "pigs," of course, take a very dim view of this evaluation.

Sursum corda.

Racism in Agriculture

Phillip Veracruz

Farm workers' children love pennies. As they grow up they begin to realize it takes more than pennies to live, to get an adequate education and survive.

In their confusion they fight among one another for the morsels that fall from the master's table. They mistake one another for the enemy. But recently, they have seen a way out of this chaos. They have begun to think together and re-evaluate their direction for coordinated action. Their spirit demands freedom, social justice, economic progress and independent political judgment and action.

We are the children of yesterday, cursed by poverty and oppression. Our inspiration comes from the lives and example of great men such as Lincoln, Gandhi, the Kennedys, King, and many others. Dim hope flares up with the unprecedented encouragement and involvement of millions of sympathizers and generous supporters who sacrificed to make life more pleasant, decent and enjoyable for others. It is just a natural response that we band ourselves together in a Farm Workers Union for mutual benefits and protection.

The local grape growers here in Delano are like the greedy dog with a big bone in his mouth. While crossing a stream he sees his shadow and tries to grab the other dog's. He drops his own bone in the process. This is what is happening in the grape strike. Growers are losing their market. Their grapes are rotting in cold storages and many of them no longer have credit with the banks.

Meanwhile, the poor workers sweat and suffer to produce the boss's wealth but are denied even a minimal wage for subsistence. They get sick from harmful pesticides and frequently become victims of malnutrition, which is a fancy word for slow starvation.

And so we fight on because even though we are the much despised and hated minorities, the blacks, the browns; we are at the same time indispensable as the labor force in the multi-bil-

Schism v.1, no.4 (Fall 1970)

lion dollar industry which is now called Agri-business. We are tolerated for convenience if we observe the ugly rules of color lines. We are permitted to cross them to work or spend our money, but not to live. We must not be allowed to dilute the super-race.

The railroad tracks in Delano are the color line. In the east-side the whites live and enjoy their sense of superiority. Though among them one is poor and ignorant, he hates Mexicans because they compete for jobs and are paid less. Besides in the cowboy movies he learned that a wild Mexican can throw a knife at his back. He believes that it would be much better and safer if there were no Mexicans at all.

Anglos in the eastside of Delano don't like blacks either. After all, black ancestors were brought here in chains to work in the cotton fields of the south, while theirs came from civilized Europe where the King of France had his head chopped off, where Napoleon butchered thousands of people and where Hitler gassed six million Jews. Perhaps many of them believe that Lincoln made a mistake of freeing the slaves because the kind act gave them hopes. They feel that blacks are "too militant and cannot be trusted in dark alleys." They resent the long-haired radicals who have the guts to say that the American Dream is a nightmare.

In their ranches, the growers maintain segregation. Anglos, Filipinos, Mexicans, Puerto Ricans, Japanese, Arabs, etc., have their own respective groups with their bunk houses and kitchens. Each group is completely a stranger to the other even if both worked for the company for years. The sinister ideas is to keep workers divided. When one group forms a union and strikes for recognition and collective bargaining, the others scab on their fellow-workers. So, exploitation goes on for big profits and prosperity in the agricultural industry and it is never shared by the workers.

People who are segregated by race, nationality or language from others have no mutual understanding nor trust. Isolation fosters suspicions, fear and racial hatred. Thus discussion, agreement and unity among workers is impossible to achieve for the ultimate goal of unionization. On the other hand, the growers become richer, more powerful and ruthless under the shield and influence of the farm bureau federations.

In the farm workers union, all races meet and join together

to achieve an ideal—mutual understanding, sincere cooperation and true brotherhood. The farm workers movement in Delano is the closest approximation of the ideal that I have seen in many years. My hope is that our unity and brotherhood will be permanent.

Straight Talk

Tom Anderson

A racist is a person who believes in genetics, history and his eyes. The epithet "racist" is something few people, including many scientists who know that truth is being smothered, can stand to be labeled with.

If "racist" means a person who hates another person because of his race, it applies to very few white people. More Negroes hate whites because they are white than vice versa. My dictionary says racism is "a belief that race is the primary determinant of human traits and capabilities and that racial differences produce an inherent superiority of a particular race." An overwhelming percentage of white Americans obviously are racists, then, whether they admit it or not. As Voltaire said: "Prejudice is opinion without judgement."

To talk of superiority and inferiority today is to mention the unmentionable. Truth has become bigotry. Fact has become racism. Discrimination has become hate. Hereford breeders don't hate Angus cows merely because they don't want to cross breed with Angus.

Hubert Humphrey honestly believes the average Negro is as good as he is. And I do too. But to get honest comparisons, one must compare average with average, that is, average white with average black.

To feel superior to someone or to a race of people, is not

Schism v.1, no.4 (Fall 1970)

Reprinted with permission of Southern Farm Publications, Nashville, Tenn.

to hate them. There are few Whites whom I like and admire as much as I do a Negro preacher who works part-time for us. He is a Christian gentleman. And I wish I were as good a Christian as he is, because that is infinitely more important than education, money or positon. I *like* him—better than I do Richard Nixon.

There is no such thing as equality. There is not even such a thing as "equal opportunity." If the same opportunity is offered a child prodigy and a moron, they do not have an equal chance. Everything, including the stars, is unequal. "One star differeth from another in glory." (I Corinthians 15:41.) The baby given to an orphanage at birth hardly has the same opportunity as the baby who has one million dollars put in his name at birth. Although the unearned wealth *could* turn out to be a disadvantage.

What stable and civlized republic in all history was predominantly or even substantially Negro? What high culture have Negroes anytime anywhere produced themselves? What high culture, once achieved, ever *remained* a high culture once it became substantially mixed with Negro bloodlines? What Negro republic or free civlization now or ever has shown the necessary attributes of self-control, self-reliance, self-responsibility and self-help to build and maintain a great civilization? Despite what you've been told, Negro history has not been obliterated. There wasn't any. During the past 5,000 years the history of Black Africa is a blank. Not just *here*. Everywhere. It's blank in Africa too. Until other races arrived, there was no literate civilization south of the Saraha Desert. The Black African had not invented a plow or a wheel, domesticated an animal or a crop. He had no written language, no numerals, no calendar or system of measurement. The only buildings he had ever built were a thatched, windowless mud hut and a stockade. His external trade consisted only of his own slaves, ivory, palm oil and mahogany. He carried things only in his hands or in human skulls. His medicine was administered by witch doctors. He was sometimes cannibalistic. He was, in short, a savage.

Instead of saying the Negro is everywhere and at all times "inferior" to the white man, let us say that he is different. About that there is no doubt. When two things or two groups differ, one has to be better in some ways than the other. The Black, on the average, scores significantly below the White in abstract intelligence. The Negro lacks the White's ability to deal with symbols. He can memorize equally, (but he cannot reason equally. He cannot compete with the White in science, statesmanship, arts, literature.

Most of the Negroes who have achieved greatness had White blood. An exception is Dr. George Washington Carver. But peanut butter is not exactly the invention of the ages.

Color of skin has nothing to do with it. The Japanese, 25 years after suffering one of history's most devastating defeats, are now third, behind the United States and Russia, in national production. They are doubling national output every seven years. They are now the most dynamic society in the world. They now do more with what they've got than any other people. They are *not* equal. They are superior. And *not* white. Even "Liberal" historian Toynbee admits that "when we classify mankind by color, the only one of the primary races . . . which has not made a creative contribution to any one of our 21 civilizations is the Black Race." And then Toynbee apologetically adds that only 6,000 years have elapsed since the first civilizations appeared on earth, which is, perhaps, too early to judge whether the Negro is "in a daydream . . . paralyzed . . . or out of the running." To which another writer rejoined: "If 60 centuries is too short a period for man to draw general inference about his past, then Toynbee's life work has been a waste of time."

Few other races, and least of all the Negro, have even approached the cultural, scientific, material and moral achievements of the Anglo-Saxons. In comparing race, to get a true picture, you must compare average with average, or best with best. Some Blacks are of course, superior to some Whites. As someone has said: "However weak the individual white man, his ancestors produced the greatness of Europe; however strong the indivdual black, his ancestors never lifted themselves from the darkness of Africa."

History shows that once the support of other races is withdrawn from the Negro, he retrogresses, as in Haiti.

Washington, Jefferson, Madison, Lincoln, Clay and Franklin all believed the Negro to be basically inferior to whites, unsuited to our society, and all advocated that Negroes be sent back to Africa.

Negro slaves were barbarians, most of whom had been slaves in Africa. They were sold to white traders by other Negroes. And when they got to America, they had never had it so good. The American Negroes came from a race which had never had what could truly be called a "civilization" of its own. Declaring them equal heirs of a civilization Anglo-Saxons had taken thousands of years developing into history's best is as absurd as calling Bishop Pike a Christian.

The best thing that ever happened to the Negro was that he was sold into slavery. Otherwise he'd still be in Central and North Africa.

I'm for allowing the Negro the opportunity to develop himself to his fullest capabilities, to contribute his utmost to mankind, and to develop pride of race which will not let him force himself upon those who do not want to associate with him on equal terms.

Millions of Americans have been brainwashed into believing that the Negro is simply a dark-skinned white man; that all the Negro lacks to live and compete equally in our society is equal environment and equal opportunity. The "Liberal" bleeding hearts have tried to keep it a deep dark secret, but an accumulation of scientific evidence indicates that Negroes possess a genetically lower intelligence potential than Caucasians and Orientals. Dr. William Shockley, Nobel Prize winning physicist, says he fears the Negro's position in American society will deteriorate rather than improve because of a "disproportionately high birth rate among Negroes of lowest potential intelligence." He added that many Negro welfare mothers "have children as pets," and said he believed consideration should be given to sterilization of welfare recipients who produce an excessively large number of children.

Dr. Shockley says a scientific study conducted in London indicates that heredity is about three times more important than environment in determining one individual's intelligence. Emotionalism concerning this subject, he says, has prevented "a sound diagnosis, agonizing though it may be, which might prevent worse agony in the future."

Dr. Shockley is not a Ku Kluxer but a scientist who is unwilling to be bought off by the educational establishment and the do-gooders.

Ours is the age of distortions, half-truths and Big Lies. Even the panel on the Jefferson Memorial in Washington is a lie—because a deletion has been made which distorts his meaning. President Jefferson's complete statement on slaves, emancipation and future race relations as contained in the "Jeffersonian Cyclopedia," page 816, published by Funk and Wagnalls in 1900, says: "It was found that the public mind would not bear the proposition (gradual emancipation) nor will it bear it even at this day (1821). Yet the day is not distant, when it must bear and adopt it, or worse will follow. Nothing is more certainly written in the book of fate, than that these people are to be free; nor is it less certain, that the two races, equally free, cannot live in the same government. Nature, habit, opinion have drawn indelible lines of distinction between them. It is still in our power to direct the process of emacipation and deportation, peaceably, and in such slow degree, as that the evil will wear off insensibly, and their place be, 'paripassu,' billed up by free white laborers. If on the contrary, it is left to force itself on, human nature must shudder at the prospect held up."

The brainwashers' all-out effort to tell it like it ain't, reminds me of when one of the best marksmen in the country was passing through a small town and noticed numerous bulls' eyes drawn everywhere, on fences, trees, walls. Every target had a bullet hole *exactly* in the center. *'Who* is this great marksman?" he asked. They took him to the town idiot.

'This is amazing marksmanship! I've never seen its equal!" enthused the marksman. "How in the world do you do it?"

"Easy, I shoot first and then draw the circle."

The White Power Program

David Ernest Duke

This platform is directed primarily to the White student who believes in the greatness of his race, and who wants to see the White race preserved and protected against all enemies. The main objective of the *White Student Alliance* is to defeat the adversaries of the White race, and to form the groundwork which will not only enable our race to persevere, but also to progress and improve.

Our aim is political *Power;* power not for the satisfaction of any personal egotism, but *Power* to protect, preserve, and advance the White race. Politics is simply a struggle for *Power*. *Power* will be in the hands of people who support *White Interests,* or *Power* will be in the hands of those who serve *Non-White Interests*. It is a harsh either/or. Either our enemies will have power, or we will. Unfortunately, political power in America today is held by the *Anti-White* minority which not only controls the government, but also the powerful media of publications, radio, and television. The plain truth is that our race is losing. We're losing our schools to Black savagery, losing our hard-earned pay to Black welfare, losing our lives to *No-Win* Red treason and Black crime, losing our culture to Jewish and Black degeneracy, and we are losing our most precious possession, our White racial heritage, to race-mixing. As students we can readily see that our high schools and college campuses are the focal points for the *Anti-White* revolution in America. To save our race, we must save our campuses, and make them centers for White Racial activism.

Through courage, strength, and idealism our White race fought disease, famine, and a savage Non-White population to build this nation out of the wilderness. Today, White America is again being threatened by Non-Whites, and yet we find few willing to defend what our people once suffered and died for. The White Student Alliance offers to White students an opportunity to defend their race, and more importantly, its giving White students the chance to become the vanguard fighters for the new philosophy of *Racial Idealism,* a philosophy which will carry our race to even greater achievement and glory. The White Student Alliance is not fighting for what is, it is crusading for what will be.

Racial idealism, or *racialism*, is the idea that a nation's greatest resource is the quality of its people. It means examining all questions of government on the basis of whether the proposed measure is good or bad for our race. It means that racial interests should never be subordinated for momentary materialistic advantage. And, it means that although economics must play a vital role in our system, the primary emphasis of our system must be the physical, mental, and spiritual health of our people. With Racial Idealism as the guiding principle of government, the state ceases to be an end in itself, and instead becomes a vessel carrying its contents: the people, to the highest levels of achievement and greatness. Unfortunately, our country's system could now be correctly termed as an economic one, namely *Capitalism*. Even though we may agree with some of the principles of Capitalism, we must keep it in mind that our nation was not founded for any economic doctrine and that our government was originally established for the protection, preservation, and advancement of our people, and also to secure for our people the right to be master of their own destiny. This is the *racial idealist* cause in which we must invest ourself. Neither Communism, Capitalism, nor any other materialistc doctrine can save our race; our only racial salvation lies in the White racial alliance uniting our people with the common cause of *racial idealism*.

The
White Student Alliance
program is a racial program
consisting of ten points

1. *We must insure the protection, preservation, and advancement of the White Student Alliance*. This is the fundamental principle of the White Student Alliance. The other nine points are simple extensions of this powerful statement. For the White race to be assured protection, preservation, and advancement it is imperative that an all-white America is eventually established. We cannot blame the Blacks for the fact that they are born innately inferior to White people, but neither can we tolerate the dangers they constitute to the White race. Black crime has literally made it unsafe for White people to walk on their own streets. Schools have become racial battlefields when the less-intelligent Blacks have taken out frustrations on White students. The Jewish controlled media of motion pictures, publications, radio, and television have plainly become mass propaganda machines which are feeding every imaginable kind of filth and lies to our people.

White men are losing their jobs to less qualified Blacks, while the White taxpayer is forced to pay huge sums for Black welfare. Furthermore, race-mixing occurs whenever any two races are in close proximity. Separation is the only solution. The White race must again become the master of its own destiny.

2. *We must have a foreign policy that serves White racial interests.* Whether our White racial interests were originally at stake in the jungles of Viet Nam is highly doubtful, but once the decision was made to engage the Communist enemy, every means at our disposal should have been used to defeat the enemy in the shortest possible time, and with the smallest possible loss of American fighting men. Our anti-White leadership bogged us down in an Asian war, and neither will return the American fighting man home, nor let him use the tactics which are necessary for immediate victory. Further examples of our insane anti-White foreign policy are the trade restrictions we have imposed against the pro-White nations of Rhodesia and South Africa, and the billions of dollars of aid and development we have given to non-White nations while millions of White people here and abroad need our help. We must learn to look at other White people around the world, whether they reside in Europe, South Africa, Australia, or elsewhere, as our racial brothers and natural allies. Furthermore, we must never let America be led again into suicidal, fratricidal wars, like the last two world wars, for the sake of alien, minority interests. We must have a foreign policy truly based on the long term interest of our race.

3. *We must have an honest economy.* The White Student Alliance maintains that private property and free competition should be the basis of our economy, but that measures must be taken to root out any and every trace of the economic exploitation of our people. In particular, we must put an end to the economic robbery of our people through he usury of high interest rates, through inflation, and through high-level money manipulation. The system that forces a working man to work over one-third of his life just to pay interest must be completely and uncompromisingly changed. Furthermore, we contend that a man has just as much right to be secure in his job as he is in his home, and that he deserves a decent standard of living as long as he does his work, no matter what type it is,

efficiently and to the best of his ability. Finally, we propose that a man's real value and worth should not be assessed by the amount of money he may make, but by the way he performs his work in relation to his ability, by his character, and by his overall contribution to his race and nation. We must have an economy that serves the interests of our race, and not a race that serves the interests of the economy.

4. *We must have an educational system based on ability.* We must make it possible for young people to achieve the maximum potential in life, and in society. For this to be accomplished, education must become solely based on the principle of student ability, and not on individual students financial resources. Under this principle, all students would be able to obtain the maximum development for their individual abilities. The benefit of this program on the quality of education, and on the quality of the nation, would be invaluable. And, it must not be forgotten that the government should have just as much responsibility to secure the proper development of a student physically. We must have an educational program which will instill into the youth maximum physical fitness, as well as one which insures the maximum deveopment of students mental capability.

5. *We must insure a healthy environment.* We must never forget that our race is a product of Nature, and that it must abide by her laws if it is to survive and prosper. It must be an imperative duty of our government to protect the gifts that Nature has bestowed to America and to insure the maintenance of a clean, wholesome, and healthy environment for our people. We must eliminate pollution and conserve our natural resources, and we must view all technological development not as an end in itsef, but as a means of advancement for our race. Any endeavor which advances us materially and technologically, yet is detrimental to the over-all welfare of our people, must be prohibited. Our race must not be sacrificed to technology, instead technology, as all things, must serve the interests of our race.

6. *We must safeguard the physical well-being, and health of our people.* We must have an America in which our people are healthy and happy; an America in which they can live and work in their homes, and on the streets of their cities without

fear. Drug slavery, venereal disease, subversion, perversion, and crime must be utterly stamped out, using whatever means that are necessary to cleanse our nation of these social cancers. Our government must not only guarantee public safety and order, and the right of our people to keep and bear arms, but it also must maintain an eternal crusade against the internal enemies of our racial well-being. It is a necessity that the basic quality of American life be improved if these national afflictions are to be amended. In other words, we must take our people from the industrialized, congested, neon and asphalt, urban rat-race that many are in, and give them a way-of-life in which they can establish a meaningful and healthy relationship between themselves, their community, their race, and Nature.

7. *We must preserve, protect and promote white culture.* As our race is the product of a higher development of mankind, so our culture is a higher manifestation of our race. Today, formless, anarchistic garbage created by Negroid and Jewish degeneracy is paraded to our people as "art," "music" and "literature." We are told that dog waste on a canvas is art just as great as a painting by Rembrandt, 'it is all the way you look at it!' The great culture heritage of our race must be protected from the present, insane *non-White* degeneracy. Our government must promote every true White cultural endeavor, and it must instill in our youth an appreciation for the order and beauty that symbolize a genuine White culture. We must awaken a new understanding of our racial and cultural heritage, so that the creative instincts of our people can once again find expression in a direction that will continually renew and advance that heritage instead of degrade and debase it.

8. *We must have an honest, free press.* Right along with the principle; Fredom of the press, we must guarantee our people: Freedom from the press. Freedom of the press, in reality, is a myth in America. The mass communication media is simply a dictatorship in Jewish and other non-White elements. Not only does our press feed every imaginable kind of lies and filth to our people, but more importantly, it blacks out the Racialist arguments from the American people. Our people must have freedom from the press, freedom from its lies and misrepresentations, freedom from its massive propaganda de-

signed to encourage race-mixing, freedom from the degradation and degeneration it heaps upon our culture, freedom from the perversion and subversion it fosters in this nation, in general, our people must be free from its varied and incessant attacks upon the White race. The dictatorship of the press must be destroyed; it must cease to serve the interests of an alien minority and begin to serve the interests of our race, by reflecting the spirit of our people.

9. *We must have a government that serves White racial interests.* Our national leaders must be *racial idealists.* The utilization or rejection of proposed government policy must ultimately rest on whether that polity would be beneficial or detrimental to our race. We must have a government of responsible leaders, not the destructive system of irresponsible government, and self serving party politics which rules today; a system in which few but the hypocritical and unscrupulous reach the top. We must have a clean civil service, wtih the severest penalties for anyone in a position of public trust who uses that position to rob from the people. In America, we must have a system which elects for every level of government, the best, the strongest and the wisest men our race has to offer. Our government must not be an end in itself, but simply a means for the preservation, protection, and advancement of the White race.

10. *We must give our people a new faith based on racial idealism.* We must turn our people away from their present materialism, despair, cynicism, nihilism, and emptiness. Our people must be given a true sense of racial brotherhood and idealism. America's White people must be truly brought together as one people and one nation. The spirit of racial brotherhood and togetherness must permeate all our dealings with other White people, and we must have an America in which all our people can have faith in, and be proud of. Furthermore, we must make it our most sacred task to secure the betterment of our race in the future. With determination we must see to it that each new generation of our people will be of a higher quality than the previous generation. We must, to the best of our ability, attempt to eliminate the flaws and weaknesses of our race, while encouraging the best qualities of our people. Our duty to the future is greater than any selfish whims

of the present. Through racialism, our people will have a greater life, and the possibility of unlimited development.

In order to achieve the objectives outlined in the platform of the White Student Alliance, political power must be achieved. The youth of America will one day be the leaders of tomorrow, it must be carried by the youth of today. The road to future political power, as the non-Whites have recognized long ago, is through the young. Finally, there is a national Pro-White youth organization, and it is growing fast and gathering momentum. Here are some of the reasons for the success of the White Student Alliance.

(1) *The White Student Alliance is filling the demand for a pro-White organization.* On America's high school and college campuses there has been a notable lack of any organization fighting for White racial interest, yet there are hundreds of organizations which are Anti-White; a few good examples include the Young Socialist Alliance, the Black Student Union, the Black Panthers, and the SDS. It is easy to see why our race has been losing, since there has been no real opposition against Non-Whites. There are millions of students that believe in the greatness of the White race, but, up till now there has been no real attempt to organize them. The White Student Alliance is nationally organized, dynamic, and racial idealist.

(2) *The White Student Alliance is honest.* To achieve victory for an idea, that idea must be stated, defended, and promoted. Our truthfulness in expounding what we believe, especially concerning racial matters, is the strength of our movement. Not only does racial honesty edify our own ranks, but it also promotes a strong and courageous image. The White Student Alliance will not compromise the truth.

(3) *The White Student Alliance is not a club, it is a fighting organization.* The White Student Alliance is not a pantywaist organization. We are not about to drink tea and eat muffins while our race goes to hell. Our organization is taking the initiative away from our racial enemies by seizing every opportunity to forward our beliefs. Every member of the White Student Alliance realizes the importance of our task, and the importance of taking the offensive in the struggle.

(4) *The White Student Alliance is fighting for a philosophy of life.* A movement conceived only as a defense against an-

other, is doomed to fail because a movement fighting for something can attack and advance, while an organization in defense can only defend and retreat. Our race has been waging a defensive struggle for fifty years with the result that our race has been fighting for a philosophy of life: *racial equality*. The White Student Alliance is fighting for a philosophy of life: *racial idealism*. We are fighting for something more than fighting against something. Now our race can take the offensive: the only road to success.

(5) *The White Student Alliance is neither "left" nor "right" politically.* White people have been divided too long into arbitrary, squabbling groups. Half of the White people are Republicans, and half are Democrats; half are Northerns, and half are Southerns; half are rich and half are poor; half are Catholics, and half are Protestants; half are labor, and half are management; half are "left" and half are "right." White people are so busy fighting among themselves, that non-Whites, by working together as a block, have been able to overcome the White majority. As White students, it is time to cast aside our petty differences and disagreements, and to form an alliance uniting under the common bond of *racial idealism*. Every point of our program was formulated within the concept of *racialism*. For a movement trying to form an alliance of White students, it would be a mistake to hold a position on anything except that which is in the realm of *racialism*.

(6) *The White Student Alliance is national in scope,* with members all over the United States, and a national headquarters right outside of Washington, D.C. A nationwide organization is essential for the realization of our goals; we have that organization.

(7) *The emphasis of the White Student Alliance is on action.* Action is essential to any political movement; in our movement it does not stop. Our action draws public attention, which in turn draws support and members. White Student Alliance action ranges from mailing out fliers, to tearing down Viet Cong flags. Any and every means possible is used to convey our ideas to the public; the White Student Alliance especially relies on public speaking. Whether in addressing a huge audience, or in talking with a friend, the spoken word is an essential part of the tactics of the White Student Alliance. The cardinal rule

for each member is to do something every day for the movement. Action is bringing us results.

The White Student Alliance is presenting a program based on ten principles that are beautiful and uncomplicated, and the White Student Alliance has a platform that will bring ultimate victory to these principles, and our race.

Join the struggle for your race; Join the White Student Alliance.

Black Liberation Impossible without Communists

Claude Lightfoot

The Communist Party has a long and glorious record in the struggle for Negro freedom. This record has been deliberately blurred over and distorted by the enemies of the Party. Today, unfortunately, some who are sincerely working for Negro freedom parrot ruling-class falsehoods that the Communist Party has become "irrelevant."

Communists have made contributions which to this day illuminate the path to Negro freedom. For example, the growth and extension on varying levels of Negro and white unity came directly as a result of the Communists' pioneering efforts. St. Clair Drake and Horace Cayton document this in their celebrated work, *Black Metropolis* (New York, 1945). They state:

> During the early thirties, marchers in Left-wing demonstrations in Midwest Metropolis frequently carried placards bearing the slogan, "Black and White, Unite!" Close interracial cooperation became associated in the popular mind with "the Reds." Of course Negroes and whites, as

Schism v.1, no.2 (Winter 1970)

we have seen, have always cooperated in Midwest Metropolis, but usually in white employer-Negro employee relations, or as Negro-white patron. These Communist slogans, however, signified something that was new to the city: a small band of white men proclaiming a total cooperation of Negro and white workers in a joint struggle to build a new society. Not even the Abolitionists had stood for that.

More recently Msgr. J. D. Conway, a courageous Catholic priest declared in the *St. Louis Review,* official organ of the St. Louis Diocese of the Roman Catholic Church:

> The Communists were 26 years ahead of the U.S. Supreme Court, 35 years ahead of the New Frontier, eons ahead of some prejudiced politicians and who knows how much ahead of Congress and some of our reluctant bishops.

These writers display great courage in speaking the truth as they see it. They also show a deep insight into social problems. Today their numbers are few, but tomorrow they will be far greater.

Through the 1930's and 1940's the Communists were pioneers in building the foundations of struggle against race and class oppression in ever-widening areas. They carried the fight against jim crow into every aspect of American life. They blazed the trail that revealed the real nature of Negro oppression and its real perpetrators. They introduced a new militancy into the freedom fight, reminiscent of the abolitionists and Frederick Douglass. They brought the nature of Negro oppression to the attention of the entire world and thereby made the fight against it worldwide.

In their ranks a new group of Negro leaders emerged, totally dedicated and totally committed to whatever would be required to free their people, regardless of personal sacrifices. Of these we shall speak later.

Drake and Cayton write:

> With the Depression "the Reds" emerged as leaders, fighting against evictions, leading demonstrations for more

adequate relief, campaigning to free the Scottsboro Boys. Their reservoir of goodwill was filled to overflowing, with even the *Defender* writing an editorial on "Why We Cannot Hate Reds."

"Respectable leaders," all during this period, fought against these struggles led by the Communists. But today some of these black leaders are forced by the circumstances of the times to adopt the same techniques and methods which only yesterday they condemned.

The leaders who oppose Communist participation in the black freedom movement claim that Communists are not truly interested in advancing Negro rights, but only seek to use the discontent of the Negro for the purpose of advancing the interests of a "foreign power," namely the Soviet Union. Hence, they claim, the Communists' interest in the Negro question is secondary.

To bolster this contention, some seek to exploit certain tactical errors made by the Communists during World War II. During that war, we Communists declared that the central task was to defeat Hitler, who represented the most reactionary, the most chauvinistic, the most rotten and the decadent forces in the entire world. We maintained further that the emergence of a strong Soviet Union in the Postwar world would be a key pillar in erecting a new world order based on social and racial justice.

Now, in the pursuit of this generally correct goal there was for a time a failure on the part of Communists to push the struggle for Negro rights vigorously enough, out of fear of jeopardizing the war effort. Wherever Communists made such errors, we Communists today join in criticism. But it is one thing to criticize and another to use such errors in an attempt to destroy the validity of a broad basic truth.

What the Communists said during World War II, it is now generally acknowledged, was correct. Their far-sightedness in regard to the Soviet Union's role in the postwar world was prophetic. Today, more than two decades after World War II, the Soviet Union has emerged as the main force against national oppression, generating enough power to give to peoples of color the world over the confidence that they can break the shackles of world imperialism. Were it not for Soviet power, offering an alternative to the domination of imperialism, it is doubtful that over one and a half billion people could have succeeded in freeing themselves from colonial oppression.

During the cold-war years the ruling circles of our country, using anti-Communism to undermine the people's movements, demanded the expulsion of Communists from all areas of American life. The word "Communism" has been made synonymous with the devil. Hundreds of Communists were jailed. Many were deported. Many more lost their jobs and were excluded from chosen fields and professions.

Many former Communist sympathizers and friends were forced to run for cover. The assault of reaction led many weaker ones to "cry for mercy." Never in the annals of American history has an organization been subjected to such persecution. It is doubtful if any other organization could have survived such attacks. Yet, though the Communist Party was compelled to raise millions of dollars to defend itself, it still had the capacity to strike some heavy blows against jim crow and segregation at the very time when its enemies and even some of its freinds were declaring it impotent.

The veteran black Communist leader, William L. Patterson, at a time when he himself faced jail and had the job of providing legal and mass defense for thousands of his Communist co-workers, struck telling blows against jim crow and segregation. He organized and led many historic civil rights struggles during those years. Just as he had organized the campaigns to free the Scottsboro Boys and Angelo Herndon during the thirties, he now took to the bar of world opinion the court frameups of Willie McGee in Mississippi and the Martinsville Seven in Virginia.

In the early 1950's Pattern presented in Paris a petition to the UN against genocide, documenting cases of lynching in the South, both in courtrooms and public squares. This was one of the boldest and most comprehensive exposures ever made of the lynch system in the United States. . . .

The acquiescence of certain civil rights leaders in a policy of purging Communists has proven costly. It has been reliably reported that some of these leaders met regularly with the FBI and were briefed on who was and who wasn't a Communist. Thus, J. Edgar Hoover had the power to purge dedicated fighters for Negro freedom from the ranks of their own organizations. . . .

Anti-Communism (and with it the purging of Communists) is harmful to the nation as such. It is a product of a sick society, mirroring the insanity which has gripped a large segment of our ruling class. It has harmed the interests of the American people more than it has hurt Communists themselves. We have spent hundreds of billions of dollars and have fought several wars, yet socialism continues to spread to all points of the earth. No more than King Canute can we command the tide of history to recede. It is the American people who bear the growing costs of the vain efforts to do so.

If purges of Communists are harmful to the nation in general, they are even more harmful to the struggle for Negro freedom—because their purpose is to deprive the black revolution of the services of some of the most dedicated and self-sacrificing forces our people have ever produced. Especially tragic is the spectacle of white forces, in many instances outright racist elements, dictating to Negro organizations which Negroes may participate in freedom's fight and which may not —compounded by the acquiescence of some so-called "respectable," "responsible" or "safe" Negroes to such a policy.

It is this policy which sought to deprive the liberation movement of such great freedom fighters as the late Dr. W. E. B. Du Bois, the late Benjamin J. Davis, the late James W. Ford, William L. Patterson, Henry Winston, the late Edward E. String, the late Louis Burnham, James E. Jackson, the late Pettis Perry, Hosea Hudson, and countless others, living and dead. These are names which, along with such a renowned fighter as Paul Robeson, would bring honor to any people anywhere in the world in their quest for freedom. Today's freedom fight rests on the solid foundation that these men did so much to help build in the thirties, forties and early fifties.

Dr. Du Bois devoted almost a century of Negro freedom, and yet reaction dared to strike him down. Thanks to a grateful African nation and an outstanding leader, Kwame Nkrumah, this great man was able to spend the last years of his life in full human dignity in Ghana, and to continue to strike blows against racism, colonialism and imperialism. This was with no thanks to many of his former pupils and colleagues who deserted him when reaction reared its ugly head.

Paul Robeson became the main target of reaction in Negro life during the period of McCarthyite hysteria. Here was a giant among men. His powerful voice was raised in concert halls, on public platforms, at home and abroad, always in defense of Negro rights. For this he won the undying hatred of the white ruling class. At Peekskill in 1949 a lynch mob tried to kill him. Again many cowardly Negro leaders sat on the sidelines and were silent as Robeson was attacked for advocating actions to destroy the whole institution of jim crow. What he fought for has become commonplace in the Negro movement today, as his book, *Here I Stand*, testifies.

James W. Ford, twice a Communist candidate for Vice President of the United States, was an architect of the forward thrust of the Negro movement in the thirties and forties. He was a prime mover, alongside A. Philip Randolph in building the National Negro Congress in 1936. The Congress set the pace during that period for the entire Negro movement. It helped elevate the whole struggle to new and higher levels.

To obtain full economic, political and social equality for Negro citizens requires not only Communist participation in freedom struggles but a strong, influential Communist Party as well. For Communist and Left progressive forces are prepared to do everything required to win freedom for Afro-American people. No other force is prepared to play such a role alongside of and in the Negro movement.

Since the early thirties when white Communists, almost alone among whites, advanced and fought for full equality, other white forces have increasingly come into the struggle. In the latter part of the thirties, through the forties and fifties, a new force consisting of labor (especially the CIO) and New Deal liberals emerged as advocates of Negro-white unity. In recent years, while many liberals of the New Deal days, along with corrupt labor officials, have backtracked, new forces have come forward: students and educators on college campuses and a significant section of religous groups. . . .

True, there are many staunch and dedicated people who have emerged in recent years. They are symbolized by the

Moores, the Reebs, the Schwerners and the Liuzzos, who have paid for their convictions with their lives. Dedication and courage, together with an understanding of the need to make changes in our social system and a readiness to fight for such changes, are necessary to hasten progress on all fronts.

The broader white forces are prepared to work for a partial solution, for adjustments in the system that bore and nourished jim crow and segregation. They are not yet ready to work to uproot that system, to change the economic and political power structure of the country as a whole, as are the Communists and other Left forces. Yet, without changing the system, we cannot conceive of the black man's securing his full equality and his freedom.

The Communist Party, as we have pointed out, was the vanguard force promoting Negro and white unity at the grass-roots level in an earlier period. It compelled a number of concessions to the black people, and played an important role in preventing America from goose-stepping aongside Hitler and the Axis powers. . . .

Interracial unity, though still a prerequisite for meaningful social changes for both black and white, as it existed in the past is inadequate today. The black man has found that he can be integrated and still remain a second-class citizen. This is true not only in regard to the power structure, but also in many of those institutions and organizations among the people who proclaim that they represent both black and white. In recent times, the Negro found that he is often an unequal partner even in his own civil rights organizations.

The problem, therefore, requires more than proclaiming the necessity for the unity of Negro and white. What is needed is a force that will create situations in which black people have equal voice with white majorities over the internal problems of the black communities. The problem now is to guarantee the equality of a black minority in a majority white society. Setting norms and standards to reach this goal is the challenge to all pro-democratic white people. It is in this respect that the Communist Party still remains the outstanding force working in the white community. Once again it is called upon to pioneer in the field of race relations. . . .

When struggles reach a point of indecision, when they stray

unto paths of secondary importance, the result is a feeling of frustration, hopelessness and a sense of going around in circles. For these reasons an organized force is needed, advanced in thought, revolutionary in practice and outlook, a force that is on top of the total picture. It is necessary to have an organized force that at each moment of indecison can break the pattern of going around in circles, that can answer the question: "Where do we go from here?" Only a force that understands the overall nature of capitalist society, the inherent laws that make this society tick, that understands the role of classes can indicate the path ahead. Only a movement that has a clear concept of the new and higher social system that will replace capitalism can give clear answers. It uses science as a tool with which to probe all factors in depth and thereby gives the mass struggle a higher level of consciousness, a vision, a deeper sense of confidence. A movement that knows where it is going cannot be defeated.

The Communist Party is such a force. This explains why it is a veteran in this battle. It has a proven record in the struggle for equality. It can make an even greater contribution. The path to black liberation involves not only a program for the immediate period but also a long range program for socialism. Both are unattainable without the participation of the Communists.

J. Edgar Hoover and the Jews

National Chronicle

Surveys prove that a large majority of White Christian Americans are Conservatives. They can be ascribed to the Right-Wing of the political spectrum.

Unfortunately there exists in America a police force that has fallen under the control of the Jews—that organization is known as the FBI. It has been built up in Jewish publications and Jewish owned Hollywood as a "hallowed institution" that should be placed beyond the bounds of criticism. As long as you are an average supporter of any White Racist organization, you will not be bothered by the FBI, but the moment you become publicly active and a leader in your community— you will soon be paid a Visit by the FBI. They will in subliminal terms advise you to disassociate yourself from any critcism of the Jews. They will suggest that it is unwise to be an open leader of any group that does not like the Jews. They will ask questions about that group's local activities as their "excuse" for visiting you—even though they most likely already know the answers to these phony questions.

How have the Jews been able to gain such influence over the FBI? The situation has reached the point where the FBI has become Jewry's most effective weapon to silence all criticism. The visit of an FBI agent to any Patriot's home has but one purpose—*not to gain information* but to intimidate—that indivdual into ceasing his work for the Rightist cause.

There is no such similar treatment of people in the Left Wing by the FBI. Many Leftist leaders have publicly proclaimed that they have never had a vist from the FBI. The FBI actually protects and guards their demonstrations from attacks by the indignant "silent majority." Only when Leftists bomb buildings, does the FBI ever step in.

Through very clever manipulation by two of the slickest Jews in America, have the Jews been able to build their influence within the highest echelons of the FBI. These two men are Roy Cohn and Lewis Rosenstiel.

Roy Cohn was able to successfully cultivate the personal friendship of J. Edgar Hoover during the Joe McCarthy Anti-Communist investigations.

Proof of how close Cohn was able to get to Hoover was his ability, just recently, to have Hoover transfer three New York FBI agents out of the state before they could testify in a current case against Cohn.

Roy Cohn has been standing trial in Federal Court being charged with "bribery, conspiracy, extortion and blackmail." In essence it is charged that Cohn bribed a city appraiser for information involving a condemnation case against Fifth Avenue Coach Lines. Cohn is both a director and a major stock-holder in the company.

It is charged that Cohn paid Jew Bernard Reicher (the appraiser) some $30,000 to give a favorable report greatly raising the supposed value of the Fifth Avenue Coach Lines, Inc.

The New York U.S. District Attorney Morgenthau had sub-poenaed the three local FBI agents to testify before a Grand Jury about their investigations into Cohn's illegal activities. Roy Cohn got wind of this and phoned J. Edgar Hoover direct at FBI Headquarters in Washington, D.C. He demanded that Hoover get rid of these agents. Hoover immediately and per-sonally gave orders those three FBI agents be transferred within 14 days, to destinations from which they would not be avail-able to testify.

(Note: Judge Morgenthau, a Jew, and a Democrat, was just recently asked to resign from the bench in New York. He refused, but he stepped down as it was Tricky Dick who made the request. He claimed that he had several other cases he wanted to follow through, was the reason for his refusal. Ed-HWH.)

U.S. Attorney Morgenthau "got wind" of this move to sabo-tage the case and moved up the date for their testimony. Cohn also "got wind" of this and phoned Hoover once again and ordered him to move faster. J. Edgar Hoover this time moved with unprecedented speed and gave the three FBI agents only 24 hours to get out of town—*THIS THEY DID!* Their wives and families, no doubt, had to move household belongings later, and this no doubt was record speed for moving FBI agents.

Actually charges of conspiracy to obstruct justice could be laid to Cohn and Hoover for this act.. Despite these admitted facts, the daily press has remained silent and there has been no demand for any investigation of Roy Cohn's tremendous influence within the FBI. Neither you nor I could ring J. Edgar Hoover on the phone and tell him to get three FBI agents out of town before they could testify before a U.S. Grand Jury against us.

Roy Cohn's and Lewis Rosenstiel's control over the FBI in behalf of U.S. Jewry is detailed in the article below, but, at this point we would stress that these indisputable facts show how the Jews have been able to successfully remake the FBI into a private intimidation squad to silence every American who might stand up and openly criticize the Jews. They are part of the Jewish "thought control" network, (B'nai B'rith?) which would squelch free speech.

This is very dangerous and is a grave threat to the progress of those who seek to save America from Jewish tyranny and monopoly. Some who are even leaders in the Right Wing have become vcitims of the Jewish brainwashing technique exemplified by the Jew, Efram Zimbalist, star in the FBI TV Show —"The FBI," and produced by the Jewish Metro-Goldwyn-Mayer studios.

Some Patriots actually think the FBI is some kind of "sacred cow." They falsely think the FBI can do no wrong and must never be criticized—and should only be praised! Those who are actually on the battle front against Jewish control of America, know that the Jews' first line of defense against us is the FBI. The FBI moves in quickly to question a sincere active Christian Patriot, when the Jews complain against him.

Read on and you will learn Rosenstiel's power within the FBI:

Several years ago a strong book was published, called "Masters of Deceit." It was purported to have been written by J. Edgar Hoover. It said the Jews had no connection with Communism, but, many patriots saw in this effort a masterstroke of the Jews to white-wash their own people's involvement in the International Communist Conspiracy.

The McCarthy investigation proved that 95% of the Communist spies captured in America were Jews. Also, public revelation proved Jews were in a majority in the leadership of the U.S. Communist Party. The leading spies caught were such Jews as the electrocuted Rosenbergs and their cohorts, Morton Sable, David Greenglass, Judith Coplin, etc., and the loyalty of Jews all across the land was a deep question by Christian-Americans.

Right-Wing Patriots couldn't believe their eyes when none other than J. Edgar Hoover himself came out to the rescue of the Jews in his book "Masters of Deceit."

At long last we can document J. Edgar Hoover's close connections with one of America's most influential Jews. It seems as though Hoover is deeply indebted to Lewis Rosenstiel, President and founder of the Schenley Whiskey Industry. (The makers and owners of a large part of the U.S. liquor market.)

It all began back during the days when the late Senator Joseph McCarthy was exposing hundreds of Reds and other security risks in Government. (Most all of whom turned out to be Jews.) To try and ward off smears which came streaming in from the U.S. Communist Party and their liberal allies that Joe McCarthy was "anti-Semite"—he hired two young upstart Jews as his chief investigators.

Their names were David Schine and Roy Cohn. Their insincere actions and brash carelessness was one of the main points which was later used by the enemy to discredit much of the good accomplished by the late Sen. McCarthy's investigations.

One of the immediate aftermaths of the McCarthy era was the frantic attempt by the Jews to offset the "Communism is Jewish" label which was clearly beginning to stick. Lewis Rosenstiel, the Schenley Liquor tycoon then helped Roy Cohn set up a phony letter-head front called "The American Jewish League Against Communism." Despite the fact that it has no membership, it's press releases were gobbled up by the pro-Jewish daily press, eagerly seeking to appease its big Jewish advertisers. Lewis Rosenstiel was the very first to give money to help finance Cohn's front to help white-wash Jewry.

In relation to all this are some highly interesting sidelights which came to light during the recent investigations into private tax-exempt Foundations. Here are the facts laid out in chronological order.

1. In 1957 Louis B. Nichols stepped down as No. 2 man in the FBI for a job with Schenley Whiskey Corp. (with the title of Executive Vice-President.)

2. Lewis Rosenstiel becomes a very close friend of J. Edgar Hoover through their mutual friend Nichols.

3. In 1964 J. Edgar Hoover gives Nichols and Rosenstiel the OK to organize "The J. Edgar Hoover Foundation" dedicated to "perpetuating the ideals and purposes to which the Honorable J. Edgar Hoover has dedicated his life."

4. In 1965 Rosenstiel gives the J. Edgar Hoover Founda-

tion 1,000 shares of stock in Schenley Whiskey Industries worth $35,000.

5. In 1966, Rosenstiel transfers $50,000 from his own tax-exempt Foundation, "The Dorothy H. and Lewis Rosenstiel Foundation" to the tax-exempt "J. Edgar Hoover Foundation."

6. In 1968, the Rosenstiel Foundation gives the Hoover Foundation an additional $1,000,000 in the form of bonds from the Glen Alden Corp., which was bought up in 1967 by the Schenley combine.

7. Rosenstiel is almost the sole financial contributor to the Hoover Foundation.

The following are the officers of the J. Edgar Hoover Foundation: Louis B. Nichols, President; Donald J. Parsons, Vice-President and a former FBI agent William G. Simon, Vice-President and a former Jewish FBI agent N. J. Pieper, treasurer and a former Schenley officer Patricia Corcoran, Assistant Treasurer and a former Nichol's private secretary employed at Schenley's.

The headquarters of the J. Edgar Hoover Foundation is located in the law offices of Attorney Robert Sagle in Washington, D.C.

The present secretary of the J. Edgar Hoover Foundation is C. D. Deloach, right now No. 3 man in the FBI and a strong possible choice to succeed Hoover.

Up to the present time the J. Edgar Hoover Foundation has not sent any appreciable amount of the large sums given by Rosenstiel. On June 2nd, 1969, Washington writer, Maxine Cheshire revealed that Rosenstiel had purchased tens of thousands of copies of Hoover's book *Masters of Deceit,* for FREE distribution in Universities, Colleges, and important people throughout the United States.

It is thusly clear that certain *RICH JEWS* have been able to flatter J. Edgar Hoover, setting up Foundations designed to appeal to his ego to forever keep his name and "ideals and purposes" alive. It all goes back to Rosenstiel's financing Roy Cohn's fake Jewish anti-Communist group to the free distribution given Hoover's book, "Masters of Deceit," which hands out the real deceitful lie to the effect that Jews are not Communists and that Jewish organizations are the chief bulwark against Communism in America.

There you have the real J. Edgar Hoover story at last, his own private tax-exempt Foundation, Totally Financed and Controlled by the stooges of Rosenstiel—a man of ill fame who came into control of the liquor industry during the bloody days of Prohibition to become a multi-millionaire.

Resignation from the John Birch Society

T. R. Eddy

Hal W. Hunt
Editor
THE NATIONAL CHRONICLE
P. O. Box AC
Burney, Calif. 96013

Dear Hal:
This is a copy of my resignation from the Birch Society.
Dear Sir:
I am writing this letter to cancel my membership in the John Birch Society and to tell you why. I base my reasons on the teachings of the Christian Faith mostly, and on some other rather obvious facts.

Mr. Welch and others of the Society have continually and pointedly welcomed into membership certain people who proclaim themselves "Jews." In view of the fact that the overwhelming majority of "Jews" are openly in sympathy with all forms of left-wing agitation including "Communism," I think any organization that admits them as such, ("Jews,") and then fails to tell about the "Jewish" finance behind the Bolsheviks and the same hand behind our own usurious money system known as the "Federal Reserve System" is highly suspect to say the least. As so many of your publications have stated "the Communists are expert at leading their own opposition."

This is not my only complaint against these people. As a Christian, I am forbidden by my Lord and Saviour, Jesus Christ, to be joined in any way to those that do not believe in Him. The writings of the Apostles, Paul and John speak for themselves. First, John 2:22-23. It is quite plain from these inspired scriptures that so-called "Jews" are first liars, and second, anti-Christs, that do not believe in the Father either as they claim. Now the only other being that requires worship in this world is the devil, so if they workship one they call "God," it must be OUR devil. Another quote is from II John 7. Do you know of any self-proclaimed "Jews" that confess that Jesus the Christ is come in the flesh? For that matter the head of the Society professes only what most people term humanism or naturalism both of which are but paraphrases of most Asiatic beliefs in diety including so-called "Judaism" which is a misnomer for a Babylonian cult carried back to Palestine in the days of the Hebrew captivity.

One last verse dealing with my reason for quitting comes from Corinthians 6:14-15. If the Birch Society is not openly, avowedly and energetically pro-Christian it will fail utterly in what it says are its aims. It cannot be "pro-Jewish" and pro-Christian at the same time.

Since my scriptures forbid being yoked to these unbelievers in any way that I can avoid I formally request you to cancel my membership in the John Birch Society.

Respectfully,

T. R. Eddy

Women's Liberation

Reprinted *in Schism* v.2, no.1 (Winter 1971) from *Good Times*.

Resolution on Women's Liberation

Randee Russell, Jerry Salak
and Kathy Rakochy

Last June, the SDS National Convention passed the resolution "The Fight for Women's Liberation is Basic to Defeating Imperialism." It said that the real basis of male chauvinism is the profits made off the double exploitation of women workers. Male chauvinist ideas are created and perpetuated by the ruling class of this country to justify this extra oppression of women. More important, these ideas are used to divide men and women in their fights against the bosses, imperialism, and racism, by keeping women from doing things as "unladylike" as fighting, and by telling men that it's unnatural to follow the often more militant leadership of women. Thus the fight against male chauvinism cannot succeed if it is seen as separate from the struggle of workers and students against imperialism. This proposal does not intend to repeat what was written and discussed last June; rather, it will try to go further, to relate some of the lessons that we have learned in building CWSA, and give some concrete suggestions of ways to fight male chauvinism.

Male chauvinism, and the extra oppression of women, is not just a bad idea. It is grounded in the basic need of the ruling class to constantly increase profits from the exploitation of workers, and its need to maintain power against the workers by any means necessary. This includes dividing working people, and all oppressed people, in many different ways—including by sex. So women's liberation cannot be achieved by treating it as an idea, a question of life style ("become a liberated woman"), etc. It has to be attacked not only ideologically, but also at its roots—the double oppression of women workers.

Schism v.1, no.3 (Summer 1970)

A look at the situation of campus workers shows that universities use male chauvinism in hiring, pay, etc. Women (often black women) get the lowest paying jobs—as food service workers, secretaries, maids. Usually there is a pay differential between these jobs and similar—sometimes exactly the same —jobs given to men (as food service workers, clerks, and janitors, for example). (A good example of this from U. of Chicago: a sign went up in a dorm cafeteria for two male workers, $2.24/hour. Two weeks later, that sign was replaced by one for two women: same job description, different name —$2.11/hour.)

These ideas are taught in all disciplines. In art and literature, women are presented mainly as sex objects. Psychology explains why that, in fact, is in the nature of things. Sociology ascribes some of the 'problem with black people' is that they are brought up by their mothers and not their fathers!! (Ideas like these have to be smashed!) And history acts like women never even existed, and certainly never did anything which might influence the course of events. In fact, in many countries around the world, and certainly in the U.S., women workers fought some of the bitterest class struggles in the history of the entire country. Things like this are covered up by our 'education.'

Like racism, and many other ideas we have been brought up with and taught all of our lives, male chauvinism has weakened SDS. Some questions which we should think about in terms of our chapters and friends:

What is the percentage of women in the chapter? Why not more?

Do women in the chapter speak up? Do they argue about their ideas? Do they speak at rallies, demonstrations, etc.?

When there are couples: Who does the housework, cooking, etc.? Who speaks up most? Does he encourage or discourage her about struggling politically, ideologically, and physically?

Often—too often—the anwers to these questions show that women are not encouraged to really get involved in fighting the ruling class, in learning and teaching ideas, etc. This does not just apply to new people in chapters, but also to people who have been involved for a while. (For instance, we know one case in which an SDSer was attacked by three Weathermen while putting up SDS posters. Three SDS women were with him, but did not help him defend himself!) When struggle with the ruling class gets sharp, there is no reason why women should not be out on the front lines fighting!! Male chauvinism robs the movement of fighters!

The ruling class—in this case in the form of the university —justifies this situation by saying that women are 'only secondary income earners.' That is a lie: Women work (often earning only $60 to $70 a week) because they have to. When they get home from work, they also have the job of taking care of their children and home. Often, a large percentage of women workers' wages goes to paying babysitters so mothers can work. This whittles the real takehome pay of many working mothers to $30 to $40 per week.

In addition, male chauvinist ideas are used to keep women campus workers from fighting back. The most common of these is the idea that women fighting, and particularly taking the lead in fighting, is 'unladylike.' Another is to convince men workers to look down on 'women's' jobs, and women workers. Thus the bosses can create situations in which men and women workers are divided. (For instance, at U. of Chicago last year, busboys in a cafeteria wildcatted demanding free meals on the job. Women in the cafeteria resented the fact that the men were paid more than they, and the fact that the men had not consulted them about the walkout—and they didn't walk out together. The strike was broken.) What really scares the rulers is when these ideas are overcome and the workers unite, like they did at US hospitals in last year's wildcat strike. When that happened, the administration sent in cops, phony union officials, and everything else they had to break the strike.

In buildng the Campus Worker Student Alliance, we have all too often overlooked blatant cases of male chauvinist pay differentials and other practices. When we haven't overlooked them, we've been much too mild about exposing and attacking them.

The US ruling class runs the educational system here, including colleges and universities. This means that, although they are often very subtle about it, they teach students all kinds of lies, distortions, and divisive ideas in the courses we take. Male chauvinism is part of this. Most importantly: (1) students are taught to disregard the oppression of women workers (and, of course, all workers, especially black); and (2) we are taught that women in general, including women students, are mainly for the pleasure and service of men, and that they should not fight, be interested in politics, etc.

A. CWSA. SDS should take the lead in exposing and fighting male chauvinist abuses of campus workers, male chauvinist abuses of campus workers, male chauvinist pay differentials, etc. We should closely examine the situations on our campuses, learn how male chauvinism is used, and fight it. For example, we could fight for free day care for the children of campus workers. This would be clearly in the interests of all campus workers, men and women, but would help to lift the additional burden that women workers have.

B. In Class. Instead of letting the ruling class put over its ideas unchallenged, we should be in there fighting. We should try, in class and in the papers we have to write (we have to write them anyway—why not make them useful?), to convince other students not to accept the various ideas the ruling class is teaching them, especially male chauvinism. Also, this should not be done abstractly: we should show classmates an aternative—fight male chauvinism, and ally with campus workers.

C. In Chapters. The question of male chauvinism should be taken up in chapters—not just discussed in workshops every few months at NCs. This resolution and last June's resolution can be used as a basis for discussion in chapters, chapter educational meetings or workshops, special forums on the subject, etc. These discussions should also be practical, and apply the ideas to the particular campus (see A. above). In addition, chapters should figure out ways of getting more women involved in SDS activities: canvassing women's dorms, holding special meetings, etc. Women in the chapters should be encouraged to speak at rallies, etc., also.

Of course, these are only a few suggestions. Much more can be done. If we start taking some steps in this direction now, SDS will be a bigger, stronger force for imperialism to have to deal with in a few months!

The Battle of the Sexes

The Herald of Freedom

Women in the United States are being conned into "demanding" the conditions *forced upon them* in the Communist countries. The ultimate maneuver to bring about the complete breakdown of family life has begun under the appealing name of the Women's Liberation Movement. The personnel to get the movement on the road has been culled from the female Civil Rights activists who had grown bored and dissatisfied wtih the role as liberators of the oppressed Negroes. As leaders of the new movement to "liberate" women, they are drawing in support from thousands of misguided women and even some men who do not know that this is all part of the Communist plan. Many years ago, before the American women came under attack by skilled propagandists who have been spreading the word that women are "oppressed," a former high ranking member of the Communist Party U.S.A. informed this writer that the final divisive efforts of the Communists would be aimed at the sexes.

The late Dr. Bella V. Dodd discussed some long range plans of the Communists which she learned of while a member of the National Committee of the C.P.U.S.A. In the United States, where there is no peasant class and where factory workers are quite satisfied with their lot as owners of homes and cars, the Communists decided to concentrate on the Negroes in order to stir up "class hatred," and they have been most successful. Another plan of the Communists, according to Dr. Dodd, was to promote animosity among the various religions but, since this did not work, they decided to infiltrate religion and destroy it from within; at this they have also been successful. The final phase was to be the breaking down of resistance by undermining the structure of family life, one of the main obstacles to the success of Communism. This was to be accomplished by promoting pornography, permissiveness, sexual freedom, and finally women's "liberation" and the Battle of the Sexes.

Schism v.1, no.4 (Fall 1970)

Back in the early days of the Kennedy Administration the "status of women" became a matter of political concern and a presidential commission was formed in 1961. Today Commissions on the Status of Women exist in 43 states, the District of Columbia, Puerto Rico and the Virgin Islands and the Interstate Association of these commissions was formed at their convention in Washington, D.C. in June, 1970. The National Organization of Women (NOW) was formed in 1966 by Mrs. Betty Friedan after the success of her book, "The Feminine Mystique." Mrs. Friedan was president of the organization, which reportedly has 35 national chapters with up to 100 members each, until early this year when she stepped down and was succeeded by Aileen Hernandez.

While she was still president of NOW, Mrs. Friedan issued a "call" for a 24-hour general strike by women throughout the country on August 26, 1970, the 50th anniversary of the 19th Amendment which gave women the right to vote. This was to be "an instant revolution against sexual oppression." Other and more radical groups will join in the Women's Strike for Equality which held a benefit party Aug. 9th at the elegant garden and pool of Mr. and Mrs. Robert Scull of East Hampton, Long Island, N.Y. The Sculls were described as patrons of "the avant-garde." The party was described as something other than an unqualified success, with two hundred people having paid $25 for the privilege of attending. One guest complained that he had expected to be allowed to see the interior of the Scull's home but that it had been carefully locked up.

Co-hostesses of the party were Mrs. Friedan, Mrs. Richard S. Coulson (Edith De Rham), writer Gloria Steinem, the pool-owning Mrs. Scull and the fabulously wealthy Gloria Vanderbilt, who also supported the Black Panthers at a cocktail party. Gloria failed to show up, however, reportedly due to the objections of her husband, Wyatt Cooper. Representative Patsy Mink of Hawaii was flown in from Washington, D.C., but was among the missing when it was announced that she would speak. Mrs. Mink became a heroine to the "movement" when she did battle with Dr. Edgar F. Berman who had the audacity to say that women were unfit (emotionally) for high executive jobs because of such factors as the menstrual and menopause. Although Mrs. Mink consented to attend the "liberation" party, she denied that she was a women's liberationist.

Among the other guests attending the fund-raising party were actress Tammy Grimes and Mrs. Timothy Cooney (Joan Ganz) who is president of the Children's Television Theater which produces the sensationally successful children's program, "Sesame Street." A scheduled speaker was William J. Goode, professor of sociology at Columbia University and president of the American Sociological Association, who talked about the new spread of (woman) power and delivered his remarks clad in a blue velvet suit with a multi-striped shirt. An unscheduled event was the shedding of clothes by Jill Johnston, a writer for the left-wing *Village Voice,* who then proceeded to put on an exhibition swim, wearing only her black panties. Music for the party was provided by the Scull's 19-year-old son Stephen, his shoulder-length hair and his rock group.

The nude swimming upset the party a bit causing a commotion which made it impossible for the speeches to continue and Mrs. Friedan, after muttering about "one of the biggest enemies of this movement," announced that there would be singing. Evidently she felt that "extremists" like Miss Johnston would not be helpful in attaining the political power that can be wielded when 53% of the population is properly organized. Among the other extremists involved in the Women's Liberation Front is Ti-Grace Atkinson, founder of the militant Feminists, who was a national fund raiser for NOW when it was being organized. Ti-Grace believes in total separation of men and women, has no personal life other than the movement and will not appear in public with a man except in a "class-confrontation" debate. She has been going around the country starting "lib groups" and says, "It's easy to mobilize women."

Another "extremist" is Rosanne Dunbar, described as "increasingly Marxist in her views," who states that the last feminist movement failed because "it was never able to make an alliance with working-class women." Roxanne is against all institutions which bind woman to man—marriage, babies, love and sex and was the first liberationist to publicly advocate masturbation as an alternative to the "slavery of heterosexuality." She switched her interests from the black revolution to the women's revolution and has been organizing among Southern women, the black poor, Mexican-Americans and poor whites. This feminist movement will not fail because of lack of contact with working-class women if Roxanne can help it.

Another busy organizer is Jo Freeman who also is a product of the Civil Rights movement. She and other women radicals raised the question of women's liberation at the 1967 National Convention of New Politics where the Communists called the shots. In 1968 she started the first newsletter, "Voice of the Women's Liberation Movement." She also helped to set up the first center in the U.S. (in Chicago) where women can live, meet and study feminist problems, the Women's Liberation Center, which is used as a meeting and "crash pad" for visiting "sisters." Like Ti-Grace, Miss Freeman wants no other life but her work and she feels that the movement's potential is unlimited.

She is undoubtedly right there since there are many organizations involved in the over-all lib movement and each offers something different under the banner of "equality"—free sex, no sex or homo-sex; the choice of having a baby or having an abortion; a chance to be in with the "in-crowd" and get a "piece of the action," a chance to escape the "drudgery" of being a wife or mother or both; a chance at top jobs in the business, professional or political world; a chance to look fat, sloppy and unattractive and feel "liberated" instead of embarrassed or ashamed; a chance to be "independent" if that happens to be your bag.

There are the Feminists founded by Ti-Grace Atkinson; the National Organization of Women, founded by Betty Friedan; the New York Radical Feminists, founded by Shulamith (Shuli) Firestone; the Feminist Repertory Theater in New York, founded by Anselms Del-Olio; the Redstockings, the League for Women's Rights, the Older Women's League, the Media Women and the Women's International Terrorist Conspiracy from Hell (WITCH), among others. There is a female liberation program, produced by Nanette Rainone, over the radical left-wing radio station, WBAI.

NOW is the oldest and probably the least radical of the lib groups; among its campaigns have been the demand for equal employment opportunities for women, day care centers where mothers who want to work can leave their children, and the repeal of abortion laws. Mrs. Betty Berry, the Marriage and Family Coordinator of NOW, wants something done about the fact that "a woman's time is worth nothing if she doesn't work outside the home." NOW advocates mandatory high school courses in the legal and financial aspect of family living and a premarital conference with a lawyer. (Goodbye romance, hello finance.)

A new organization, the League for Women's Rights, would like to see a handbook prepared on the legal status of women before, during and after marriage and have it given out to everyone applying for a marriage license. "It would be like a driver's manual and no license would be given without passing a test on whether the book has been read and absorbed." Some women wish to be completely "liberated" from alimony where as others feel the dissolution of a marriage should be handled in the same financial manner as the dissolution of a business partnership. Florynce Kennedy, an activist lawyer, has suggested that housewives be paid for their time, based on the state's minimum wage and that, if the marriage is dissolved, the amount should be given her as "severance pay," with no deduction for upkeep during the marriage.

These proposals apply to women who are married or who plan to marry but many lib activists want no part of men or family life as it is generally known. Morton Hunt, a knowledgeable writer on the subject, states: "The women's lib extremists make such an issue of hatred for men, marriage and mothering that they don't offer women liberation at all—just a way of cutting off many things that are gratifying to many women." Dr. Abram Kardiner, former head of the department of psychiatry at Columbia University, believes the extremists are irrationally motivated, stating: "From what I've seen of the liberationists, their most conspicuous feature is self-hatred. I see tremendous vituperativeness and lack of feeling. They think it's a curse to be female and have exaggerated opinions about the merits of being a male."

The Feminists have picketed the N.Y. marriage license bureau, charging "fraud with malicious intent," and stating "Marriage is slavery . . . the wife is cheap labor, unpaid except for bed and board." The Redstockings have issued a manifesto which states in part: "Women are oppressed, class-exploited as sex objects, breeders, domestic servants and cheap labor." The oppressors are "all men." Maybe these gals just haven't met the right guy.

The radical background and the radical future of the Women's Liberation movement was indicated in an announcement of International Women's Day, March 8, 1970, which stated:

"Women's struggles have a history. The first Women's Day was on March 8, 1908 when thousands of working women from the lower East Side of New York City demonstrated in the streets for the right to vote, better working conditions, shorter working hours, and legislation against child labor. In 1911, Clara Zetkin, a socialist leader in Germany, proposed that March 8 be proclaimed International Women's Day. Since then, women have used this day to celebrate their struggles, to protest and to demand."

Describing today's "struggles," the announcement read as follows:

"Black and brown women are leading the struggles of women in this country . . . Black and brown people have been oppressed and exploited as people for hundreds of years. Their labor helped build this country but they have not shared in the benefits of this labor. . . .The cops are used like an occupying army in black and brown ghettos, interested in protecting the property of businessmen, not protecting the lives of ghetto residents. The cops use terror and brutality to keep black and brown people down.

"Black and brown people have a long history of resistance to such oppression. The Panthers, Los Siete, the Young Lords, are leading the struggles of their people against brutality and for liberation. . . .

"Black and brown women, in the fight for the liberation of their people, are showing all women how to win our own liberation. It is only by becoming fighters for liberation and by uniting with our real friends—working people around the world, black, brown, and white—to fight our real enemies— the imperialists—that we can win our liberation as women. . . .

"White women in this country are getting together too. . . . Side by side with our sisters here and around the world, we are saying that the world must be controlled by and for the people who live in it and produce its wealth."

Like all other "movements" in which the Communists are interested, there is something to appeal to non-Communists, some basically good and fair demands to which are added little by little the extra ingredients which spell out C-O-M-M-U-N-I-S-M to the experienced eye. The formula of combining legitimate grievances with Communist objectives is ever a favorite for lining up mass support. The various "grievance groups" are then used as a political lever and we move further and further to the left. The new Women's Liberation Front is just another of the many Communist-promoted and inspired movements which have been accomplishing this purpose. The "liberation" of women (The Communists called it "emancipation.") was supposedly one of the great accomplishments of the Communist cabal which took over Russia. As of 1939 they proudly proclaimed:

The great October Socialist Revolution emancipated woman, giving her full equal rights with man.

Article 122 of the Constitution of the U.S.S.R. declares:

"Women in the U.S.S.R. are accorded equal rights with men in all spheres of economic, state, cultural, social and political life.

The possibility of exercising these rights is ensured to women by granting them an equal right with men to work, payment for work, rest and leisure, social insurance and education and by state protection of the interests of mother and child, pre-maternity and maternity leave with full pay, and the provision of a wide network of maternity homes, nurseries and kindergartens. . . ."

To help women take an active part in production and in public life in general the Soviet state has established numerous nurseries and kindergartens, where the mother can leave her child while she is at work. . . .

Soviet legislation on marriage and the family protects the interests of mother and child. In the Soviet Union marriage is a voluntary union of free and equal persons. Registration of marriages in the U.S.S.R. is encouraged both in the interests of the state and society as a whole and in order to facilitate the protection of the personal and property rights of the wife and the children. However, unregistered marriages are just as registered marriages in the eyes of Soviet law. There are no "illegitimate" children in the Soviet Union, all children are accorded the same rights.

A marriage may be dissolved either by mutual agreement of the husband and wife, or at the desire of either one of them. . . .

The care manifested for children in the U.S.S.R. is not confined to their school years. From their very youngest days the children are the objects of an attention which ensures them the opportunity of growing up into worthy citizens of Socialist society. The working mother may work in the factory or office, and the collective farm mother in the field, with their minds at rest, knowing that their children are safe in nurseries under the supervision of experienced doctors and nurses.

In the kindergarten and the school the growing child is provided with everything necessary for his physical and mental development.

In the sparsely inhabited regions of the Far North, the steppe lands and the forest regions, boarding schools and dormitories have been built, so that the children are not obliged to walk for miles to get to school. . . .

What the "emancipation" of women in the Soviet Union means and what the "liberation" of women in the United States will mean is that women can be made to work like men while their children are raised (and indoctrinated) in state-controlled or owned nurseries and schools. Women here will be "liberated" to work harder than they ever did taking care of their homes and children, but with none of the happiness and satisfaction that accompanies what to most women is a "labor of love."

It is one thing when obviously "kooky" extremists demand outrageous forms of "liberation" but when seemingly respectable government officials go them one better the time has come to sit up and take notice. The N.Y. *Times* of August 11, 1970 reported that Mrs. Rita E. Hauser, the U.S. Representative to the U.N. Human Rights Commission, said in a speech that laws banning marriages between persons of the same sex were unconstitutional. Mrs. Hauser spoke in St. Louis at a meeting of the American Bar Association on the subject of "Women's Liberation and the Constitution" and stated that such laws were based on an outdated notion that reproduction is the purpose of marriage and that over population had made this rationale outmoded. Since limiting reproduction has now become the social goal, according to Mrs. Hauser, she said "I know of no better way of accomplishing this than marriage between the same sexes." Yes, that would surely take care of the "population explosion" but we would hope that it would create another kind of explosion—of outrage from normal men and women.

Another less revolting but more costly (to the U.S. taxpayers) plan has been proposed by Rep. Bertram L. Podell of New York who has announced that he plans to introduce legislation to provide a pension plan for housewives. This would apply to 26,845,000 women classified by the Labor Department as housewives. A new constitutional amendment has also been started on its way by passage through the House of Representatives as a result of the efforts of Rep. Martha Griffiths. It must now pass the Senate and be passed by three fourths of the state legislatures. The amendment guaranteeing women equal protection under the law was first proposed in 1923 and has been sitting around awaiting the proper climate to present itself again.

That "proper climate" is definitely here but the Women's Silent Majority would do well to avoid the Battle of the Sexes. Legally "guaranteeing" more and strange "rights" to women will only bring the government more and more into our private lives and produce the same kind of totalitarian government that exists in the Communist countries, by easy stages and because "the people" demand it.

National Defense

Reprinted in *Schism* v.1, no.4 (Fall 1970) from *Liberty Letter*.

A Profile of Defeatism: Dismantling the Nation's Defenses

Anthony Harrigan

History shows that soft thinking and faint-hearted leadership form a path to national destruction. Students of the Roman civilization point to the Roman Senate's loss of will to win as a major cause of the downfall of the empire. At the last, the Senate seemed to serve the barbarian aggressors rather than the national interest of Rome.

A generation ago, the representatives of the French people took refuge in a Maginot Line mentality, saying that the shift in the strategic balance to Nazi Germany would not endanger France. They rejected appeals for stronger defenses, arguing that new cycles of weapons took money needed for social purposes and insisting that there was no absolute security in more weapons. They sought peace through negotiation and favored concessions such as were made at Munich.

Today, many thoughtful Americans are deeply concerned that a similar mood is settling over the United States. They are alarmed at the growth of the anti-preparedness sentiment in the U. S. Senate and the impact of this sentiment upon sections of public opinion. They fear a rapid decomposition of American morale as a result of defeatism among men in high places—defeatism masked as a "struggle for peace."

For many months, senator after senator has chipped away at various features of the nation's defenses—at aircraft carriers, the C-5A transport, the Army's new battle tank, military aid to allies, anti-ballistic missiles, selective service, ROTC, fighter-bombers, and numerous other weapons and programs basic to the security of this nation. Companies which produce weaponry needed for national safety have been libeled as

Schism v.1, no.4 (Fall 1970)

merchants of death. American soldiers in the field, fighting an utterly unprincipled enemy that resorts to trickery and terrorism, have been criticized for making the tough battlefield decisions that combat troops must make if they hope to stay alive.

This harassment of the nation's defense forces apparently is only the beginning. Some people, it seems, won't be satisfied until the American defense establishment is dismantled. In this connection, it is instructive to review the massive opposition to the ABM (anti-ballistic missiles) and MIRV (multiple warhead missiles).

Pressure for a slowdown in America's defense effort is intense and comes from many sources. For example, a group of Americans met at Arden House, Harriman, N.Y., March 31-April 2 under the auspices of the American Assembly of Columbia University to consider arms limitation. At the conclusion of their meeting they issued a statement, saying: "We ask the President to defer for six months the impending deployment of multiple independently targetable re-entry vehicles (MIRV)."

The MIRV missiles constitute one of the few areas in which the United States is ahead of the Soviet Union. A U.S. halt at this time might probably give the Soviets a chance to catch up with the United States. Thus a halt could well be a military technological disaster for the United States.

The American Assembly describes itself as a "non-partisan educational institution." But consider the signers of the anti-MIRV statement. One of them was Adam Yarmolinsky, former assistant to Secretary of Defense Robert S. McNamara. Mr. Yarmolinsky, was a guiding spirit behind the campaign to muzzle the military in the early 1960's. Another signer was Dr. George W. Rathjens of the Massachusetts Institute of Technology, a leading contributor to Senator Edward Kennedy's anti-ABM book published in 1969. Two other contributors to the Kennedy volume also signed the American Assembly report. A close reading of the entire list of signers shows that it was a "stacked deck" and blatantly partisan.

Arguments against a strong stand on national defense find innumerable outlets. McGeorge Bundy, former adviser in the Kennedy and Johnson administrations and now president of the

Ford Foundation, testified in Washington on the "arms race." Predictably, he urged suspension of deployment of offensive and defense strategic weapons. He was quick to recommend American concessions, saying for instance, that "if we are to get any early limit on SS-9 (Russian missile) deployment, we ourselves must put MIRV on the bargaining table." Mr. Bundy's most curious statement, however, was his comment that "there are times and topics for toughness with Moscow, but the Strategic Arms Limitation talks (SALT) in April is not one of them." That will strike many citizens as strange advice. Mr. Bundy recommends that the U.S. not be tough in talks that effect the security—the lives—of the American people. Does he imagine that the Soviets will cease to be tough in their demands?

An air of unrealism permeates the statements of anti-preparedness elements in the country. Congressman William S. Moorehead of Pennsylvania said in April that he saw no need for the U.S. to maintain 15 aircraft carriers "since none of the communist nations have any attack carriers." One wonders whether Rep. Moorehead meant what he said. Does he believe the U.S. should scrap the weapons system in which it has a clear lead over the Soviet Union? The interior logic of his statement is that the U.S. shouldn't maintain carriers because it has an advantage over the Soviets in carrier deployment. That's a sure prescription for second class status in the world, if not outright defeat by the USSR.

For naivete, Americans have only to read the comments of Sen. Edward W. Brooke (R-Mass.). In a recent Senate debate on the ABM and MIRV, Sen. Brooke remarked: "I believe that the Soviet people centainly cannot want to continue the spending of billions of dollars on nuclear weapons when they could best put that money to better use."

Since when have the wishes of "the Soviet people" ever mattered for anything in the shaping of Soviet policy or programs?

Centainly, Sen. Brooke must be aware that there is no representative government—no voice of the people—in the Soviet Union and that the party, military and organizational hierarchs make all the decisions, irrespective of what the people want. Indeed, there is no free press and no freedom of petition, so the real desires of the Soviet peoples cannot even be articulated or find expression at the national level. Thus Sen. Brooke's question can be seen as an extraordinary piece of irrelevance, which is damaging because it obscures the nature of the threat facing the United States.

The thought processes of the members of the anti-preparedness bloc understandably strike realistic citizens as strange indeed. Take, for example, the statement of Sen. Edmund S. Muskie (D-Maine) that "more nuclear weapons do not buy more security." Statements to this effect have been issued by many of the opponents of new defensive systems. What does Sen. Muskie mean? Is the statement logical? Suppose a senator were to say "more hospitals don't buy better medical care." Would anyone believe him? Logically, nuclear weapons are as to national security as hospitals are to medical care. In the case of weaponry, there is an additional element, namely that the adversaries of the United States—the enemies of American freedom—are increasing their stock of nuclear weapons. Relatively, therefore, the U.S. has a smaller stockpile of nuclear weapons. The logical conclusion to be drawn from this situation is that America's security is diminishing. Hence the need for the ABM, MIRV and other offensive and defensive systems.

The intense antagonism to strengthened American defenses has even reached the point where the editors of The New York Times assert (as they did in reference to the opening of the SALT talks April 16) that "hopes for halting the nuclear missile race ride for the moment with the Soviet delegation." The Times followed this up with Leonid Brezhnev's statement that prospects for the SALT talks would be favorable "if American opinion succeeds in overcoming resistance by the arms manufacturers and the military." It is interesting to wonder what might have been the U.S. public reaction in 1941 if a leading American newspaper had indicated the U.S. was doing nothing to halt an arms race and quoted the Imperial Japanese government as saying that peace prospects would be good if American shipbuilders and the military could be overcome.

It is unfortunate that the editors of The Times don't share the realistic views of C. L. Sulzberger, The Times' chief correspondent. In a dispatch from Belgium this spring, Mr. Sulzberger declared: "The menace against America is being heightened while Moscow seeks to continue the impression that it sticks to the Khrushchev era strategy. . . . More and more ICBMs are aimed at the United States which is increasingly in the front line."

Such is the situation the United States faces in the world today. The American people live in a global environment of increasing danger from the nuclear-armed Soviet Union.

The facts of the changing strategic balance have been spelled out to the President, the Secretary of Defense, the House Armed Services Committee and authoritative strategic studies groups in the U.S. and Western Europe. Nevertheless, the anti-preparedness elements choose to ignore the accumulation of facts concerning the nuclear and missile threats. Perhaps the most extraordinary aspect of the entire anti-preparedness drive is the extent to which the disarmers are willing for the country to go. The battle against conventional weapons such as aircraft carriers, transport planes and heavy tanks—is but a prelude to the central assault on America's basic deterrent power against Communist aggression.

Sen. George McGovern (D-S.D.) revealed the full scope of the disarmers' hopes and plans April 9 in debate in the Senate on an anti-MIRV resolution. For the first time, a member of the Senate anti-preparedness bloc called for dismantling of a key portion of the nation's defense against Soviet aggression.

"I think we are forced to consider this year," said Sen. McGovern, "whether it would not be wise to allow the phasing out of the entire fixed site ICBMs. At the very least we should forego expenditures on futile improvements in the Minuteman force pending an investigation of whether land-based missiles can be a viable component of our retaliatory forces in the future." He called for a flat prohibition on funds for the Minuteman procurement program.

There's no mistaking Sen. McGovern's intent, for he emphasized that he favors "phasing out" the Minuteman. Hopefully, the meaning of this statement will not be lost on the American public. The Minuteman missiles are an absolutely indispensable element in the nation's defense against surprise Soviet nuclear attack on the United States. If the Minuteman force were eliminated, the American people would be naked to direct and disastrous destruction at the hands of the men in the Kremlin.

That a member of the U.S. Senate would make such an appalling proposal is a frightening revelation of the lengths to which the anti-preparedness bloc is prepared to go. It would almost seem that some members of this bloc have concluded that the struggle against the Soviet empire is hopeless and, secretly, are prepared to make the American people adjust and accommodate themselves to Soviet domination.

The McGovern statement plainly indicates that the pressure is on for unilateral disarmament by the United States—a one-sided abandonment of nuclear defenses which would leave the United States weak and ultimately helpless. It is hard to believe that the American people approve of unilateral disarmament or accept the idea of a Soviet victory in the cold war. Yet that is the direction in which Sen. McGovern and other disarmers and defeatists are pushing the United States. The American people must support national defense programs if the Munich men of our time are not to triumph.

National Defense without Armaments

Gene Sharp

Now, more than ever, we need to question some of our basic assumptions about defense, security and peace, and to examine possible new policies that might help achieve those goals. The dangers and limitations of modern military means—conventional, nuclear, and chemical-bacteriological—are too obvious to need repetition. What has not been clear is what alternative we have. This article is focused on one alternative system of defense, which is most commonly called civilian defense.

The often-posed choice between the acceptance of tyranny

Schism v.1, no.4 (Fall 1970)

The following is a chapter from Mr. Sharp's *Exploring Nonviolent Alternatives,* Extending Horizons Books (Boston: Porter Sargent Publishers, 1971).

and the waging of war has been aggravated by developments in weapons technology, communications, and transportation. The technological changes in methods of war have brought about the concentration of large-scale military power in the hands of a few countries which possess scientific know-how, a technological and industrial base, and vast resources. In particular, the supremacy of the United States and the Soviet Union in capability for large-scale conventional and nuclear warfare cannot yet be seriously challenged.

In consequence, most countries have found that their capacity for self-defense has been drastically reduced or destroyed altogether. This is true even for highly industrialized Western European countries, and the matter is more extreme for less developed countries.

At the same time, local conflicts have gained worldwide significance and led to direct involvement in one form or another by the super powers. This gravitation of deterrence and defense tasks to the most powerful and most technologically developed countries has had a variety of undesirable results for the other countries.

For example, alliance with a super power is no sure guarantee of national security. The ultimate defense lies in foreign hands, and despite treaties a small power may be left helpless when the chips are down, as the fate of Czechoslovakia was attacked by its own allies!

Likewise, military help from a super power can be highly dangerous for the people being "defended." Witness Vietnam. And what would happen to West Berlin, or even West Germany, in case of powerful American military help to throw back a Russian invasion?

Dependence on stronger powers for defense may have other disadvantages. For example, do not the very people who want American military support frequently resent being dependent on it? Does not dependence on others for defense sometimes lead to reduced willingness to contribute to one's own defense? Does not such dependence often lead to an unwise stifling of one's own political judgment and autonomy in both domestic and foreign policies?

This shift of responsibility for the security of many nations to the super powers has more than doubled the latter's defense tasks. Military commitments of the U.S. extend far beyond its own defense. Dozens of countries around the world depend on American support and pledges for their security. A similar situation exists on a smaller scale for the Soviet Union. Someday China may have a comparable status.

These foreign commitments (assuming good motives behind them) are for the United States an extraordinarily difficult and often thankless task. Even from a military perspective, there are severe problems involved in carrying out this world role, as is illustrated by the war in Vietnam and the tensions in Korea.

The political problems are also severe. It is hard, for example, to pose as a defender of freedom when that role seems to require alliances with reactionary dictatorships. Great sacrifices intended to help people avoid dictatorial rule are sometimes seen as unwanted efforts of Uncle Sam to be the world's policeman. Or, less flatteringly, as ruthless attempts to impose a new imperialism.

It is hardly necessary to mention that the local involvement of a super power carries with it the additional danger of escalation into a larger international war. All this is to say nothing of the drain of resources on the United States, the killing of American soldiers, the effects of such violence abroad on the society at home, or the distraction from other important domestic and international tasks.

This could all be changed if countries fearing military aggression or the imposition by violence of minority dictatorships had the capacity to defend themselves—in other words, if countries throughout the world were able, primarily by their own efforts, to defeat domestic or foreign-aided dictatorial groups, of *any* political stripe, and also were able to deter and defeat international aggression against themselves.

The world security situation would then be very different, and would not "require" global American military involvement. There would then be neither the need nor the excuse for worldwide military commitments of the United States or any other country. The super powers could instead concentrate on their own defenses and devote their technical and financial superiority to constructive humanitarian ends.

But is this possible? How can the capacity for self-defense be restored, if it has been destroyed by the very nature of modern military technology? We need to ask: Can there be a new concept of defense which is *not* dependent on military technology, but which could nevertheless be effective against real dangers? That could only happen if defense could be provided *without* military means—an idea which to most people has been inconceivable.

Defense has almost always meant military defense. I will argue that this need no longer be true. The main question is: How can there be a nonmilitary defense?

We must start with basics. We have usually assumed that defense capacity and military power are identical, and that military occupation means political control. But these assumptions are not valid.

Military power today often exists without real capacity to *defend* in struggle the people and society relying upon it. Often it only threatens mutual annihilation. More importantly—and this is the main argument of this article—defense capacity can today be provided without military means.

Military occupation does not necessarily give the invader political control of the country, and the occupation can be destroyed *without* military resistance.

Since military technology in most cases has abolished the possibility of effective geographical defense, we are thrown back to the people for the defense of their freedoms and society. This approach is called *civilian defense* (not to be confused with civil defense).

Civilian defense aims to defeat military aggression by using resistance by the civilian population as a whole to make it impossible for the enemy to establish and maintain control over the country. This is a direct defense of the society by the citizens. The priorities of action are crucial. The maintenance of a free press, for example, or keeping the invader's propaganda out of the schools is each of more direct importance to democracy than, say, possession of a given mountain or the killing of young conscripts in the invader's army. Large-scale preparation and training would be necessary to maximize the effectiveness of social, economic and political power against an invader or an internal take-over.

The citizens would prevent enemy control of the country by massive and selective refusal to cooperate and to obey, supporting instead the legal government and its call to resist. For example, police would refuse to locate and arrest patriotic opponents of the invader. Teachers would refuse to introduce his propaganda into the schools—as happened in Norway under the Nazis. Workers and managers would use strikes, delays and obstructionism to impede exploitation of the country—as happened in the Ruhr in 1923. Clergymen would preach about the duty to refuse to help the invader—as happened in the Netherlands under the Nazis.

Maintaining Control

Politicians, civil servants and judges, by ignoring or defying the enemy's illegal orders, would keep the normal machinery of government and the courts out of his control—as happened in the German resistance to the Kapp *Putsch* in 1920. Newspapers refusing to submit to censorship would be published illegally in large editions or many small editions—as happened in the Russian 1905 Revolution and in several Nazi-occupied countries. Free radio programs would continue from hidden transmitters—as happened in Czechoslovakia in August, 1968. In civilian defense struggles, the general citizenry and the society's institutions are themselves combatants. When successful, civilian defense of the society would lead to the collapse or withdrawal of the invader or internal usurper. But the victory would follow from the successful direct defense of the society, not from battles over the control of geography.

In addition, in case of invasion, civilian defense would set in motion restraining influences both in the invader's own country (stimulating dissension at home, splits in the regime and, in extremes, even resistance) and in the international community (creating diplomatic pressures, political losses, and sometimes economic sanctions) that would be inimical to the invader's interests and to his attempts at consolidating an occupation.

This may sound unlikely. But there is more evidence that civilian defense can work than there was 30 years ago for the practicability of nuclear weapons, intercontinental rockets and trips to the moon.

Nevertheless, the idea that national defense may be exercised more effectively by the vigilance and trained nonviolent resistance of citizens than by military means seems startling to some and ridiculous to others. There is no denying that there would be risks and dangers involved in such a policy. But these need to be measured against the risks and dangers of military deterrence policies.

Contrary to present assumptions, there is a long history of nonviolent political struggle. Despite lack of knowledge of its requirements, and in the absence of training and preparations, this technique has produced some impressive results, even against high odds.

There are as yet no cases in which prepared civilian defense has caused an invader to withdraw—because there has never yet been a case of prepared civilian defense being used as a country's official defense policy. (There are, of course, cases of effective unprepared resistance in occupied countries, such as colonial India and World War II Norway.) The formulation of a civilian defense policy is a deliberate attempt to advance beyond where we are now, an attempt based upon a serious calculation of political realities and possibilities.

Given the resources and the commitment, there is reason to believe progress can be made in devising political strategies of nonviolent action calculated to control tyrants and preserve political freedom. With political research and analysis, it seems to me that we could locate and come to understand the weaknesses of occupation regimes and of totalitarian systems. Then we could concentrate resistance against them on their weak points, using what might be called a form of "political karate."

Even *without* advance preparations, the people of Czechoslovakia provided an experiment in the use of nonviolent struggle in their response to the Russian invasion and occupation. Given the options open to them, their successes, while moderate, were temporarily impressive. The Russians have not yet withdrawn; they have won important points, although at greater cost than expected. The Dubcek regime held out from August until April, while the Russians expected to be able to overcome possible Czech military resistance within days. We need to learn from the strengths and weaknesses of this case.

Civilian defense ought to be subjected to an examination and conisideration at least as rigorous as that devoted to any proposal for a major change in defense policy. Concrete examination has to be given to the many practical problems involved in waging civilian defense, to possible strategies, to types of repression that would need to be anticipated, and to the question of the casualties. My plea, therefore, is not for the adoption of civilian defense now, but for research, investigation and official consideration. My intent is not to win converts, but to provoke thought.

Begin with the Known

As a first step, civilian defense must draw upon the known experience of nonviolent struggle, without being limited by it, in order to develop viable strategies to deter and defeat attacks on a country.

The study of cases of nonviolent action has been largely neglected by strategists, historians and social scientists. Serious research to correct this neglect has only begun. Moreover, the situation has been aggravated by a series of misunderstandings about the nature of nonviolent action which need to be corrected.

Nonviolent action, the major instrument of a civilian defense policy, is the opposite of passivity and cowardice. It is not simply persuasion, but the wielding of power. It does not assume that man is inherently "good." It has been mostly used by "ordinary" people. It does not absolutely require shared principles or a high degree of common interest between the contending groups. It may work by "nonviolent coercion." *At least* as "Western" as it is "Eastern," the technique is designed for struggle against a repressive violent opponent. It may be used to defend as well as to change a government, and has been widely applied against foreign occupations and even against totalitarian systems.

There are many instances of effective nonviolent action, including: the early resistance by American colonists, 1763-1775; Hungarian passive resistance vs. Austrian rule, especially 1850-1867; Finland's disobedience and political noncooperation against Russia, 1898-1905; the Russian 1905 Revolution, and that of February, 1917 (before the October Bolshevik coup); the Korean nonviolent protest against Japanese rule, 1919-1922 (which failed); the Indian 1930-1931 independence campaign; German government-sponsored resistance to the Franco-Belgian occupation of the Ruhr in 1923.

Later examples include: resistance in several Nazi-occupied countries, especially Norway, the Netherlands and Denmark; governmental and popular measures to nullify anti-Jewish measures in several Nazi-allied and Nazi-occupied countries, such as Bulgaria, Italy, France and Denmark; the toppling by popular noncooperation and defiance of the dictators of El Salvador and Guatemala in 1944; the 1963 and 1966 campaigns of the Buddhists against the Saigon regimes in South Vietnam.

Other recent cases involve resistance, uprisings and less dramatic pressures for liberalization in communist-ruled countries, including the 1953 East German uprising, strikes in the Soviet political prisoner camps in 1953, major aspects of the 1956 Hungarian revolution, Polish popular pressures for reforms, efforts for de-Stalinization in the Soviet Union, popular pressures for liberalization in Czechoslovakia early in 1968 and popular and governmental noncooperation following the Russian invasion in August.

Thus, it is evident that nonviolent resistance has occurred even against totalitarian systems, on an improvised basis and despite the absence of training, preparations and know-how. It should be noted that totalitarians like Hitler deliberately sought to promote the impression of their regime's omnipotence, both domestically and internationally, to discourage any potential opposition. Such systems contain critical weaknesses in the form of inefficiencies, internal conflicts and tendencies toward impermanence. It is precisely these features that offer themselves up for exploitation by civilian defense strategies. However, the basic reason why civilian defense can be effective against totalitarian systems is that even such extreme political systems cannot free themselves entirely from dependence on their subjects. As an articulated strategy, civilian defense is designed to deny totalitarian rulers the compliance, cooperation and submission they require.

Over 146 specific methods of nonviolent action have been identified (defined, with examples, in my forthcoming The Politics of Nonviolent Action). These methods are classified under three broad categories: protest, noncooperation and intervention.

The methods of nonviolent protest are largely symbolic demonstrations, including parades, marches and vigils (40 methods). Noncooperation is divided into four sub-categories: a) boycotts of social relations (six methods), b) economic boycotts (24 methods), c) strikes, and d) acts of political noncooperation (34 methods). "Nonviolent intervention," by psychological, physical, social or political means, includes 18 methods (such as the fast, nonviolent occupation and parallel government).

The use of a considerable number of these methods—carefully chosen, on a large scale, persistently, with wise strategy and tactics, by trained civilians—is likely to cause any illegitimate regime severe problems.

Nonviolent action resembles military war more than it does negotiation; it is a technique of struggle. As such, nonviolent action involves the uses of power, but in different ways than military violence. Instead of confronting the opponent's apparatus with comparable forces, the nonviolent actionists counter with political weapons. The degree to which noncooperation itself will threaten the opponent's power position will vary, but its potentiality is illustrated most obviously in the disruptive effects of massive strikes and in mutinies of the opponent's own troops.

The violent antagonist's repressive measures are hardly insignificant, but *in themselves* they are not decisive. In fact, the opponent's repression is evidence of the power of nonviolent action, and is no more reason for despair than if, in a regular war, the enemy shoots back.

If the civilian defenders maintain their discipline and persist despite repression, and if they involve significant sections of the populace in the struggle, the opponent's will can be retarded and finally blocked. If leaders are arrested, the movement may carry on without a recognizable leadership. The opponent may declare new acts illegal, only to find that he has opened up new opportunities for defiance.

There is a strong tendency for the opponent's violence and repression to react against his power position. This is called "political jujitsu." Against disciplined and persistent nonviolent actionists, his violence can never really come to grips with the kind of power they wield. Under certain conditions repression may make more people join the resistance. The opponent's supporters may turn against him; uneasiness may lead to disobedience in his own camp. The numbers of resisters may become so large that control becomes impossible. His police may give up, his officials occasionally resign, and sometimes his troops may even mutiny. Massive nonviolent defiance by the population has by then made the enemy government powerless. This is the potential. But it will not be easy to achieve. Defeat of the nonviolent actionists is always possible, just as defeat occurs in traditional war. Victory with this technique will come only to those who have developed it into a refined and powerful political tool.

Thus, civilian defense depends primarily on a trained civilian population to defend the country's freedom and independence by social, psychological, economic and political means. The population could be prepared through regular democratic processes and government decisions. Long before the changeover from military defense to civilian defense—a process called *transarmament*—considerable research, investigation and analysis would be needed. Highly important, too, would be widespread public study, thinking, discussion and debate on the nature, feasibility, merits and problems of civilian defense and all of the forms its exercise might take.

After the decision to transarm, a Department of Civilian Defense might be set up to provide planning, analysis, coordination and some leadership. All this would probably be more complex than planning for military defense.

No country is going to abandon military defense without confidence in a substitute defense policy. Therefore, for a significant period, civilian defense preparations would be carried out alongside military measures, until the latter could be phased out as no longer needed. Because of their different natures, however, the two policies would probably require separate institutional arrangements. During the transarmament period, personnel and money would be needed for both.

A major educational program for the whole country on the nature and purpose of civilian defense would be required. Federal, state and local governmental bodies, assisted by independent institutions such as schools, churches, trade unions, business groups, newspapers, television and the like could undertake this. People would be informed about the broad outlines of the new policy, the ways it would operate, and the results expected.

Certain occupational groups, including those wishing to participate in advanced aspects of the policy, would need specialized training. Such training would vary in its character and purpose, ranging from that required by local neighborhood defense workers to specialist education at civilian defense counterparts of West Point. This is not to say that there is no role for spontaneity within the scope of civilian defense, but that it is a limited role and even then needs to be self-disciplined and rooted in thorough understanding of the requirements of nonviolent action and the chosen civilian defense strategies.

In crises, specialists in civilian defense would play an important role in initiating resistance, especially at the beginning of an occupation or a coup. In various situations they could serve as special cadres for particularly dangerous tasks. Some specialists might be kept in reserve to guide the later stages of the resistance. However, they could not—and should not be expected to—carry out the resistance for the general population. Responsibility for the main thrust of civilian defense must be assumed by the citizenry. Since the leaders generally would be among the first imprisoned or otherwise incapacitated by the usurper, the population must be able to continue on its own initiative.

Maximizing Impact

Preparations for civilian defense would not consist simply of instructions arrived at by a centralized leadership and carried out at the lower levels. An effective strategy would require an analysis of the potentialities of many factors—means of transportation, government departments, schools, and so forth—to identify the specific points at which noncooperation might have a maximum impact in preventing any illegal group from seizing control. Ordinary people in jobs at those places would often be the best sources of the intelligence information needed to make these decisions. To make accurate tactical judgments, however, one would need knowledge of the forms and strategies of nonviolent resistance, the enemy's weaknesses, the kinds of repression to expect, the crucial political issues on which to resist, and many practical questions of how to implement the resistance.

The setting up of an underground system of contacts would probably have to wait until a crisis, to make it harder for the opponent to know the exact personnel and structure of the resistance organization. However, "war games" and civilian defense maneuvers could offer the specialists a chance to examine the viability of alternative strategies and tactics for dealing with various types of threats. Training maneuvers in which imaginary occupations or takeovers would be met by civilian resistance could be acted out at levels ranging from local residential areas, offices or factories to cities, states and even the whole country.

Technical preparations would also be necessary for civilian defense. For example, provisions and equipment would be required for communication with the population after the enemy had occupied key centers and seized established newspapers, radio stations and other mass media. Equipment to publish underground newspapers and resistance leaflets and to make broadcasts could be hidden beforehand. It might be possible to make advance arrangements for locating such broadcasting stations or printing plants in the territory of a friendly neighboring country as part of a civilian defense mutual aid agreement.

Since an enemy might seek to force the population into submission by starvation, and since certain resistance methods (e.g., a general strike) would disrupt distribution of food, emergency supplies of staples should be stored locally. Alternative means of providing fuel and water during emergencies could also be explored. For certain types of crises, plans might be considered for the dispersal of large groups of people from big cities to rural areas where the oppressor would find it more difficult to exercise control over them.

Because civilian defense requires the active support and participation of the populace (*not* necessarily unanimity, however), the citizens must have both the *will* and *ability* to defend their society in crises. For citizens to have the will to defend their democratic system does not imply that they believe the system is perfect. But it does mean that the system is preferable to any regime likely to be imposed by interal take-over or by foreign invaders, and that any necessary changes in the system should be made by democratic decision. For effective civilian defense, people have to *want* to resist threats to their freedom and independence. They must genuinely cherish the democratic qualities of their society.

Measures to increase the effectiveness of civilian defense (including the decentralization of control in order to make citizens more self-reliant in facing emergencies) are likely to contribute to the vitality of democratic society, and to increased participation in it. With civilian defense, therefore, there is no rivalry or contradiction between defense requirements and domestic needs; they are complementary. In the case of the U.S., this would be a considerable advance over present military policy, which has delivered us into exactly that contradiction.

Civilian defense is thus a democratic defense of democracy. Just as tyranny and war, in their cyclical appearances, may be mutually-reinforcing causes, so political freedom and peace may be intimately connected. A civilian defense policy may provide concrete means for producing a condition of life that allows for the interplay and perpetual renewal of the last two qualities in place of the first two.

Aggressor's Considerations

An aggressive regime deciding whether or not to invade another country will usually consider: 1) the expected ease or difficulty of the invasion and subsequent control of the country, and 2) the anticipated gains as compared to costs (human, economic, political, ideological, prestigial, military and other). Except in the case of a nation acting on a huge gamble or pure irrationality, the likelihood of considerably greater losses than gains will probably deter the invader.

Invasion is not an objective in and of itself. It is a way to achieve a wider purpose, which almost always involves occupation of the invaded country. If, however, a successful invasion is followed by immense difficulties in occupying and controlling the country, its society and population, the invasion's "success" becomes for its perpetrators a dangerous mirage. Certainly the Russians invading Czechoslovakia encountered at the early stages great and unanticipated difficulties. Advance civilian defense preparations and training could have considerably increased these. Where preparations and training are thorough, a would-be invader might perceive that he will not be able to rule successfully the country that he might easily invade. Civilian defense has at that moment revealed itself as a powerful deterrent.

There are other contingencies a would-be aggressor would need to think through. A population's spirit and methods of resistance could well spread to other countries and again be applied against his tyranny. In such a light, civilian defense has to be considered as a possible post-nuclear deterrent to conventional attack.

Could civilian defense deter a nuclear attack? It is sometimes argued that civilian defense is nonsense in the nuclear age, since it would provide no defense should nuclear bombs start falling. The question, however, is whether the conditions likely to be produced by transarmament to civilian defense will encourage or discourage a decision to launch a nuclear attack on the country involved.

Who fears and expects a nuclear attack the most today, and who the least? It is precisely the nuclear powers who most fear nuclear attack, partly because each side is afraid of the other. Brazil, Mexico, Indonesia, Canada and Australia—all *without* nuclear weapons—fear and expect nuclear attack far less than the U.S. and U.S.S.R.

Fear of nuclear attack, then, or fear of military defeat in a major conventional war, may be a strong reason for launching a nuclear attack on the enemy. Civilian defense, which can only be used for *defensive* purposes, would remove that motive, and hence, if not cancel out the danger, at least greatly reduce it. It is certainly significant that several military men to whom this problem has been presented do not see much likelihood of a nuclear attack against a country employing only civilian defense as a deterrent.

No deterrent can ever be *guaranteed* to deter. And, of course, the failure of the nuclear deterrent could permanently end all talk of alternative deterrents as well as the talkers and non-talkers. But the failure of the civilian defense deterrent would still permit human life to continue and long range hope for a just solution to remain, while the struggle against tyranny would enter a new stage with a more direct confrontation of forces. When the deterrence capacity of civilian defense fails, a series of contingency plans to deal with the new situation comes into operation with the potential to win a real political and human victory.

Although resistance is never easy, it is less difficult to resist a tyrannical regime while it is seeking to establish itself than after it has succeeded. George Kennan points out that for a successful seizure of power by a totalitarian regime "a certain degree of mass bewilderment and passivity are required." Advance preparations and training for civilian defense are designed specifically to prevent that condition. The invader will encounter a population well prepared to fight for its freedom with methods which, precisely because they are nonviolent, will be especially insidious and dangerous to the occupation regime. And in the end, the invader may well lose.

Of course, civilian defense cannot keep enemy troops from entering the country. But the enemy's entry is an illusion of easy success; it operates as a political ambush. The people will not have allowed themselves to succumb to the psychological condition that Hitler prescribed for successful occupation; they will not have admitted defeat and recognized the occupation regime as their conqueror and master.

Under civilian defense, the country and the defense capacity would not have been defeated. The combat strength would not yet have been applied. The citizenry, trained and prepared, would not feel dismayed or confused. They would understand that the distribution of enemy soldiers and functionaries throughout the country did not mean defeat but instead was the initial stage of a longer sruggle at close range. This would be difficult. But the civilian defenders would hold advantages. Setbacks might occur; these could lead, however, to rebuilding strength for future campaigns. There are no white flags of surrender in civilian defense.

Although civilian defense cannot defend the geographic borders, some limited action could be taken even at the initial stage. The deployment of troops could be delayed by obstructionist activities at the docks (if troops came by sea), by refusal to operate the railroads, or by blocking highways and airports with thousands of abandoned automobiles.

Such acts would make clear to the individual enemy soldiers that, whatever they might have been told, they were not welcome as an invasion force. As other symbolic actions the people could wear mourning bands, stay at home, stage a limited general strike, defy curfews, or urge the invading soldiers not to believe their government's propaganda. Such actions would give notice to friend and foe that the occupation will be firmly resisted at the same time build up the people's morale so as to prevent submission and collaboration.

The invader's parades of troops through the cities would be met by conspicuously empty streets and shuttered windows, and his public receptions would be boycotted. Efforts would be made to undermine the loyalty of his individual soldiers and functionaries. They would be informed that there will be resistance, but that the resistance will be of a special type, directed against the attempt to seize control but without threatening harm to them as individuals. If this could be communicated, the soldiers might be more likely to help the resisting population in small ways, to avoid brutalities, and to mutiny at a crisis point, than they would if they expected at any moment to be killed by snipers or plastic bombs.

Forms of Noncooperation

There would be early forms of more substantial political and economic noncooperation. For example, the invader might meet a blanket refusal by the government bureaucracy and civil servants to carry out his instructions. Or, these officials might continue the old policies, ignore his orders, and disrupt the implementation of new policies. The police might refuse to make political arrests for the invader, warn people of impending arrests, selectively refuse certain orders or carry them out with great inefficiency.

Attempts to exploit the economic system might be met with limited general strikes, slow-downs, refusal of assistance by or disappearance of indispensable experts, and selective use of various types of strikes at key points in industries, transportation and the supply of raw materials. News of resistance might be publicized through prearranged channels throughout the world, and also be beamed at the invader's homeland. These are only illustrations. Since each case is different, and the enemy's objectives are crucial, obviously there can be no one blueprint for all situations. And it would be important to plan different possible types of strategies for dealing with diverse threats.

Over the long run, both injuries and deaths are to be expected, though they are likely to be much fewer than in military struggles. If the citizens are unwilling to face the prospect of such casualties in their defense action, the resistance will surely collapse; similarly, in a conventional war defeat is certain if the troops when fired upon run the other way or surrender. In this, as in any struggle, casualties must be seen in the context of the campaign as a whole. It is remarkable how many people who accept as natural millions of dead and wounded in a military war find dangers of execution and suffering in civilian defense a decisive disadvantage; this is especially puzzling when there is evidence that casualty rates in nonviolent struggles are vastly smaller than in regular warfare.

As the occupation deveops, the enemy may try to gain control of various institiutions, such as the courts, schools, unions, cultural groups, professional societies and the like. If that control is achieved, the future capacity for resistance will be weakened for a long period. Therefore, civilian defense must firmly resist any efforts of the invader to control the society's institutions. A few examples will show how this could be done.

The courts would declare the invader's bureaucracy an illegal and unconstitutional body; they would continue to operate on the basis of pre-invasion laws and constitutions, and they would refuse to give moral support to the invader, even if they had to close the courts. Attempts to control the schools would be met with refusal to change the school curriculum or to introduce the invader's propaganda, explanations to the pupils of the issues at stake, continuation of regular education as long as possible, and, if necessary, closing the schools and holding private classes in the children's homes.

Efforts to dominate trade unions or professional groups could be met by persistence in abiding by their preinvasion constitutions and procedures, denial of recognition to new organizations set up by or for the invader, refusal to pay dues or attend meetings of any new pro-invader organizations, and the carrying out of disruptive strikes and economic and political boycotts.

In considering the possibility of failure of civilian defense, or of only very limited success, two factors need to be kept in mind. First, even failure after an heroic struggle by civilian defense would be preferable to any outcome of a major nuclear war. At worst, it would mean a long, difficult and painful existence under severe tyranny, but life would go on, and with life the hope for eventual freedom. Non-violent action is not a course for cowards. It requires the ability and determination to sustain the battle whatever the price in suffering, yet it would, in the most disastrous case imaginable, still allow a future for mankind. And secondly, in this kind of struggle, failure to achieve total victory would not mean total defeat. Even if the population were unable to drive out the invader, it could maintain a considerable degree of autonomy for the country, and for its institutions upon whose independence any country's freedom largely depends.

The other side of the argument for civilian defense is that under present international and technological conditions this system offers a greater chance of real success in opposing occupation or regaining political freedom than does military defense. When the usurper fails to bring the occupied country to heel, a miasma of uncertainty and dissent would grow within his regime and among his soldiers and officials. International pressures would further weaken the oppressor and strengthen the civilian defenders. Very likely, the usurper would find that he faced not only the opposition of world opinion but significant diplomatic moves and economic embargoes. Continued repression in the occupied country would feed further resistance. The multiplication of noncooperating and disobedient subjects would thus be calculated to defeat the would-be tyrant and bring about a restoration of liberty, enhanced with new meaning, vitality and durability.

The exact way that victory would come would vary from one situation to another. In one case it might coincide with a change of government in the invading country. Or there might be negotiations, with some face-saving formula for the invader. In extremes, the occupation force itself might be so near disintegration and mutiny that with or without such a formula the troops and functionaries would simply go home. In any case, the real meaning would be clear: the occupation would have been defeated.

Another way of looking at civilian defense is to realize that it is not disarmament, if disarmament means the reduction or abandonment of defense capacity. Instead, the changeover to civilian defense is transarmament—the substitution of a new defense capacity that provides deterrence and defense without conventional and nuclear military power. It also contributes to world peace, since unlike military means civilian defense cannot be used for, or misperceived as intended for, international aggression.

A Policy, Not a Creed

Nor is civilian defense a new doctrine for which unquestioning "believers" are sought. It is a defense policy, not a creed. The stage of development of civilian defense, in theory and practice, is still primitive. Those who have examined the idea differ in their judgments of the types of defense problems, and of enemies, for which it might be suitable. For example, some say it is not possible against a Nazi-type regime, but that it would work against occupation regimes of medium severity. I hasten to add that there is also anything but uniformity of opinion about military defense policies!

Another crucial point about civilian defense is that it is possible for only one or a few countries to adopt the policy initially, without treaties and while most countries remain militarily armed. When convinced of its effectiveness and advantages, other countries too may transarm. Aggressive regimes may well have to be taught lessons in the resistance capacity of civilian defense countries.

The first nations to adopt civilian defense are likely to be those that most want self-reliance in defense but which lack the ability to do this with their own military means. The super powers may well follow far behind. It does not, of course, have to be that way, and surprises may occur. A considerable period would doubtless exist in which some countries had transarmed to civilian defense while many others retained military defense —and some of the latter might never change over.

There would inevitably be strongholds of resistance to adoption of this policy. Democratic countries with large military establishments are unlikely, and probably unable, to eliminate these in a short span of time. They might, however, add a civilian defense component, if its effectiveness could be convincingly demonstrated. They might increasingly rely on the component, gradually phasing out the military sector, until the substitution was completed. Some military personnel could no doubt be retained to fit into the new civilian defense system.

Dictatorial regimes and unstable governments probably would cling hardest to military capacity for both domestic and intenational purposes. However, even dictatorships could be influenced toward civilian defense, both by removal of fear of foreign military attack (contributing to internal political relaxation) and by nonviolent pressures for change from their own population.

It is impossible to predict with certainty the international consequences of the initial case of transarmament. A nation's decision to adopt a policy of civilian defense and its effectiveness in carrying it out will depend on the state of knowledge of this kind of struggle, the adequacy of the strategic planning, the quality and extent of preparations and training, the geographical location of the country, the nature of its enemies, and the determination, skill and heroism of the people.

The succesful defeat of a seizure of power or an occupation by a systematic civilian defense policy might make a significant contribution toward the adoption of such a policy by other countries. Initial successes of this policy are likely to lead more and more countries to investigate it and finally to transarm.

Countries that had already adopted civilian defense could directly encourage other nations to transarm. Under "Civilian Defense Mutual Assistance Pacts" several countries could share knowledge, research results and experience. They could provide certain aid in emergencies (such as food, supplies, finances, diplomatic and economic pressures, a haven for refugees, safe printing and broadcasting facilities). They could give technical advice to countries considering civilian defense, and undertake joint activities to deter aggression by this means.

In contrast with military planning, a sharing of results of civilian defense research, planning and training would not endanger future combat effectiveness. It would instead accelerate the rate at which countries transarmed to civilian defense. This would be of major importance in a step-by-step removal of war from the international scene, and in increasing world security. It is important to note also that even if some countries never abandon military capacity, this would not be a reason for abandoning civilian defense, but rather for expanding it and improving its effectiveness.

Some of the important consequences of civilian defense will be social and economic. For example, transarmament to civilian defense by poor developing countries would probably mean that a large percentage of their present inordinate military budgets could be spent on dealing with poverty and development. Likewise, the developed countries would be able to give more help to the developing world after they convert to civilian defense.

Civilian defense can also deal with domestic or foreign-aided coups d'etat against the legal government, for which military defense is not designed. (Furthermore, it is usually the military establishment which overthrows the legal government, as in Greece in 1967).

In the long run, civilian defense would be significantly cheaper than military defense, although it would not be inexpensive. And the transition period, with both military and civilian defense preparations, might be quite expensive.

Another side benefit of civilian defense is that it is likely to make the means of defense serve democratic political ends positively, rather than requiring a foreign policy and alliances that violate a country's avowed democratic principles. No longer would it be necessary in the name of "defense" to make military alliances with dictatorships or to give tacit support to oppressive governments in order to keep military bases. In short, civilian defense would very likely become a potent force around the world for liberalizing or overthrowing tyrannical regimes.

But most importantly, civilian defense could be expected to restore a very high degree of self-reliance in defense to all countries. It would do this by shifting the source of defense power from modern technology to the people themselves, to their determination and ability to act. If the nations of the world were able, predominantly by their own efforts, and above all without military assistance from the super powers, to defend themselves from internal usurpation by violent minorities and from foreign invasions, the security problems of the world would be altered fundamentally.

The Large Assumption

All of this discussion, of course, is based upon a large assumption: that today's elementary idea of civilian defense can be refined and developed to produce a new kind of defense policy at least as effective as military means. A considerable period of time given over to specific problem-oriented research will be needed to develop the general principles and theoretical frameworks of this policy, to produce models that may lend themselves to adaptation to a particular country's needs, and to complete planning, preparations, training and other difficult tasks for the transarmament period.

Certainly all would agree that no reasonable possible solution to the problems of modern war and tyranny, and of effective defense against aggression and internal takeovers should be left uninvestigated. It is important now to start the exploration, thought, discussion and research that are needed to make possible a fair evaluation of this concept, and, if it turns out to be workable, to provide the basic knowledge necessary for transarmament, which could be completed within our lifetimes. We are now at a stage in the development of civilian defense at which major advances could be achieved relatively quickly.

Increased confidence in civilian defense and liberation by nonviolent action could produce a chain reaction in the progressive abolition of both war and tyranny. If this happened, the whole course of history would be altered. Some of the gravest fears and insecurities of the modern world would be lifted. Civilian defense could make it possible to face the future realistically, without fear or panic, but with courage, confidence and hope.

Church and State

Reprinted in *Schism* v.2, no.1 (Winter 1971) from *Secular Subjects* no.247 (Oct. 1970).

The Good Lord
and the Government

William Hoffer, interview with
Sen. Sam J. Ervin, Jr.

Senator Sam J. Ervin, Jr. (D-N.C.) is the recognized Congressional authority on matters dealing with basic human rights as guaranteed in the United States Constitution.

Recently he discussed his philosophy of separation of church and state, particularly as it applies to attempts by religious groups to finance their activities with tax money.

Q. What is the basic conviction that undergirds your philosophy of religious freedom? On what sine qua non does religious freedom rest?

A. I have a conviction that there can be no political freedom where religion dominates the state and no religious freedom where the state dominates religious organizations.

So I think it's essential to the preservation on my kind of liberty to maintain the doctrine of separation of church and state.

Q. What is the most elemental threat to religious freedom in America today?

A. We are confronted with increasingly insistent demands from some religious groups that their activities be financed out of tax money. Their success would strike a mortal blow at religious freedom. State support of a church is bad not only because it violates the First Amendment but because it's bad for a church. The church that depends upon tax money for the support of its activities—rather than upon the voluntary gifts of its adherents—loses spiritual strength.

Q. Some people might call your stand irreligious.

A. Support of separation of church and state tends to promote, rather than disparage, religion. Our forefathers who wrote the principle into the Constitution did so because they were religious men.

Q. In March, President Nixon advocated Federal assistance to nonpublic school children. How will Congress react to such legislation?

A. I would hope that Congress would not embark upon the support of religious institutions with tax money. As a matter of fact, I introduced a proposal four times in the Senate—twice in the form of amendments to the education bills and twice in the form of separate bills—making it certain that Federal courts should have jurisdiction to determine the constitutionality of grants and loans of Federal tax money to religious institutions. And the Senate adopted the measure on all four occasions.

I could not get the bill through the House because the Judiciary Committee of the House would not act upon it.

Q. Are you still attempting to get the bill passed?

A. No. The 1968 Flast decision by the Supreme Court made it unnecessary.

Q. What happened in the Flast case?

A. The Flast case originated in the District Court of the United States in New York. The court held that a Federal court does not have jurisdiction to entertain a suit by a single taxpayer who claims that there has been a misapplication of Government money. In other words, there was no way to enforce the First Amendment by challenging Federal tax funds going to religious groups.

The case was appealed to the Supreme Court, and I was asked to file a brief and argue the case. The Supreme Court laid down the principle that as far as the First Amendment is concerned, a private taxpayer can bring suit in a Federal court to challenge the validity of grants and loans of Federal tax money to religious denominations.

Q. Did the ruling accomplish all that you hoped to accomplish through legislation?

A. Yes. As a matter of fact, my proposed bill had a lot of limitations and restrictions that I had to put in to get passed, which would have tied the jurisdiction of the Federal court far beyond where the Supreme Court left it.

Q. What is the attitude of Congress toward providing any type of aid to religious institutions?

A. I am unable to say what the consensus would be. The fact that my bill passed the Senate four times would indicate that the majority of the Senate, at least, was opposed to the use of tax money for religious purposes.

When my bill was first offered as an amendment to the education bill, it met strong opposition. When I offered it the second time, only two Senators voiced opposition. And the other two times it was adopted by the Senate virtually unopposed. But I never could get a bill around the roadblock in the House Judiciary Committee.

Q. Will the attitude of the Supreme Court toward separation of church and state be affected by the addition of Chief Justice Warren Burger and Associate Justice Harry Blackmun?

A. I wouldn't think so. The Flast case was an 8 to 1 decision. It was written by Chief Justice Warren and the only dissentor was Justice Harlan. I would guess that Burger and Blackmun would go along with that decision. Both are pretty fundamental on constitutional questions.

Q. Several recent polls have indicated that most Americans oppose Government aid to church institutions. Do you believe this to be an accurate representation?

A. Most of our early settlers came to the United States to escape being required to support religious institutions whose doctrines they disbelieved. And I think that most Americans would agree with Thomas Jefferson: "To compel a man to furnish contributions for the propagation of opinions he disbelieves . . . is both sinful and tyrannical."

Q. Is not the financial crisis in many parochial schools itself an argument for Government aid?

A. Not a valid one. The Government takes tax money, and it supports public schools. If a parochial school is not willing and able to finance its activities, it ought to go out of business and let the children receive public education.

One of the bad things about giving parochial schools access to the United States Treasury and State treasuries is that you injure the public school system. I have no doubt that many public school systems don't get adequate financing—either from the Federal Government or the State governments.

Q. But what would happen if the parochial school system broke down? Or if large numbers of parochial school youth were "dumped" into the public system, as has been threatened by church educators in several areas? Would the public school system be able to handle the load?

A. The public school system would necessarily have to expand, and to do so would require a substantial outlay of money. But the reason parochial school systems exist is because parents want their children to receive religious instruction, which is unconstitutional to offer in a public school system. And if they want to have this extra thing—and I think religious instruction is a wonderful thing for children—they ought to be willing to pay for it.

You can't tell me that in a country like this, where there's so much money available for luxuries, people can't finance parochial schools. If they got enough devotion to want to instruct their children in religious matters, they can finance it.

Q. Several states have recently adopted plans channeling tax money into the secular area of parochial school curricula. That is, into salaries of teachers of mathematics, English language, and so forth. Sometimes the money goes to supply teaching aids and equipment. Since no money goes for teaching religion, is such aid constitutional?

A. No. The Supreme Court has declared in several cases that when a religious institution is financed in any one of its activities by tax money, the state is financing that religious institution as a whole. You cannot put secular education in one package and religious instruction in another in the hands of the same people and say there's separation of church and state.

If you furnish tax money to finance the nonreligious activities of a religious organization, you are financing that religious organization, because you enable it to take other funds and use them to teach religion.

Q. In May the Supreme Court upheld tax exemption of churches. Do you believe this decision to be consistent with separation of church and state?

A. I think the decision of the Supreme Court on this point is in entire harmony with separation of church and state. The decision rests fundamentally upon the proposition that if the state taxes church property, the state is compelling the church to support the state. To do this would be just as unconstitutional as to require the state to support the church.

Q. Some who have studied that decision believe that the

court modified the language of the Everson case, which prohibited the state not only from passing laws which aid one religion or prefer one religion over another but also from aiding all religions equally. Catholic spokesmen, for example, have conjectured that the court has opened the way to aiding church supported schools in the secular areas of their curriculum. Do you have any comment?

A. I disagree with this view. The decision supports the doctrine of separation of church and state because it holds that church property must be exempt from taxation in order that the church might not be compelled to support the state. Hence it is consistent with the principle that the state must not support the church and the church must not support the state.

Q. The Supreme Court recently approved of free textbooks being supplied to children enrolled in a parochial school. Do you agree that this is constitutional?

A. If you furnish the textbooks strictly to the child, and they're the same books as are furnished to the public schools, a very good case can be made for non-violation of that Constitution.

But you've got to recognize this: if you begin to give money to parochial schools for one purpose, you'll wind up giving it for all purposes, and you'll be paying people to teach religion.

Q. If a religious school is in financial trouble, wouldn't it be better from the school's viewpoint to accept governmental aid, rather than to close down?

A. No. It's not good for a religious denomination under any circumstances to consent—even for its seeming benefit—to violate separation of church and state.

Q. Do you anticipate any bills being introduced into the next session of Congress that will threaten church-state separation?

A. Education bills, which originate in the House, will have to be scrutinized carefully to see that they do not contain a sleeper authorizing use of Federal tax money for religious purposes.

Q. What would happen if, in the future, religious organizations did persuade the Federal Government to finance their activities?

A. If you start giving tax money to religious denominations, you are going to stir up dissension throughout the country, because the amount of money that a religious group would get would be contingent upon its political power. You would embroil the nation in quarrels among different denominations.

Q. What has caused you to become so involved in the question of religious freedom?

A. My conviction that the greatest gift the good Lord and the Government can give to a person is freedom.

That's the most precious value of civilization.

Have Churches Carried Social Action Too Far? Some Have!

The Reverend J. Lester McGee

The so-called "crisis-centered activists and humanists" in the churches have certainly carried social action too far. They have nothing else to do. They know nothing else to do, so it is natural for them to get caught up in the emotional secularistic swirl of the times. And remember, secularists get emotional too. In fact, I have seen more emotional fanaticism for the social gospel these last three years than I have for revivalism all the rest of my ministry.

Of course, the so-called "heaven-glancing traditionalists" in the churches who argue that the church's mission is to save souls and not cities have not carried it anywhere. They haven't even picked it up.

But in the main, most of our churches have not gone too far. They have perhaps not gone far enough. I would prefer being labeled and catalogued with this group, in spite of its shortcomings, rather than with the activists or the traditionalists. Most of these churches are just catching up after dragging their social concerns feet too long.

If I am levying a criticism today, it must be against those who have gone too far, for I am convinced that too many have gone too far. After all, isn't it a little more glamorous to go to the mayor's office and in the presence of newsmen and grinding cameras talk about the city blight, scum and poverty than to kneel with a lone distraught sinner and tell him about Jesus the Saviour?

But I am not going to be too harsh with these Humanists. I deplore their evangelistic barrenness, but more—I grieve for their utter disdain of dealing with people as persons. They prefer demonstrations, protests, parades and power pressures to persons. And I don't like the impertinence of the worldly-wise but historically-ignorant secular do-gooders who are critical of the church, calling her obsolete and no longer relevant, and continually spouting off that the church must stop talking "pie-in-the-sky-when-you-die" and get out into the ghettos and minister to modern man.

Where in heaven's name do they think the church has been all these centuries? They are not saying anything startingly new. Don't they know the church has ever been out in the world? St. Francis of Assisi was a social reformer, a worker with the poor, and he was a churchman, not a secularist. Wasn't he out in the world? St. Augustine of Hippo, John Wesley of England, Grenfel in Labrador, Livingstone in Africa, Kagawa in Japan were all men of deep social concerns. Yet they were churchmen, not secularists.

The Methodist Church alone has hundreds of missionaries scattered around the world. By-and-large their work is social and remedial. Christianity was pioneering in the world with social ministries long before any of us was born. Hull House in Chicago, Star of Hope Mission in Houston, Wesley House in Louisville, The Bowery Mission in New York, Kingdom House here in St. Louis—settlement homes, homes for the aged, orphanages, hospitals—were all church initiated, instituted and operated. What do they think the Salvation Army and Volunteers of America have been doing all these decades? Many of our colleges and universities were church established institutions. We are not novices in the social ministry.

Denominations and Councils of Churches had Social Creeds and were making social pronouncements long before the politicians started talking about new deals, fair deals, great societies, human rights and war on poverty. In fact, most of them got their ideas from these pronouncements. But none of these suggested programs was ever intended to be exclusively a secular ministry.

Virtually every modern social reform was spearheaded by the church in one form or another, from Universal Suffrage to Labor Unions, to social agencies, hospitals and universites. In fact, you name it and you will find that the church initiated it and promoted it for human betterment. It is almost amusing to hear some of the activists talking about new forms of ministry. Not a one of them is really new. It is just a mock-up or adaptation of a form introduced millenniums ago.

To me, there can be no either/or—either Social Gospel or Individual Salvation ministry. It must be both/and. I don't want you to forget my text: "These you ought to have done without neglecting the others." And you can fire that from either vantage point. Unless the church deals with the moral and social ills, and sins of the world as a whole, it cannot deal with these problems in the lives of individual persons. And on the other hand, we must save the individual persons composing society or we cannot save society as a whole. So you see, I am not against social concerns. I just lament those who say there isn't anything else.

Some of our fathers fell victim to the idea that Christianity was nothing more than a social program of good works. They were sure that by the end of the 20th century the world would be Christian. People were going to be good by taking them out of the slums. Public education was supposed to remove all crime. But their idealism soon ended in disillusionment and frustration. Two world wars shattered the rosy dream of the goodness of man. And once more the theologians were jolted into the realization that Christianity was a matter of a right relationship between God and man through Christ. We learned that to have a redeemed society there had to be redeemed men.

Now we are in danger of repeating the same mistake. The philosophy is the same, but the methods are different. We are now being taught that the world and society will be saved by sociology. The trend is for Christians to become secular and live in a secular city. We are taught that the thing to do is to be identified with the world, but we overlook the fact that

Christians face the probability of being overcome by the world. Radical theologians claim we should forsake person-to-person evangelism and seek to change the structures of society. But they don't stop to realize that those in charge of the structures, are not about to let anybody tear down their playhouses.

Of course, I do not say Christians should live in a ghetto of unconcern, hopelessly accepting the status quo. Christians have a responsibility to identify themselves with the world and fight every injustice. But this is not the total mission. "These you ought to have done without neglecting the others."

I am not a disciple of Norman Vincent Peale, but I do like what he says in this regard. I quote him: "The minister does have an obligation to relate the Christian Gospel to social situations in which human and moral values are definitely involved. But when he becomes a political crusader, with exclusive emphasis upon social preachments, he is one-sided, narrow and recreant to his basic function as a pastor of human souls. I suspect that many of the clerical and super-social zealots are merely compensating for having little or no personal life-changing religon at all. Or else they are sophomoric adherents to a loud-mouthed but small group of so-called religious leaders. A balanced combination of personal religion and socially minded Christianity is the soundest form of ministerial leadership."

Think of Jesus saying: "You've got first to perfect your government, to perfect your social system, to perfect your economic system, then come take up your cross and follow me." The late Archbishop William Temple once said: "If we have to choose between making men Christian and making the social order more Christian, we must choose the former." But I maintain we don't have to make that choice. These you ought to have done without neglecting the others."

The main objection I have to those who say we must get out of our cloistered halls and from behind our stained glass windows and go out and work with the poor and the disadvantaged—is that they would have us believe this is all we have to do. They are so sure the church must work *only* with the poor. They forget the bourgeois—the middle classes—and the upper classes who need Christianity as badly as any poverty ghetto I know.

From somewhere the silly idea has come that Christianity

must lose all distinctiveness and become like everything else in order to communicate with people in the world. This is nonsense!

Medicine has not thrown away its distinctiveness, and what it has learned over years of painstaking research, in order to make its dosages more palatable.

Science has not given up its distinctiveness, and agreed to follow an easier path of noncritical research, in order to please a lazy and indulgent world.

And, my friends, the church exposes its greatest weakness if it gives in to the suggestion that it must be like everything else in order to speak meaningfully to men. Certainly Jesus lived and moved in the marketplace, but He moved with His message, not theirs. He proclaimed the Christian Gospel, not the pagan philosophy.

The ultimate question, then, is: What is the supreme task, the consummate mission of the church?

Here it is as I see it: To end man's estrangement from God, to proclaim the great good news that "God was in Christ reconciling the world to Himself."

The church is in danger of forgetting that its supreme task is to bring men and women into a living relationship with God. So we are completely off-center when we spend all our energies fashioning social institutions and service projects only. We are off-center if we are so mesmerized by counseling and psychiatric techniques that we have no more to say to broken personalities than the secularist specialists have to say. We are off-center if we imagine that we are doing anybody and good just sitting in a coffee house scared stiff we are going to forget ourselves and mention the name of God and thus offend some sloppy beatnik or guitar-strumming hippie. And we are certainly off-center if in seeking peace among the nations we forget passionately to say to individuals: "Be you reconciled to God." "These things you ought to have done without neglecting the others."

Now if you think I have shied away from the racial issue which seems to be bound up body and soul with all contemporary social movements, let me tell you a true story:

A Southern layman was noted for his anxiety about being in the company of fellow creatures of another race. In other words, he was a Southern segregationist. He just didn't like Negroes. But he attended a Laymen's Retreat and received a rich religious experience he had not previously known. Several weeks later someone attempted to test his new faith and asked him how he felt about his church admitting Negroes to worship. With a new grip on winsomeness, he replied: "I have discovered that the closer I get to Christ the less I worry about who is standing next to me."

Maybe our proximity to Jesus Christ has a whole lot to do with how important or inconsequential are all these social issues. When we know Him and have close fellowship with Him in a rich abiding experience with Him, the race issue is not an issue at all. We accept every person as a child of God and our brother or sister in Christ. Not only that, we become interested in his welfare. We seek to help him if his plight is worse than ours. We become the good samaritan. We minister to his needs . . . "Inasmuch as you have done it unto one of the least of these" becomes our passion.

But when we are following our Lord afar off—as I fear many are today—we become "touchy" and irritable. We see the molehills as mountains. We go off on tangents. We forget our divine commission.

I am convinced social action cannot be carried too far, if it is true Christianity in action and is motivated by hearts and lives truly surrendered and obedient to the will of our Lord. Otherwise, God pity those whose actions however humanitarian, however sympathetic, however merciful they might be, are only secularly motivated.

Religion and American Foreign Policy

Walter Hoops

Freethinkers are a suspicious lot. They have good reasons to be wary. Their enemies, especially the Roman Catholic

Church, are sly, deceitful, devious and powerful adversaries. Edd Doerr, our associate editor, has shown in his book "The Conspiracy that Failed" how Roman Catholic tacticians have taken over the maxim of the Jesuits: The end justifies the means. We know that vigilance is the price of religious freedom. We observe that the "League for Free Education" continuously works to break down the wall of church and state separation. These bigots have taken a leaf out of the Communist Book of Falsifications: The countries under the heel of the Kremlin dictatorship are always called "Democratic Republic" or "People's Republic" when everybody knows that democracy is dead in Czechoslovakia, Hungary, Poland, East Germany and the three Baltic countries. There are no free elections as the majority of the people have no voice in determining policy. Catholics are not for free education: they want taxpayers to support their parochial schools (now called non-public schools in all press releases).

But vigilance can become an obsession. In order to dramatize our cause, it is tempting to exaggerate the influence of religious organizations. This is the case, I believe, of Viet Nam. The war in that unhappy country is not popular in America (no war ever is if it continues without a decisive result) mainly because most Americans are not aware of the real nature of the enemy. To go along with popular resentment, some Freethinkers have invented their own rationale. Martin A. Larson, distinguished author and assistant editor of *The American Rationalist,* makes the statement that "the R. C. Church demanded the war in order to maintain their last foothold in that part of the world," but presents no proof whatsoever in his article "The War in Vietnam," which he first offered to *The American Rationalist* but which I refused to publish because I was afraid it would tarnish the reputation of so prominent a scholar. (It was subsequently printed in American and foreign Freethought and other journals and this editorial is my reaction to it.)

It is, of course, true that people of the Catholic faith are dominant in South Viet Nam politics. When the French made a colony of Cochin China, they brought the Catholic system with them. Churches, schools, hospitals were built, property was acquired in the age-old tried and true formula. It recruited promising young men for the career of priesthood. Although the majority of the Viet Namese are Buddhist, for all practical purposes Viet Nam was and is a Catholic country. The elite in business, education, administration, army, was trained in Catholic schools, the only ones offering a complete education. Many converts were the result because Catholic membership opened the best ways for advancement. When the Communists took over North Viet Nam, Catholics were oppressed because Communists do not believe in Freedom of Religion. Almost one million Catholics fled to the South after and before the Geneva agreement which divided the country. The Communists agreed to withdraw their men to the North but they never had the intention to live up to this promise. Large contingents remained in the South and began at once a murderous and cruel campaign against the peasants in order to "prepare" them for the 1956 election. Communists do not believe in *free* elections because they would be thrown out of every country they now control if they did. Can you imagine what would happen in Czechoslovakia, Hungary, East Germany, and all the other satellites if really *free* elections took place? I even believe that the rulers in Moscow and Peking would be toppled if the masses of people were given a chance to voice their honest opinions without fear of retribution. The election of 1956 was called off because there was no chance to guarantee an unbiased outcome. Meanwhile, the Viet Cong—the name of the Communist Party in Viet Nam— had murdered thousands upon thousands of helpless and innocent villagers in a campaign that recalled the cruelties of the extermination of the Albingesers in the 13th century. Anyone familiar with the terror-tactics of the Communists was not surprised: Stalin killed or starved into submission 12-15 million Russians dwarfing even the horrendous crimes of the Nazis against the Jews; Mao killed millions of middle-class Chinese to set up his communes; the extermination of the freedom-fighters in Hungary and Czechoslovakia is still a vivid memory. The National Liberation Front which should be called Enslavement Front because Communists never liberate anybody, was determined to make South Viet Nam Communist. There are millions of people in the South who do not want to live under Communism because they know what would happen to their freedoms, as limited as they are.

Many of these people are Catholics and quite a few of them are today in leading positions. Is that a crime? (Years ago, when we fought the disastrous influence of the Communists in the Automobile Workers Union I used the mimeograph of a Catholic Church in New York to put out our side of the arguments. We beat the hell out of them and prevented further raids on our treasury. Soon the *Daily Worker* which we called the "Daily Liar" folded.)

The turmoil in South Viet Nam, the changes of regimes, the various putsches and the laws against dissenters have not endeared this country to the U.S.A. It is not easy for a country used to colonial exploitation by the French to emerge into a stable state of, for and by the people. It took us a long time, and I remember very well the upheavals in Germany after the defeat of the Kaiser, the many elections, the political murders and finally Hitler.—The constant changes of governments before DeGaulle took over in France should not be forgotten. Any nation at war, fighting for its very existence, has to pass laws against traitors and, of course, not all dissenters are traitors. Any thorough-going reforms of land ownership, compensation of confiscated property, any regulation of public education etc. etc. will have to wait until the conflict is over. Russian Communists proclaimed land reform during the 1917 revolution and the peasants believed it. But a few years later, with the Communists firm in the saddle, the homesteads were taken away and made into collective farms.

The *main* enemy in South Asia is not the Catholic Church but *Communism,* whether is is monolithic or not. True, Catholicism and Communism are twin evils and one is tempted to say with Mercutio in "Romeo and Juliet": The plague on both your houses. But Communism is the deadlier enemy at present; it kills daily hundreds of our young men and men, women and children of the South Vietnamese. The Communists have never given up their avowed aim to conquer the world. America stands in the way of this conquest. Therefore, it must be eliminated whether by hot or cold war. Direct warfare is too risky now, so the Kremlin strategists have decided on attacks wherever they seem to find a weakness: Cuba, Dominican Republic, Guatemala, Laos, Cambodia, Thailand, Viet Nam. Cecil Rhodes once put his hand on the map of Africa saying: "I see all this, from

Cape Town to Cairo, British." The Communists conspirators and promoters of the "Enslavement" fronts are gleefully looking at the map of Asia and see it as part of their slave-empire, including Indonesia, New Zealand and Australia. Unless we are willing to turn over the 17 million Vietnamese and later hundreds of millions to the Communist regimes of Russia or China, we must come out of Viet Nam with a peace guaranteeing the free independence of all South Asian countries. The cost in man-power and money is tremendous but as Thomas Paine so well put it, the cost of freedom is high.

I know that this is not a popular position to take but I am used, as Thomas Paine was, to swim against the stream. I have worked with Communists, I have seen them in action, I have seen them make common cause with fascists and betray former friends if it serves their purpose of victory over us. They are the eternal enemies of freedom, liberty and the pursuit of happiness of which we Americans are so justly proud. To these ideals I dedicate this editorial.

Sex Education

"What's to worry about? They'll teach sex like they do the rest of the subjects and the kids will lose interest."

Reprinted in *Schism* v.1, no.3 (Summer 1970) from *Industrial Worker* v.67, no.12 (Dec. 1970).

The Case against Sex Education in the Schools

William A. Marra

Call it by any name you wish, but it is the SIECUS mentality which is the real issue in the bitter fight over sex education in the schools. The fight is not over a bona fide course in high school biology, even if this includes a section on human reproduction; nor is it over a half-hour film on menstruation shown to girls only in the fifth grade. The fight is not about religious or moral exhortations to purity, either. It is about the K through 12 sex-saturation program, with not a gland or organ or square inch of skin missed; with every action, even every perversion, between the sexes fully and graphically treated and endlessly discussed.

The SIECUS Mentality

SIECUS may be technically correct in insisting that it does not set up and implement sex education courses for children. No one claims that it has juridical control over each school district so that it can literally dictate the contents of all curricula. But SIECUS definitely has a "mentality"—a clearly expressed philosophy on "human sexuality." It is this mentality which seems to have hypnotized key members in virtually every school district, public and private, in all fifty states. The sex education programs, now in force, or planned for September, have an uncanny resemblance to one another—not to say a downright identity. Their principle of unity is this very SIECUS mentality, as actualized in the sequence of topics, substantial content, visual aids, list of recommended books, and even in the language used to press for thirteen years of sex education and to shout down opponents of the same.

Schism v.2, no.1 (Winter 1971)

Case against Sex Education

Typical SIECUS inspired curriculum examples would be, for public schools, the Parsippany-Troy Hills program and the New Jersey "Guidelines" which it faithfully follows; for parochial schools, the notorious Rochester Program already in force in the Catholic Diocese of Rochester, New York. In truth, however, just about any existing or planned K through 12 program "in human sexuality" would serve equally as well for an example. Almost all of these programs are ineffective. They do great harm by killing the bashfulness which a person ought to nurture concerning his intimate life; and they have certain ominous moral implications.

Ineffectiveness of the Program

Many well-intentioned persons favor sex education in the schools because they have been led to believe, by clever rhetoric, that such courses will somehow reverse or at least arrest the sorry trends in sexual behaviour which we witness today. They have been alerted to the alarming increase in teen-age promiscuity, veneral disease, unhappy marriages, homosexuality and extra-marital pregnancies.

The point is insinuated by the proponents of sex education that "we have failed the youngsters" in this crucial area of sex. We have left them to shift for themselves in this manner, to accept half-truths, old wives' tales, misinterpretations and distortions. We have not made available to them "all that science now knows" about the "wonder of human sexuality."

A moment's reflection, however, soon convinces us that what lies at the root of the depressing sexual mores today is not lack of information. Rather it is obviously the lack of all "formation." A teen-age girl does not engage in promiscuity because she is "ignorant of scientific facts." Nor do marriages fail because of "old wives' tales" which somehow inhibit the couple from "achieving orgasm." All these problems are clearly rooted in character, in religious and moral weakness, and not at all in ignorance, least of all ignorance of "science."

But it may be argued that at least with VD and unwanted pregnancies, information may indeed help. Let us for the moment grant this. The question then arises: do we require 13 years to teach the youngsters about VD and conception—or better, contraception? The Army does a splendid job on VD with a half-hour film. And even an advanced course on contraception would hardly take more than an hour. What will be done with the rest of the proposed 13 years of instruction? "Remedial sexology?"

In fact, however, there is no evidence at all that even these problems plainly related to information will be ameliorated by sex instruction, even 13 years of it. No clinical or statistical proof exists that VD, for example, decreases as sex education increases.

The sex-education proponents are not too concerned about this, however. After all, to prevent VD, unwanted pregnancies, homosexuality, and the like, would simply be a "negative" goal. Their sights are much higher: positively, they want all children to "have an understanding of their own sexuality." They especially want to help the children with gender identity. Now who would dare to object to this?

If we cut away all the jargon, this euphemism of a curriculum which teaches gender identity is seen to be a hoax, educators pretend that young girls need courses on "what it means to be a woman?" Will they be less feminine if they are denied 13 years of study involving naked bodies, masturbation, and positions of intercourse? Must they be told what their "peer groups" are doing in "various cultures?" Do they need to be kept informed on acceptable contemporary behaviour for girls, e.g. playing with dolls as opposed to hunting with spears?

The Killing of Bashfulness

If the sex education courses were convicted merely of being useless, they would not thereby be totally discredited—at least in the eyes of many apathetic Americans. In fact, they might then seem perfectly congenial to those elementary and high school curricula over-laden with equally useless, non-academic material.

But the sex education courses, I submit, will inflict irreversible damage on the minds of children exposed to them. To develop this charge, I will begin with a set of facts admitted by all; I will then analyze the two major contradictory explanations for the facts. This will prove that, far from being merely useless, the sex-education courses—because of their public structure—constitute the rape of intimacy and are, for this reason, totally unacceptable no matter how qualified the teachers and how scientifically accurate the contents.

The facts are these: all decent adults veil their nakedness and, still more, their sexual activities; they veil even their speech about such things. And they attempt to instill a similar attitude in their children. Moreover, they designate as "shameless" those who publicly flaunt their nakedness or their sexual acts; and even those who chatter about their "love life" in public.

Now what explains all this reserve about sex and nakedness? Those pushing for sex education courses have a handy, plausible, and extremely effective explanation: the adults in question (that is, most of us who have not yet been enlightened by science) have been victimized by the puritanical, Jansenistic, prudish view that human sex is somehow dirty, ugly or sinful. In a word —their favorite, indispensable word—we adults have "hang-ups" about sex. The sex-educationists look with alarm upon the possibility that we will transmit our crippling hang-ups to our children and thus perpetuate the cycle of adults who hush-hush the wonderful realm of sex; who are embarrassed by the existence and even the very mention of sex.

This concern to liberate the young from "hang-ups" explains in part the apostolic zeal with which they work to get K through twelve sex education courses in every school in the nation.

There Is a Thing Called Noble Shame

There is, however, another explanation of the facts adduced above. As far back as 1927 my great teacher and friend, Dietrich von Hildebrand, wrote a classic work on sex and love, entitled in English, *In Defense of Purity*. He analyzed the complete difference between shame over ugly things and noble shame over intimate things. This latter is the case with human sex: its intimate character, not any ugliness or sinfulness, is what demands a noble reserve and bashfulness from us.

There may, of course, exist today a few prudes and puritans (in truth, though, I have yet to meet even one such) who actually believe that God somehow made a mistake when he created the reproductive organs. But most married persons are clearly conscious that their sexual union in marriage is good in the eyes of God. Far from seeming ugly or sinful, it is gratefully understood as enobling and beautiful. These same married persons believe that sex and nakedness belong to the inner sanctum of each person, that only the sexual parts of the body have this character of intimacy, and that a noble bashfulness with respect to all things sexual is absolutely called for.

Sex Not Like Other Bodily Processes

As von Hildebrand noted, it is just because sex (in contra-distinction to any other strictly bodily process) is intimate that it can serve as the adequate bodily expression and completion of wedded love. A man can achieve a self-disclosure by reveal-ing his nakedness before a woman; and he can achieve a self-donation in the full sexual union. If sex were like the strictly bodily processes and concerned merely the periphery of a person, neither achievement would be possible.

But, it may be asked, what has this intimacy to do with sex education? Simply this: the public treatment—for 13 years—in a most detailed, vivid way of such an intimate matter as sex will kill modesty and bashfulness in the youngsters. Intimacy demands a delicate reserve, the cloaking with a veil of modesty and bashfulness. This very veil will be pierced and finally torn down in some youngsters; in others it will never be allowed to come into being in the first place.

What Should Our Sex Education Goal Be?

Let each of us parents ask ourselves this: will it be such a happy outcome, such a triumph of science over prejudice, if our 12 year old daughter or son finally becomes able to discuss orgasm, ejaculation, masturbation and contraception in an "ob-jective way"—without a blush—"freed from all hang-ups?" Can we not see, rather, the terrifying harm such a pseudo-scientific "objective" approach will do to something so fragilely intimate as human sex?

Bashfulness is already on the defensive, of course, even without sex education in the schools. The unbelievable public "entertainment," with its raw and often brutal eroticism, assaults and offends the modest reserve of all decent persons. And dirty jokes, told in the presence of decent persons, are precisely aimed at piercing the veil of bashfulness so as to evoke a blush. But these unfortunate violations are unofficial and are thus clearly things to shun and resist. Once similar images and endless discussions of sex are enshrined in a school curriculum, however, the assault on bashfulness will become authoritative, something to cooperate with.

Extreme Delicacy Needed

If we agree that some sex instruction for youngsters is desirable and necessary, we must see that the intimate character of sex rules out any public treatment. Even private instruction must be carried out with tact and extreme delicacy, so as not to pierce or fray the veil of noble bashfulness which ought to be spun by each child as he grows.

As so many before have said, parents are the God-designated teachers for their children in these matters. They have the opportunity, the loving motivation, the knowledge of individual readiness to speak with each child at the right time, with just enough detail, in an atmosphere of reverence and trust. If the parents do not fulfill their responsibilities here, let the energies of the sex-educators be expended in their direction—to encourage and exhort them, to provide suitable terminology when needed, to give them access to good books on the subject either for parents or for the youngsters themselves.

The schools can help by having trusted persons available for counseling about matters of sex—whether about biology or morality—which certain children may hesitate to discuss with their parents. None of this will take thirteen years; nor will it demand integration into every academic subject.

Two ominous consequences for morality flow from the SIECUS inspired sex education curriculum. The one is practical; the other may be called religious and the commandments of God.

The practical consequence is this: although 13 years of exposure to vivid details of sex will certainly kill bashfulness and noble shame, it will in no way protect youngsters from temptations against purity. Quite the contrary; sex saturation courses will simply multiply the occasions of sin, especially for adolescents, especially for boys. The last thing a 15 year old boy needs is to see a colored slide showing a naked woman on her back with her legs spread apart, or to engage in "objective" discussions of masturbation and oral-genital intercourse. One would think that, at least among professing Christians, charity would move adults to minimize and not increase, the occasions of sin against purity.

The religious consequence is still worse: using sex as a wedge, the sex education programs—at best, amoral—tend to overthrow the absolute character of biblical morality and to replace the latter with situation ethics or with ethical relativism based on "changing cultures."

We, who believe in the Bible as the Word of God, believe that God is a personal being, a transcendant consciousness brooding in eternity, an infinite holy Person: our Creator, Lord and Judge. We believe that in the decalogue God has declared His holy will for us in all essentials of morality. Of the Ten Commandments, we note that two refer to human sexual behavior. (None refers to breathing or digestion, a fact which suggests that God, too, considers the sexual parts of the human body as something special.)

Sex: A Closed Garden Outside Marriage

The Biblical teaching on sex may be summed up by the French Catholic formulation of the Ninth Commandment: "Thou shalt not seek the work of the flesh outside marriage." In these words God teaches us that sex, good and holy in marriage, is a closed garden outside marriage—that is, outside the firm mutual commitment of wills whereby two persons vow to share each other's fate and to remain together until death.

The Bible also teaches that the Word of God endures forever. Too many of those now pushing sex education in the schools believe just the opposite. They believe, and teach—whether directly or not—that "values" on the younger generation. And they say that this is, in any case, impossible. We would just "turn the youngsters off" if we insisted on lecturing them on the "thou shalts" and "shalt nots" of an age long since passed away.

Thus the message of cultural relativism in ethics goes to the children in many different ways, especially upon the occasion of sex morality, by obviously having implications for all morality. This cultural relativism is often combined with the nefarious but intellectually seductive lie of situation ethics. This pretends that no behaviour—and here again reference is especially made to sexual behaviour—can ever be wrong in itself and thus, absolutely prohibited in the sight of God. When the actuality of temptations against purity is added to this weakening of the religious conviction that certain deeds are always sinful, the result is predictably grave: the precious virtue of purity will become still more difficult for youth to achieve.

How late it is now to erect dikes against this mounting tide of amorality and anti-morality must be evident to every thoughtful Christian today. Indeed the Christian must look to himself and his own church when he seeks to apportion the blame for the catastrophic decline of all morals, but especially those linked to decency. The frightening collapse of public decency and the ever stepped-up assaults by "professional" bureaucrats against the morals and minds of our children could never have occurred with such sickening speed were it not that churches have lost their savor.

If men and women in sufficient numbers had been kept vividly conscious of the presence of God, they would not have endured for one moment the public outrages against purity which now pollute the spiritual atmosphere everywhere. If they had been led to grasp the awesome character of the beginning of human life, involving as it does the creative power of God, they would not suffer their children to be exposed to the tasteless obsessions with sex of the sexologists. They would look in unbelieving horror upon the humanistic cliques increasingly coming to power in educational circles today composed of persons who know the name of every sexual organ and perversion but who sneer contemptuously at the Biblical truth that sex is a holy faculty. Such as these do not hold in reverence wedlock.

All who are rightly alarmed by the eruptions of indecency everywhere, most certainly including the vicious imposing of

SIECUS-type sex education courses in school, would do well to ponder the only strategy that offers even a small hope for success. This is the strategy of a genuine conversion, first of the self, and then of others where this is possible. We must possess again, if indeed we ever had it, the firm consciousness of the reality and the presence of God. We must cherish His holy Word. We must frame the elements of our earthly life under the supernatural vault which locates and defines them and provides the only true measure of anything temporal. We must see birth, death, sexual union and conception, and love itself against the eternal splendor of the reality of God.

Meanwhile, we may and we, in fact, must look for temporary weapons, at least to stay the advent of sex education in the schools. On every level the fight must be waged: local school board meetings and elections; state legislatures; courts; letters to newspapers; statements to school officials indicating our determination to have our children undergo not one hour of the wretched sex education planned for them.

Perhaps the best weapon is the private school. The time has come to challenge the monopoly—always wasteful, but now intolerably dangerous—of government managed and financed schools. Let us nurse back to health our weakened individual freedoms.

The "Latest" Book in Sex Education

Arthur Hoppe

Good news! The forward-looking Southern Baptists, meeting in Nashville, have voted to give sex education courses in their churches based on "a sound Biblical approach."

This is a wise step. There certainly is no better textbook for a sex education course than the Bible!

We'll pass over the Song of Solomon here, mainly because we

Schism v.2, no.1 (Winter 1971)

can't reprint the text in a family magazine. But let us envision a typical, happy, eager Sunday School, Sex Education Class.

Miss Primm: Now that we all understand begatting, are there any questions, children?

Johnny: How old was Methuselah when he begat Lamech?

Miss Primm: He was 187, Johnny.

Johnny: Wow! What's next. Miss Primm?

Miss Primm: Wife swapping, Johnny. Let us turn to Genesis 12:15 and read how Abraham swapped his wife; Sarah, who "was very fair," to the Pharaoh of Egypt?

Billie: Did the Pharaoh give him his wife in return?

Miss Primm: No, Billie, he gave Abraham "sheep and oxen, and he asses, and menservants, and maidservants, and she asses, and camels."

Billie: Man, what a groovy deal! I'm going to get married when I grow up.

Miss Primm (pleased): I'm so glad, Billie. One thing we want you to learn in Sunday School is the value of matrimony.

Billie (nodding enthusiastically): It sure beats swapping bubble-gum cards.

Miss Primm: And the other is the value of having a family. Now if you'll turn to Genesis 19:8 we'll read about how Lot and his two beautiful daughters were surrounded in their house in Sodom by a mob of angry sex fiends.

Millicent: Oooo. Miss Primm, what did poor Lot do?

Miss Primm: Why he bravely stepped out the door and addressed them, saying—let's see here—"Behold now. I have two daughters which have not known man; let me, I pray you, bring them out unto you, and do ye to them as is good in your eyes."

Johnny: You mean what's good in a sex fiend's eyes? Boy, that's socko, Miss Primm. What's next?

Miss Primm: Incest, Johnny. You see, Lot and his daughters escape to a cave and the older daughter says to the younger (Genesis 19:32): "Come, let us make our father drink wine, and we will lie with him, that we may preserve the seed of our father." Now you can read the lurid details yourselves. The story ends: "Thus were both the daughters of Lot with child by their father." That's all for today class.

Billie: Gosh, Miss Primm, what will we study next week?

Miss Primm: Mass orgies. We will begin with Numbers 31:8-

42 which describes how Moses and the Israelites defeated the Midianites, slew all the men, gave the women gynecological examinations and kept 32,000 virgins for their sport.

Johnnie: Man o' man, Miss Primm, Sunday School sure is fun!

So, hats off, I say, to the Southern Baptists for coming up with a brand new textbook on sex education (only several thousand years old).

Of course, there will be some prudes who'll contend that such material, has no place in our nation's churches. Let's pray the Baptists don't get themselves arrested.

Narcotics

"WHEN US SYNDICATE FELLERS HEARD THESE BLACK PANTHERS WAS CHASIN' O PUSHERS OUTTA DA GHETTO WE SEEN OUR DUTY WAS TO HELP YOU LAW N' ORDER FELLERS!"

Reprinted in *Schism* v.1, no.3 (Summer 1970) from *Spokane Natural* v.4, no.4 (Feb. 20-May 5, 1970).

Marihuana

The Brian Bex Report

What is marihuana?

Marihuana is a drug found in the flowering tops and leaves of the female Indian hemp plant, cannabis sativa. The plant grows in mild climates around the world, especially in Mexico, Africa, India, and the Middle East. It also grows in the United States, where the drug is known by such names as "pot," "tea," "grass," "weed," and "Mary Jane."

The drug is made by crushing or chopping into small pieces the dried leaves and flowers of the plant. This green product is usually rolled and smoked in short cigarettes or pipes, or it can be eaten mixed with food. The cigarettes are commonly known as "reefers," "joints," and "sticks." The smoke from marihuana is harsh and smells like burnt rope or dried grasses. Its sweetish odor is easily recognized.

The strength of the drug differs from place to place, depending on where and how it is grown, how it is prepared for use, and how it is stored. The marihuana available in the United States is much weaker than the kind grown in Asia, Africa, or the Middle East.

What is its use?

Marihuana is one of the least understood of all natural drugs, although it has been known for nearly 5,000 years. According to a UN survey, it has been most widely used in Asia and Africa. Very early in history, the Chinese used it to relieve pain during surgery, and the people of India used it as a medicine. Today it is used mainly for its intoxicating effects and has no known use in modern medicine.

Traffic in and use of drugs from the cannabis plant are now legally restricted in nearly every civilized country in the world,

Schism v.2, no.1 (Winter 1971)

including countries where marihuana is used in religious ceremonies or as a native medicine.

How widely is it used in the United States?

The use of marihuana as an intoxicating drug was introduced in the United States in 1920. In 1937, the Federal Marihuana Tax Act outlawed its general use and every State followed with strict laws and enforcement. In the mid-1960s, authorities reported a sharp increase in the use of marihuana. Arrests on marihuana charges have more than doubled since 1960, according to the President's Commission on Law Enforcement and Administration of Justice.

No one knows the exact extent of marihuana use in the United States. Some health authorities believe that 4 to 5 million Americans may have used the drug at least once in their lives. Other estimates are as high as 20 million. Research studies are under way to determine more precisely just how widely the drug is used.

How does the drug work?

When smoked, marihuana quickly enters the bloodstream and acts on the brain and nervous system. It affects the user's mood and thinking, but medical science still has not discovered just how the drug works in the body, what pathway it takes to the brain, and how it produces its effects. Some scientist report that the drug accumulates in the liver. Because it may cause hallucinations when taken in very large doses, it is classed as a mild hallucinogen.

What are its physical effects?

The long-term physical effects of taking marihuana are not yet known because no one has done the kind of research needed to learn the results of chronic use. The more obvious physical reactions include rapid heartbeat, lowering of the body temperature, and sometimes reddening of the eyes. The drug also changes blood sugar levels, stimulates the appetite, and dehydrates the body. Users may get talkative, loud, unsteady, or drowsy and find it hard to coordinate their movements.

What are its other effects?

The drug's effects on the emotions and senses vary widely,

depending on the amount and strength of the marihuana used. The social setting in which it is taken and what the user expects also influence his reaction to the drug.

Usually, when smoked, the drug effect is felt quickly—about 15 minutes after inhaling the smoke of the cigarette. Its effects can last from two to four hours. The range of effects can vary from depression to a feeling of excitement. Some users, however, experience no change of mood at all. The sense of time and distance of many users frequently becomes distorted. A minute may seem like an hour. Something near may seem far away.

How does marihuana effect judgment?

A person using marihuana finds it harder to make decisions that require clear thinking, and he finds himself more responsive to other people's suggestions. The drug has an adverse effect on any task that takes good reflexes and thinking. For this reason it is dangerous to drive while under the influence of the drug.

What are the latest findings about the drug?

Working with man-made tetrahydrocannabinol, one of the active ingredients of marihuana, a leading scientist recently found that high dosages of the drug brought on severe reactions in every person tested. The National Institute of Mental Health study also showed that psychotic reactions sometimes occur, for unknown reasons, in some individuals who take smaller amounts.

The scientist observed that a dose equal to one cigarette of the United States type can make the smoker feel excited or silly. After an amount equal to four cigarettes, the user's perceptions change. Colors seem brighter, and hearing seems keener. After a dose equal to 10 cigarettes, other reactions set in. The user experiences visual hallucinations (seeing or imagining shapes in objects that are not there). His mood may swing from great joy to extreme anxiety. He may become deeply depressed, or have feelings of uneasiness, panic, or fear.

Authorities now think in terms of drug "dependence" rather than "addiction." Marihuana, which is not a narcotic, does not cause physical dependence as does heroin or other narcotics.

This means that the body does not become dependent on continuing use of the drug. Neither does the body, probably, develop a tolerance to the drug, which would make larger and larger doses necessary to get the same effects. Withdrawal from marihuana does not produce physical sickness.

A number of scientists think the drug can cause psychological dependence, however, if its users take it regularly. All researchers agree that more knowledge of the physical, personal, and social consequences of marihuana use is needed before more factual statements can be found.

Does it lead to use of narcotics?

A 1970 Lexington study of narcotic addicts from city areas showed that more than 80 percent had previously used marihuana. Of the much larger number of persons who use marihuana, scientists agree that few go on to use morphine or heroin. No direct cause-and-effect link between the use of marihuana and narcotics has been found. Researchers point out, however, that a person predisposed to abuse one drug may be likely to abuse other, stronger drugs. Also, users of one illicit drug may be exposed to a variety of them through contacts with drug sellers and other users.

What are the laws dealing with marihuana?

Under federal law, which classifies marihuana as a narcotic, to have, give or sell marihuana in the United States is a felony. Federal laws and many State laws deal with the drug as severely as if it were a narcotic.

The Federal penalty for possessing the drug is 2 to 10 years imprisonment for the first offense, 5 to 20 years for the second offense, and 10 to 40 years for further offenses. Fines of up to $20,000 for the first or subsequent offenses may be imposed.

State laws also control the illicit use of these drugs. For transfer or sale of the drug, the first offense may bring a 5-to-20 year sentence and fine up to $20,000; two or more offenses, 10 to 40 years in prison. If a person over 18, sells to a minor under 18 years of age, he is subject to a fine of up to $20,000 and/or 10 to 40 years in prison for the first offense, with no suspension ~ntence and no probation or parole.

What are the special risks for young users?

Breaking the laws that deal with marihuana can have serious effects on the lives of young people. They may find their education interrupted and their future shadowed or altered by having a police record. A conviction for a felony can complicate their lives and plans at many turns. It can prevent a person from being able to enter a profession, such as medicine, law or teaching. It can make it difficult for him to get a responsible position in business or industry. Special individual evaluation is necessary to obtain a government job. Before a student tries marihuana, he should know these facts.

Expers on human growth and development point out other risks. They say that a more subtle result of drug abuse on the young person is its effect on his personality growth and development. For young people to experiment with drugs at a time when they are going through a period of many changes in their transition to adulthood is a seriously questionable practice.

"It can be especially disturbing to a young person who is already having enough of a task getting adjusted to life and establishing his values," says an NIMH scientist engaged in studies of young marihuana users.

Another reason for caution is the lack of scientific evidence to support statements being reported by students that the use of marihuana is "medically safe." It is hoped that research now under way may add to the little currently known about the effects of the use of marihuana.

Why is so little known about the drug?

Medical science does not yet know enough about the effects of marihuana use because its active ingredient—tetrahydrocannabinol—was not available in pure form until recently. In the summer of 1966, the chemical, first synthesized by an NIMH-supported scientist in Israel, was made available for research purposes. Now for the first time researchers can accurately measure the drug's effects and study its short-and-long-term action on the body.

What research is being done?

The National Institute of Mental Health, an agency of the

Public Health Service, is responsible for supporting and conducting research to learn more about marihuana and to present this knowledge to the public.

The program of the NIMH Center for Studies of Narcotic and Drug Abuse includes surveys of how people get the drug, how widely students and others use it, and what physical and psychological effects different amounts and periods of use have upon people. With NIMH support, scientists are now studying the specal drug qualities of marihuana and its physical effects.

The NIMH Addiction Research Center in Lexington, Kentucky, is developing studies to discover exactly how marihuana effects memory, perception (or awareness), mood, and physical movement. Other studies are planned to learn more about the drug's long-range effects on the body and mind.

Ginsberg Talks about Speed

Allen Ginsberg

Let's issue a general declaration to the underground community, contra speedamos ex cathedra. Speed is anti-social, paranoid making, it's a drag, bad for your body, bad for your mind, generally speaking, in the long run uncreative and it's a plague in the whole dope industry. All the nice dope fiends are getting screwed up by the real horror monster Frankenstein Speedfreaks who are going around stealing and badmouthing everybody.

The answer to it, I would say, is somehow put the speedfreaks in relation to doctors in nature, again. What the government ought to do is establish quiet farms—mountain—wilderness—fresh air-heated log cabins, where the speedfreaks can go with their girl friends or boy friends, if they have any, and get out of the city where speed is available and get back to the refreshing influence of nature. They're getting all sorts of electronic horror vibrations. It's the worst thing in the whole drug scene that I know of, the one thing I can't figure out what to do.

I've used speed, briefly, like for a day for writing, but the use of speed over two days tends to lead to irritability and inconsistency and a kind of Hitlerian fascist mentality, which may be the byproducts of real perceptons of interest. But generally, the interpretations are over-forced, with too much will power and insistency, so they're always leaning on everyone else around them, trying to force everybody else into their universe. It's not a common universe that is the problem, it's one everyone can participate in—the speed-crystal universe. Speed was originally invented by the Germans for use by the pilots in bombing England, so it's originally a kind of totalitarian synthetic.

The physiological problem is that if you stay up three or four or five days, you tend not to eat well enough to nourish your body, and pretty soon there comes to be a metaphysic of despising your body out of that crystal universe. Since you don't sleep, you don't get your 45 necessary minutes of dreaming each night, and so after a while the unconscious dream life begins to erupt during walking, walking around consciousness and you begin to act out your dream life and mistaking hallucinations from the unconscious as being manifest sensory realities that other people can pick up on, which is not true, so there's disjunction of realities. Or there's the insistence on your reality being the only reality, if you're on the speedfreak, which is undemocratic, and that's where it's totalitarian.

Since 1958, it's been a plague around my house. People that I liked or who were good artists, have gotten all screwed up on it, and come around burning down the door, stealing. All the stuff I brought back from India was stolen by speed-freaks.

The junk problem's an easy problem to handle compared to the speed problem. With speed you don't have a physiological addiction, but you do have a psychic adiction, which is strong and is followed by a long depression that lasts during this time. Apparently getting off speed requires a great deal of attention and care and love and nature. But the speed addic has generally so offended everybody by the time he wants to get off that he's created a social void for himself.

The ideal government agency to deal with speed freaks would be a whole bunch of lumberjacks up in the mountains and strong peasant girls to cook flapjacks and make a fire; and let the speed demon sleep off his depressions and lie around for a couple of weeks until he finally feels like going out and smelling the evergreens and then maybe building a fence or a bridge back.

Legalization of Heroin

Jeffrey Rogers Hummel

Heroin is obviously a dangerous drug. Its deleterious effects are too widely known to require enumeration; they are usually not even denied by the most zealous advocates of today's drug culture. Yet, despite this concession of the harmfulness of heroin, it nevertheless ought to be legalized. In fact, heroin has been chosen rather than one of the other drugs over which the merits and demerits are more controversial, because these aspects of the question are irrelevant to a consideration of whether or not government should make a drug illegal.

Government action in the case of heroin, as in any other case, involves the use of coercion. Government holds a monopoly on force, and the only way it can act it to use that force on individuals. In this case, it is employing force to (1) prevent the consumption of heroin, and (2) to prevent its exchange. Of course, the most fundamental objection to this is that it is morally wrong. No individual has the right to violently interfere with the peaceful pursuits of another, nor does government. If someone is doing something to which you object, you are not justified in using physical force to stop him—unless he has violated your right to life or property. The heroin user is harming no one but himself: he violates the rights of no one. Nor is there any violation of rights involved when two individuals contract with each other to exchange heroin. The argument that rests on the assertion that the use of heroin leads to other more aggressive crimes is specious: individuals should be simply prevented from committing these other crimes. To use the power of government to initiate force against an individual for consuming heroin or for exchanging it is grossly unjust.

Furthermore, this use of coercion does not solve the problem. It is at best futule, and probably counter-productive. The consumption, distribution, and production of heroin occurs because there exists a demand for this commodity. Government intervention may disturb the market processes, it cannot eliminate the demand. By outlawing heroin, its production, distribution, and consumption are not prevented, but merely transferred to the black market. This results in numerous undesirable effects: (1) The price of additional expense and risk that government intervention introduces. Thus, a commodity which is very cheap to manufacture and transport is made so expensive that its users are led to theft and other crimes in order to be able to purchase it. (2) When any business is transferred from the free to the black market, it becomes the sole province of the underworld, and a lucrative source of income is diverted to the coffers of crime syndicates. At the same time, despite these ill effects, nothing constructive is done towards reducing the demand for heroin.

For persons who earnestly wish to reduce this demand, the only proper approach is to attempt to change people's mind and convince them that using heroin is harmful and wrong. Heroin use can be eliminated only in a society in which the values of its members are such that the use of heroin is generally viewed with distaste and disgust. Such values can only be promoted by persuasion. A law which proscribes a particular practice in a society where the practice is generally accepted—or at least accepted by a large segment of the population—is totally useless. It will not be enforced, or, if it is, only at the cost of total repression. It is absurd to think that a government can by force maintain the morality of a morally degenerate population. Unless the government is tyrannical, it will be the product of its society. The futility of legislating morality is best exemplified by Prohibition, a measure which not only failed to decrease he consumption of alcohol, but probably augmented it, and, in addition, brought about the birth of America's first big crime syndicates. On the other hand, if a society generally disapproves of a practice, a law against it will be superfluous and unnecessary. It cannot reinforce the society's disapproval; it is a product of that disapproval.

Such was the case in America before World War II. The use of heroin was so abhorrent to most Americans, that laws were not needed. Today, the law hasn't changed, but the attitude of Americans has.

If heroin were open to the free market—and by this I mean a 'free' market and not a restricted and controlled market as exists in other drugs—its price would immediately drop within a range that could be afforded by any heroin addict. This has led some to suggest that heroin addicts could acquire overdoses so cheaply that they would kill themselves off. Perhaps, but probably not. Competition in the heroin market would induce firms to innovate with new drugs that satisfy the demand without harmful side effects—the use of methadone foreshadows this possibility. However, the only way to really prevent people from using heroin is to convince them that it is wrong and irrational. Institutionalized coercion, is always immoral and usually counter-productive. It is not the answer.

Penology

Sweeping Crime From The Streets

Reprinted in *Schism* v.1, no.3 (Summer 1970) from *The Thunderbolt* no.122 (Feb. 1970).

"Justice"—
A Tragedy in One Act

Park Chamberlain

CHARACTERS

>Judge Gusshie Lybbral
>Prosecuting Attorney
>Clerk
>Reporter
>John Smith
>Mrs. John Smith
>Tom Smith, the son, the accused
>Acey L. Yew, Defense Counsel
>Night Watchman

The Clerk: People against Smith, ready for trial by the Court, jury having been waived. Judge Gusshie Lybbral presiding.

Judge Lybbral: Proceed, please.

The Prosecuting Attorney: May it please the Court, I have one witness only, and a number of objects to be offered in evidence. Mr. Smith, will you take the stand, please?

(Mr. Smith is sworn and takes the stand.)

The Prosecuting Attorney: Mr. Smith, will you tell the Court your story in your own words, please?

Mr. Smith: Yes sir. Judge Lybbral—I mean, your honor— I am John Smith, the father of Tom Smith, who is seated over there as you can see, and who is accused of breaking into a store, stealing some money and other things, and beating up a night watchman—there he is over there—blinding him in one eye, in fact. Tommy got arrested because someone saw him running from the store, but that fellow has disappeared, I understand.

Anyhow, judge, I want you to know that I have been worried about Tommy for some time, and finally his mother and I had a good talk with him at home—he's out on bail, you know.

Well, we told him that if he really did these awful things he should come clean and serve his sentence if your Honor gives him one, and then go straight for the rest of his life. And that he should pay the night watchman for the terrible hurt he did him—you see, he has inherited money of his own, your Honor. I pleaded and pleaded with him, and so did his mother; in fact, she cried and cried, and, well, your Honor, I cried too. We've never had criminals in our family, your Honor, except Tommy. Anyway, the result was that he finally confessed everything, and wrote it all down, and here it is. He told us, just how he did it, and took us to where he hid the burglar tools, so I have them here, and he took us to where he hid the money and all the other things he stole and he even gave us the watchman's spectacles—they're all smashed—and even his own shirt that has the watchman's bood on it. I have all those things right here, your Honor.

(He opens a large suitcase and empties it on the table in front of him.)

Prosecuting Attorney: I offer in evidence this confession, and all of these objects, which I shall now describe for the Reporter . . .

Mr. Smith (interrupting): Now, your Honor, I keep wanting my boy to change his plea to guilty and throw himself on the mercy of the Court. Why don't you, Tommy?

Tom Smith: Why should I? Everything you said is correct, Pop, I'm not complaining about that, but my lawyer here, Mr. Acey L. Yew, says your old court can't do a thing to me. You tell 'em, Mr. Yew.

Mr. Yew: I object to the offer of evidence, your Honor. I have just one question for Mr. Smith. Mr. Smith, before all this went on between your wife and yourself and your son, did you or your wife warn your son that he need not answer any questions, and that anything he might say to you could be used against him, and that he was entitled to a lawyer?

Mr. Smith: Who, me? Or Tom's mother? Why, no.

Mr. Yew: Very well. You heard the answer, your Honor. Your Honor, you well know that I have spent the better part of my life redressing wrongs committed upon persons accused of crime and especially seeing that the rights guaranteed them by the Bill of Rights are ever broadened, preserved and strengthened.

Judge Lybbral: I know you have, Mr. Yew. Your efforts along that line cannot be too highly praised.

Mr. Yew: Thank you, your Honor, and the same must be said of your efforts, too, along that line—not as flattery but as simple fact—for it is common knowledge that Judge Lybbral has always taken pride, as he should, in being well ahead of the Supreme Court of our land in expanding the constitutional rights of persons accused of wrongdoing.

(The Judge bows and beams.)

And therefore, your Honor, I know that you were as shocked as I was by the disgusting violation of the constitutional rights of this young man at the hands of his unscrupulous parents. You heard this man here—who admits to being the boy's father—stand here in this American court of justice, and brazenly gloat how, without warning this poor boy of his rights, he and his wife—the defendant's mother—snivelled and wept him into an alleged confession! Can you imagine more unjust pressure than a sobbing mother and even a sobbing father? And all this within the four walls of the boy's own home, where there would be a sentimental atmosphere that would be unbearable to a dutiful son, and which would inevitably bring out the truth—I mean, no, excuse me, your Honor, I meant to say—

Judge Lybbral: I understand, Mr. Yew.

Mr. Yew: Yes, thank you—I meant to say, which would inevitably bring out what his parents wanted him to say, wouldn't it, now?

Of, course, I well know, your Honor, that up to the present, the rules governing coerced confessions, as stated in the glorious *Miranda* and other like cases, have to do only with interrogation by a governmental agent, such as a police officer. However, if it is reprehensible for a stranger, such as a police officer, to wangle a confession out of a pathetic helpless youngster like this, how much worse is it for his own Mom and Dad to do it to him—people in whom he should be able to repose—and obviously did repose—his deepest and most loving confidence! Your Honor should therefore joyously seize this opportunity to entend the rule of *Miranda* so that it may become for the future an even broader and stronger bulwark against the violation of the constitutional rights of the individual.

I therefore move that the Court refuse admission into evidence of everything that has been presented thus far—the confession, the burglar tools, the money and other things allegedly stolen and the bloody shirt and the watchman's spectacles—all these things you should hold totally and completely inadmissible in evidence. And since that is all the evidence there is, I urge that you here and now find this child not guilty of any and all charges against him.

Judge Lybbral: Well spoken, Mr. Acey L. Yew. It is true, of course, as you say, that the *Miranda* rule and other relevant rules have hitherto been applied only in the case of interrogation by police or other governmental agents. However, as you also say, there seems to be no good reason to confine the rule to them, and every good reason why the rule should not be confined, for, after all, the purpose of the rule is to protect the guilty—excuse me— Mr. Reporter, strike that last word—to protect the accused, I meant to say, of course—the *ACCUSED*—from being coerced into confessing, or indeed, into unfairly admitting anything that might be used against him. And what pressure could be more coercive and unfair than that which Mr. Smith—this boy's father! —has described here? I therefore rule—no, I am constrained to rule—that the accused's constitutional rights were grossly, nay, unspeakably violated, and that therefore all of the so-called evidence that has been offered to this court must be rejected. And since admittedly there is no other evidence, as I understand that the night watchman was struck from behind and never saw his assailant—I find the accused not guilty on all counts and order his immediate release.

The Prosecuting Attorney: But, your Honor, there are prior convictions of this defendant for violent assault and—

Judge Lybbral: I fail to see their relevance. No, Mr. Prosecuting Attorney, there is nothing for you to say—unless, of course, you do not believe in the Constitution of the United States.

Mr. Yew: Thank you, Judge Lybbral.

Judge Lybbral: The court is now adjourned.

The Night Watchman: Just a minute. Look here, I lost an eye to this punk. I'm gonna sue him, and maybe I can collect something because he's got money, and I want to use his confession and all this here stuff as evidence. I'm an individual too, aren't I? Don't I have any rights?

Mr. Yew: That will be a matter to be settled in a civil suit for damages. But you may have my opinion, Mr. Night Watchman, and it is this, that evidence contaminated for one purpose must be regarded as contaminated for all purposes. What good are constitutional rights if they do not protect a citizen in *ANY* prosecution, civil or criminal, against the use of evidence that has been unconstitutionally obtained?

Judge Lybbral (coldly): I trust, Mr. Night Watchman, that you will not be a party—as were these so-called "parents" here —to any further violations of this poor boy's constitutional rights.

(All persons, except Mr. and Mrs. Smith and the Night Watchman, start toward their respective doors):

Tom Smith (in stage whisper): Mr. Yew, do you think I can get back that money I stole?

Mr. Yew: (same whisper): We shall see, dear boy, we shall see.

Thy Brothers' Keeper

Leviathan

A few weeks ago some of us at Leviathan were told about and asked to interview a young, black correction officer, who was interested in organizing the inmates. A radical jailer? Someone who wears the uniform of authority while the inmates are carefully stripped of their identity? How was he able to resolve this contradiction and what, in fact, provoked his own thinking this way?

We learned that the contradiction between "jailer" and "radical" remains; that his street experiences have been the same as the inmates he sees every day; and that his own political consciousness developed over the last 3 years and not on the job but in the streets of the ghetto where he struggled alongside his brothers and sisters.

But we learned something more from the answers to these questions than perhaps the reader will from the transcribed interview. In part, because we talked about things which could

Schism v.1, no.3 (Summer 1970)

not be taped, but that's not the only reason. For we were made to realize during the time we spent together that our initial understanding of certain concepts and words were based on "white" thinking. When this black officer spoke about "rehabilitation" he was not talking about helping prison inmates adjust to the open wound (society as is). Rather, rehabilitation meant recovering one's own identity and uncovering that natural urge for self-determination; and this kind of rehabilitation—which black and brown inmates relate to and which, addicts in particular need—leads to changing individual life-styles so that inmates can, for example, identify with and join the Black Panthers or the Young Lords.

In the interview that follows, we've omitted or changed any reference that could identify the correction officer.

CO: Correction Officer   I: Interviewers

I: Can you tell us how you became a correction officer in the first place?

CO: First of all, let me go back, because it would be a little unfair to get right there, before giving you some indication of how I came up. I was always in the street, from the time I was fourteen. When I was coming up, I was thrown into a situation with my peers. At that time we had nothing constructive to do. I did go to school, I worked after school, and after work we would stand on the corner, and the first thing we would do was get a bottle of wine and get high. We formed gangs, I was a member of a gang, I was a war counselor of a big gang in Brooklyn, and I got to the point where I was really stretching myself out in terms of criminal activities. I was thrown out of school when I was sixteen, and I was fortunate in one regard that my old man, my father, put a collar to me and so he gave me a choice, either I worked full-time or I went into the service. I did not really want at that time to get a full-time job, so I did join the service, and I am thankful that he did do it at that time, and that the choice that I made was a good choice.

I: Why?

CO: Drugs were on the scene at that time. And had I not gotten away from that atmosphere, I would today be one of the biggest junkies that you have ever seen. We smoked at that time. I have several individuals in my family, my close family, that are drug addicts and it was around me at all times. The only reason I did not turn to drugs at that time, was that I was afraid of the needle. I had plenty of opportunity to. This incidentally is one of the reasons why a lot of our kids today are junkies. But getting back to why I joined the correction department. After I got out of the service, I was so indoctrinated into a military type of approach to my personal problems.

I: Was that the Army?

CO: The Marine Corps, I really did not know what correction was, but there was something that I thought was manly about wearing a uniform and about carrying a gun. It took a long time, after I had joined the correction department, before that had worn off. As I said, I did not know what correction was all about. I have never in my ten years considered this a permanent job. I was always here temporarily. But as you grow, certain responsibilities come on. And I never really gave myself the opportunity to stretch out, to go for higher horizons. And I think I found a niche here. I found where I can really work, especially in the area that I want to work, which is not the way the man defines the job, but the way I define what the need is. So about three years ago, I made some very basic decisions that I would stay here and attempt to do two things: organize correction officers to the lie that was going on, to organize inmates, to create that kind of situation that would make institutions, such as this, a more humane place . . .

. . . Let me talk about the game that correction, as part of the entire system, is playing. Correction, the term was formulated in 1933. It changed from prisons because of the philosophy of rehabilitation. And it is under the guise of rehabilitation that all of the job titles and institutions changed from prisons to correction institutions, from prison keeper to correction officer, and so on down the line. In terms of rehabilitation, in terms of changing peoples' way of life, I would say that the system, as it is now, is working in the opposite direction. What they are doing, is providing an atmosphere for the study of higher crime. Jails are just gathering places for unfortunate people, people who are downtrodden, and who have always been on the lower levels of society, to gather and further communicate with each other and to learn new ways of crime and so on. As I have said before, little if any rehabilitation is taking place in prison, it is impossible in that environment. Our prisons today are so overcrowded that we are forced to transfer inmates to state prisons because we just can't handle them. They are building physical facilities—they are giving that great priority—they want bigger, better, houses—places to house people. Period. No thought of rehabilitation. They have various programs within their individual institutions that operate under the guise of rehabilitation, but they are not realistic type programs.

In terms of rebab. I have some very definite ideas from my ten years of working within the system. And that is what I am principally concerned with at this time. Most of the people that we get, the kids that we get, have been failures in the school system, as failures have been defined by the man, and the schools are just jumping off places to the prisons and what not. The relationship between an officer and an inmate is very definite. First of all the uniform puts you on one side of the line, and their uniform puts them on the other. The officer, when he is handling four hundred and some odd adolescents, can do nothing in terms of taking care of the physical needs of these individuals. Consequently, everything and anything that happens in society, happens worse in there. The whole environment is a hostile environment. It is hostile towards the inmate, it's hostile towards the officers, it's hostile towards the administration. The inmate can acclimate himself to the prison. And who suffers? The inmate suffers. I was reading in the paper today, that the only one who really feels uncomfortable in the prison are the officers and the administration. The inmate can acclimate himself to the prison environment. But that's a lie. The environment is one in which you cannot relax at all, you are always on guard, you are sort of thrown into the jungle, which is exactly what the prison is today. I was speaking a while ago about rehab. The principle purpose for what are called rehab programs is to get money from the state and federal governments, to perpetuate the system. But the man at the bottom, the man who is supposed to be benefiting from the program, does not. In terms of statistics, the recidivism rate, that means those who return, is somewhere in the neighborhood of 85 to 90%. This bears out what I said before, jail being a hostile society and the type of society which does not change anyone's mind, but does make them more bitter and teaches them better ways of criminal activities.

I: When you talk about rehabilitation programs, do they also include work programs where the prisoners produce products that are sold?

CO: Yes, the programs do have individuals working in certain capacities where they produce things that are sold. License plates are one. They also produce bread. The bread produced in the city hospitals and in the public schools. There is also a print shop which prints all the paper for the Department of Correction and various other institutions.

I: Are they paid for that?

CO: We have three pay scales for city prisoners. For what we would consider on the outside experienced trades, we pay them 10 cents an hour, for inexperienced, we pay them 5 cents an hour, and for all others, we pay them 3 cents an hour.

I: Is the bread, for example, sold by the city to public institutions?

CO: I think there is a transfer of funds involved here. I don't know what exactly the arrangement is, but I do know that they produce products that are consumed by other city agencies. As far as pay is concerned, you all know that it is no better than slave labor, and that's one of the areas that obviously has to be worked on. There have been certain individuals who have devoted some time—I'm talking of inmates—attempting to organize strikes for living wages and what not, but when the situation occurs what the administration does, is to isolate the individual and see that he does not get into the prison population.

I: How did you begin to start feeling the need to organize in prison? How did you come to change your attitude from what it was when you first started?

CO: I think it was because of what I was involved in on the outside. I am very active in school. And once you become active in school, you see where prisons and schools are interrelated. I saw where the boys I was working with in our schools were ending up in prison, and I just couldn't work in one and neglect the other. Then the whole game started to be exposed in my eyes. I am the sort of person that can't work with someone every day and not relate to him in some ways. I started rapping to kids who were coming back, trying to find out why they did not learn from their experiences in jail. Why they just assumed a life where this is one of the risks that they take. Jail sort of gears them into a life of the desire for fast money, the will to risk going back to jail, and thinking about the outside and waiting for the day when they can go out and make that fast money again. So it's just one continuous circle, and it becomes harder to break the older you get. One thing I have found, is that there is a certain age—and for most individuals it is different —but it is around 26 or 27, when they wake up and they say, wow, am I going to do this all my life? This is the critical age, where I feel I could really influence and direct.

I: You said before that you have one uniform and the prisoners have another and that this puts you on two different sides of the line. How does this effect your ability to work with prisoners?

CO: Well, personally, I don't find it hampers me at all, because, as far as they are concerned I come from way out in left field. I don't holler at anyone while I am there. My approach is not a hostile approach, the approach of authority, and everything is on their side and the inmate has no say in the manner.

I: How long does it take them to understand that you are really with them, since at first they must judge you by the uniform?

CO: There is a system that the institution has where there is no steady officer in any of the housing areas. They keep on rotating you. I work on rotating shifts, so that there are always different officers, so that you can't get that personal a relationship going. So they take the correction officer, who they say is the most important part of the rehab. program and they make it impossible for him to build any kind of relationship with the inmate. But for myself, I am fairly well known within the department, because of my approach, that is number one. A lot of kids have older brothers and friends out in the street, you'd be surprised how closely knit a society this really is. So they know me out in the street and in the institution and they know they can trust me in certain situations.

There are certain individuals who can't be reached. They are already damaged, they are too far damaged to do anything with. We had an incident recently with a boy who likes to take off other boys. He lured a boy into his cell and tried to take him off. This other kid wasn't giving up nothing, so the boy beat him with a pipe and pretty much mangled him. Well this boy is obviously sick. He does not belong in a jail, he belongs in a hospital. But the hospitals are overcrowded. So, what they do is, they keep him locked in a cell, and chances are he will never see the outside again.

I: Have any of the kids that you worked with become active in the street when they left?

CO: Yes, they have. I have instituted an entire program, which is obviously what has to be done. A program that is not only functioning with the institution, but has that kind of after-release care, not only supervision, but identification, communication, relationship, and whatnot. One rule the department has is that they bar fraternization with inmates once they are released. I obviously have broken that one. Kids find it difficult, after they have taken a fall and have gotten this on their record, to get any meaningful or gainful employment. They can't drive cars because they can't get licenses. They can't get any kind of job as truck drivers. When they are on parole or probation, it is difficult to get jobs because of the guidance and watchdog effect of a parole or probation officer. And then again they are thrown back into that same kind of environment from which they came. That's why nowadays, when the kids who I work with are released, I refer them directly to the Black Panthers or the Young Lords.

I: On the street there is a real barrier between young people and cops. So what's the difference in prison, since basically you are a cop?

CO: It's the same kind of separation, it is the same kind of feeling.

I: By what means could you instigate something in the prisons, it would seem to me that they would be very suspicious of anything you were involved in.

CO: Today I had an argument with a captain. This was a completely personal thing. I was assigned to a detail that I was not supposed to be assigned to. What I had to do was take the 30 or 40 inmates that I had and transfer them to a different quad, and do mess hall duty. That's in fact what I did. When I got to the mess hall, I told the captain—I attempted to pull him over to the side—to tell him, babe, you just ain't right. First of all, you know damn well I ain't supposed to be here. I made the decision, he said, I don't want to deal with personalities going to mess hall. Later on he came back and he said, I don't appreciate when I give an order people getting pissed off. I said, what are you talking about? This is a person here, and if I think I am being screwed, I am going to tell you I am being screwed. Now let's get that set. The entire mess hall was filled at that time, but everyone dug where it was at and there was an immediate silence, so the only two voices that could be heard were mine and the captain's. Well, he said, let's go to the warden and let him settle this, you know, you ain't said nothing slick. So we were on our way to the warden, but he was the mess hall captain and he had more people to feed, so he couldn't leave at that time. So he says, we will go after chow. After chow we never went. I knew I was right. This is some of the things that they will do. I identify more with the same experiences that the kids have in the streets than I do with the man's system. And they know it. When I walk in with the Panther newspaper, and I say—this is yours, and brother pass it, and then I go to the next quad and pass it, they know where I am coming from. I work in a reformatory with sixteen housing areas. In the area where I work I get inmates from all of the other areas coming up and they say, where I am at. And they also know that I am about to leave the job. They don't want to see me go, but I don't know how much longer I can last. What I want to do is, when I do move, I want them, first of all, to put pressure on me to move, and I want to exploit it. That's the way I want to go. I wanted to do it in the school struggle when I was on the barricades there, but they didn't do it at that time. This is a more natural activity that (for his political activity-ed.) and a more natural activity that I should have been involved in a long time ago. And this activity in the jail is something that I am sure they will move on.

I: Do you think that if you were fired there would be any kind of demonstration or protest by the inmates?

CO: At this point it would be difficult to tell. They are going to be there for the length of their sentences and they realize that. And the man has ways of cutting off what little privileges they get. The privilege of receiving mail, the privilege of going on visits, the privilege of eating three meals a day, the privilege of attending religious service. A prisoner has no rights, these are all privileges.

I: This is a different kind of question altogether. From what you are saying I gather most of your relations are with males.

CO: Yes.

I: Do the prisoners at any point get together with females?

CO: No. They are even segregated from the homosexuals that we have. When a homosexual is detected, she is segregated.

I: Then all the correction officers for women are women?

CO: Yes.

I: What kind of pressure have you gotten already from the prison authorities as a result of your activities?

CO: If they knew the extent of my activities here, they would stop it immediately. Fortunately I have been able to continue to do it for the past three years. It's beginning to come to a head now. Since I have been in the Department, I have been brought up on disciplinary charges four times for petty reasons: excessive lateness, disrespecting a superior officer, etc. They give me the most undesirable work assignments. They more or less institute the same kind of repression that is found in the wider segment of our society. But they can't do too much, because if they go too far, they would be leaving themselves open to charges of discrimination, and this they are not willing to do at this point.

I: Are most of the officers white, or are they black or brown?

CO: Most of the officers in the Department are white, but most of the new officers that are coming in are black, so that a change is coming. That's why one area that I am working in is with officers, telling it like it is. Unfortunately, I have had too much success in this area because there is a barrier that has to be broken down. The job of law-enforcement represents today the highest level that the masses of black and Puerto Ricans can aspire to. By the masses, I mean if you are lucky enough to get a high school diploma or equivalency, stay out of jail, and keep your record clean, you can get into that field. They feel it is a good paying job, and it is. A correction officer or a police officer makes more than a school teacher with a college degree. The man pays his troops well. Most individuals that are in law enforcement today came out of the military directly.

I: Why do you feel that you have not had much success working with officers? Is it primarily the effect of the whole prison system on them?

CO: I feel that I have not been too successful in this area

because they are not actively organizing like I am outside of prison. Maybe I am impatient in that regard . . . I see wide-scale repression. One thing that every black and Puerto Rican officer understands today is that when he leaves the job and he goes back into the wider segment of the black or Puerto Rican, he gets to depend on that badge and that gun that he has. I have been in situations out in the street with the police officers, where I was thrown up against the wall and frisked because I was out on the street in the middle of the night. And when they found a gun, they said wow, we've got something here, and then they would look in the other pocket and find the badge. This is the kind of experience that can be repeated and is repeated and just about every correction officer I have spoken to has had a similar experience. I have gotten something from it. Unfortunately, they have not gotten to the point where they can see exactly what this is, and identify it and work actively against it.

I: Do you have the same kind of racism in the structure of the prison as you do with the way an inmate is treated?

CO: We do have that same racism that is prevalent in the wider society, but in the last four or five years the situation has gotten better. One of the things that is very significant now is that our prison systems could not exist if we did not have black and Puerto Rican officers. Because a white correction officer today, from the work that we have all been doing, cannot control, cannot look at, cannot even say anything to the majority of black and Puerto Rican inmates.

I: Would that mean, that if black and brown correction officers were organized to leave, that that would in some way disrupt the system?

CO: Organize them to leave the job? If that happened, yes. I don't see that happening now.

I: Is there a hierarchy in prison? Like who is the enemy to the officers? Who is the boss?

CO: Yes, the chain of command is warden, deputy warden, captain, and correction officers. We have in the city of New York 9 wardens, I think one of them is black. The hierarchy is predominantly white. Also, one of the things in civil service that is another reason why it represents a "good" profession for minority groups is that they have to abide by the rule of law. Everyone has to take a test and your promotion is geared to what mark you make on the test. The tests are usually color-blind, so that there is nothing that they can do in that area to perpetuate that kind of racism.

I: Then how come there have been so few black and Puerto Rican men working as officers before now?

CO: Previously, they had been excluded. Puerto Ricans were excluded because of height requirements. Blacks were excluded because of ways of advertising the position, and years ago, it was pretty much like unions, it was a father and son thing, and you had to pay a patronage to get a job. Not so, today.

I: Have you found much difference in the way that black and Puerto Rican guards treat black and Puerto Rican prisoners, as opposed to the way white guards do?

CO: Yes, prisons represent to me today a microcosm of the wider society, magnified. You can relate better to an individual that comes from your environment, if you give yourself a chance. That's number one. And by relate I mean there is a language that is prevalent in black communities that if you are not a part of, that if you have not been a part of, you just can't understand. And by language I mean we talk an awful lot, and the way we talk to each other—I am talking about, say two blacks—we are constantly gaming with each other, and you got to be able to game right back. You got to be slicker and flyer than the other cat. And by slick and fly I think you know pretty much what I mean. Unfortunately, an individual that does not come from that environment, does not understand it and does not relate to that individual on those terms. I am able to do that, and this is one of the ways in which I gain the confidence of the individuals I work with.

I: Are the white officers overtly racist, though?

CO: We are dealing with two things. We are dealing with racism and we are dealing with that authority thing, where—I told you to do something, and if you don't do it, I am going to kick you in your ass. And if you ask whether people get kicked in their ass, yes, every single day of the week. If you ask whether brutality exists—yes, and I can name you incidents that happened yesterday, and today. Yes, racism does exist, but it is not as overt as it was say, yesterday, or the day before yesterday. Now, with more and more blacks and Puerto Ricans coming into the job, it just can't go on the way it did years ago.

I: Have you ever been placed in a situation, where you were ordered by a warden or by an officer above you to handle or treat a prisoner in ways that you didn't want to? How did you and how would you today respond to that?

CO: When I first got on the job, as I said before, I was wrapped into this military thing, I was wrapped into this authority thing, and I thought that this is the way to manhood. This is also a feeling on the part of the inmates—he who is best with his hands is best. The rule of the jungle, pretty much. Yes, when I was first on the job, I was in situations where I was ordered by individuals to, as you say, handle individuals, the way I wouldn't handle them today. Physically abuse inmates, and what not, yes.

I: Would you refuse it now?

CO: I have not put my hands on anyone in two or four years.

I: What is then the response of that officer who thinks you should?

CO: I could care less, to tell you the truth. There are certain situations that happen in that environment when you have to protect yourself, let's put it that way. But I never initiate any action on my own part, and if ordered to do so, I still refuse to, and damn what he thinks.

I: Do you work closely with any other correction officers?

CO: You have to choose your comrades very selectively and it is difficult for me to order priorities. Right now I am in a situation where I am dealing with adolescents, predominantly, for eight hours a day, so my work is in this area. As far as correction officers are concerned, at every opportunity I get, I don't tell them, you know, you shouldn't hit anyone, but I say, dig babe, whether you know it or not, it's a brother you are knocking down, think about that.

I: What's the response?

CO: Mixed. There was a woman correction officer I know. We were sitting together yesterday rapping, and she told me that she had decided in her own mind that she can no longer work for this man. She is also moving in the direction that I feel, that that I am. So it's happening.

I: Do you think that the way kids, especially black and brown kids, have lived their everyday life outside of prison in a sense allows them to survive in prison?

CO: Yes, prison is not a traumatic shock for long, because all their friends are in jail. So they are able to assimilate very quickly. And once they are there, what they attempt to do is to form their own clique and identify with that clique and hope for the day when they are released. They are pretty much left on their own in terms of their subculture, because there is not that kind of give-and-take relationships with those who are, quote, rehabilitating them. What I do is exactly the opposite, I try to get into that culture and rap about things that I know, my experience in the streets, drugs, I stole cars, you know, all of these things and relate them in very real terms. And to try to make them see that if they are looking for the immediate, they are going to take a fall. The street is very, very hot, and I try to bring them a little bit along in terms of their awareness of what is going on in their lives.

I: Do you know of many of the kids that have left and related to the Panthers or the Lords?

CO: Yes. Let me say this also, drugs represent our major problem.

I: You mean heroin?

CO: Heroin. Any kind of drug that makes an individual dependent on it—and my approach to that is not the puritanical approach where you say, you should leave that alone, don't touch it, it is bad for you, spank you on your hand. I say, if you are going to do it, control it, don't let it control you. We have rap sessions on it, where I attempt to bring this kind of awareness to them. I am faced with a problem. We need warriors, we need young blacks and Puerto Ricans who are willing to give of their life, of their time, when they get back into society, to bring about necessary changes in society. Without the individual approach, without changing this individual, the first thing they are looking for, most of them, and I don't like categorizing people, but the majority of the cats in there, the first thing is to go looking for drugs. Right back where they came from. So you do two things: you have to change this individual's life style, and bring them to the point where he sees where that problem originated from.

I: What kind of other so-called "crime" are kids in there for, other than drugs?

CO: Stealing—cars, pocketbooks; also they are coming up now with some beauties. Conspiracy to commit trespass, conspiracy to commit burglary, malicious mischief, a six month sentence for malicious mischief.

I: What position is that kid in when that happens—are they burglars?

CO: To be perfectly honest, like I said I don't like to pre-judge an individual, but nine times out of ten, yes.

I: What do you think you would do if a rebellion broke out in a jail where you worked?

CO: A rebellion. This is exactly what I am trying to organize to happen. Hopefully, when it does happen, I won't get caught in the middle and get washed along with everyone else. That is the only way I can answer that.

I: Do you know about the movie rebellion at Rikers Island? What was that all about?

CO: The Daily News likes to create situations that are unreal. No one was responding to the movie, that is number one. The incident that happened was a fight between two individuals. The auditorium is located in the penitentiary, the Adolescent Remand Shelter. What really happened was that there were, I believe, 1200 inmates in the auditorium watching the movie. It seems that one of the detention inmates recognized a sentenced inmate that ratted on him when they were involved in a crime. He walked over to this guy and punched him in the jaw and knocked him down. The individual who was knocked down picked up a chair and threw it at the other individual. When the chair flew, peo-ple—inmates, tried to get out of the way. All hell broke loose. What they were trying to do was to get out of the auditorium. The officer who was trampled—and that is what he was, tram-pled—was trampled because he was an old man and could not get out of the way. That was the extent of that big riot. There was no rebellion.

I: What's your sense of the kind of organizing that is going on among prisoners in prison today? The Muslims, the Pan-thers?

CO: The Muslims do not organize politically, they organize, if at all, on a religious level. A Panther, if identified, is removed from prison population and placed in solitary confinement. A case in point, the Panther 21. They have no right holding them in the federal detention pen, and the only reason they are holding them there is that they can't turn them loose in a city prison, or they would tear it apart in terms of organizing. You have to realize that we are in a controlled environment—and the man has rats throughout the system and he can control everything that happens. He can pretty much tell who is organizing and remove them from the population. If they suspect political organizing is going on, or meetings, or anything of that nature, what they do is segregate that individual.

I: Then there is less overt political activity among black prisoners today than there was, let's say, five years ago, when a lot of radical Muslims and Panthers were getting organized in the prisons?

CO: Yet. I was around when the Five Percenters first came on the scene, and they were very, very active. But as of late they sort of died out. The man has learned how to cope with the situation.

I: Is the militancy of the kids increasing such that if one or two people spontaneously stood up to protest something, other people would rally behind and support them?

CO: Yes.

I: Did that happen anywhere that you know of recently?

CO: Yes. It happened when Ralph Poynter was in the reception center—Ralph is a political organizer from way back—he devoted his full four months to political organizing. They had three situations, three incidents there where the man had to assemble all the inmates in the auditorium and attempt to placate the prisoners in terms of what their demands were. Their demands were: the right to organize, the right to get a paper within the prison, the right to get decent food, and there were two other demands that I don't remember. But since Ralph has been discharged that big push has died out.

I: Do you see any difference between the kids from 16-19 that come into the prisons now, as opposed to two years ago?

CO: Yes. Now one thing that is very significant and very heartening is the fact that most of the blacks no longer go to Catholic, Protestant religious services. They no longer walk around with rosary beads and crosses, they walk around with a star and a crescent. Unfortunately, it has not as of yet carried on further. It is a big thing to get Muslim services included in the prison agenda, but it is just a start.

Appendix

Directory of Contributing Periodicals

The descriptive statements following the titles below were either provided by the periodical's office or taken from its masthead.

The American Rationalist, P.O. Box 1762, St. Louis, Mo. 63199

The American Rationalist is an independent nonpartisan monthly journal of fact, opinion, criticism and of service for all who share, or are in sympathy with, the basic Rationalist-Humanist world view or philosophy, regardless of the labels by which they may choose to identify themselves. Bimonthly $4.50 yr.

Black Politics, P.O. Box 1233, Berkeley, Calif. 94701

An independent journal whose purpose is to provide a forum for vanguard theories and ideas that deal with currently crucial issues.
Bimonthly $3 yr.

The Bond, Room 538, 156 Fifth Ave., New York, N.Y. 10019

The voice of the American Servicemen's Union.
Monthly Free to servicemen

The Brian Rex Report, Chamber of Commerce Bldg., Indianapolis, Ind. 46204

The Brian Rex Report, Inc. is a nonpolitical nonprofit educational champion of private property, the free market, the profit and loss system, and limited government. Biweekly Free

Catholic Worker, 36 East First St., New York, N.Y. 10003

Organ of the Catholic Worker Movement. 9 issues 25c yr.

Christian Anti-Communism Crusade, P.O. Box 890, 124 E. First St., Long Beach, Calif. 90801

The newsletter of the Christian Anti-Communism Crusade presents up-to-date information on the attitudes and activities of the branches of the world communist movement. Information is obtained by critical study of the communist press. While the information is objective, the Crusade acknowledges its own bias. It rejects the materialistic philosophy and totalitarian structure of communism, and upholds Christian evangelism.
Monthly Free

Christian Crusade Weekly, P.O. Box 977, Tulsa, Okla. 74102

Published by Christian Echoes National Ministry. Weekly $2 yr.

Christian Economics, Christian Freedom Foundation, Inc., 3030 West Sixth St., Los Angeles, Calif. 90005

We uphold the Constitution of the United States and the limited government which it inaugurated; we believe in the free market economy and the faithful application of Christian principles to all economic activities. Fortnightly $3 yr.

The Conference Board Record, 845 Third Ave., New York, N.Y. 10022

Published by the National Industrial Conference Board, one of the great nonprofit fact-finding laboratories of the world. For more than fifty years, it has continuously served as an institution for scientific research in the fields of business economics and business management. Its sole purpose is to promote prosperity and security by assisting in the effective operation and sound development of voluntary productive enterprise. Monthly $30 (qualified non-Associates)

Counterattack, 1775 Broadway, New York, N.Y. 10019

On the fighting front since 1947. Published by American Business Consultants, Inc. Biweekly $24 yr.

The Dan Smoot Report, Box 9538, Dallas, Tex. 75214

Weekly $12 yr.

The Davis Arena, P.O. Box 631, Davis, Calif. 95616

Dissent, 509 Fifth Ave., New York, N.Y. 10017

Dissent is a journal devoted to radical ideas and the values of socialism and democracy. Each writer speaks for himself; there is no effort made to exact editorial consensus or uniformity. Bimonthly $6 yr.

Door to Liberation, P.O. Box 2022, San Diego, Calif. 42112

Biweekly $4 yr.

The Fifth Estate, 1107 West Warren St., Detroit, Mich. 48201

A Newspaper of Detroit. Monthly $3 yr.

Freedom Magazine, 6413 Franklin Ave., Los Angeles, Calif. 90028

Freedom is published for the Liberty Amendment Committee of U.S.A. and is devoted to the promotion of the Liberty Amendment which will restore our Constitution to full force and effect, stop the tax and spend cycle, take the bureaucracy out of competition with private enterprise, and federal invasion of state sovereignty and repeal the U.S. personal income tax. 12 issues $5

Freedom Talk, Life Line, Dallas, Tex. 75206

A daily radio commentary by *Life Line.*

The Freeman, The Foundation for Economic Education, Irvington-on-Hudson, N.Y. 10533

The Foundation for Economic Education is an educational champion of private ownership, the free market, the profit and loss system, and limited government. Monthly Free

Good Times, 2377 Bush St., San Francisco, Calif. 94115

We stand for the peaceable and orderly abolition of money and dissolution of government. Weekly $6 yr.

The Herald of Freedom, P.O. Box 3, Zarephath, N.J. 08890

For God and Country. Biweekly **$10 yr.**

Heterodoxical Voice, P.O. Box 24, Newark, Del. 19711

Published by the Newark Free Community, Inc.

20 issues $5; students $4

Human Events, 422 First St., S.E., Washington, D.C. 20003

In reporting the news, HUMAN EVENTS is objective; it aims for accurate presentation of the facts. But it is *not* impartial. It looks at events through eyes that are biased in favor of limited constitutional government, local self-government, private enterprise and individual freedom. These principles represented the bias of the Founding Fathers. We think the same bias will preserve freedom in America.

Weekly $15 yr.

Industrial Worker, 2440 N. Lincoln, Chicago, Ill. 60614

The working class and the employing class, having nothing in common, are engaged in a struggle that must go on until the workers of the World organize as a class, take possession, and abolish the system of wages.

Monthly $2 yr.

The Intercollegiate Review, 14 South Bryn Mawr Ave.,
Bryn Mawr, Pa. 19010

A journal of scholarship and opinion.   Quarterly $4 yr.

Issues, American Council for Judaism, 201 East 57th St.
New York, N.Y. 10022

A Journal of Independent Jewish Inquiry.

Semiannually $1.50 yr.

The Kentucky Farmer, 1407 Laurel Ave., Bowling Green, Ky. 42101

Kentucky's farm trade magazine, devoted exclusively to Kentucky's agriculture for 105 years.   Monthly $3 for 10 yrs. (Ky. residents)

Lancaster Independent Press, 120 South Queen St., Lancaster, Pa. 17603

Biweekly $10 yr.

Leviathan, 330 Grove St., San Francisco, Calif. 94102

Published by Movement people active in antiwar work, racial research and writing, community organizing, and draft resistance. The magazine is organized to reflect the diversity of experiences which have contributed to the Movement's growth, and to unite these experiences in the common task of building its future.   10 issues $5

Liberal, 5233 North Fifth St., Philadelphia, Pa. 19120

Bulletin of the Friendship Liberal League, presenting a LIBERAL and RATIONALIST viewpoint.   Monthly $2 yr.

Liberation, 339 Lafayette St., New York, N.Y. 10012

Monthly $7 yr.

Liberty, 6840 Eastern Avenue, N.W., Washington, D.C. 20012

We believe in religious liberty and believe this is best accomplished when there is separation of church and state. We believe in civil government as divinely ordained, but we do not feel that the government's jurisdiction extends into the area of an individual's conscience.

Monthly $1.25 yr.

Liberty Letter, 300 Independence Ave., S.E., Washington, D.C. 20003

Liberty Lobby is a legislative action organization for grass-roots America! It is your lobby in Washington, which fights for a constitutional government.   Monthly $2 yr.

Life Lines, 4330 North Central Expressway, Dallas, Tex. 75206

LIFE LINES is chartered as a nonprofit, nondenominational, religious-patriotic organization and is dedicated to the preservation of American Freedoms through an informed public.   3 times weekly $5 yr.

El Malcriado, P.O. Box 130, Delano, Calif. 93215

EL MALCRIADO, The Voice of the Farm Worker, is published twice monthly by the United Farm Workers Organizing Committee, AFL-CIO.   Twice monthly $3.50 yr.

Manas, P.O. Box 32112, El Sereno Station, Los Angeles, Calif. 90032

Manas is a journal of independent inquiry, concerned with study of the principles which move world society on its present course, and with search for contrasting principles—that may be capable of supporting intelligent idealism under the conditions of life in the twentieth century.   Weekly $5 yr.

Manion Forum Newsletter, St. Joseph Bank Bldg., South Bend, Ind. 46601

The Voice of Freedom Loving Americans.   Weekly $7 yr.

The Match!, P.O. Box 3684, Tucson, Ariz. 85700

       Monthly $5 yr.

Monthly Review, 116 West 14th St., New York, N.Y. 10011

       Monthly $7 yr.

National Chronicle, P.O. Box AC, Burney, Calif. 96013

The *National Chronicle* is a regularly government authorized publication, legally recognized by the Government and by the State of California. Our state authorization is No. 19,0091. We can look any man in the eye and tell him to "go to Hell" for we wear no man's collar and for that reason we can call a spade exactly what it is.   Weekly $5 yr.

National Renaissance Bulletin, National Renaissance Party, Box 10, New York, N.Y. 10024

A political party devoted to the restoration of the American Republic, the preservation of American sovereignty and the establishment of an American regime based on the principles of racial nationalism and social justice.   Monthly $3 yr.

National Socialist World, P.O. Box 5505, Arlington, Va. 22205

Published by the World Union of National Socialists.

       Quarterly $10 yr.

New America, Room 402, 1182 Broadway, New York, N.Y. 10001

New America is a democratic socialist newspaper in the tradition of Eugene Victor Debs, Norman Thomas and Michael Harrington. It advocates a movement of the democratic left and a strategy of coalition politics to unite labor, negroes, liberal reformers, and democratic radicals to fundamentally transform American society in an equalitarian direction.   Semimonthly $5 yr.

The New Right, Michigan National Youth Alliance, P.O. Box 202, Center Line, Mich. 48015

The National Youth Alliance is an organization dedicated to fighting for capitalism and individual rights.   Monthly $5 yr.

New World Review, N.W.R. Publications, Inc., Suite 308, 156 Fifth Ave., New York, N.Y. 10010

A magazine dealing with life in the socialist countries, our country's relations with them, and the need of closer ties in the interests of world peace. Quarterly $3.50 yr.

News & Letters, 415 Brainard, Detroit, Mich. 48201

A Marxist-Humanist publication which represents a unique combination of workers and intellectuals, black and white. Edited by a black production worker, it is written by workers, youth and black people who speak for themselves in its pages, and is attempting to end the division between mental and manual labor. Monthly $1 yr.

The North Carolina Anvil, P.O. Box 1148, Durham, N.C. 27702

Weekly $7.50 yr.

People's World, 81 Clementina St., San Francisco, Calif. 90014

Weekly $7 yr.

Political Affairs, 23 West 26th St., New York, N.Y. 10010

Theoretical Journal of the Communist Party, U.S.A.

Monthly $6 yr.

Racialist, 2507 N. Franklin Rd., Arlington, Va. 22201

Published by the White Student Alliance.

Monthly $5 yr. (includes membership)

Rat, 241 East 14th St., New York, N.Y. 10003

Published every two weeks by an all-women's collective.

Biweekly $6 yr.

SDS New Left Notes, 173a Massachusetts Ave., Boston, Mass. 02115

Published by the Students for a Democratic Society.

Weekly $10 yr. (nonmembers)

Secular Subjects, P.O. Box 2931, St. Louis, Mo. 63130

To separate state and church, oppose supernaturalism and injustice, promote the study of the sciences. Monthly $5 yr.

Social Questions, 11 Forest Blvd., Ardsley, N.Y. 10502

The Methodist Federation for Social Action, an unofficial membership organization, founded in 1907, seeks to deepen within the Church, the sense of social obligation and opportunity to study, from the Christian point of view, social problems and their solutions and to promote social action in the spirit of Jesus. 9 issues $3 yr.

Sons of Liberty, P.O. Box 1896, Hollywood, Calif. 90028

The Southern Patriot, 3210 W. Broadway, Lousville, Ky. 40211

The Southern Patriot reports on the peace, freedom and labor movements in the South and developments which affect them. It is published by the Southern Conference Educational Fund whose goals are ending poverty, racism, and war. The main thrust of SCEF's work is organizing in the white community for coalitions with the black movement.

Monthly $3 yr.

Spokane Natural, Box 1276, Spokane, Wash. 99210

Serving the Northwest. Biweekly $5 yr.

The Technocrat, 433 East Market St., Long Beach, Calif. 90805

Offering to the American public a medium by which it can learn the facts regarding the transition period in which we are moving toward a New America of technological abundance.   Quarterly $1.40 yr.

The Thunderbolt, P.O. Box 6263, Savannah, Ga. 31405

Workers and farmers fight communism and race mixing.

Monthly $5 yr.

The Torch, P.O. Box 122, Grove City, Pa. 16127

A publication of the Conservative Club of Grove City College supporting the anti-collectivist Consensus.   10 issues $2

Trud!, P.O. Box 114, Essex Falls, N.J. 07021

From the White Underground.   Monthly $5 yr.

War/Peace Report, 218 East 18th St., New York, N.Y. 10003

Fact and opinion on progress toward a world of peace with justice. Published by the Center for War/Peace Studies.   Monthly $5 yr.

The Western Socialist, 295 Huntington Ave., Boston, Mass. 02115

Capitalism is based upon the existence of a generally propertyless majority of the population: the wage and salaried employees. World Socialism will make possible the free right of access by all mankind to all that is in and on the earth.   Bimonthly $1 yr.

White Power, Box 5505, Arlington, Va. 22205

The newspaper of White Revolution.   12 issues $3

The White Sentinel, P.O. Box 9013, Ft. Lauderdale, Fla. 33310

The truth that should be printed. Published by the Christian Constitutional Educational League, Inc.   Monthly $3 yr.